Transparency and Secrecy

Transparency and Secrecy

A Reader Linking Literature and Contemporary Debate

Edited by Suzanne J. Piotrowski

LEXINGTON BOOKS
A division of

ROWMAN & LITTLEFIELD PUBLISHERS, INC.
Lanham • Boulder • New York • Toronto • Plymouth, UK

Published by Lexington Books
A division of Rowman & Littlefield Publishers, Inc.
A wholly owned subsidiary of The Rowman & Littlefield Publishing Group, Inc.
4501 Forbes Boulevard, Suite 200, Lanham, Maryland 20706
http://www.lexingtonbooks.com

Estover Road, Plymouth PL6 7PY, United Kingdom

British Library Cataloguing in Publication Information Available

Library of Congress Cataloging-in-Publication Data

Transparency and secrecy : a reader linking literature and contemporary debate / [edited by] Suzanne J. Piotrowski.
    p. cm.
  ISBN 978-0-7391-2751-3 (cloth : alk. paper) — ISBN 978-0-7391-2752-0 (pbk. : alk. paper)
  1. Government information—Access control—United States. 2. Freedom of information—United States. 3. Transparency in government—United States. 4. Government information—Access control. 5. Freedom of information. 6. Transparency in government. I. Piotrowski, Suzanne J., 1973–
  JK468.S4T74 2010
  323.44'50973—dc22   2010006377

∞™ The paper used in this publication meets the minimum requirements of American National Standard for Information Sciences—Permanence of Paper for Printed Library Materials, ANSI/NISO Z39.48-1992.
Printed in the United States of America

To my major professor,

David H. Rosenbloom

Contents

Preface

The idea for this reader was born while sipping coffee next door to the Chinese consulate in New York City. I was with Marc Holzer, the dean of the School of Public Affairs and Administration, and we were waiting for our visas to be approved so we could attend the Third Sino–U.S. Conference on Public Administration in Beijing. Marc encouraged me to develop a reader along the lines of my research interests and the burgeoning subfield of transparency. I listened to Marc, not only because he was my dean but also because I value his opinion. Without Marc's initial encouragement and support, this project would not have come to fruition. For this, I thank him.

A generous grant from the Lois and Samuel Pratt Program for Freedom of Information, based at Rutgers School of Law–Newark, N.J., supported this project and made it possible.

This project, more than any other I have worked on, has benefited from the input of my students. Since Spring 2007, I have been teaching a master of public administration seminar on *Administrative Transparency*. This reader is an outgrowth of the syllabus for that class. The students in these classes gave me excellent feedback on which articles and pieces worked and did not work for them. They also tested out the assignments and study questions at the back of the chapters. Without my students' thoughtful comments, this reader would not be the final, coherent book that it is today.

Multiple research assistants from the School of Public Affairs and Administration (SPAA) at Rutgers–Newark, N.J., have been exceptionally helpful in the development of this book. Erin Borry, now a doctoral student at the University of Kansas, helped choose the original selection of material. Yuguo Liao and Jyldyz Kasymova, both doctoral students at SPAA, read close to final drafts of the reader, gave valuable comments and asked excellent questions. John Sowden, a Master of Public Administration student, provided excellent research assistance and requested some of the permissions for the excerpts.

I worked closely with an excellent copy editor while developing this reader, Lisa DeLisle. Lisa's attention to detail and organizational suggestions greatly improved the final product.

Two friends and mentors helped me substantially on this project and throughout my career: professors Alasdair S. Roberts and David H. Rosenbloom. I first met Alasdair when I was a graduate student conducting my dissertation research on the U.S. federal Freedom of Information Act. From day one, he has been extremely supportive of me. He rightly encouraged me to broaden the focus of the reader and include more international readings and examples. David was my major professor while at American University. David's commitment to his students is unmatched. Seven years after graduating I can, and still do, call him up to ask for his advice on papers and projects. The only difference is now I am calling Hong Kong instead of Bethesda.

I would like to thank the following institutions for granting me the permission to reprint their publications: Oxford University Press (Weber's "The Power Position of the Bureaucracy"); Cambridge University Press (Rourke's "Administrative Secrecy"); Springer Science+Business Media (Kitiyadisai's "Privacy Rights and Protection"); Campbell Public Affairs Institute, The Maxwell School of Syracuse University (Blanton's "National Security and Open Government in the United States"); State University of New York Press (Piotrowski's "Governmental Transparency in the Path of Administrative Reform"); Sage Publications, Inc. Journals (Rosenbloom and Piotrowski's "Outsourcing the Constitution and Administrative Law Norms"); Blackwell Publishing Ltd. (Roberts's "A Partial Revolution"; Moon's "The Evolution of E-Government among Municipalities"; Feinberg's "Mr. Justice Brandeis and the Creation of the Federal Register"; Rhinard's "The Democratic Legitimacy of the European Union Committee System"; Baker, Addams, and Davis's "Critical Factors for Enhancing Municipal Public Hearings"); Taylor & Francis Group (Lee's "At the Intersection of Bureaucracy, Democracy, and the Media"); Harvard Law Review Association ("Open Meeting Statutes"); Pantheon Books, a division of Random House, Inc. (Bok's "Whistleblowing and Leaks"); and The American Society for Public Administration (Lovell's "The Enduring Phenomenon of Moral Muteness").

Finally I need to thank my family for suffering through with me as I pulled this project together. The support of my parents, Pat and Rich Piotrowski, and my husband, Richard Heap, is seemingly endless and for this I am in their debt.

My hope is that you find this book useful and that this is the first of many editions of this reader. If you have critiques or suggestions for other articles, assignments, or material for future editions please e-mail them to me at spiotrow@newark.rutgers.edu.

Suzanne J. Piotrowski
Hoboken, N.J.

Introduction

The UK Members of Parliament expense scandal that began in the spring of 2009 is in many ways a story about governmental transparency. The story began with a Freedom of Information Act request seeking information on the expenses submitted by Members of Parliament. This request would not have been possible five years ago. The UK Freedom of Information Act was passed in 2000 and became fully implemented in 2005. In this particular case, the Freedom of Information Act request was denied. The decision was appealed to the Information Commissioner, and the case eventually went all the way to the Information Tribunal (Rosenbaum 2009). The expense records were going to be released but with key information deleted or redacted from the documents. A complete set of the records without the portions redacted was then leaked to—and paid for by—*The Daily Telegraph*, a British newspaper (BBC 2009).

The documents brought to light a variety of expense reimbursements—from questionable mortgage payments to wasp-nest removal to a duck island (*Daily Telegraph* 2009). Because of these revelations, there has been major political fallout, and the scandal has occupied time during the Prime Minister's Questions, which is available for viewing online. The documents are now posted on the Parliament's website (UK Parliament 2009). A freedom of information request, leaked documents, open sessions of parliament, and the posting of documents to government websites are aspects of different components of transparency.

There are four primary avenues of access to government information. Proactive dissemination of information is the primary way governments release information. Large amounts of information are released based on statutory or regulatory requirements, tradition, or public relations and trust-building efforts. Information released through proactive dissemination can either be through communications from public affairs offices, formal publications, releasing historical documents to depository libraries or agency reading rooms, or, the most common way recently, posting documents on websites.

The proactive information dissemination model is contrasted with the requestor model. With the requestor model, document releases are initiated either through formal or informal avenues. Informal requests can be made over the phone, by fax, through e-mail, or in person. Formal requests typically occur when documents are requested citing a specific law, such as requests made to a federal agency invoking the Freedom of Information Act or requests sent to a local government referencing the relevant state open records act. Requests are processed and documents are then released or not released, in accordance with statutory guidelines or administrative discretion. Once documents are identified to be released, they may be given to individuals or placed in reading rooms.

Open public meetings are the third avenue of access to government information. At the U.S. federal level, the Federal Advisory Committee Act allows public access to advisory committee meetings. All states have sunshine laws that allow access to public meetings. Whistleblowing and leaking information are the final avenues through which government information is released. Whistleblowers generally see some administrative wrongdoing and circumvent the chain of command to publicize an issue. Employees may blow the whistle by contacting inspector-general offices or similar auditing bodies, calling established phone lines, or using website reporting tools. Individuals who leak material make information that is not releasable through formal channels available to media outlets. Leaking is usually done confidentially or anonymously. Unlike the other forms of release, leaks may be illegal.

OUTLINE OF BOOK

Excluding this segment, this book is broken into six parts. The first part serves as an introduction to the concept of transparency. Within the section there is a selection of historical and contemporary pieces tracing the development of governmental secrecy and transparency. Part two introduces some of the concepts that are at times in tension with the transparency in practice. The competing values addressed in this section are security, privacy, and efficiency. Freedom of information, in an international context, is the focus of the third group of readings. The fourth part of the book examines ways in which governments proactively release information. Open public meetings, at varying levels of government, are the subject of the fifth part and its associated readings. The sixth and final part of the reader addresses whistleblowing in public organizations and leaking information.

RECOMMENDED BOOKS

Adams, G. B., and D. L. Balfour. *Unmasking Administrative Evil.* 3rd ed. Armonk, N.Y.: M. E. Sharpe, 2009.

Alford, Fred. *Whistleblowers: Broken Lives and Organizational Power.* Ithaca, N.Y.: Cornell University Press, 2001.

Becker, L. C., and C. B. Becker, eds. *Encyclopedia of Ethics.* New York: Routledge, 2001.

Behn, R. D. *Rethinking Democratic Accountability.* Washington, D.C.: Brookings Institution Press, 2001.

Bertelli, A. M., and L. E. Lynn. *Madison's Managers: Public Administration and the Constitution.* Baltimore, Md.: Johns Hopkins University Press, 2006.

Bok, Sissela. *Lying: Moral Choice in Public and Private Life.* New York: Vintage, 1999.

———. *Secrets: On the Ethics of Concealment and Revelation.* New York: Vintage, 1989.

Bozeman, B. *Public Values and Public Interest.* Washington, D.C.: Georgetown University Press, 2007.

Carter Center. "Atlanta Declaration and Plan of Action for the Advancement of the Right of Access to Information." *International Conference on the Right to Public Information.* 29 February 2008. www.cartercenter.org/documents/Atlanta%20Declaration%20and%20 Plan%20of%20Action.pdf (14 July 2009).

Cooper, Terry. *The Responsible Administrator.* 5th ed. San Francisco, Calif.: Jossey-Bass, 2006.

Cross, Harold. *The People's Right to Know.* Ams Press (reprint), 1953.

Florini, Ann, ed. *The Right to Know: Transparency for an Open World.* New York: Columbia University Press, 2007.

Foerstel, H. *Freedom of Information and the Right to Know: The Origins and Applications of the Freedom of Information Act.* Westport, Conn.: Greenwood Press, 1999.

Franck, T. M., and E. Weisband. *Secrecy and Foreign Policy.* New York, 1986.

Frederickson, H. George, ed. *Ethics and Public Administration.* Armonk, N.Y.: M. E. Sharpe, 1993.

Fung, Archon, Mary Graham, and David Weil. *Full Disclosure: The Perils and Promise of Transparency.* New York: Cambridge University Press, 2007.

Hoffman, Daniel. *Governmental Secrecy and the Founding Fathers: A Study in Constitutional Controls.* (Contributions in Legal Studies) Westport, Conn.: Greenwood Press, 1981.

Hood, Christopher, and David Heald. *Transparency: The Key to Better Governance?* New York: Oxford University Press, 2006.

Lee, Mordecai, ed. *Government Public Relations: A Reader.* Boca Raton, Fla.: CRC Press, 2007.

Lord, Kristin. *The Perils and Promise of Global Transparency: Why the Information Revolution May Not Lead to Security, Democracy, or Peace.* Albany, N.Y.: State University of New York Press, 2006.

Marsh, Marcus. *Access to Government: Genuine Freedom of Information for the United Kingdom.* London: Bow Group, 2000.

McDermott, P. *Who Needs to Know? The State of Public Access to Federal Government Information.* Lanham, Md.: Bernan Press, 2007.

Moynihan, Daniel Patrick. *Secrecy: The American Experience.* New Haven, Conn.: Yale University, 1998.

Piotrowski, Suzanne. *Governmental Transparency in the Path of Administrative Reform.* Albany, N.Y.: State University of New York Press, 2007.

Roberts, Alasdair. *Blacked Out: Government Secrecy in the Information Age.* New York: Cambridge University Press, 2006.

Wiener, Jon. *Gimme Some Truth: The John Lennon FBI Files.* Berkeley, Calif.: University of California Press, 1999.

RECOMMENDED CASE STUDIES

The Case Program at the Harvard Kennedy School (www.ksgcase.harvard.edu/) has some excellent cases that relate to the material in this reader. These can be ordered electronically by students individually.

- A *Duty* to Leak? CR15-04-1728.0
- Spilling the Beans in Owaho. CR15-04-1745.0
- A Problem at the Housing Authority. C16-90-946.0
- Reforming Prague City Hall: The Efforts of Mayor Jan Kasl to Increase Transparency and Fight Corruption (A). C15-05-1797.0
- Reforming Prague City Hall: The Efforts of Mayor Jan Kasl to Increase Transparency and Fight Corruption (B). C15-05-1798.0

RECOMMENDED VIDEOS

- *The Insider.* 1999. www.imdb.com/title/tt0140352
- *The U.S. vs. John Lennon.* 2006. www.theusversusjohnlennon.com/site/
- *Secrecy.* 2008. www.secrecyfilm.com/
- *Are We Safer in the Dark?* 2006. www.sla.org/marketplace/stores/1/DVD_-_Are_We_ Safer_in_the_Dark_P90C2.cfm
- *The Pentagon Papers.* 2003. www.amazon.com/Pentagon-Papers-James-Spader/dp/ B0000WN1N6/ref=sr_1_2?ie=UTF8&s=dvd&qid=1247576728&sr=8-2

ASSIGNMENTS

1. This book introduces you to the different avenues of access to information (proactive dissemination of information, requestor model, open public meetings, whistleblowing, and leaking information). These avenues of access allow for the release of government information and greater transparency. Transparency and these avenues of access are at times in tension with competing values. Three such competing values are personal privacy, security, and efficiency.

   For this paper, students should reflect upon the issue of transparency in the case study *Spilling the Beans in Owaho.* How is the concept of transparency at work in this case study? In your response to this question, you should discuss the key issues surrounding each of the avenues of access to information. If you believe that one of these avenues is not applicable to this case study, you should state so explicitly. Are any of the competing values at play in this case study?

2. You need to write a ten-page paper on some aspect of transparency. Your paper should be written as a white paper to an executive. For example, your paper could be addressed to President Obama, your state's governor, the mayor of your city, or the executive director of a not-for-profit organization.

   The components of the white paper are: (1) introduction/summary; (2) background; (3) solution; (4) conclusion; (5) bibliography. The entire paper, including the bibliography should be ten pages. You may find Purdue University's online writing center helpful when preparing your white paper: http://owl.english.purdue.edu/owl/resource/546/02/. You need to be very clear about the following issues when writing your paper:

   - How is your topic related to transparency?
   - What is the problem? You should be able to write a summary of the problem in one sentence.
   - What is your solution?
   - Who is the white paper going to be addressed to? It should have a very specific audience, i.e., President Obama, Governor Corzine, etc.

3. *Note to instructor*: While this assignment is set up as a review of a local government, it can easily be adapted to apply to a state- or national-level agency. This project has been given as a final project in a semester-long class.

   Students must complete a comprehensive transparency analysis of a local government of their choosing. Students will have to do original research to gather the data for this project. The paper should be between fourteen and twenty-three double-spaced pages, not including the appendix. The organization of the final project should be as follows:

I.   Introduction (1–2 pages)
II.   Open Meetings Analysis (3–5 pages)
III.   Document Request Analysis (3–5 pages)
IV.   Website Analysis (3–5 pages)
V.   Conclusions (2–3 pages)
VI.   References (not included in page limit)
VII.   Appendix (not included in page limit)

I. Introduction

The introduction should give background information on the town you picked and why you picked it. It should also explain briefly what your paper is about.

II. Open Meetings Analysis

Students must attend an open meeting in the town they are reviewing. When attending the meeting, you need to keep these questions in mind and make sure you answer them in your final project. The open meetings section of the paper should be between three and five pages of text (aside from any handouts you may include). You should stay at the meeting for at least two hours.

Background info

Give some background information on the meeting. What meeting did you go to? What were the topics addressed? Why did you choose that meeting? What time was the meeting held?

Facilities

Think about the physical location of the meeting. Was the room big enough for the people who were there? Could everyone hear? Was the meeting videotaped?

Participation

Explain what the public participation was like at the meeting. How many people attended? How did people sign up to speak? How many people spoke? What were the topics addressed at the public comment session? Were there any "gadflies" at the meeting?

Running of meeting

Give an overview of how the meeting was run. Were Robert's Rules of Order invoked? What was the overall tone of the meeting? Did it go into closed session?

Notice and minutes

Describe any issues surrounding notice of the meeting and the minutes. How did you hear about the meeting? Did the town post the agenda online before the meeting? Are minutes from the meeting available online?

Gain access to the minutes of the meeting you went to. How do the official minutes compare with your recollections and notes? Include with the final project a copy of the meeting agenda and any other information handed out.

Reflection on meeting

Conclude this section with any other reflections you have on the open public meeting you attended or the process in general.

III. Document Request Analysis

Every student should make two records requests. To learn more about making document, or freedom of information, requests in the United States, go to the website of the Reporters Committee for Freedom of the Press (www.rcfp.org/foia/). So as not to unduly burden any one municipality, students should make no more than three records requests to any one local government.

What should be requested?

The request will be made to the local government you are studying. One possibility for a document request is the most recent salary information for the top-ten highest paid employees of the municipality. Citing the relevant law, you can ask for the local government to indicate if these individuals receive overtime pay and the dollar amount of the overtime pay they received for the last fiscal year. Freedom of information–type requests may take weeks to be filled, so students should plan accordingly.

Document request written section

This section of your project will focus on the document requests you made and should be between three and five double-spaced pages. You should address the following three substantive topics:

Process Which requests did you make? Describe the process you went through to request the documents. Were there any particularly large bureaucratic hurdles you had to get over? Were the people you were dealing with exceptionally helpful? Did you get responses to your requests? If you made requests to more than one town or under a different law (such as another state's law or the federal Freedom of Information Act), include a comparison of the process under the different laws. Include copies of all your correspondence with the government(s) from which you requested documents in the appendix to the report.

Findings Briefly describe the material you received from the document requests. Were there any surprises in the material you received? If you were not successful in receiving any material, note that and leave this section blank.

Analysis, critiques, and suggestions Give your reaction to the process as a whole. Overall, how did your town do in filling the requests? What suggestions would you make to the town on how to improve their document request process? Did you have any other thoughts on the document request process?

IV. Website Analysis

This section of your project deals with municipal websites as conduits of transparency for local governments. Review your town's website and see if the town has the following information posted:

- Contact information: Is there contact information posted (name, phone number, mailing address, and e-mail address) for the mayor or town manager, municipal hall, municipal clerk, council members, each of the municipal departments, and municipal court?
- An employee directory including the employees' work phone numbers and e-mail addresses
- Mission statement and strategic plan
- Financial documents including bond documents, debt statements, budgets, and property-tax rates. Is historical information also posted?
- Meeting minutes (regular and closed session) and agendas. Is historical information also posted?
- Copies of the state's freedom of information and open public meeting acts
- Document request form and information on how to file a request
- Town's master plan
- Privacy statement
- Town newsletter
- Listing of employment opportunities
- A section for feedback or suggestions

This section of the report should be between three and five double-spaced pages. When writing up this section of the paper, describe the website generally. Is the above information accessible? How would you rate the town with regard to its website and transparency? Are there any major problems with the website? Is there anything particularly good about the website? If the town you are researching does not have an official website, you should note this and then review the website of a comparable or nearby town.

V. Conclusions

Within the conclusion section you should reflect on the project as a whole. Did your town have any particular strengths or weaknesses with regard to transparency? What recommendations would you make to the town to improve its transparency? Can you draw links with any of the readings for class?

1

What Is Transparency?

INTRODUCTION

In 2003, Webster's *New World College Dictionary* bestowed the title of Word of the Year onto *transparency*. This honor was given because the editors at Webster decided that "transparency is an answer to the public's impatience with secrecy and deceit on the part of leaders, institutions, and processes everywhere" (Associated Press 2003). Indeed the term *transparency* has seen resurgence in recent years. On President Barack Obama's first day in office, he signed an executive order on the topic. The executive order on *Transparency and Open Government* states, "Transparency promotes accountability and provides information for citizens about what their Government is doing." While the term *transparency* is achieving a level of public renaissance, the concept itself is a well wrought one.

Max Weber, a German theorist writing in the late 1800s and early 1900s, produced *Economy and Society: An Outline of Interpretive Sociology*. Weber, a sociologist, was an acute observer and theoretician on bureaucracy. He reflects on the great power of bureaucracies and how even elected officials are frequently at a loss when faced with the expertise of career bureaucrats (p. 991). Weber goes on to comment on the inherent nature of bureaucracies to be secretive: "This superiority of the professional insider every bureaucracy seeks further to increase through the means of *keeping secret* its knowledge and intentions" (emphasis in original, p. 992). Weber was one of the earliest theoreticians to write about the relationship between secrecy and bureaucracy with respect to monarchs, elected officials, and the general public. Weber's writing provoked such questions as: Is it a losing battle to pry secrets from bureaucrats? Is bureaucracy by its very nature *not* a democratic institution?

The political scientist Francis Rourke addressed the issue that secrecy is a function not just of bureaucracy and the executive branch but also of legislatures. His *American Political Science Review* article "Administrative Secrecy: A Congressional Dilemma" was published in 1960, but the themes he brings up are in many ways contemporary ones. Among the issues he raises are the excessive use of the personal privacy argument to keep information secret, the role of Congress in perpetuating government secrets, closed Congressional meetings, and the criticism that government secrecy surrounding scientific information is in many cases unnecessary. Rourke concludes that "nothing could be more axiomatic for a democracy than the principle of exposing the processes of government to relentless public criticism and scrutiny" (p. 691).

In 1998, Sen. Daniel Patrick Moynihan published his book *Secrecy: The American Experience*, in which he presents a history of secrecy in the United States. Memorably, Moynihan argues that "secrecy is for losers" (p. 227). He makes the case that organizations with a high level of restriction on information flow are more likely to fail. He concludes with a call to action: "It is time to dismantle government secrecy, this most pervasive of Cold War–era regulations. It is time to begin building the supports for the era of openness that is already upon us" (p. 227).

Christopher Hood and David Heald edited a volume addressing multiple aspects of governmental transparency. In chapter 1 of *Transparency: The Key to Better Governance?* (2006), Hood traces the history of the term *transparency*, which he refers to as "quasi-religious in nature" (p. 135). In chapter 2, David Heald presents the reader with a description of four directions of transparency: upward, downward, outward, and inward. Transparency upward is when organizational hierarchical superiors can observe the behavior and conduct of their subordinates. Transparency downward is when the subordinates can gain information on the conduct of their superiors. According to Heald, these two vertical directions of transparency can coexist. Transparency outward, a form of horizontal transparency, is when individuals can observe what is taking place in the environment outside of the organization. The other form of horizontal transparency, transparency inward, relates to when outsiders can observe what is happening inside an organization (pp. 27–28). Much of what is being presented in this volume relates to what Heald defines as transparency inward.

Is freedom of information (FOI) a fundamental human right? Professor Patrick Birkinshaw, director of the Institute of European Public Law at University of Hull, tackles this question and concludes that "FOI is a fundamental human right both in civil law and common law systems" (2006, 178). The Inter-American Court of Human Rights in the case of *Claude Reyes et al. v. Chile* found that freedom of information is a fundamental human right. In this case, plaintiff Marcel Claude Reyes was seeking, and was denied, environmental information from the Chilean government. The case went to the Inter-American Court of Human Rights, which found in favor of Claude Reyes. This case is excerpted in this volume. The section "What Is Transparency?" begins with a reading by Max Weber and ends with a reading by President Barack Obama. They are meant to give the reader a better understanding of some of the historical, theoretical, and practical issues surrounding transparency.

Assignments and Study Questions

1. Students must identify and bring to class three newspaper articles that touch on some aspect of transparency. In one-paragraph summaries, explain what the key issues are, with respect to transparency, in each article. When looking for articles, consider the following areas: open meetings, public records, document management, freedom of information, whistleblowing, and leaks. Make an effort to look through a range of newspapers including those with a local, regional, national, and international scope.
2. The readings lay out varying definitions of transparency. Which ones do you associate with most closely? Why?
3. Is a more transparent government necessarily a more ethical government?
4. German sociologist Max Weber argued that bureaucracies are inherently secretive. Does this sentiment still hold today? Why have or why have not things changed?

* * *

The Power Position of the Bureaucracy

Max Weber

A. THE POLITICAL IRRELEVANCE OF FUNCTIONAL INDISPENSABILITY

The democratization of society in its totality, and in the modern sense of the term, whether actual or perhaps merely formal, is an especially favorable basis of bureaucratization, but by no means the only possible one. After all, bureaucracy has merely the [limited] striving to level those powers that stand in its way in those concrete areas that, in the individual case, it seeks to occupy. We must remember the fact which we have encountered several times and which we shall have to discuss repeatedly: that "democracy" as such is opposed to the "rule" of bureaucracy, in spite and perhaps because of its unavoidable yet unintended promotion of bureaucratization. Under certain conditions, democracy creates palpable breaks in the bureaucratic pattern and impediments to bureaucratic organization. Hence, one must in every individual historical case analyze in which of the special directions bureaucratization has there developed.

For this reason, it must also remain an open question whether the *power* of bureaucracy is increasing in the modern states in which it is spreading. The fact that bureaucratic organization is technically the most highly developed power instrument in the hands of its controller does not determine the weight that bureaucracy as such is capable of procuring for its own opinions in a particular social structure. The ever-increasing indispensability" of the officialdom, swollen to the millions, is no more decisive on this point than is the economic indispensability of the proletarians for the strength of the social and political power position of that class (a view which some representatives of the proletarian movement hold).[1] If "indispensability" were decisive, the equally "indispensable" slaves ought to have held this position of power in any economy where slave labor prevailed and consequently freemen, as is the rule, shunned work as degrading. Whether the power of bureaucracy as such increases cannot be decided a priori from such reasons. The drawing in of economic interest groups or other non-official experts, or the drawing in of lay representatives, the establishment of local, inter-local, or central parliamentary or other representative bodies, or for occupational associations—these seem to run directly against the bureaucratic tendency. How far this appearance is the truth must be discussed in another chapter, rather than in the framework of this purely formal and pological (*kasuistisch*) discussion. In general, only the following can be said here:

The power position of a fully developed bureaucracy is always great, under normal conditions overtowering. The political "master" always finds himself, vis-à-vis the trained official, in the position of a dilettante facing the expert. This holds whether the "master," whom the bureaucracy serves, is the "people" equipped with the weapons of legislative initiative, referendum, and the right to remove officials; or a parliament elected on a more aristocratic or more democratic basis and equipped with the right or the *de facto* power to vote a lack of confidence; or an aristocratic collegiate body, legally or actually based on self-recruitment or a popularly elected president or an "absolute" or "constitutional" hereditary monarchy.

B. ADMINISTRATIVE SECRECY

This superiority of the professional insider every bureaucracy seeks further to increase through the means of *keeping secret* its knowledge and intentions. Bureaucratic administration always tends to exclude the public, to hide its knowledge and action from criticism as well as it can. Prussian church authorities now threaten to use disciplinary measures against pastors who make reprimands or other admonitory measures in any way accessible to third parties, charging that in doing so they become "guilty" of facilitating a possible criticism of the church authorities. The treasury officials of the Persian Shah have made a science of their budgetary art and even use a secret script. The official statistics of Prussia, in general, make public only what cannot do any harm to the intentions of the power-wielding bureaucracy. This tendency toward secrecy is in certain administrative fields a consequence of their objective nature: namely, wherever power interests of the given structure of domination *toward the outside* are at stake, whether this be the case of economic competitors of a private enterprise or that of potentially hostile foreign polities in the public field. If it is to be successful, the management of diplomacy can be publicly supervised only to a very limited extent. The military administration must insist on the concealment of its most important measures with the increasing significance of purely technical aspects. Political parties do not proceed differently, in spite of all the ostensible publicity of the party conventions and "Catholic Congresses" (*Katholikentage*).[2] With the increasing bureaucratization of party organizations, this secrecy will prevail even more. Foreign trade policy, in Germany for instance, brings about a concealment of production statistics. Every fighting posture of a social structure toward the outside tends in itself to have the effect of buttressing the position of the group in power.

However, the pure power interests of bureaucracy exert their effects far beyond these areas of functionally motivated secrecy. The concept of the "office secret" is the specific invention of bureaucracy, and few things it defends so fanatically as this attitude which, outside of the specific areas mentioned, cannot be justified with purely functional arguments. In facing a parliament, the bureaucracy fights, out of a sure power instinct, every one of that institution's attempts to gain through its own means (as, e.g., through the so-called "right of, parliamentary investigation")[3] expert knowledge from the interested parties. Bureaucracy naturally prefers a poorly informed, and hence powerless, parliament—at least insofar as this ignorance is compatible with the bureaucracy's own interests.

C. THE RULER'S DEPENDENCE ON THE BUREAUCRACY

The absolute monarch, too, is powerless in face of the superior knowledge of the bureaucratic expert—in a certain sense more so than any other political head. All the irate decrees of Frederick the Great concerning the "abolition of serfdom" were derailed in the course of their realization because the official mechanism simply ignored them as the occasional ideas of a dilettante. A constitutional king, whenever he is in agreement with a socially important part of the governed, very frequently exerts a greater influence upon the course of administration than does the absolute monarch since he can control the experts better because of the at least relatively public character of criticism, whereas the absolute monarch is dependent for information solely upon the bureaucracy. The Russian Tsar of the *ancien regime* [before the appointment of a Prime Minister in 1905] was rarely able to put across permanently anything that displeased his bureaucracy and violated its power interests. His ministries, which were subordinated directly to him as the autocrat, represented, as Leroy-Beaulieu very correctly observed, a conglomerate of satrapies which fought among each other with all the means of personal intrigue and bombarded each other with voluminous "Memoranda," in the face of which the monarch as a dilettante was quite helpless.[4]

The concentration of the power of the central bureaucracy in a single pair of hands is inevitable with every transition to constitutional government. Officialdom is placed under a monocratic head, the prime minister, through whose hands everything has to go before it gets to the monarch. This puts the latter to a large extent under the tutelage of the chief of the bureaucracy. Wilhelm II, in his well-known conflict with Bismarck, fought against this principle, but had to withdraw his attack very soon.[5] Under the rule of expert knowledge, the influence of the monarch can attain steadiness only through continuous communication with the bureaucratic chiefs which is methodically planned and directed by the central head of the bureaucracy. At the same time, constitutionalism binds the bureaucracy and the ruler into a community of interests against the power-seeking of the party chiefs in the parliamentary bodies. But *against* the bureaucracy the ruler remains powerless for this very reason, unless he finds support in parliament. The desertion of the "Great of the Reich," here the Prussian ministers and top Reich officials, brought a monarch into approximately the same situation in November 1918 as did the parallel event under the conditions of the feudal state in 1076.[6] This, however, is an exception for the power position of a monarch is on the whole far stronger vis-à-vis bureaucratic officials than it was in any feudal or in a "stereotyped" patrimonial state. This is because of the constant presence of aspirants for promotion with whom the monarch can easily replace inconvenient and independent officials. Other circumstances being equal, only economically independent officials, that is, officials who belong to the propertied strata can permit themselves to risk the loss of their offices. Today as always, the recruitment of officials from among propertyless strata increases the power of the rulers. Only officials who belong to a socially influential stratum which the monarch believes to have to take into account as support of his person, like the so-called *Kanalrebellen* in Prussia, can permanently and completely paralyze the substance of his will.[7]

Only the expert knowledge of private economic interest groups in the field of "business" is superior to the expert knowledge of the bureaucracy. This is so because the exact knowledge of facts in their field is of direct significance for economic survival. Errors in official statistics do not have direct economic consequences for the responsible official, but miscalculations in a capitalist enterprise are paid for by losses, perhaps by its existence. Moreover, the "secret," as a means of power, is more safely hidden in the books of an enterprise than it is in the files of public authorities. For this reason alone authorities are held within narrow boundaries when they seek to influence economic life in the capitalist epoch, and very frequently their measures take an unforeseen and unintended course or are made illusory by the superior expert knowledge of the interested groups.

Weber, Max. "The Power Position of the Bureaucracy." Pp. 990–94 in *Economy and Society: An Outline of Interpretive Sociology.* New York: Bedminster Press, 1968. Reprinted by permission of Oxford University Press.

* * *

Administrative Secrecy: A Congressional Dilemma

Francis E. Rourke

Attacks upon administrative secrecy are a commonplace of congressional politics. By resolution, investigation, and the threat of even more punitive sanctions, Congress has repeatedly asserted its belief that executive officials should not be allowed to withhold documents and testimony at their own discretion.[1] The most graphic recent evidence of this legislative concern has been provided by a House Special Subcommittee on Government Information.[2] Over the past three years, this group, headed by Representative Moss of California, has made far-ranging efforts to expose and dramatize the evils of executive secrecy.[3]

The long-standing congressional resentment against administrative efforts to conceal information has very visible roots in considerations of institutional self-interest, since the performance of legislative functions in central areas of policy-making and administrative oversight demands frequent access to facts that only executive officials can supply. In the field of defense policy, especially, congressional dependence upon executive information is acute, and bitter controversy has been sparked by executive refusals to release data bearing on such matters as the missile defense program, foreign aid expenditures, and differences within the high command over the best way to spend the defense dollar.[4]

Among recent instances where Congress has found executive secrecy a handicap in its efforts to oversee administration, none has gained more publicity than the Dixon-Yates affair. In 1955 congressional critics of the administration's proposals to finance private construction of a utility plant in the Tennessee Valley for the benefit of the AEC [Atomic Energy Commission] were exercised to discover that a Bureau of the Budget consultant, Adolphe H. Wenzell, had simultaneously been an officer of the First Boston Corporation. This was the investment house that had represented Dixon-Yates in negotiations with the AEC and the Budget Bureau.

Although the administration at first insisted that Wenzell had not actually participated in contract discussions, subsequent inquiry disclosed that he had indeed played the role of intermediary in the affair.[5] The difficulty Congress encountered in obtaining full and accurate information on this and other matters connected with the Dixon-Yates investigation prompted Senator O'Mahoney to the conclusion that "there has been an utmost effort on the part of witnesses from the government to conceal the facts." Among the government officials who at one point or another refused to give testimony on their part in the contract negotiations were the Budget Director, Rowland Hughes; the chairman of the Atomic Energy Commission, Lewis L. Strauss; the chairman of the Securities and Exchange Commission, J. Sinclair Armstrong; and Presidential Assistant Sherman Adams.[6]

Testimony to the continued strength of the congressional determination to preserve access to data in the hands of executive officials may also be found in the refusal of the Senate in 1959 to confirm the nomination of Lewis L. Strauss to be Secretary of Commerce—an event which marked only the eighth time that a Cabinet nominee has been denied confirmation. One of the principal charges levelled against Strauss was of excessive use of the doctrine of executive privilege to withhold information from the legislature—a refusal that Senators believed was based principally on the damage that disclosure might do to Strauss' own reputation. Senator Anderson, a leader of the opposition to him, called the rejection of Strauss "a signal victory for those who still believe this is a government for the people and that the public should be protected against a man who might use executive privilege to hide the truth."[7]

One issue that has generated persistent heat over a period spanning the terms of the last three Presidents has been the question of congressional inspection of loyalty-security files. Roosevelt, Truman, and Eisenhower have each in turn had occasion to exercise their presidential prerogative to refuse Congress permission to inspect documents of this sort.[8] This refusal has been based partly on a desire to protect the individuals whose records were requested from the damage they might incur through the exposure of some of the material contained in their files—scurrilous accusations, for example. It has also been justified on the ground that secrecy is necessary for the efficient administration of the loyalty-security program, since it protects the identity of confidential informants to the government from a disclosure that might jeopardize their usefulness.

Pressure to obtain material contained in these files has come mainly from the conservative sectors of the legislature—in both the Democratic and the Republican parties. But the general notion of open government is at least as much a liberal as it is a conservative doctrine. The assaults upon secrecy in both the Dixon-Yates and Strauss affairs were mounted mainly by legislators of liberal persuasion, and two of the chief protagonists today of the "people's right to know," Congressman Moss of California and Senator Hennings of Missouri, would generally be classified as liberal in political outlook. Moreover, the fight against secrecy has been carried on with equal vigor whether Congress was under Democratic or Republican control. It is thus an issue upon which all ideological and partisan factions in the legislature can make common cause.

I

In its criticism of executive secrecy, the legislature has always drawn strong support from a powerful constellation of interests in American society—the organized press, including the American Society of Newspaper Editors, the American Newspaper Publishers Association, and the Associated Press Managing Editors Association. For reasons of economic self-interest as well as ideological dedication, the newspaper industry's condemnation of governmental secrecy has been even more sweeping and persistent than that of the legislature. (It includes the legislature among its targets.) The passage of resolutions attacking governmental secrecy has now become a standard item on the agenda whenever newspapermen meet in state or national conventions.

The strong interest of the press helps insure widespread newspaper coverage of legislative attacks upon executive secrecy. Representative Hofmann of Michigan, a minority member of the House Subcommittee on Government Information has in fact taken public notice of the benefits accruing to the chairman from the nationwide publicity given the committee's critical inquiry into administrative secrecy.

Whatever the chairman's intent may have been, the effect of this subcommittee's conspiracy with the press has been his personal glorification. The effectiveness of this press agentry may be evident in Mr. Moss's success in capturing both the Democratic and Republican nominations in California's Third Congressional District.[9]

The desire of the press to open up channels of information extends to state as well as national government, and during recent years newspaper groups have been instrumental in bringing about the passage of laws limiting governmental secrecy in a number of states, including Illinois, Ohio, and Pennsylvania."[10]

Since World War II executive secrecy has also come under heavy fire from the nation's scientific community. This criticism has its roots in the growing involvement of the federal government in scientific research—an involvement that has brought technical development in many fields, particularly atomic energy, under substantial government control. Today scientists in and out of government service have a vested interest in governmental procedures and policies concerning the release of information in their professional field. In this area the web of executive secrecy extends beyond government itself, and embraces projects operated by private institutions under governmental auspices.

Much of the scientific criticism of secrecy rests on the premise that it is unnecessary, because it attempts to conceal matters that are part of the general fund of scientific knowledge in the Western world, or that can be easily discovered by scientists working outside the classification system. There is, of course, general agreement that the weapons developed through modern science may themselves need to be kept secret, but as one scientist put it:

> A field as basic as that of magnetism is known to all competent scientists throughout the world already. If there is something new ready to be discovered in that field, it will also be discovered by people in other countries. An attempt to keep such a discovery secret in this country would handicap ourselves, I am sure, more than it would withhold from others."[11]

One striking fact which this comment points up is the changing character of the so-called "state secret." In the past such secrets dealt mainly with purely military matters—troop dispositions, fortifications, battle plans and the like. This was information that a potential adversary could only obtain through espionage. Now increasingly, even the strictest counterintelligence measures cannot hide a secret that another country can uncover through scientific research and exploration in its own laboratories. Of course, if one scientific community keeps its inventions secret, it may be able to delay the speed of comparable discoveries elsewhere. This is one of the compelling considerations behind the proliferation of restrictions on disclosure of scientific information. But insofar as such restrictions serve to stimulate more intensive counter-efforts toward secrecy or toward fresh discoveries in rival camps, they may yield little or no net advantage. And the U-2 affair provides a graphic illustration of the stimulus secrecy gives to retaliatory espionage.

The difficulty of keeping secrets is related to what is perhaps the most basic of all scientific criticisms of governmental secrecy. This is the charge that it has become unduly negative in its effects through its stress upon the necessity of concealing rather than uncovering information. In the view of an influential part of the scientific community, innovation and development depend essentially upon a widespread flow of communications among scientists working on related problems. Insofar as governmental secrecy stifles such communications, it hampers scientific progress. From this perspective, the benefits to be gained in terms of a high rate of scientific discovery more than offset whatever element of risk may be present in removing restrictions on communications. Scientific achievement is itself regarded as the firmest basis for national security.

Not the least of the advantages of a policy of maximum disclosure is the fact that it strengthens the possibility of the chance discovery that has played so important a role in the history of science, and assists in the "hot pursuit" of a scientific problem from its genesis to its solution. As one scientist has noted:

> . . . The really significant new concepts of Science are often, if not always, the result of associations of widely diverse facts and ideas that may not hitherto have seemed remotely connected.
>
> Such ideas as the laws of mechanics and the concepts of space and time derived from astronomy, together with the work of Planck on high temperature radiation, led Einstein to postulate the equivalence of mass and energy. On this concept is based the development of nuclear energy.
>
> Yet today, any intelligent military organization, operating under the present security rules, would certainly classify the equivalent of Planck's work so that it would be denied to a potential Einstein.[12]

Needless to say, reasonable men still disagree as to whether the gains from a high rate of discovery equal or offset the loss that may be involved in opening up a one-way system of communications with a potential national adversary.

The direct and indirect support given the legislative attack upon executive secrecy by both the press and the scientific community reflects the degree to which the legislature serves broader interests than its own in its efforts to prevent the withholding of executive information. But it need hardly be noted that a legislative crusade against administrative secrecy would necessarily compel wide support from all those who prize informed public deliberations and executive accountability. Students of political institutions themselves have a special stake in the success of legislative efforts to expose the processes of government to unremitting scrutiny, since disclosure here is so valuable an aid to effective scholarship. Congressional attacks upon executive secrecy thus have the sanctity of serving a broad range of community interests while at the same time maximizing legislative self-interest.

Rourke, Francis E. "Administrative Secrecy: A Congressional Dilemma." *American Political Science Review* 54, no. 3 (1960): 684–87. Copyright © 1960 American Political Science Association. Reprinted with the permission of Cambridge University Press.

* * *

Claude Reyes et al. v. Chile
Inter-American Court of Human Rights

In the Case of Claude Reyes et al.,
the Inter-American Court of Human Rights (hereinafter "the Inter-American Court" or "the Court"), composed of the following judges:*

Sergio García Ramírez, President
Alirio Abreu Burelli, Vice President
Antônio A. Cançado Trindade, Judge
Cecilia Medina Quiroga, Judge
Manuel E. Ventura Robles, Judge and
Diego García-Sayán, Judge;

also present,

Pablo Saavedra Alessandri, Secretary, and
Emilia Segares Rodríguez, Deputy Secretary pursuant to Articles 62(3) and 63(1) of the American Convention on Human Rights (hereinafter "the American Convention" or "the Convention") and Articles 29, 31, 56 and 58 of the Rules of Procedure of the Court (hereinafter "the Rules of Procedure"), delivers this judgment.

I
INTRODUCTION OF THE CASE

1. On July 8, 2005, in accordance with the provisions of Articles 50 and 61 of the American Convention, the Inter-American Commission on Human Rights (hereinafter "the Commis-

---

*Judge Oliver Jackman did not take part in the deliberation and signature of this judgment, because he advised that, due to circumstances beyond his control, he would be unable to participate in the seventy-second regular session of the Court.

sion" or "the Inter-American Commission") lodged before the Court an application against the State of Chile (hereinafter "the State" or "Chile"). This application originated from petition No. 12,108, received by the Secretariat of the Commission on December 17, 1998.

2. The Commission submitted the application for the Court to declare that the State was responsible for the violation of the rights embodied in Articles 13 (Freedom of Thought and Expression) and 25 (Right to Judicial Protection) of the American Convention, in relation to the obligations established in Articles 1(1) (Obligation to Respect Rights) and 2 (Domestic Legal Effects) thereof, to the detriment of Marcel Claude Reyes, Sebastián Cox Urrejola and Arturo Longton Guerrero.

3. The facts described by the Commission in the application supposedly occurred between May and August 1998 and refer to the State's alleged refusal to provide Marcel Claude Reyes, Sebastián Cox Urrejola and Arturo Longton Guerrero with all the information they requested from the Foreign Investment Committee on the forestry company Trillium and the Río Condor Project, a deforestation project to be executed in Chile's Region XII that "c[ould] be prejudicial to the environment and to the sustainable development of Chile." The Commission stated that this refusal occurred without the State "providing any valid justification under Chilean law" and, supposedly, they "were not granted an effective judicial remedy to contest a violation of the right of access to information"; in addition, they "were not ensured the rights of access to information and to judicial protection, and there were no mechanisms guaranteeing the right of access to public information."

4. The Commission requested that, pursuant to Article 63(1) of the Convention, the Court order the State to adopt specific measures of reparation indicated in the application. Lastly, it requested the Court to order the State to pay the costs and expenses arising from processing the case in the domestic jurisdiction and before the body of the inter-American system.

. . . .

Concerning Marcel Claude Reyes and Arturo Longton Guerrero's Request for Information from the Foreign Investment Committee and the Latter's Response

57(12) Marcel Claude Reyes is an economist. In 1983, he worked in the Central Bank as an adviser to the Foreign Investment Committee and in the Environmental Accounts Unit; also, he was Executive Director of the Terram Foundation from 1997 to 2003. One of the purposes of this non-governmental organization was to promote the capacity of civil society to respond to public decisions on investments related to the use of natural resources, and also "to play an active role in public debate and in the production of solid, scientific information [. . .] on the sustainable development of [Chile]."[1]

57(13) On May 7, 1998, Marcel Claude Reyes, as Executive Director of the Terram Foundation, sent a letter to the Executive Vice President of the Foreign Investment Committee, indicating that the foundation proposed "to evaluate the commercial, economic and social aspects of the [Rio Condor] project, assess its impact on the environment [. . .] and exercise social control regarding the actions of the State entities that are or were involved in the development of the Río Cóndor exploitation project."[2] In this letter, the Executive Director of the Terram Foundation requested the Foreign Investment Committee to provide the following information "of public interest":[3]

1. Contracts signed by the State of Chile and the foreign investor concerning the Río Cóndor project, with the date and name of the notary's office where they were signed and with a copy of such contracts.

2. Identity of the foreign and/or national investors in this project.

3. Background information from Chile and abroad that the Foreign Investment Committee had before it, which ensured the soundness and suitability of the investor(s), and the agreements of the Committee recording that this information was sufficient.

4. Total amount of the investment authorized for the Río Cóndor project, method and timetable for the entry of the capital, and existence of credits associated with the latter.

5. Capital effectively imported into the country to date, as the investors' own capital, capital contributions and associated credits.

6. Information held by the Committee and/or that it has requested from other public or private entities regarding control of the obligations undertaken by the foreign investors or the companies in which they are involved and whether the Committee is aware of any infraction or offense.

7. Information on whether the Executive Vice President of the Committee has exercised the power conferred on him by Article 15 bis of D[ecree Law No.] 600, by requesting from all private and public sector entities and companies, the reports and information he required to comply with the Committee's purposes and, if so, make this information available to the Foundation."[4]

57(14) On May 19, 1998, the Executive Vice President of the Foreign Investment Committee met with Marcel Claude Reyes and Deputy Arturo Longton Guerrero.[5] The Vice President handed them "a sheet with the name of the investor, the company name, and the amount of capital he had asked to import into the country"[6] when the project was approved, the companies involved, the investments made to date, the type of project and its location.[7]

57(15) On May 19, 1998, the Executive Vice President of the Foreign Investment Committee sent Marcel Claude Reyes a one-page letter, via facsimile, in which he stated that "with regard to our conversation, the figures provided correspond only to capital, which [was] the only item executed. The Project [was] authorized to import 'associated credits' of US$102,000,000, but ha[d] not availed itself of this authorization[, and the authorized capital] amount[ed] to US$78,500,000."[8]

57(16) On June 3 and July 2, 1998, Marcel Claude Reyes sent two letters to the Executive Vice President of the Foreign Investment Committee, in which he reiterated his request for information, based on "the obligation of transparency to which State agents are subject and the right of access to public information established in the State's Constitution and in the international treaties signed and ratified by Chile." In addition, Mr. Claude Reyes indicated in these letters that he had "not received an answer from the Foreign Investment Committee to his request," and made no comment on the information that had been provided (*supra* para. 57(14) and 57(15)).[9]

57(17) The Vice President of the Foreign Investment Committee did not adopt a written decision justifying the refusal to provide the information requested in sections 3, 6 and 7 of the original request for information (*supra* para. 57(13)).[10]

57(18) On June 30, 2005, during the proceedings before the Inter-American Commission (*supra* para. 13), the State forwarded the Commission a copy of the foreign investment contracts and the assignment contracts relating to the "Río Condor" project.[11]

57(19) The State provided Mr. Claude Reyes and Mr. Longton Guerrero with the information corresponding to sections 1, 2, 4 and 5 of the original request for information orally and in writing (*supra* para. 57(13)).[12]

57(20) On April 3, 2006, the Executive Vice President of the Foreign Investment Committee at the time when Mr. Claude Reyes submitted his request for information, stated during the public hearing held before the Inter-American Court, *inter alia*, that he had not provided the requested information:

(a) On section 3 (*supra* para. 57(13)), because "the Foreign Investment Committee [. . .] did not disclose the company's financial data, since providing this information was contrary to the public interest," which was "the country's development." "It was not reasonable that foreign companies applying to the Foreign Investment Committee should have to disclose their financial information in this way; information that could be very important to them in relation to their competitors; hence, this could have been an obstacle to the foreign investment process." It was the Foreign Investment Committee's practice not to provide a company's financial data that could affect its competitiveness to third parties. The Committee and the Vice President defined what was in the public interest;

(b) On section 6 (*supra* para. 57(13)), because information on the background material that the Committee could request from other institutions "did not exist" and the Committee "does not having policing functions"; and

(c) On section 7 (*supra* para. 57(13)), because "the Foreign Investment Committee had neither the responsibility nor the capacity to evaluate each project on its merits; it had a staff of just over 20 persons. Furthermore, this was not necessary, since the role of the Foreign Investment Committee is to authorize the entry of capitals and the corresponding terms and conditions, and the country had an institutional framework for each sector."[13] . . .

VII
VIOLATION OF ARTICLE 13 OF THE AMERICAN CONVENTION REGARDING TO ARTICLES 1(1) AND 2 THEREOF (FREEDOM OF THOUGHT AND EXPRESSION)

The Commission's arguments

58. Regarding the alleged violation of Article 13 of the Convention, regarding Articles 1(1) and 2 thereof, the Commission indicated that:

(a) The disclosure of State-held information should play a very important role in a democratic society, because it enables civil society to control the actions of the Government to which it has entrusted the protection of its interests. "Article 13 of the Convention should be understood as a positive obligation on the part of the State to provide access to the information it holds"; this is necessary to avoid abuses by government officials, to promote accountability and transparency within the State, and to allow a substantial and informed public debate that ensures there are effective recourses against such abuses;

(b) There is a growing consensus that States have the positive obligation to provide the information they hold to their citizens. "The Commission has interpreted Article 13 to include a right of access to State-held information";

(c) "According to the broad terms of Article 13, the right of access to information should be governed by the 'principle of maximum disclosure.'" "The burden of proof corresponds to the State, which must demonstrate that restrictions to access to information are compatible with the inter-American provisions on freedom of expression." "This means that the restriction must not only be related to one of the [legitimate] objectives [that justify it], but it must also be shown that disclosure could cause substantial prejudice to this objective and that the prejudice to the objective is greater than the public interest in having the information" (evidence of proportionality);

(d) Most States of the Americas have regulations concerning access to information. The respective Chilean laws were not applied in this case because they were promulgated after the facts that gave rise to the petition. "The State of Chile has made a series of legislative modifications; however[, . . .] these do not guarantee effective and broad access to public information." "The exceptions established by law [. . .] grant an excessive degree of discretionality to the official who determines whether or not the information is disclosed";

(e) In the instant case, the Commission focused its attention on the information concerning the FIC assessment of the pertinence of the foreign investors, which was not provided to the alleged victims, and which was not officially refused;

(f) Regarding the State's argument that, if the type of information requested had been revealed to the alleged victims, it would have violated the right to confidentiality of the companies concerned, it should be recalled that restrictions to the right to seek, receive and impart information must be expressly established by law. "The State has not cited any provision of Chilean legislation or any legal precedent which expressly establishes that information on the decision-making procedure of the Foreign Investment Committee is confidential." The decision to retain information appears to be "totally at the discretion of the Vice President of the Foreign Investment Committee." Additionally, in its answer to the application, the State departs from the line of argument on confidentiality, alleging that the Foreign Investment Committee did not have the time, capacity or legal powers to investigate the circumstances of the investors;

(g) The Foreign Investment Committee never provided a written response with regard to the missing information and has not shown how retaining the information in question was "necessary" to achieve one of the legitimate objectives established in Article 13 of the Convention. Moreover, it never presented any argument to prove that the disclosure of the information would have resulted in substantial prejudice to these objectives, and that this prejudice was greater than the public interest of disclosing the information as required by the said Article 13. In addition, the State's assertion that the role of controlling Government entities is the exclusive competence of Congress is "unsustainable"; and

(h) "The Chilean State did not guarantee the right of the [alleged] victims of access to information because a State entity refused access to information without proving that it was included in one of the legitimate exceptions to the general rule of disclosure established in Article 13. Also, when the facts that gave rise to this application occurred, the State did not have mechanisms to ensure the right of access to information effectively." . . .

The Court's findings

61. Article 13 (Freedom of Thought and Expression) of the American Convention establishes, *inter alia*, that:

1. Everyone has the right to freedom of thought and expression. This right includes freedom to seek, receive, and impart information and ideas of all kinds, regardless of frontiers, either orally, in writing, in print, in the form of art, or through any other medium of one's choice.

2. The exercise of the right provided for in the foregoing paragraph shall not be subject to prior censorship but shall be subject to subsequent imposition of liability, which shall be expressly established by law to the extent necessary to ensure:
   a. respect for the rights or reputations of others; or
   b. the protection of national security, public order, or public health or morals.

3. The right of expression may not be restricted by indirect methods or means, such as the abuse of government or private controls over newsprint, radio broadcasting frequencies, or equipment used in the dissemination of information, or by any other means tending to impede the communication and circulation of ideas and opinions.[. . .]

62. Regarding the obligation to respect rights, Article 1(1) of the Convention stipulates that: The States Parties to this Convention undertake to respect the rights and freedoms recognized herein and to ensure to all persons subject to their jurisdiction the free and full exercise of those rights and freedoms, without any discrimination for reasons of race, color, sex, language, religion, political or other opinion, national or social origin, economic status, birth, or any other social condition.

63. Regarding domestic legal effects, Article 2 of the Convention establishes that: Where the exercise of any of the rights or freedoms referred to in Article 1 is not already ensured by legislative or other provisions, the States Parties undertake to adopt, in accordance with their constitutional processes and the provisions of this Convention, such legislative or other measures as may be necessary to give effect to those rights or freedoms. . . .

XI
OPERATIVE PARAGRAPHS

174. Therefore,
THE COURT DECLARES,
Unanimously, that:

1. The State violated the right to freedom of thought and expression embodied in Article 13 of the American Convention on Human Rights, to the detriment of Marcel Claude Reyes and Arturo Longton Guerrero, in relation to the general obligations to respect and guarantee the rights and freedoms and to adopt provisions of domestic law established in Articles 1(1) and 2 thereof, in the terms of paragraphs 61 to 103 of this judgment.
   By four votes to two, that:
2. The State violated the right to judicial guarantees embodied in Article 8(1) of the American Convention on Human Rights, to the detriment of Marcel Claude Reyes and Arturo Longton Guerrero, with regard to the administrative authority's decision not to provide information, in relation to the general obligation to respect and guarantee the rights and freedoms established in Article 1(1) thereof, in the terms of paragraphs 114 to 123 of this judgment.
   Dissenting Judge Abreu Burelli and Judge Medina Quiroga.
   Unanimously, that:
3. The State violated the rights to judicial guarantees and judicial protection embodied in Articles 8(1) and 25 of the American Convention on Human Rights, to the detriment of Marcel Claude Reyes, Arturo Longton Guerrero and Sebastián Cox Urrejola, with regard to the judicial decision concerning the application for protection, in relation to the general obligation to respect and guarantee the rights and freedoms established in Article 1(1) thereof, in the terms of paragraphs 124 to 144 of this judgment.
   Unanimously, that:
4. This judgment constitutes, *per se,* a form of reparation in the terms of paragraph 156 hereof.
   AND DECIDES,
   Unanimously, that:

5. The State shall, through the corresponding entity and within six months, provide the information requested by the victims, if appropriate, or adopt a justified decision in this regard, in the terms of paragraphs 157 to 159 and 168 of this judgment.

6. The State shall publish, within a period of six months, once in the official gazette and in another newspaper with extensive national circulation, the chapter on the Proven Facts of this judgment, paragraphs 69 to 71, 73, 74, 77, 88 to 103, 117 to 123, 132 to 137 and 139 to 143 of this judgment, which correspond to Chapters VII and VIII on the violations declared by the Court, without the corresponding footnotes, and the operative paragraphs hereof, in the terms of paragraphs 160 and 168 of this judgment.

7. The State shall adopt, within a reasonable time, the necessary measures to ensure the right of access to State-held information, pursuant to the general obligation to adopt provisions of domestic law established in Article 2 of the American Convention on Human Rights, in the terms of paragraphs 161 to 163 and 168 of this judgment.

8. The State shall, within a reasonable time, provide training to public entities, authorities and agents responsible for responding to requests for access to State-held information on the laws and regulations governing this right; this training should incorporate the parameters established in the Convention concerning restrictions to access to this information, in the terms of paragraphs 164, 165 and 168 of this judgment.

9. The State shall pay Marcel Claude Reyes, Arturo Longton Guerrero and Sebastián Cox Urrejola, within one year, for costs and expenses, the amount established in paragraph 167 of this judgment, in the terms of paragraphs 167 and 169 to 172.

10. It will monitor full compliance with this judgment and will consider the case closed when the State has fully executed its operative paragraphs. Within a year of notification of this judgment, the State shall send the Court a report on the measures adopted to comply with it, in the terms of paragraph 173 of this judgment.

Judge Abreu Burelli and Judge Medina Quiroga informed the Court of their joint dissenting opinion concerning the second operative paragraph. Judge García Ramírez informed the Court of his separate concurring opinion on the second operative paragraph. These opinions accompany this judgment.

Claude Reyes et al. v. Chile, Inter-American Court of Human Rights (2006): 1–61.

* * *

Memorandum for the Heads of Executive Departments and Agencies. Subject: Transparency and Open Government
Barack Obama

My Administration is committed to creating an unprecedented level of openness in Government. We will work together to ensure the public trust and establish a system of transparency, public participation, and collaboration. Openness will strengthen our democracy and promote efficiency and effectiveness in Government.

Government should be transparent. Transparency promotes accountability and provides information for citizens about what their Government is doing. Information maintained by the Federal Government is a national asset. My Administration will take appropriate action, consistent with law and policy, to disclose information rapidly in forms that the public can readily find and use. Executive departments and agencies should harness new technologies to put information about their operations and decisions online and readily available to the public. Executive departments and agencies should also solicit public feedback to identify information of greatest use to the public.

Government should be participatory. Public engagement enhances the Government's effectiveness and improves the quality of its decisions. Knowledge is widely dispersed in society, and public officials benefit from having access to that dispersed knowledge. Executive departments and agencies should offer Americans increased opportunities to participate in policymaking and to provide their Government with the benefits of their collective expertise and information. Executive departments and agencies should also solicit public input on how we can increase and improve opportunities for public participation in Government.

Government should be collaborative. Collaboration actively engages Americans in the work of their Government. Executive departments and agencies should use innovative tools, methods, and systems to cooperate among themselves, across all levels of Government, and with nonprofit organizations, businesses, and individuals in the private sector. Executive departments and agencies should solicit public feedback to assess and improve their level of collaboration and to identify new opportunities for cooperation.

I direct the Chief Technology Officer, in coordination with the Director of the Office of Management and Budget (OMB) and the Administrator of General Services, to coordinate the development by appropriate executive departments and agencies, within 120 days, of recommendations for an Open Government Directive, to be issued by the Director of OMB, that instructs executive departments and agencies to take specific actions implementing the principles set forth in this memorandum. The independent agencies should comply with the Open Government Directive.

This memorandum is not intended to, and does not, create any right or benefit, substantive or procedural, enforceable at law or in equity by a party against the United States, its departments, agencies, or entities, its officers, employees, or agents, or any other person.

This memorandum shall be published in the *Federal Register*.

BARACK OBAMA

Obama, Barack. Memorandum for the Heads of Executive Departments and Agencies. Subject: Transparency and Open Government. (2009). http://www.whitehouse.gov/the_press_office/ TransparencyandOpenGovernment/ (9 July 2009).

2

Transparency and Competing Values:
Privacy, Security, and Efficiency

INTRODUCTION

Transparency is one of those concepts that very few people actually want to go on the record as being against. Governmental transparency has been equated to motherhood and apple pie. Who isn't for them? Thoughtful observers of government realize that there are legitimate arguments to limit governmental openness. To invoke a metaphor, a representative democracy is like a swan: "all elegance and tranquility above the surface, all hustle and bustle below the surface, and unseen" (Birkinshaw 2006, 191). Is there a need to see the chaos happening below the surface, or can the public be content with watching the elegant swan swim by? Patrick Birkinshaw (2006, 191–93) presents students of transparency with a list of arguments against openness and freedom of information. His list begins with the swan metaphor and includes, among others, the arguments that follow.

Efficiency and strong government: It is a core responsibility of government to protect its people. Fulfilling openness requirements, such as freedom of information requests and open meeting provisions, can be very costly. Resources used to meet openness requirements are deflected away from more important governmental functions.

Danger to security and innocent third parties: Government holds mountains of information that if in the wrong hands can be a danger to society. Even seemingly benign information in the wrong hands may turn into a threat if held by terrorists.

Unjustified Invasion of Personal Privacy or Commercial Confidentiality: Governments not only hold information sensitive to security and law enforcement, they also hold information concerning individuals and private entities. Freedom of information laws typically include some sort of personal privacy provisions. The difficulty is finding the correct balance between the public's right to know and the individual's and corporation's desire to keep their information out of the public domain.

FOI undermines trust and panders to irrelevance: There is a necessary trust that must exist between the governed and governors. The unnecessary and districting fixation on openness undermines this trust.

This section of the book focuses on three concepts that are at times in tension with transparency: personal privacy, security, and efficiency. These tensions mirror some of the arguments against freedom of information that Birkinshaw lays out for us.

Personal privacy is an often cited reason to withhold information that is requested from government. Louis Brandeis and Samuel Warren wrote a seminal *Harvard Law Review* article on "The Right to Privacy" in 1890. Many of the issues that Brandeis and Warren touch on are still relevant today. They speak to the roles media and ever-evolving technology play with respect to personal privacy. Technology is changing the way we store, access, and retrieve government records. Charles Davis (2005) writes about the very contentious issue of digital access to court records. Court records, including sensitive information on personal events such as bankruptcies and divorces, have historically been available in paper form to individuals who visit a courthouse. Davis traces the evolution of privacy law as it has evolved in part due to a response to technological advances.

Krisana Kitiyadisai, in the article "Privacy Rights and Protection: Foreign Values in Modern Thai Context" (2005), challenges some basic assumptions of privacy and makes the reader consider if the notion of privacy is a culturally relative one. Kitiyadisai explains how the concept of privacy is viewed in Thailand and forces Western readers to reconsider their basic understanding of what the right to privacy means.

Security—national security, homeland security, local law enforcement—is the second area that is typically cited as being in tension with transparency. Thomas Blanton, in his book chapter "National Security and Open Government in the United States: Beyond the Balancing Test" (2003), contends that this is a false dichotomy. To build his case, he presents a history of secrecy in the United States, including a discussion of the post-9/11 environment. He concludes his well-substantiated position with what some would argue is a radical conclusion: openness actually contributes to security.

The third and final concept presented in this section is efficiency. Filling freedom of information requests, advertising public meetings, keeping websites current, and managing archives are all resource-consuming tasks. The implementation of right to know policies can be expensive and labor intensive. Government bureaucrats frequently feel that complying with these rules and regulations takes them away from their "real" work. Many government agencies are underfunded and understaffed, and fulfilling transparency requirements must be done in addition to employees' regular daily tasks. Before becoming a Supreme Court justice, Antonin Scalia commented on this issue:

> They are foolish extravagances only because we do not have an unlimited amount of federal money to spend, an unlimited number of agency employees to assign, an unlimited number of judges to hear and decide cases. We must, also, set some priorities—and unless the world is mad the usual Freedom of Information Act requests should not be high on the list. (Scalia quoted in Markman 1988)

While Scalia was speaking directly about the U.S. federal Freedom of Information Act (FOIA), the same argument could be made against the implementation of other transparency-related policies.

In her book *Governmental Transparency in the Path of Administrative Reform* (2007), Suzanne Piotrowski discusses how the quest for government efficiency is at times in tension with transparency requirements such as the U.S. Freedom of Information Act. Piotrowski explains how business-model management reforms when applied to the U.S. federal government had unintended consequences for implementation of the FOIA and democratic accountability more generally.

Privacy, security, and efficiency are three areas that are frequently seen to be in tension with the fulfillment of right to know goals. When reading the excerpts throughout this book on freedom of information, proactively released information, open meetings, whistleblowing, and leaks, be sure to consciously consider how each of these tensions is at play. At the beginning of this section you will read arguments against openness. Birkinshaw also gives us seven arguments in favor of freedom of information and open government (2006, 194–96):

- Information is used in the public interest and the interests of all individuals.
- Information is a necessity for accountability.
- Information, particularly reliable information, is a prerequisite to establish effectiveness and efficiency in government.
- Information is a necessary right of citizenship.
- Information is power and its exclusive possession is especially so, both in terms of policy formulation and invasions of personal privacy by government.
- Secrecy is a cloak for arbitrariness, inefficiency, corruption, and so on.
- FOIA reciprocates the trust that people place in government.

When considering the three tensions—privacy, security, and efficiency—outlined in this chapter, also consider how they balance with the reasons for increased openness in government.

Assignments and Study Questions

1. Are national security and openness in government inherently in tension with one another?
2. In what ways has changing technology affected the debate around personal privacy?
3. Should court records be made available online? Should "pajama surfers" be able to access divorce records in the middle of the night from their computer when it once would have required a trip to the courthouse? If a record is deemed "public," is the medium of release relevant?
4. In what ways could a government help protect the privacy interests of the people it serves? Consider the roles of technology and the possibility that governments currently collect personal information that is not necessary for the task at hand (i.e., collecting social security numbers to process a dog license).
5. Make up a list of five broad types of government information that should not be released to the public. What are your reasons for not releasing each category of information? Can you come up with counterarguments to each of these points?
6. Can you think of any other tensions with openness and governmental transparency? Explain.

* * *

The Right to Privacy

Samuel D. Warren and Louis D. Brandeis

That the individual shall have full protection in person and in property is a principle as old as the common law; but it has been found necessary from time to time to define anew the exact nature and extent of such protection. Political, social, and economic changes entail the recognition of new rights, and the common law, in its eternal youth, grows to meet the demands of society. Thus, in very early times, the law gave a remedy only for physical interference with life and property, for trespasses *vi et armis.* Then the "right to life" served only to protect the subject from battery in its various forms; liberty meant freedom from actual restraint; and the right to property secured to the individual his lands and his cattle. Later, there came recognition of man's spiritual nature, of his feelings and his intellect. Gradually the scope of these legal rights broadened; and now the right to life has come to mean the right to enjoy life,—the right to be let alone; the right to liberty secures the exercise of extensive civil privileges; and the term "property" has grown to comprise every form of possession—intangible, as well as tangible.

Thus, with the recognition of the legal value of sensations, the protection against actual bodily injury was extended to prohibit mere attempts to do such injury; that is, the putting another in fear of such injury. From the action of battery grew that of assault.[1] Much later there came a qualified protection of the individual against offensive noises and odors, against dust and smoke, and excessive vibration. The law of nuisance was developed.[2] So regard for human emotions soon extended the scope of personal immunity beyond the body of the individual. His reputation, the standing among his fellow-men, was considered, and the law of slander and libel arose.[3] Man's family relations became a part of the legal conception of his life, and the alienation of a wife's affections was held remediable.[4] Occasionally the law halted,—as in its refusal to recognize the intrusion by seduction upon the honor of the family. But even here the demands of society were met. A mean fiction, the action *per quod servitium amisit,* was resorted to, and by allowing damages for injury to the parents' feelings, an adequate remedy was ordinarily afforded.[5] Similar to the expansion of the right to life was the growth of the legal conception of property. From corporeal property arose the incorporeal rights issuing out of it; and then there opened the wide realm of intangible property, in the products and processes of the mind,[6] as works of literature and art[7], goodwill,[8] trade secrets, and trademarks.[9]

This development of the law was inevitable. The intense intellectual and emotional life, and the heightening of sensations which came with the advance of civilization, made it clear to men that only a part of the pain, pleasure, and profit of life lay in physical things. Thoughts, emotions, and sensations demanded legal recognition, and the beautiful capacity for growth which characterizes the common law enabled the judges to afford the requisite protection, without the interposition of the legislature.

Recent inventions and business methods call attention to the next step which must be taken for the protection of the person, and for securing to the individual what Judge Cooley calls the right "to be let alone."[10] Instantaneous photographs and newspaper enterprise have invaded the sacred precincts of private and domestic life; and numerous mechanical devices threaten to make good the prediction that "what is whispered in the closet shall be proclaimed from the house-tops." For years there has been a feeling that the law must afford some remedy for the unauthorized circulation of portraits of private persons;[11] and the evil of the invasion of privacy by the newspapers, long keenly felt, has been but recently discussed by an able writer.[12] The alleged facts of a somewhat notorious case brought before an inferior tribunal in New York a few months ago,[13] directly involved the consideration of the right of circulating portraits; and the question whether our law will recognize and protect the right to privacy in this and in other respects must soon come before our courts for consideration.

Of the desirability—indeed of the necessity—of some such protection, there can, it is believed, be no doubt. The press is overstepping in every direction the obvious bounds of propriety and of decency. Gossip is no longer the resource of the idle and of the vicious, but has become a trade, which is pursued with industry as well as effrontery. To satisfy a prurient taste the details of sexual relations are spread broadcast in the columns of the daily papers. To occupy the indolent, column upon column is filled with idle gossip, which can only be procured by intrusion upon the domestic circle. The intensity and complexity of life, attendant upon advancing civilization, have rendered necessary some retreat from the world, and man, under the refining influence of culture, has become more sensitive to publicity, so that solitude and privacy have become more essential to the individual; but modern enterprise and invention have, through invasions upon his privacy, subjected him to mental pain and distress, far greater than could be inflicted by mere bodily injury. Nor is the harm wrought by such invasions confined to the suffering of those who may be made the subjects of journalistic or other enterprise. In this, as in other branches of commerce, the supply creates the demand. Each crop of unseemly gossip, thus harvested, becomes the seed of more, and, in direct proportion to its circulation, results in a lowering of social standards and of morality. Even gossip apparently harmless, when widely and persistently circulated, is potent for evil. It both belittles and perverts. It belittles by inverting the relative importance of things, thus dwarfing the thoughts and aspirations of a people. When personal gossip attains the dignity of print, and crowds the space available for matters of real interest to the community, what wonder that the ignorant and thoughtless mistake its relative importance. Easy of comprehension, appealing to that weak side of human nature which is never wholly cast down by the misfortunes and frailties of our neighbors, no one can be surprised that it usurps the place of interest in brains capable of other things. Triviality destroys at once robustness of thought and delicacy of feeling. No enthusiasm can flourish; no generous impulse can survive under its blighting influence.

It is our purpose to consider whether the existing law affords a principle which can properly be invoked to protect the privacy of the individual; and, if it does, what the nature and extent of such protection is.

Warren, Samuel D., and Louis D. Brandeis. "The Right to Privacy." *Harvard Law Review* 4, no. 5 (1890): 193–97.

* * *

Privacy Rights and Protection: Foreign Values in Modern Thai Context

Krisana Kitiyadisai

The concepts of liberal Western values dramatically entered into Thai consciousness and culture as a result of the 1932 coup with the abolition of absolute monarchy and the introduction of a parliamentary system under a Constitution based on liberty, equality, and freedom. However, the democratic development was short-lived and Thailand went through a series of coups and military regimes. After the Cold War, the influences of economic expansion, globalization and subsequent political struggles have changed Thailand into a country with a modern, industrialized and cosmopolitan outlook. But the traditional Thai values and culture are not conducive to the assimilation of the concepts of human rights, privacy rights and protection, as Thai culture is based on collectivism and non-confrontation. For the new generations, changes are taking place in the new cultural space. By observing various web-board discussions, the issue of privacy protection is fast becoming one of the hot topics among the educated, urban middle-class and Internet surfers or netizens, especially regarding the issues of 'smart' ID cards (that would contain personal and medical information) and the enforced registration of prepaid SIM cards for mobile phones. The first part of this paper discusses the Thai conception of privacy and the influences of Buddhism on privacy rights and the background to the development of privacy legislation. The second part discusses the legal provision on privacy rights and the debates on the smart ID cards project and the control of SIM cards for national security.

THAI PERSPECTIVES ON "PRIVACY"

Most writers on the concept of Thai privacy agree that the western concept of "privacy" is not applicable to Thai social reality. But this may be changing in the age of the Internet, insofar as culture is forever dynamic and as some argue, a desire for privacy is a panhuman trait.[1] According to Thais, the first connotation of privacy is negative in the sense that the loss of privacy would bring shame, disrespect, or loss of face in public. The word "private" was assimilated into Thai culture around the reign of King Rama V (1868–1910) as the Thai word "*pri-vade*" (modified from "private") was used for "*shud-pri-vade*" which means casual clothes vis-à-vis military uniforms; "*shud-pri-vade*" are clothes people would wear at home, which could range from pyjamas, dressing gowns, or old tatty clothes to informal attire. Normally, these clothes would be quite casual or "unrespectable" so that one would be embarrassed if caught wearing them at formal occasions or in public. During the period of Kings Rama IV and V (1851–1868), Western military uniforms, costumes and royal regalia were much admired and assimilated into Thai culture. So, this meaning corresponds to the concept of "privacy" in Thai language of "being private" or "living privately" (*khwam pen yu suan tua*).

It is important to further notice that this conception of privacy is basically *collectivistic*—not, as Westerners tend to assume, *individual*. That is, as Ramasoota makes clear, "being private" in traditional Thailand applies primarily to the shared family space in which family members undertake a wide range of activities—including rituals, cooking and eating, and sleeping—as demarcated from the world outside: "It is the kind of privacy that is shared by *intimate members of the same household*. By this token, individualistic privacy is said to have no place in traditional Thai culture."[2]

Niels Mudler likewise points out that privacy and individualism are Western concepts that are not applicable to Thai society, for Thai life is played out in public.[3] However, a person's private affairs should be kept private which implies that a Thai has both a right and obligation in the sense that he has to hide his own psychological problems within the bounds of expected behavior; this includes the right to expect other people to respect his private affairs which would cause him to lose face if made public.

The second meaning of "privacy" in Thai culture connotes the right to be left alone or non-interference which can be equated to "private affairs" or "my private affairs" or "my business" ("*rueng-suan-tua*" or "*ruengsuan- tua-khong-chan*" or "*tu-ra-khong-chan*"). Personal or private businesses or affairs should not be interfered with in Thai culture, e.g., quarrels within the family, the punishment of a child by his parents, and so forth. This notion is the legacy of the feudal heritage of Thai society where the master or lord of the household owned and commanded the lives and destinies of all his subordinates under his autocratic rule.

The lack of a Thai word for "privacy" reflects the traditional Thai village life and the heritage of the feudalistic values in Thai history. The traditional Thai village house consists of a large room which is used as kitchen, living room, dining room, and bedroom. This one-room house is where all members of the immediate extended family share their social lives. For this lifestyle to be kept in order and harmony, necessary cultural values and norms had been established, evolved and shared among people for generations. According to Holmes and Tangtongtavy, the two cornerstones of Thai culture are conflict avoidance and the hierarchical society.[4] In order to create strong relationships and to maintain them, conflict avoidance or non-confrontation is diligently observed, because the result of a confrontation can be disastrous as it results in "losing-face" ("*siar-na*") by either side of the conflict. "Face" represents one's social and professional position, reputation and self-image, so that a loss of face is to be prevented or avoided at all costs—which further means that face-saving or "*koo-na*" has to be instigated at critical junctures. This intense need for gaining, and not losing, face has been explained in terms of cultural collectivism from which members are afraid of being excluded.[5] Consequently, power and status within a group depend on respect and admiration accumulated through gaining "face." The more "face" a person has, the higher his credit rating—so much so that he can buy goods from local shops on credit and exert substantial influence in a group's decision-making.

The second cornerstone, the hierarchical society, is the product of Thai feudalism or *Sakdi-nar* which was established during the fifteenth century and abolished by King Rama V less than 300 years ago. *Sakdi-nar* was a system of ranking each individual according to the size of allocated land or rice-field; therefore a person's power and rank depended on his level of *Sakdi-nar* (*Sakdi* = power, ranking; *nar* = rice field). The patronage system existing within the vertical networks of relationship helped in maintaining the flexible and interdependent structure of Thai society. Several values and norms for supporting this hierarchy includes "to know who's high, who's low" ("*roojak thee soong, thee tum*"), "to give respect or show honor" ("*hai-kiad*") to high-ranking superiors, while the high ranking *Sakdi-na* shows benevolence ("*parame*") and gives favor ("*boon-khun*") to those under their patronage. Thai society can be perceived as an affiliation society whose members depend upon each other and seek security in dependence and patronage.[6] Therefore, a low ranking person's behavior would be very polite and submissive in order to avoid any transgression which could be construed as showing disrespect and lead to "losing face."

Asian countries generally stress the importance of abiding by the rules of politeness protocols, including the face-saving rituals of bowing ("*wai*" for Thais), profuse apologies, formal turn-taking during negotiations and other deferential yet obligatory protocols.[7] In Thai culture, there is a whole series of protocols ranging from body language, spoken and written communications, and prescribed manners—all aiming at "showing respect" or "saving face." Therefore, the notion of privacy in traditional Thai society could be close to "saving face" ("*raksa-na*") in which "*haikiad*" (to give honor or respect) represents the valuable currency. The more "*kiad*" and "*na*" (honor and face) a person receives, the higher the status, power and social credit the person has acquired in that society.

The combination of privacy as "private affairs" ("*rueng-suan-tua*") and the right of "non-interference" works in support of "saving face"—and hence, interference by outsiders is interpreted as a "disrespect" that is dangerous insofar as it can lead to "losing face." In this light, the Thai Prime Minister's reactions of outrage against the US Congressional report on human rights violations during the country's "war on drugs" was perceived by most Thais as quite justifiable.[8] Paradoxically, the interference in "private affairs" is welcome and acceptable when conducted with "saving face" ("*raksa-na*") motivation. Frequently, a third party (who has a lot of "face") may be asked to help in reconciling a high level of confrontational negotiation which, if not properly managed so as to "saving face" on both sides, may slide into an aggressive and violent conclusion, e.g., the disputes between neighboring countries over frontiers and claims to natural resources in Asia.

BUDDHIST PERSPECTIVES ON PRIVACY RIGHTS

According to Buddhism, human beings have no rights in the sense that we are not born with auto-matically endowed human rights such as privacy rights and protection. In Buddhism, the rights of ownership of land, water, lake, trees, natural resources, and even our own bodies are all illusory, but which we accept as necessary for operating at this realm of existence. They are social conventions for getting on with life and the pursuit of personal development, self-improvement and ultimately enlightenment. So, the concepts of human rights and privacy rights are perceived as man-made, whereby the corresponding social and legal norms have been developed to enable the achievement of personal and societal objectives. But this does not mean that Buddhism ignores the sanctity of life, animals, other living beings, or the whole of nature. Indeed, Buddhists texts are full of teachings on moral and respectful conduct towards all sentient beings and the law of karma warns the transgressors of the results of bad karma (actions).

The Buddhist precaution reflects the fact that man-made rules and laws would inevitably be in conflict within themselves as these are created to serve human avarice; so these mechanisms are fragmented and reflect the prevailing force in the society. This would lead to further competition and aggressive posturing for protecting and furthering the interests among various groups. Phra Dhammapitaka points out the underlying flaw of Western approaches by the example of the concept of "equality."[9] This concept should be democratically interpreted as sharing together in times of "*suk-lae-duk*" (happiness and sorrow), that is, in times of plenty and poverty. But—in what to Buddhists appears to be a central contradiction or paradox—the general application of "equality" in the capitalistic world implies the competition or struggle for an equal share in the stake. By contrast, the Thai concept of equality is reflected in "*ruam-duk-ruam-suk*" (sharing-suffering-sharing-happiness) which has the same spirit of "in sickness and in health; for richer, for poorer." Thus, Phra Dhammapitaka stresses the importance of educating people to respect other people's rights while being aware that all these rights are the means for human development and that they are not ends in themselves, lest we would become so attached to the concepts of rights that we would forget the purpose of Life.

Thus the Buddhist approach to human rights which includes privacy rights is more practical and spiritual at the same time. The Buddha's teaching, which is especially conducive to the protection of human rights, includes the teaching on the Ideal Person, the Virtuous Person, the Social Benefactor, and the King's Duties.[10] These teachings cover all aspects of righteous bodily conduct, righteous speech and mentality with comprehensive details so that the practice of these teachings can significantly contribute towards human rights protection. Instead of creating and assigning rights, Buddhism prescribes the ground rules for conducting a moral and virtuous livelihood in which all types of transgressions and bad karma are forbidden and subject to the law of karma.

The influence of Buddhism in Thai culture is amply reflected in the elements of *kreng-jai*, *nam-jai*, *hen-jai* and *sam-ruam*, including the law of karma. The quality of kreng-jai refers to an attitude of having consideration for others and being thoughtful in maintaining a smooth social atmosphere. So, *kreng-jai* facilitates avoiding unpleasantness and interpersonal confrontation. Holmes and Tangtongtavy observe that the manifestation of *kreng-jai* can range from complying with others' requests to the avoidance of asserting one's opinion or needs in order to maintain a cooperative relationship.[11] *Nam-jai* (water-heart), one of the most admired values in Thai culture, means "water from the heart"—that is, genuine kindness and generosity without expecting anything in return. This reflects the Buddhist teaching on kindness (*Metta*) and compassion (*Karuna*). On the other hand, *hen-jai* (see into the heart), which means understanding, sympathy, and empathy, which can be practically expressed by being willing to listen, being flexible and forgiving, and accommodating towards one's fellow human beings in time of distress.

The term *sam-ruam* refers to moderation in expressions and conduct which is based on the Buddhist teaching on equanamity (*Upekkha*) and appreciative gladness (*Mudita*). When a person is *sam-ruam*, he would restrain his emotions, whether being elated or in grief or in anger so as to avoid excessive display of emotions which could cause embarrassment and discomfort to others. The law of karma ensures that Thais are generally very motivated towards righteous conduct, for fear of the results of bad karma and for counting on the benefits of good karma as well. Therefore, the major task for practicing Buddhists is to encourage more inactive Buddhists to become diligent practitioners, thereby increasing the level of human rights protection in Thailand and in pursuit of spiritual liberation.

With kind permission from Springer Science+Business Media: Kitiyadisai, Krisana. "Privacy Rights and Protection: Foreign Values in Modern Thai Context." *Ethics and Information Technology* 7, no. 1 (2005): 17–20.

* * *

National Security and Open Government in the United States: Beyond the Balancing Test

Thomas S. Blanton

National security is not a value in itself, but rather a condition that allows a nation to maintain its values.[1] In contrast, open government is both a condition and a value of democratic societies. Thus, putting the two concepts on the same spectrum, or speaking of them as in some kind of balance with each other, gives excessive weight to the former, and diminishes the necessary suspicion that should greet any attempt to reduce openness on national security grounds. We need a new paradigm beyond the balancing test, else security concerns of the day will continue to erode fundamental values.

Such erosion is not new in the United States, since secrecy attended the birth of this country at the Constitutional Convention of 1787. But the government's enormous information security and classification system is a more recent phenomenon, an aging child of the Cold War that not only refuses to go quietly into retirement, but finds a fountain of youth in wars of all kinds.

The new secrecy trend actually began before the Bush administration, during the partisan battles of the late Clinton years. In turn, the Bush administration's retrenchment began before 9/11, but the shock of 9/11 provided the government with political capital and U.S. public support for greater secrecy in the name of national security. The current information war features battles on many fronts: scientific and technical information, presidential records, implementation of the Freedom of Information Act, online censorship, public safety information, and more. The bottom line is that the new secrecy is not as bad as it could be, but much worse than it should be.

At the same time, a new paradigm is beginning to emerge—partly based on the scientific critique of secrecy, but even more so on the secrecy failures surrounding 9/11—that posits instead of a balancing act, an extreme limitation on secrecy and an emphasis on openness as the most important guarantor of security.

The following provides a highly selective historical background for U.S. limitations on openness in the name of national security, a brief and idiosyncratic description of how the Cold War created the modern national security secrecy system, a revisionist review of the roots of U.S. retrenchment in the late 1990s, a theological discussion of the origins of Bush administration secrecy, a succinct tour guide's map of the main battlefronts in the current information wars, and finally, more of a wish list than a prognosis for the new paradigm that is emerging in large part from the ashes of the World Trade Center. . . .

NEW PARADIGM—OPENNESS IS SECURITY

A new paradigm is struggling to emerge from the ashes of the World Trade Center. Originally, this paradigm had nothing to do with terrorism but came directly from the scientific method—tested hypotheses, complete citations, replicable results, peer review. The most articulate exponents of openness—even and particularly in the new Cold War hothouse of nuclear secrets—were precisely the scientists who had developed the Bomb, and they argued not so much on behalf of democratic values, or civil rights and liberties, but on scientific efficiency, and national security. Vannevar Bush, for example, President Roosevelt's key science adviser during World War II, stated the following in 1945: "Our ability to overcome future enemies depends upon scientific advances which will proceed more rapidly with diffusion of knowledge than under a policy of continued restriction of knowledge now in our possession."[2]

The Tolman Committee appointed by General Groves in 1945 to assess any declassification of Manhattan Project information, stated its general philosophy as follows:

> It is not the conviction of the Committee that the concealment of scientific information can in the long-term contribute to the national security of the United States. It is recognized that at the present time it may be inevitable that the policy of the Government will be to conceal certain information in the interest of national security. Even within this limitation there are many matters whose declassification would greatly help the progress of science without violating that policy. If we are looking to the national welfare or national security as they may be two decades from now the Committee has no doubt that the greatest strength in both fields would come from a completely free and open development of science. Thus, the Committee is inclined to the view that there are probably good reasons for keeping close control of much scientific information if it is believed that there is a likelihood of war within the next five or ten years. It is also their view, however, that this would weaken us disastrously for the future—perhaps twenty years hence.[3]

A more modern iteration of the same analysis came from Dr. Edward Teller, co-inventor of the hydrogen bomb and avatar of ballistic missile defense. Teller wrote [in] *The New York Times* in 1973:

> I urge the United States to move . . . toward unilaterally abandoning all forms of scientific and technical secrecy. . . . I advocate this in the enlightened self-interest of the United States. . . . First [because] in science there are very few real secrets. . . . Second [because of] the long term [adverse] effects of secrecy on scientific progress, especially in the United States.[4]

The most current critique of secrecy in the United States rises directly from the lessons of the September 11th terrorist attacks. During the Congressional hearings on what went wrong in law enforcement that otherwise might have prevented the attacks, the Immigration and

Naturalization Service and the Federal Aviation Administration testified that excessive secrecy was the problem. The intelligence agencies and particularly the CIA had not shared with either the INS or the FAA the urgency of searching for the two September 11th hijackers who were living in the United States and booked their September 11th tickets under their own names. "Had we had information that those two individuals presented a threat to aviation or posed a great danger, we would have put them on the list and they should have been picked up in the reservation process," the Transportation Security Administration testified.[5]

One of the leaders of the 1990s retrenchment began singing a new tune. Sen. Richard Shelby (R-Alabama), apparently saw no contradiction between his role as chief sponsor of the proposed "official secrets act" that was vetoed by President Clinton, and his minority report critique of the CIA's information "hoarding" as one of the underlying causes of the intelligence failures leading to September 11th. According to one *Washington Post* reporter who paid attention to Shelby's gripes, some of the hoarding occurred because the intelligence agencies didn't have the technology to make sharing possible. Some took place because they didn't even know what they had in their own case files and on their intercept tapes. And some came because they thought certain secrets were too sensitive to share, either to protect sources and methods, or preserve their own unique standing in the intelligence pecking order. Shelby wrote:

> This is particularly true in an Intelligence Community institutional culture in which knowledge literally is power—in which the bureaucratic importance of an agency depends upon the supposedly "unique" contributions to national security it can make by monopolizing control of "its" data-stream.[6]

The Congressional inquiry into September 11th exposed dozens of examples of intelligence hoarding and excessive secrecy—a form of bureaucratic competition not for better intelligence but for status and power. The staff director of the September 11th inquiry summed up the findings in her summary statement:

> Finally, the record suggests that, prior to September 11th, the U.S. intelligence and law enforcement communities were fighting a war against terrorism largely without the benefit of what some would call their most potent weapon in that effort: an alert and committed American public. One need look no further for proof of the latter point than the heroics of the passengers on Flight 93 or the quick action of the flight attendant who identified shoe bomber Richard Reid.[7]

This fundamental point is key to the future debate over national security secrecy. The current climate is one of information phobia. But information is security and openness is our best defense. Americans, whether they want to or not, need to know when airport security is lethally porous. They need to know if and when and where we are vulnerable to biological or nuclear attack. Only when the public is fully informed about such vulnerabilities will there be sufficient pressure to move our leaders to act.

The only way we will beat thoughtless restrictions on information is to show how those restrictions actually stop us from fighting terrorism. The mantra of the moment is an old familiar one from wartime, "loose lips sink ships." Perhaps the Enron scandal will come up with a new alliteration, maybe along the lines of "off-the-books means off-the-wall." Because the first casualty of excessive secrecy is honest policy, policy the American people will support, policy that will be effective. Thinking back to the Iran-contra scandal, where secrecy hid a cabal of zealots like Oliver North doing the President's bidding against the will of Congress and his own Cabinet, maybe the rhyme would be "secret Ollies make more follies."

Only a few months before September 11th, a group of former CIA and White House officials and Cuban exiles went back to the beach at the Bay of Pigs, for a fortieth anniversary autopsy on that debacle. We now know the CIA didn't even share the secret invasion plans with its own Cuba analysts, who could have told the operators there was no chance of an army uprising against Castro. Back in 1961, President Kennedy called up the publisher of *The New York Times* to try to spike that paper's pre-invasion expose, and afterwards JFK said he wished the *Times* had published everything—maybe then they'd have called off the invasion before it became "a perfect failure."[8]

Secrecy is the enemy of efficiency, as well. Look at Enron, now the poster child of a perfect failure, founded by a Ph.D. economist and devoted to turning everything into a market, but hiding its own debts and inflating its profits as if the rules of transparent information that make all markets work somehow didn't apply in Houston. Those same rules also apply in the war against terrorism: Just listen to the testimony before Congress from the mayors and police chiefs, including New York City mayor Rudy Giuliani himself, complaining that the big problem is the federal government does not share information with the locals.

Perhaps the single biggest success against domestic terrorism involved a major sharing of information, against the instincts of law enforcement officers, but under a threat of violence unless the information went public. This was the case of the Unabomber, the terrorist Harvard-educated Luddite who blew up scientists with letter bombs, randomly. How did the United States catch the Unabomber? After he threatened undifferentiated violence unless major newspapers published his anti-modernism manifesto, finally the FBI and the Justice Department made that recommendation to the major newspapers. *The Washington Post* printed a special section to contain the Unabomber's 35,000-word screed, and convinced *The New York Times* to swallow half the cost. Newspapers across the country circulated his crank letter file, and told the world everything we knew about him—and his brother recognized the facts and turned him in. Openness empowers citizens.[9]

The biggest U.S. success against foreign terrorism in the last ten years—that is, preventing terrorism before innocent people were killed, rather than punishing terrorists with cruise missiles—took place in Washington state, at Port Angeles, at the ferry dock from Victoria, Canada. Again, openness rather than secrecy meant security. On December 14, 1999, an alert Customs inspector named Diana Dean stopped the last car off the ferry, a large late-model Chrysler with a big trunk. The man behind the wheel was sweating in the cold, and he had driven an out-of-the-way route in order to take the ferry. So Diana Dean asked the driver to get out and open the trunk. He bolted, and Dean's co-workers caught him hiding under a car six blocks away. In the trunk were 130 pounds of fertilizer-style explosives and four homemade timers—apparently destined for Los Angeles Airport or the Seattle Space Needle for the millennium. No TOP SECRET CIA message had come in to Diana Dean that day, warning of Ahmeds smelling of ammonia. But she had read, extensively, about the Oklahoma City bombing and the 1993 attempt on the World Trade Center—all public information based on public trials.[10]

Openness empowers citizens, weeds out the worst policy proposals, ensures the most efficient flow of information to all levels of law enforcement, makes a little more honest the despots who are our temporary allies against terrorism. Openness keeps our means more consistent with our ends. But we need to drop the idea of balancing this fundamental value against national security. To admit the notion of balancing is to lose the debate over where to balance. The appropriate attitude is the one articulated by Justice Brennan in 1980 (unfortunately, in a dissent):

[T]he concept of military necessity is seductively broad, and has a dangerous plasticity. Because they invariably have the visage of overriding importance, there is always a temptation to invoke security 'necessities' to justify an encroachment upon civil liberties. For that reason, the military-security argument must be approached with a healthy skepticism . . . [11]

The government has successfully framed the debate after 9/11 as terrorism fighters versus civil libertarians, as soldiers versus reporters, as hawks versus doves. In wartime, the poundage of the former will always outweigh the latter, and the Bush administration has guaranteed wartime for the foreseeable future. So our task is to reframe the debate and leave behind the balancing act. We need to place openness where it belongs, not only at the center of our values, but also at the center of our strategy for security.

Blanton, Thomas S. "National Security and Open Government in the United States: Beyond the Balancing Test." Pp. 31–71 in *National Security and Open Government: Striking the Right Balance,* edited by A. Roberts and H. Darbishire. Syracuse, N.Y.: Campbell Public Affairs Institute, The Maxwell School of Syracuse University, 2003. Reprinted with permission from Campbell Public Affairs Institute, The Maxwell School of Syracuse University.

* * *

Governmental Transparency in the Path of Administrative Reform

Suzanne J. Piotrowski

This book was written to answer a series of questions. How do public management reforms relate to open government initiatives? How do the market-driven reforms, which gained momentum in the mid-1990s, affect access to government documents? Is the U.S. federal government a more open government, in terms of access to documents, because of these reforms? What lessons can future reformers, current public managers at all levels of government, and open government advocates glean from the past juncture of public management reforms and open government policy?

This book at its most basic form is a case study of the implementation of the federal Freedom of Information Act (FOIA). The central question of this book is: How did the National Performance Review (NPR) affect implementation of the federal Freedom of Information Act? This question is important for two reasons. The first is that while the NPR ended when President Clinton left the White House, the key components of the reform are still active within the federal government. We are living with multiple iterations of these reforms in the federal administration and will be for the foreseeable future. Second, the Freedom of Information Act is vitally important to the federal government generally and federal administration specifically. The FOIA allows individuals to gain access to government documents. The ability to access government documents is essential to finding out what the government is doing.

I learned that the reinventing government movement in federal administration, as introduced by the NPR, affected implementation of the FOIA in a variety of ways, many of which were unintended and unforeseen. Transparency of government, which promotes democratic accountability, is embodied in the FOIA. Major administrative reforms associated with the NPR included the push toward results-oriented performance and employee empowerment in government, the increased use of privatizing and outsourcing, and an emphasis on customer service.

These reinventing movement's values are at varying times in tension with, and complementary to, the goals of the FOIA.

The NPR, as a major administrative reform, had unforeseen and unintended consequences for aspects of federal administration that were tangential to its main thrust. The NPR was launched by the Clinton administration in 1993 and continued until the Bush administration took office in January 2001. Although its name was changed to the National Partnership for Reinventing Government in 1998, its main objectives were always to streamline government, making it more results-oriented and customer focused.

While there are many controversies over the implementation of the FOIA, there can be no doubt that freedom of information is a core aspect of transparency policy and central to modern democracy. For instance, in 1946, the UN General Assembly went so far as to resolve that "freedom of information is a fundamental human right and is the touchstone for all the freedoms to which the United Nations is consecrated" (Zifcak 1998, 942). It is hard to imagine that members of Congress could have predicted the scope of outcomes associated with the passage of the FOIA in 1966.

Today, implementation of the FOIA is a major governmental function. In FY 2002, $300.1 million was spent by federal agencies on processing FOIA requests and associated litigation costs. The equivalent of 5,237 full-time federal employees was dedicated to FOIA administration. Approximately 2.4 million requests for documents were received by the federal agencies and entities covered by the FOIA (U.S. Department of Justice 2003, 5).[1] In February 2002, there were approximately thirty bills pending to redefine what is released under the FOIA (Cha 2002, A1).

FOIA administration, implementation, training, and policy analysis have become a veritable cottage industry. Some attorneys specialize in making FOIA requests and litigating appeals. The American Society of Access Professionals, a nonprofit association concerned with access to government documents through avenues such as the FOIA and the Privacy Act, has government administrators, private lawyers, representatives of public interest groups, and academics as members. It conducts FOIA training programs nationwide. The University of Missouri boasts a Freedom of Information Center. George Washington University's National Security Archive is a holding facility for declassified documents largely released under the FOIA.

The FOIA is used by ordinary citizens, convicted felons, public interest groups, researchers, journalists, and businesses. By far, businesses use the FOIA more than any other group (Tapscott and Taylor 2001). Corporations frequently request information that their competitors have submitted to the government. The FBI has received so many requests for its files on Albert Einstein, John Lennon, George Orwell, and Frank Sinatra, among others, that it has posted them in its electronic FOIA reading room. Documents released under the FOIA have served the public interest in more traditional ways as well. Seth Rosenfield, a staff writer for the San Francisco Chronicle discovered that:

> According to thousands of pages of FBI records obtained by the Chronicle after a 17-year legal fight, the FBI unlawfully schemed with the head of the CIA to harass students, faculty and members of the Board of Regents, and mounted a concerted campaign to destroy the career of UC President Clark Kerr, which included sending the White House derogatory allegations about him that the bureau knew were false. (Rosenfield 2002, 1)

Files released under the FOIA show that the FBI and other agencies spied on Albert Einstein, by going through his trash and monitoring his mail and telephone calls (Overbye 2002). The FOIA is implemented within the context of the federal administration as a whole. Because of this, it is important to look at FOIA implementation within the larger context of theories surrounding public management. There are currently two competing visions of how federal administration should operate—conventional administration and New Public Management. The first, conventional administration was developed after World War II as a modification of orthodox or classical public administration. It views public administration as inherently political and seeks to bring democratic-constitutional values into public management. The values of representation, responsiveness and democratic accountability are essential and embodied in a host of major statutes and policy initiatives. These include the Administrative Procedure Act, the Federal Advisory Committee Act, the Government in the Sunshine Act, the Negotiated Rulemaking Act, and outreach efforts under the Small Business Regulatory Fairness Act of 1966 and similar measures. These statutes simultaneously work to ensure democratic-constitutional values within the federal administration. Perhaps foremost among these values is democratic accountability, achieved through transparency. In 1822, James Madison wrote in a personal correspondence:

A popular Government, without popular information, or the means of acquiring it, is but a Prologue to a Farce or a Tragedy; or, perhaps, both. Knowledge will forever govern ignorance: And a people who mean to be their own Governors must arm themselves with the power which knowledge gives. (Madison 1822, 790)

The Senate report on the Freedom of Information Act addresses Madison's sentiments:

Today the very vastness of our Government and its myriad of agencies makes it difficult for the electorate to obtain that "popular information" of which Madison spoke. But it is only when one further considers the hundreds of departments, branches, and agencies which are not directly responsible to the people, that one begins to understand the great importance of having an information policy of full disclosure. (U.S. Senate 1974, 38 [Report 813, 1965])

An "information policy of full disclosure" is not without costs. Conventional public administration necessarily emphasizes the importance of process while recognizing that it may be cumbersome and add expense to administration. Supreme Court Justice Felix Frankfurter urged us to "Remember, there are very precious values of civilization which ultimately, to a large extent, are procedural in their nature" (U.S. Congress 1940, 13664). Thus, conventional public administration posits that democracy, at least in part, is promoted through process.

The second vision of how the federal administration should operate is the New Public Management (NPM) and its United States variant, the reinventing government movement. Along with the United States, Australia, Canada, Finland, France, Germany, the Netherlands, New Zealand, Sweden, and the United Kingdom all faced some elements of reform (Pollitt and Bouckaert 2000). In *The Global Public Management Revolution* (2005), Donald Kettl lays out six core components of the New Public Management.

> —*Productivity*. How can government produce more services with less tax money? . . .
> —*Marketization*. How can government use market-style incentives to root out pathologies of its bureaucracy? . . .
> —*Service orientation*. How can government better connect with citizens? . . .
> —*Decentralization*. How can government make programs more responsive and effective? . . .
> —*Policy*. How can government improve its capacity to devise and track policy? . . .
> —*Accountability*. How can governments improve their ability to deliver what they promise? . . . (Kettl 2005, 1–2)

These core components were emphasized to different degrees depending on the country. Kettl argues that a central theme of these reforms was the replacement of "traditional rule-based, authority-driven processes with market-based competition-driven tactics" (3). Stephen P. Osborne and Kate McLaughlin offer an alternative list of eight key doctrines of the NPM. Their list includes hands-on and entrepreneurial management, standards and measures of performance, output controls, disaggregation and decentralization of public services, private sector styles of management, discipline and parsimony in resource allocation, and the separation of political decision making from direct management (Osborne and McLaughlin 2002, 9–10).

The NPM was developed in the 1980s and 1990s in a conscious effort to replace conventional public administration. The NPM focuses on redesigning administration to achieve program and policy outcomes (Kettl 1997, Lynn 2001). It views conventional public administration as preoccupied with procedure while neglectful of outputs and outcomes. Although many scholars and practitioners were supportive of the NPM, a chorus of critical public administration scholars also emerged (Riccucci 2001, Rohr 2002). The National Performance Review (NPR) was the most highly developed American version of the NPM. At times, the NPR may be at odds with transparency in seeking results through outsourcing, employee empowerment, and performance management. Conversely, some specific reforms associated with the NPR, specifically customer service initiatives, may improve governmental transparency.

These visions compete, but because neither completely denies the legitimacy of the other's values, they can be viewed as existing on a continuum. On one end, public administration must be infused with democratic-constitutional values and procedures because they are central to democratic-constitutional government. The other end of the continuum is Hamiltonian: "A feeble execution is but another phrase for a bad execution; and a government ill executed, whatever it may be in theory, must be, in practice, a bad government" (Hamilton 1788, 423–24). The NPR recognized that the purpose of administration is to achieve results cost-effectively. Conventional administration recognizes the importance of achieving results within the framework of constitutional procedures, rights, and values. The mix of Madisonian and Hamiltonian approaches varies across agencies, programs, and policy arenas.

KEY TERMS AND CONCEPTS

The New Public Management, the reinventing government movement, and the National Performance Review are all related concepts. The NPM refers to an international movement, which gained momentum in the early and mid-1990s.[2] Among other things, the NPM pushed for the application of market forces to the public sector. In Europe, the NPM emphasized the use of performance contracts to achieve administrative results. In the United States other means of holding administrators accountable for results, such as annual performance reporting, were more common.

The NPR was a U.S. federal government reform initiative launched by the Clinton administration on March 3, 1993 (Gore 1993, xxiv) and led by Vice President Al Gore until its conclusion in January 2001. The reinventing government movement encompasses both of these previous terms, the NPR and the NPM. The term "reinventing" is drawn from David Osborne and Ted Gaebler's influential 1992 book, *Reinventing Government.*

Governmental transparency allows the public to develop a more accurate picture of what is happening inside a government. Transparency is relevant to executive agencies, the Executive Office of the President, Congress, the Courts, as well as other governmental organizations such as advisory committees. Transparency is a prerequisite for democratic accountability in government. Democratic accountability enables the electorate to hold a government responsible for its actions. *Democratic accountability* is contrasted with *accountability for results,* Accountability for results, a reinventing government movement value, is usually referred to simply as accountability. It focuses on outputs (e.g., number of cases processed) and outcomes (e.g., the achievement of public policy objectives). The two concepts overlap because democratic accountability can include voters' response to government performance. However, accountability in the reinvention conception is largely unrelated to the electorate and matters of constitutional government such as the separation of powers. The NPR's larger goal was building public trust in government. Its theory was that performance would promote trust. The initial NPR report states "By 'customers,' we do not mean 'citizens.' A citizen can participate in democratic decision making; a customer receives benefits from a specific service" (Gore 1993a, xxxix). To a large extent, the NPR embraces a traditional dichotomy between politics and administration.

. . . .

ARE DEMOCRATIC ACCOUNTABILITY
AND ACCOUNTABILITY FOR RESULTS RECONCILABLE?

The potential tension between democratic accountability and accountability for results was explained early on in this book. These two related, but at times competing, visions of governmental accountability can be visualized on a continuum. The objective is to find a point on that continuum that balances the need to have both types of accountability. Each of the management initiatives studied affects this balance.

The NPR, which supported accountability for results, did not focus on the FOIA, which embodies democratic accountability. However, the NPR did affect the FOIA. While the FOIA was not a priority of the NPR, the management initiatives associated with the reform movement impacted FOIA policy. It is in the unintended consequences of NPR on the FOIA that the intersection of democratic accountability and accountability for results are seen.

While the intent of performance management and outsourcing initiatives was not to obfuscate democratic accountability that was the end result. FOIA activities were overwhelmingly left out of agency performance plans. The consequence may be reduced funding and consideration for these activities. At the federal level, contracting out leads to a reduction of democratic accountability by making it more difficult to access documents concerning outsourced functions.

If implemented correctly, the use of contractors to perform parts of the FOIA process aids in accountability. FOIA caseloads are unpredictable and depend largely on the actions of requesters. Because of this, the use of contractors could improve democratic accountability by helping process uneven workflow and more quickly filling requests.

Customer service and employee empowerment initiatives could improve democratic accountability if they were applied uniformly to FOIA processes. Most agencies do not view FOIA requesters as customers. If FOIA requesters were given comparable attention as customers of mission-based agency functions, then FOIA processes would improve. If this happened, requests would be processed with fewer delays, leading to improved democratic accountability. The relationship between democratic accountability and accountability for results is multifaceted.

In summary, these two types of accountability are reconcilable. They will not be reconciled, though, unless there is a concerted effort of students of public administration to work toward that end. Democratic accountability and accountability for results fluctuate between working toward the same goals and working against one another. If the push for results continues, and it will, then creative solutions need to be developed and implemented. Administrative changes are essential. Potential changes include giving FOIA processes equal billing with an agency's mission-based objectives and raising the awareness of the roles federal employees play in safeguarding freedom of information. Congress can do its part by clarifying the FOIA to include more contractor records and forcing agencies to include nonmission-based activities in their performance and customer service plans.

The largest federal administrative reform of the 1990s did not consider a major administrative function that affects every executive branch department and agency. The National Performance Review did have implications for implementation of the Freedom of Information Act, but these implications were unintended and unforeseen. If democratic accountability, whose spirit is embodied by the FOIA, is going to be valued along with accountability for results, then future management reforms will need to integrate both of these values into their initiatives.

Piotrowski, S. J. *Governmental Transparency in the Path of Administrative Reform.* (Pp. 1–6, 107–8) Albany, N.Y.: State University of New York Press, 2007. Reprinted with permission from State University of New York Press.

3

Freedom of Information

INTRODUCTION

More than 80 countries now have some form of freedom of information law or regime. Of note is that more than half of these laws are new within the last decade. Mexico recently revamped its freedom of information law. In 2002, Mexico passed the Federal Transparency and Access to Public Information Law. While there are still issues with respect to implementation, Mexico now has a law that other countries are using as a model. In 2007, a major overhaul of Article 6 of the Mexican Constitution was passed in the federal congress. The revised Article 6 established principles of transparency and provided minimum standards for access to public information at the federal, state, and municipal levels. Cutting-edge electronic filing systems are also being put in place in Mexico to facilitate the requesting process. (See *Article 6 of Mexican Constitution* [English Translation] 2007; Bookman 2008; freedominfo.org 2009). The English translation of Article 6 of the Mexican Constitution is included in this reader.

The United States was a relatively early adopter of freedom of information laws and initially passed its FOIA in 1966. Many of the U.S. state laws actually predated the U.S. federal FOIA. Freedom of information laws have been used in the United States to pry documents unwillingly out of government's hands. While the overwhelming majority of freedom of information requests are routine, some lead to prolonged legal battles. One such story revolves around the British musician John Lennon. Jon Wiener, a University of California, Irvine, professor sought the FBI's files on Lennon. He describes his experience with the process below:

> When FBI Director J. Edgar Hoover reported to the Nixon White House in 1972 about the bureau's surveillance of John Lennon, he began by explaining that Lennon was a "former member of the Beatles singing group." Apparently Hoover wanted to show that although he was no rock fan, at least he knew who Lennon was. When a copy of this letter arrived in response to my 1981 Freedom of Information Act (FOIA) request, the entire text was withheld, as were almost 200 other pages, on the grounds that releasing it would endanger the national security. That seemed unlikely. So, with the help of the American Civil Liberties Union (ACLU) of Southern California, I filed a lawsuit under the FOIA in 1983, asking the court to order the release of the withheld pages. Fourteen years later, after the case went to the Supreme Court, the FBI finally agreed to settle almost all of the outstanding issues of the case, to release all but ten of the documents, and to pay $204,000 to the ACLU for court costs and attorney fees. (Wiener 1999, 1)

Weiner's firsthand account of this struggle, including the final documents, is published as a book and helped inform a documentary on Lennon (Leaf and Scheinfeld 2006; Wiener 1999).

Nine principles have been identified as essential parts of an FOI regime by Article 19, an organization that promotes freedom of expression and freedom of information. In a comparative legal study of national freedom of information laws published by the United Nations Educational, Scientific, and Cultural Organization elaborates on these nine principles (Mendel 2008).

Principle 1: Maximum Disclosure—Freedom of information legislation should be guided by the principle of maximum disclosure.

Principle 2: Obligation to Publish—Public bodies should be under an obligation to publish key information.

Principle 3: Promotion of Open Government—Public bodies must actively promote open government.

Principle 4: Limited Scope of Exemptions—Exceptions should be clearly and narrowly drawn and subject to strict "harm" and "public interest" tests.

Principle 5: Processes to Facilitate Access—Requests for information should be processed rapidly and fairly, and an independent review of any refusal should be available.

Principle 6: Costs—Individuals should not be deterred from making requests for information by excessive costs.

Principle 7: Open Meetings—Meetings of public bodies should be open to the public.

Principle 8: Disclosure Takes Precedence—Laws that are inconsistent with the principle of maximum disclosure should be amended or repealed.

Principle 9: Protection for Whistleblowers—Individuals who release information on wrongdoing—whistleblowers—must be protected.

Implementation of these laws is the next important step (Neuman and Calland 2007; Piotrowski 2007). Having strong freedom of information laws without successful implementation does little to promote transparency. Another key issue is the application of freedom of information laws to third parties working for government. David Rosenbloom and Suzanne Piotrowski address this topic in their article *Outsourcing the Constitution and Administrative Law Norms* (Rosenbloom and Piotrowski 2005).

While much of the attention regarding freedom of information has centered on the national and subnational levels, transnational organizations also deserve and have received some attention with respect to freedom of information. In an article included in this reader, Alasdair Roberts (2004) discusses modest transparency reforms at transnational organizations, such as the World Trade Organization. Increasingly these organizations are coming under pressure to establish transparency guidelines and in fact the World Bank is in the process of establishing internal transparency guidelines.

The next section of this reader focuses on the proactive release of information. The requestor model of release and the proactive release of information can be thought of as two points on a continuum. At times the distinction between the two can be blurred. For example, some freedom-of-information laws have provisions that frequently requested documents must be posted online. Over time agencies may not wait for a formal request to be made before releasing the information. The requestor model can also be complicated when documents are requested but not released. Individuals and organizations may seek to pry these documents from governments through the courts or some type of ombudsman organization. While a formal document request began the release process, the final documents were involuntarily released by the government because of a judicial procedure.

Assignments and Study Questions

1. Compare the laws regarding access to government documents from two countries. Your final project should present an overview and history of each act; examine current issues surrounding each act, either proposed policy changes or implementation issues, and briefly describe how to use each act.
2. If governmental transparency and open government are such important values to our society, why are there such discrepancies in implementing freedom of information policies?
3. Do you think the proliferation of FOI laws will continue? Why or why not?
4. What do you see as some of the key differences between FOI in the United States and internationally?
5. How far should the reach of FOI laws be with respect to organizations that work for, or partner with, governments?

* * *

Article 6 of Mexican Constitution

ARTICLE 6. The expression of ideas shall not be determined by any judicial or administrative inquisition, unless it transgresses morality, the rights of a third party, provokes a crime, or disturbs the public order. The right to information shall be guaranteed by the State.

In order to guarantee the right to public information, the Federation, the States, and the Federal District, according to their own competences, will be ruled by the following precepts and principles:

I. Any information in possession of any authority, entity, or federal, state, and municipal bodies, shall be made public, and will only be temporarily retained for reasons of public interest in the terms established in the law. A principle of maximum publicity will prevail in any interpretations of such right.

II. Any information regarding private lives and personal data will be protected by the terms and exceptions determined by the law.

III. Any individual, without having to acknowledge any interests or justify its use, will be granted free access to public information, and his or her personal data, and will furthermore have the right to the amendment of such information.

IV. Expeditious mechanisms of access to public information will be established. These mechanisms will be validated by means of specialised bodies or organisations, and will be granted operational and decision-making autonomy.

V. All involved individuals will have to keep their documents in updated administrational archives, and will have to publish, by means of available electronic media, all complete and updated information on their organisational indicators and the use of public resources.

VI. The law will determine the ways in which involved individuals will make public every piece of information regarding public resources provided to either individuals or corporations.

VII. Failure to comply with dispositions regarding the access to public information will be cause of legal sanctions.

Article 6 of Mexican Constitution [English Translation]. 2007. http://www.gwu.edu/~nsarchiv/mexico/
article6%20_english.pdf (2 May 2009).

* * *

Outsourcing the Constitution and Administrative Law Norms

David H. Rosenbloom and Suzanne J. Piotrowski

The literature on privatization in public administration pays only limited attention to the stark reality that when government activities are privatized or outsourced, democratic norms embodied in constitutional and administrative law are apt to be lost. Notable exceptions include Moe (1987, 2001), Moe and Gilmour (1995), Gilmour and Jensen (1998), and Roberts (2000).[1] However, much more space has been devoted to this result of so-called third-party government in law reviews (Bass and Hammitt 2002; Feiser 1999; Freeman 2003; Gillette and Stephan 1998; Guttman 2000a; Mays 1995). Failure to more fully address the effect of privatization on constitutional and administrative law rights and protections in public administration promotes discussion and analysis that focus overwhelmingly on cost-effectiveness, techniques for privatizing and outsourcing, contract management, and performance monitoring. The field's instrumental and pragmatic approaches often give short shrift to constitutional contractarianism (Piotrowski and Rosenbloom 2002; Rosenbloom 2003, pp. 172–76; Rosenbloom and O'Leary 1997, pp. 17–22). Public administrative scholars and practitioners, anxious to improve administrative practice, often jump from accurate diagnosis of complex problems to the prescription of untested, flawed, or ill-conceived reforms—many of which fail largely because they emphasize managerial values over political and constitutional ones (Caiden 1991, pp. 1–33, 296–98). This is often manifested in proposals for third-party accountability that largely ignore law, relying instead almost entirely on nested hierarchical managerial relationships reaching through the top levels of agencies and potentially culminating in oversight by elected officials (Posner 2002). In focusing on management, contemporary public administration tends to neglect the broader issues of democratic governance, which were historically at the core of the field's concerns (Lynn 2001).

In this article, we illustrate some of the costs of privatization and outsourcing in terms of constitutional and administrative law norms as well as why competitive sourcing equations are incomplete without their full consideration. We explore the prospects for outsourcing constitutional and administrative law norms along with government activities by subjecting contractors to some of the requirements these norms impose on public agencies. For instance, should private contractors' employees have rights to whistle-blowing, privacy, and liberty that more or less match those guaranteed to government employees by constitutional law? Should freedom of information, open records, and open meetings laws be applied to private contractors? Should the public have the same constitutional and administrative law protections when they deal with private contractors doing outsourced government work as when they interact directly with government agencies? Our wider purpose is to bring such questions to the forefront of public policy discussion and decision making regarding competitive sourcing and outsourcing. We hope to frame the issues cogently for the public administration community in the interests of promoting a more comprehensive and thoughtful assessment of privatizing, one that brings public administrative expertise to the forefront of determining when and how to apply constitutional and administrative law norms to government contractors.

THE ABSENCE OF CONSTITUTIONAL AND ADMINISTRATIVE LAW NORMS IN THE PRIVATE SECTOR: SOME ILLUSTRATIONS

Apart from the Thirteenth Amendment's prohibition of slavery and involuntary servitude other than as criminal punishment, the U.S. Constitution does not apply to purely private relationships. As the Supreme Court reiterated in 1988, "Embedded in our Fourteenth Amendment jurisprudence is a dichotomy between state [governmental] action, which is subject to scrutiny under the Amendment's Due Process Clause, and private conduct, against which the Amendment affords no shield, no matter how unfair that conduct may be" (*National Collegiate Athletic Association v. Tarkanian* 1988, p. 191). A relatively narrow breach of this dichotomy, analyzed infra, occurs when a private entity becomes a state (i.e., governmental) actor for constitutional purposes and is therefore subject to constitutional constraints. Under federal constitutional law, five general types of public-private involvement are most likely to transform a private party into a state actor: (a) private engagement in a public function, as defined by the courts; (b) government control of an ostensibly private party; (c) coordinated joint public-private participation in an activity; (d) entwinement of governmental and private actors to the extent that they function as a single organization; and (e) empowering private entities to use government's coercive power such as the power to seize assets. State-level constitutional law draws similar distinctions between governmental and private action, although variation in specific applications is to be expected.

For the most part, administrative law also incorporates a dichotomy between governmental and nongovernmental activity. Except with respect to formally constituted advisory committees and negotiated rulemaking committees, federal administrative law—including its provisions for freedom of information, open meetings, enforcement proceedings, and public participation—places few, if any, constraints on private parties regardless of their relationship with government agencies. State administrative law varies considerably and is not readily summarized (see Asimow, Bonfield, and Levin 1998). However, in terms of transparency, which is of particular importance to third-party government (Roberts 2000), administrative law has broader applicability to contractors in most of the states than at the national level, as we explain later in this article.

The following examples illustrate how the legal dichotomy between governmental and nongovernmental action can apply both in the context of outsourcing public administrative functions and more generally. They demonstrate that constitutional rights and administrative transparency, taken for granted when dealing with government, may be wholly irrelevant in the private sphere.

Alicia Pedreira worked for the Kentucky Baptist Homes for Children, a religious organization under state contract to provide services to at-risk youth. By all accounts she was an excellent employee. She became an ex-employee in 1998 after an amateur photographer's picture of her at an AIDS walk appeared in an art exhibition at the Kentucky state fair. The photo showed Pedreira with another woman's arms around her waist. Leaving nothing to guesswork, Pedreira was wearing a tank top bearing a map motif that included an arrow pointing to the Isle of Lesbos in the Aegean Sea. As soon as she heard about the picture, which later made the rounds in her office, Pedreira knew she would be fired. The president of Baptist Homes explained why she could no longer work there: "To employ a person who is openly homosexual does not represent the Judeo-Christian values which are intrinsic to our mission," which is "to provide Christian support to every child, staff member and foster parent" (Press 2003, pp. 187, 188).

If Pedreira had worked for a state or local governmental agency, doing exactly the same job, a dismissal for failing to adhere to "Judeo-Christian values" clearly would have violated her

First and Fourteenth Amendment religious freedom. If she were covered by civil-service law, Pedreira undoubtedly would have been entitled to a hearing guided by state or local regulations and constitutional due process. The government agency trying to fire her probably would have borne the burden of persuasion in showing a nexus between her homosexuality and some significant detrimental effect on its administrative operations.[2] If the case went far enough, she might even have won a court decision protecting her liberty to engage in homosexual activity. In *Lawrence v. Texas* (2003), the U.S. Supreme Court recognized that

> when sexuality finds overt expression in intimate conduct with another person, the conduct can be but one element in a personal bond that is more enduring. The liberty protected by the Constitution allows homosexual persons the right to make this choice. (*Lawrence v. Texas* 2003, slip op. at 6)

It concluded that individuals' "right to liberty under the Due Process Clause gives them the full right to engage in their [homosexual] conduct without intervention of the government" (*Lawrence v. Texas* 2003, slip op. at 18). Although individuals' constitutional rights in the context of public employment are far from identical to those held by citizens generally, a government agency firing someone in Pedreira's circumstances generally must justify its infringement on constitutionally protected liberty by showing that the dismissal serves an important or compelling governmental interest in a narrowly tailored fashion (Shafritz, Rosenbloom, Riccucci, Naff, and Hyde 2001, chap. 3).

Stephen Downs bought a "No War With Iraq/Give Peace A Chance" T-shirt in a shop at the Crossgates Mall in Guilderland, New York. He put it on and went to the mall's food court where he was told by two security guards to remove the shirt or leave the mall. A lawyer, he refused and was arrested for trespass, which is punishable by up to a year in prison (CNN. com/U.S. 2003). If Downs had been sitting on the National Mall in Washington, D.C., at a table in a public park or on a public bench on the sidewalk of one of Guilderland's main streets, his right to wear the T-shirt and stay put would have been protected by the First and Fourteenth Amendments' guarantee of freedom of speech. However, when privately owned malls become the functional equivalents of public spaces and main streets—that is, when public space and main streets are effectively privatized—those amendments do not apply. Constitutional law can constrain private parties in this context only when they own an entire town, and maybe not even then (see *Hudgens v. National Labor Relations Board* 1976; *Lloyd Corp. v. Tanner* 1972; *Marsh v. Alabama* 1946).

Similar issues arise when private homeowner associations develop the equivalent of public zoning regulations. Such associations have

> enforced rules that prohibited the distribution of newspapers, prevented homeowners from entering and leaving their condominium through the back door, and interfered with the marital relationship of a newlywed couple [by determining that the woman was too young to live in the residence]. (Mays 1995, p. 58)

Owners of private dwellings regulated by municipalities are free to post antiwar and political campaign signs in their windows or on their lawns (*City of Ladue v. Gilleo* 1994). In the absence of a curfew, they can surely invite their grandchildren to visit whenever they want. Such freedoms can be wrested from those living under the private rule of homeowner associations (Mays 1995, pp. 58–59).

After the Columbia Space Shuttle tragedy in 2003, the media obtained a number of e-mails from NASA that revealed some engineers' concerns for a worst-case scenario caused by damage to the shuttle during its launch. Some of the e-mails were obtained through requests under the federal Freedom of Information Act (FOIA). NASA was generally quite responsive and garnered praise for being much more open than it had been after the Challenger Space Shuttle exploded in 1986. NASA even facilitated the flow of information by putting up a Web page for "Freedom of Information Act (FOIA): Summary of Requests Currently Being Processed Related to STS-107 Columbia" (NASA 2003).

Nonetheless, transparency regarding the Columbia was far from complete because a great deal of the launch work and operation of the shuttle fleet is done by a contractor, United Space Alliance. A NASA official explained that United Space Alliance was involved in "'nearly every aspect of NASA's decision-making processes [and an] integral member' of the team that 'reached flawed conclusions about the relative safety of Columbia and crew before and during flight'" (Reinert 2004). Like other private entities, United Space Alliance, which was formed by the Boeing and Lockheed-Martin corporations, is not covered by the federal FOIA. Although it provided summaries of some information requested by the media, it was not nearly as forthcoming as NASA. Yet, in terms of public debate regarding the accident and the future of manned space flight and the shuttle program, information about United Space Alliance's decision making and assessment of the risks to the Columbia and its crew is as vital as that held by NASA. The FOIA's "central purpose of opening agency action to public scrutiny" (*U.S. Department of Defense v. Federal Labor Relations Authority* 1994, p. 491) is frustrated when a federal agency outsources its activity to a private entity. It was due only to extraordinary measures—inquiry by the Columbia Accident Investigation Board and release of its voluminous *Final Report*—that a fuller accounting of United Space Alliance's activity became public (Columbia Accident Investigation Board 2003).

INHERENT AND NONINHERENT GOVERNMENTAL FUNCTIONS

These examples were chosen to illustrate that constitutional and administrative law norms have potential application even when private activity does not involve inherently governmental functions. Outsourcing inherently governmental activities raises additional problems for accountability and popular sovereignty. In 1989, well before the Clinton-Gore administration advanced outsourcing as a basic tenet of good public administration (Gore 1993, chap. 1; National Performance Review 1995, p. 7), Paul Light (1999) noted that the EPA's private

> consultants were analyzing proposed legislation, drafting EPA's budget documents, overseeing the agency's field investigation teams, preparing work statements for other EPA contracts, writing draft preambles to formal rules, responding to public comments on those rules as part of the formal rulemaking process, developing guidelines for monitoring other contractors, organizing and conducting public hearings, and advising senior officials on legislative reauthorizations.[3] (p. 14)

Similarly, the Department of Energy, relied

> on a private workforce to perform virtually all basic governmental functions. It relied on contractors in the preparation of its most important plans and policies, the development of budgets and budget documents, and the drafting of reports to Congress and congressional testimony. It relied on contractors to monitor arms control negotiations, help prepare decisions on the export of nuclear technology, and conduct hearings and initial appeals in challenges to security clearance disputes. In addition, a contractor workforce is relied on by the Inspector General. (U.S. Congress 1989, p. 63, as cited in Guttman 2000a, p. 873)

Senator David Pryor (D-AR) denounced such arrangements as creating "a very large, invisible, unelected bureaucracy of consultants who perform an enormous portion of the basic work of and set the policy for the Government" (Light 1999, p. 13).

Proponents of outsourcing would generally agree with Pryor that governments should retain control of inherently governmental functions. However, they differ on whether governments should be required to perform these functions in house. For instance, in *Privatization: The Key to Better Government*, E. S. Savas (1987) contends that "false alarms are raised about privatizing services that are said to be 'inherently governmental'; the responsibility for providing the service can be retained by government, but the government does not have to continue producing it" (p. 62). In his view, "the role of government is to steer, not to man the oars. Privatization helps restore government to its fundamental purpose" (Savas 1987, p. 290) Consequently, he sees no rational barrier to outsourcing adoption, airport operation, child protection, crime laboratory work, crime prevention and patrol, economic development, election administration, housing inspection and code enforcement, housing management, criminal justice probation, property acquisition, public relations and information services, and records maintenance, among many other functions (Savas 1987, p. 73).

The federal government's policy, by contrast, requires inherently governmental activities to be performed in house by federal agencies. The Federal Activities Inventory Reform (FAIR) Act (1998) requires agencies to provide an annual inventory of all their activities that are commercial as opposed to inherently governmental. Inherently governmental activities are shielded from "competitive sourcing" and should not be outsourced (U.S. Office of Management and Budget [OMB] 1998, p. 2). The OMB defines "inherently governmental" as an

> activity that is so intimately related to the public interest as to mandate performance by government personnel. These activities require the exercise of substantial discretion in applying government authority and/or making decisions for the government. Inherently governmental activities normally fall into two categories: the exercise of sovereign government authority or the establishment of procedures and processes related to the oversight of monetary transactions or entitlements. (OMB 2003a, section B.1.a)

Examples include:

- "Binding the United States to take or not to take some action by contract, policy, regulation, authorization, order, or otherwise";
- "Determining, protecting, and advancing economic, political, territorial, property, or other interests by military or diplomatic action, civil or criminal judicial proceedings, contract management, or otherwise";
- "Significantly affecting the life, liberty, or property of private persons"; and
- "Exerting ultimate control over the acquisition, use, or disposition of United States property." (OMB 2003a, section B.1.a, pp. 1–4)

Problems of definition and scope aside, both ways of dealing with inherently governmental functions rely on a familiar politics-administration distinction that is apt to be untenable in practice. Contractors engaged in some activities will inevitably exercise discretion and frame policy options. Whereas Savas (1987) discounts or ignores the potential for policymaking by contractors, OMB recognizes it and seeks to confine it to relatively narrow limits. OMB's key document on outsourcing, *Circular A-76*, defines "the use of discretion" as inherently governmental if it commits the government to a course of action when two or more alternative courses of action exist and the decision making is not already limited or guided by existing policies, procedures, directions, orders, and other guidance that (1) identify specified ranges of acceptable decisions or conduct and (2) subject the discretionary authority to final approval or regular oversight by agency officials. (OMB 2003 a, section B.1.b)

In other words, "not every exercise of discretion is evidence that an activity is inherently governmental" (OMB 2003a, section B.1.b). Contractors may use discretion within a fixed range and be "tasked to develop options or implement a course of action, with agency oversight" (OMB 2003a, section B.1.c).

OMB's approach, although more realistic than Savas', may, nevertheless, be too formalistic in anticipating bright lines between agency personnel and contractors and assuming that influence will always be exerted unidirectionally by the former over the latter. Lines may be blurred, if not eradicated altogether, by the mutual dependence and interpersonal relationships between agency personnel and contractors, as was the case with NASA and United Space Alliance and the consultants at EPA. As Paul Posner of the U.S. Government Accountability Office notes, agency management of contractors is "best characterized as bargaining relationships in which the third-party partners often have the upper hand in both policy formulation and implementation" (Posner 2002, p. 525).

Agencies may also be overwhelmed by their contract workforce. For example, Daniel Guttman, an expert on the "evolving law of diffused sovereignty," noted that

> Congress and the Executive Branch have long recognized that the Department of Energy (DOE) lacks the in-house workforce needed to supervise and control its contractors—most of whom manage and operate the nuclear weapons complex. In 2001, DOE reported that it had 14,700 employees (civil servants and officials), and more than 100,000 contractor employees. (Guttman 2000b, p. 3)

Overall, OMB estimates that of 1,609,000 federal positions being tracked under President George W. Bush's President's Management Agenda (OMB 2001), 751,000 are inherently governmental and 858,000 are commercial (OMB 2003b, p. 3). For various reasons, only 416,000 of the commercial positions are deemed suitable for outsourcing (OMB 2003b, p. 3).

OMB may also be understating the policymaking inevitably made by street-level bureaucrats. As every student of street-level administration knows,

> providers (whether public or private) enjoy considerable discretion when implementing the policy choices of elected officials. This discretion affords them an opportunity to redefine policy choices or to specify them at a level of detail unanticipated by policymakers. Decisions at the ground level of policy implementation can be as consequential as decisions, such as eligibility standards or general program directives, set directly by a centralized public authority. Even the power simply to provide the most carefully specified services creates a principal-agent problem in which a contractor may, without violating any technical contractual terms, enjoy substantial room to maneuver. (Freeman 2003, p. 1309)

Some of the potential problems with OMB's definitions of inherently governmental functions and permissible discretion came to light in the wake of the Abu Ghraib prison scandal in 2004. Interrogators employed by CACI International, a private company under contract with the Army, participated in the abuse of Iraqi detainees (Crawley and Adelsberger 2004). Whether Army personnel at Abu Ghraib knew what they were supposed to be getting from CACI is a moot point. The Army has been unable or unwilling to develop centralized information on its contract employees and the firms they work for, including those supporting military operations (Peckenpaugh 2004, p. 1). In part, this may be because the Army sometimes outsources its contracting functions to other federal agencies. Its contract with CACI was awarded through the Department of the Interior's National Business Center, which used a professional engineering services schedule to procure the interrogators (Harris 2004a, pp. 1–2). This occurred despite an earlier decision by the General Services Administration to cancel a similar contract with Affiliated Computer Services, Inc. for interrogators at Guantanamo Bay, Cuba, on the basis that it is "inappropriate to use [a] technology contract for interrogation work" (Harris 2004a, p. 1). As for who influenced whom on the ground at Abu Ghraib, the Army captain in charge of the interrogators said that military personnel were "supervised" by a CACI employee and that there was no "contracting officer representative to oversee the performance of the contract interrogators," which can make it difficult or impossible to administer a contract effectively (Crawley and Adelsberger 2004).

Abu Ghraib is clearly an outlier. However, it illustrates that relationships among government agencies, government personnel, and contractors can become attenuated and far more complicated than anticipated by OMB's directives and instructions. It is inevitable that at least some of the time some contractors will be in a position to define individual rights, withhold information that government agencies would be required to release, frame policy options, set public policy through their street-level interactions, and exercise influence—or even supervision—over public employees. Consequently, some of the value of constitutional and administrative law norms will be lost in outsourcing, whether the functions are inherently governmental or otherwise. Limiting outsourcing to noninherently governmental functions does not eliminate the potential benefits of imposing constitutional and administrative law norms on contractors.

CALCULATING WHETHER TO OUTSOURCE

It is somewhat surprising that constitutional and administrative law norms are not necessarily taken into account in calculating when to privatize and outsource governmental functions. The federal courts and Congress have invested considerable effort to developing and applying constitutional and administrative law constraints to public administration, especially since 1946 (Rosenbloom 2000a, 2000b; Rosenbloom and O'Leary 1997). This is barely recognized in OMB's *Circular A-76*, which contains sixty-three pages of detailed instructions on competitive sourcing (OMB 2003a). Its basic instructions on implementing the FAIR act consume another thirty-one pages. Competitive sourcing involves the following personnel: agency tender officials, contracting officers, competitive sourcing officials, performance work statement team leaders, human resources advisors, most efficient organization teams, source selection authorities, and source selection evaluation boards.[4] There is a streamlined competition process for agencies with sixty-five or fewer full-time equivalent employees; those with more than sixty-five engage in a standard competition. Decisions in both types of competitions are based overwhelmingly on cost-effectiveness. Costing factors include pay, benefits, insurance, contract administration, overhead, retirement, and related considerations. Nowhere are there instructions on—or even mention of—factoring in the cost—or for that matter, value—of agency compliance with constitutional or administrative law requirements such as procedural due process and freedom of information.

Constitutional and administrative law norms simply do not enter into the competitive sourcing decision. Ironically, given the results orientation of the President's Management Agenda,[5] they do have some visibility in the competitive sourcing process. For instance, agencies must make their annual inventories of commercial and inherently governmental inventories available to Congress and the public. Interested parties can challenge these inventories and appeal adverse decisions. Agencies are also required to take a number of steps in dealing with their adversely affected employees. Openness, fair decision making, and protective procedures for employees are important in government but not mandated for contractors.

JUDICIAL GUIDANCE ON OUTSOURCING CONSTITUTIONAL AND ADMINISTRATIVE LAW NORMS

Public officials and administrators have largely ceded the process of outsourcing constitutional and administrative law norms to the federal and state judiciaries. The courts have responded in at least two ways that demonstrate the potential for bringing contractors under these norms. The U.S. Supreme Court is adjusting the historic constitutional doctrine of state action to the contemporary realities of privatizing, outsourcing, public-private partnerships, and hybrid administrative arrangements such as quasigovernmental corporations. The state courts are applying transparency requirements to contractors under state FOIAs and related statutes. These responses are intended to strengthen individual rights and promote open government, not to thrust prohibitive costs on contractors. They are balanced and offer important baselines for thinking about outsourcing constitutional and administrative law norms along with government functions.

State Action Doctrine

As noted earlier, constitutional law draws a sharp distinction between governmental and nongovernmental action. Following this approach, individuals such as Pedreira, Downs, and those aggrieved by homeowner associations cannot assert any constitutional protections against interference with their freedoms by private parties. The Thirteenth Amendment aside, it is only when private individuals and organizations become state actors that their behavior is subject to constitutional constraints. This occurs when their activity "may be fairly treated as that of the State [i.e., a government] itself" (*Brentwood Academy v. Tennessee Secondary School Athletic Association* 2001, p. 295). "Fairly" is the key concept and underlying value.

State action doctrine seeks to balance three concerns. First, it protects the autonomy of the private sphere by not subjecting private conduct to constitutional constraints just because the private entity is paid, subsidized, licensed or regulated by, or otherwise connected to government. Second, it protects individual rights from abuse by private individuals and organizations that act as surrogates for government or are empowered by it. Third, it prevents government from evading "the most solemn obligations imposed by the Constitution" by privatizing and outsourcing (*Lebron v. National Railroad Passenger Corporation* 1995, p. 397).

Within this framework, "what is fairly attributable is a matter of normative judgment, and the criteria lack rigid simplicity" (*Brentwood Academy v. Tennessee Secondary School Athletic Association* 2001, p. 295). The judiciary's inquiry is "necessarily fact-bound" (*Brentwood Academy v. Tennessee Secondary School Athletic Association* 2001, p. 298), and "cases deciding when private action might be deemed that of the state have not been a model of consistency" (*Lebron v. National Railroad Passenger Corporation* 1995, p. 378). The main categories of state action, noted earlier, are neither exhaustive nor mutually exclusive. Nevertheless, they provide useful guidance.

A private party may be a state actor when it engages in a public function. To date, Supreme Court decisions characterize the following as public functions: incarceration (*Correctional Services Corporation v. Malesko* 2001; *Richardson v. McKnight* 1997), providing medical care in public or private prisons (*West v. Atkins* 1988), administering elections (*Terry v. Adams* 1953), and managing privately owned towns (*Marsh v. Alabama* 1946), although not homeowner associations (Mays 1995, pp. 56–59). A few lower court decisions have held that private organizations performing mandated governmental functions, including health care, are state actors (Freeman 2003, p. 1334). As this list makes clear, the concepts of public function and inherently governmental activity are not identical. The "operation of prison or detention facilities" is clearly a public function under state action doctrine. However, OMB's *Circular A-76* does not prohibit contracting it out on the grounds that it is an inherently governmental activity (OMB 2003a, section B.1.c.4).

The Supreme Court emphasizes that it is the judiciary's call—not that of legislatures and elected or appointed executives—to determine what is or is not a public function. For instance, in a state action case involving Amtrak, the Court reasoned that

> it is not for Congress to make the final determination of Amtrak's status as a government entity for purposes of determining the constitutional rights of citizens affected by its actions. If Amtrak is, by its very nature, what the Constitution regards as the Government, congressional pronouncement that it is not such can no more relieve it of its First Amendment restrictions than a similar pronouncement could exempt the Federal Bureau of Investigation from the Fourth Amendment. (*Lebron v. National Railroad Passenger Corporation* 1995, p. 392)

Amtrak is illustrative of a second way in which an ostensibly private party may become a state actor. This occurs when the private entity is controlled by government or, whatever its formal status, is considered a government agency for constitutional purposes. Amtrak's authorizing statute states that it "will not be an agency or establishment of the United States Government" (*Lebron v. National Railroad Passenger Corporation* 1995, p. 375). Two Supreme Court decisions seemed to agree that for commercial purposes, Amtrak is "not an agency or instrumentality of the United States Government" (*Lebron v. National Railroad Passenger Corporation* 1995, p. 393). However, the Court held that Amtrak is subject to First Amendment constraints in renting out its billboards because it is a creature of the federal government. It was created by Congress to further governmental goals, and six of its eight externally named directors are appointed directly or indirectly by the president, four with the advise and consent of the Senate. Moreover, Congress retained the "right to repeal, alter, or amend" the statutory independence of Amtrak's directors "at any time" (*Lebron v. National Railroad Passenger Corporation* 1995, p. 398).[6]

A third category of state actors are joint participants with government in an activity that trenches on individuals' constitutional rights. This category prevents the government from deliberately circumventing the Constitution by enlisting private parties to accomplish unconstitutional ends. For instance, the murders of civil rights workers Michael Schwerner, James Chaney, and Andrew Goodman near Philadelphia, Mississippi, in 1964 gave rise to federal criminal litigation against three Mississippi law enforcement agents and fifteen private individuals who were charged with conspiring to deprive the three victims of their constitutional rights under color of state law (*United States v. Price* 1966).[7] Joint participation is potentially relevant to activities such as the on-again, off-again efforts by the federal Transportation Security Administration (TSA) to develop a passenger prescreening system based on data supplied by private sources. If the collection of personal information by the TSA itself would violate Fourth Amendment privacy rights, then the private actors gathering it for the agency could become state actors, and their personnel could be subject to constitutional tort suits.[8]

Some forms of joint participation shade into what would now be considered a fourth category of state action, entwinement. In an early example, a private coffee shop that discriminated based on race was considered a state actor because it was physically and economically part of a publicly owned building and parking lot (*Burton v. Wilmington Parking Authority* 1961). More recently, the Tennessee Secondary School Athletic Association (TSSAA), formally a private organization, was challenged by a private school for violating its First and Fourteenth Amendment rights to contact potential athletic recruits. By a 5:4 margin, the Supreme Court held that the TSSAA was a state actor because 84 percent of its members were public schools, its governing council and board were selected by the participating schools, the public schools tended to dominate its decision making, and its staff was eligible to participate in the state retirement system. In the Court's words,

> The entwinement down from the State Board is therefore unmistakable, just as the entwinement up from the member public schools is overwhelming. Entwinement will support a conclusion that an ostensibly private organization ought to be charged with a public character and judged by constitutional standards; entwinement to the degree shown here requires it.[9] (*Brentwood Academy v. Tennessee Secondary School Athletic Association* 2001, p. 302)

Entwinement has obvious importance for public-private partnerships and some outsourcing arrangements.

A fifth category of state action pertains to private entities that are empowered to use government's coercive power. This category may overlap others, as in the public function of managing prisons, but it can also stand alone in actions involving assets such as garnishment, prejudgment attachment, and replevin. For instance, a private party who uses governmental power such as a writ of replevin[10] to seize property held by another may become a state actor who is liable in a constitutional tort suit for violations of due process of law (*Wyatt v. Cole* 1992). This category of state action probably has the most relevance to outsourcing the collection of delinquent taxes, which is done in forty states and currently of interest to the Internal Revenue Service (Friel 2003; Gruber 2004).

Nonjudicial Application of State Action Doctrine: Some Examples

In the hands of the courts, state action decisions are often technical, precedent parsing, and based on subtle (or flimsy) distinctions (Chemerinsky 2002; Gillette and Stephan 1998; Guttman 2000a; Mays 1995). However, the fundamental balance that state action doctrine seeks to secure among the competing interests of private autonomy, protection of individual rights, and constitutional government can be applied by legislators and executive officials as well as judges. It can also be advanced by the public administration community and private organizations.

Acting by executive order in 1941, President Franklin D. Roosevelt prohibited defense contractors from engaging in employment discrimination based on race, color, creed, or national origin.[11] Recalling Pedreira's case, contractors could also be prohibited from discriminating based on sexual orientation or at least required to provide an equivalent of due process when curtailing their employees' liberty to engage in homosexual relationships. Contracts could also protect whistle-blowing—a First and Fourteenth Amendment right in the public sector—and promote other constitutional values. Beyond the employment relationship, outsourcing contracts can include any number of provisions to protect the public in their dealings with contractors. Such protections are common when outsourcing incarceration and youth services. They can be applied to the outsourcing of public education as well. The Cleveland school-voucher program requires participating private schools, both parochial and secular, "not to discriminate on the basis of race, religion, or ethnic background, or to 'advocate or foster unlawful behavior or teach hatred of any person or group on the basis of race, ethnicity, national origin, or religion'" (*Zelman v. Simmons-Harris* 2002, p. 645).[12] The commercial nature of privately owned shopping malls, stadiums, and similar facilities, as well as the tax and zoning concessions governments sometimes make to their developers, may provide leverage for protecting the free speech and other rights of those who frequent these private yet functionally public spaces. However, private property rights, which include the right to exclude others from one's property, also command great respect (*Dolan v. City of Tigard* 1994). Regulating homeowner associations may present a similar conflict among constitutional values.

Private accrediting organizations can also include constitutional values in their requirements. The American Correctional Association, founded in 1870, is a leading example. It sets standards for prisons, jails, and juvenile detention facilities. These involve such matters as personnel, telecommunications devices for the deaf, inventory control of firearms and chemical agents, shelter in place for life-threatening airborne hazardous releases, noise levels, standards for cells (including square footage, natural light, air circulation, and temperature), external defibrillators, writing surfaces, contraband mail, guard training, and the certification of chaplains (American Correctional Association 2004). The American Association of University Professors and the National Collegiate Athletic Association are similarly in a position to promote free speech, procedural due process, equal protection, and other constitutional values in private universities and colleges.

State Courts and Transparency

As Guttman (2000a) notes, the federal

> courts have long held that contractors (and other third parties) are generally not subject to the Freedom of Information Act . . . because they are not "government agencies." The [judicial] analysis reflects the view that the qualities private actors bring to the public service will be compromised if constrained by FOIA. (p. 901)

No matter how valuable contractors' records developed with public funds may potentially be to informed public debate, the federal courts are unlikely to rule that they are covered by FOIA unless they are in the physical possession of a federal agency.[13] Guttman (2000a) cited growing pressures to resolve "the tension between third party accountability and autonomy" (pp. 901–5). Although the tension is still with us, the state courts have mapped out some instructive approaches in considering when to outsource transparency along with governmental functions.

Craig Feiser (2000) found that thirty-four state court systems have explicitly dealt with the application of freedom of information and related statutes to private entities. The courts in twenty-two states use a so-called flexible approach that can take three forms:

1. A "Totality of Factors Approach" (Connecticut, Florida, Maryland, North Carolina, Oregon, and Kansas) considers at least four factors, in combination: (a) whether the private entity performs a governmental function, (b) the level of government funding, (c) the extent of governmental involvement or regulation, and (d) whether the entity was created by the government (Feiser 2000, p. 837).

The approach is flexible because no single dimension is wholly determinative.

Florida's approach went beyond these factors to include whether the private entity is "acting on behalf of any public agency," "commingling . . . funds," conducting the activity on public property, and whether the government has a "substantial financial interest in the private entity"

(Feiser 2000, p. 839). Additional concerns are the nature of the relationship of the privately performed activity to the agency's decision making and "for whose benefit" the private organization works (Feiser 2000, p. 839).

2. A "Public Function Approach" (Georgia, New York, Ohio, California, Louisiana, Missouri, Utah, Kentucky, Delaware, and New Hampshire) looks at whether the private entity is performing a public function. Definitions vary among these ten states. Public functions include performing personnel activities and financial analysis for public agencies, maintaining a booklist for a state university, operating a private firefighting company, and operating a university alumni foundation and an industrial advisory committee (Feiser 2000, pp. 845–50).

3. A "Nature of Records Approach" (Colorado, Maine, Minnesota, Montana, Washington, and Wisconsin) focuses on the nature of the information sought rather than the composition of the entity that holds it or the functions involved. For example, documents used by "a public stadium district" were considered public records even though they were held by a private party as was information held by a private investigator under government contract (Feiser 2000, pp. 850–52).

By contrast, twelve states take "restrictive approaches limiting access" (Feiser 2000, p. 853). These look at whether public funds are involved (Arkansas, Michigan, North Dakota, Indiana, South Carolina, and Texas); whether "the private entity was created by the legislature or . . . previously determined by law to be subject to" transparency statutes (Pennsylvania, Tennessee, New Jersey, West Virginia); and whether information is held by a public entity (Iowa) or the entity holding it is under public control (Illinois; Feiser 2000, pp. 853–60).

Outsourcing Transparency

Feiser (2000, p. 863) is inclined to rank the states from most to least open. The public administration community can use his analysis more proactively—perhaps even to build a theory of transparency for outsourced functions. When should transparency be outsourced along with governmental functions and why? The state courts have identified several criteria—legislators can endorse or reject them in drafting and amending statutes, and public managers can decide whether to apply them in writing contracts when they have the discretion to do so. For example, in 2001, Connecticut amended its FOIA to incorporate, clarify, and extend state court decisions regarding the act's application to "contractors performing child care and disability eligibility decisions on behalf of state social service agencies, entities running public assistance employment service programs for the state, and the like" (Bass and Hammitt 2002, pp. 613–14). It is clear, however, that to outsource or competitively source without considering these criteria at all is a default position that abdicates responsibility to the courts and endorses private autonomy and the secrecy it protects over public sector transparency. If arrived at by reasoned analysis, these may be sensible courses of action; otherwise, they are likely to yield suboptimal balances.

FEDERAL CONTRACTING IN PRACTICE: TAKING LIMITED STEPS TOWARD OUTSOURCING THE CONSTITUTION AND ADMINISTRATIVE LAW NORMS[14]

Federal regulations treat the decision whether to outsource an activity separately from the question of the conditions that should be imposed on contractors. As noted earlier, one consequence of this division is that calculating when to contract out does not address whether to outsource constitutional and administrative law norms along with noninherently governmental functions. Much of the specific content of federal contracts for outsourcing is dictated by the Federal Acquisition Regulation (FAR): "The Federal Acquisition Regulations System is established for the codification and publication of uniform policies and procedures for acquisition by all executive agencies" (FAR 2004, section 1.101). In practice, FAR is an extensive and evolving system of regulations covering an extremely wide range of topics surrounding federal acquisitions, including general administrative matters, competition and acquisition planning, contracting methods and contract types, socioeconomic programs, general contracting requirements, special categories of contracting, and contract management. In June 2004, the General Services Administration established a new office to help ensure compliance with these and other federal contracting rules and regulations (Harris 2004b). A small component of the FAR and related regulations deals with important elements of democratic governance: individual rights, including protection of whistle-blowers and personal privacy, and transparency.

Whistleblower Protection

Federal employees who release information highlighting the potential wrongdoings of their agencies are afforded some protections against on-the-job retaliation. Subchapter A, Part 3 of FAR addresses similar issues for contract employees: "Improper Business Practices and Personal Conflicts of Interest." This section includes the following provision regarding whistle-blower protections for contract employees:

> Government contractors shall not discharge, demote or otherwise discriminate against an employee as a reprisal for disclosing information to a Member of Congress, or an authorized official of an agency or of the Department of Justice, relating to a substantial violation of law related to a contract (including the competition for or negotiation of a contract). (FAR 2004, section 3.903)

This provision exemplifies how rights enjoyed by federal employees can be extended to private employees through outsourcing.

Personal Privacy

FAR (2004) also contains a Privacy Act Notification clause specifying that

> if a contract specifically provides for the design, development, or operation of a system of records on individuals on behalf of an agency to accomplish an agency function, the agency must apply the requirements of the [Privacy] Act to the contractor and its employees working on the contract. (section 24.102.c)

The Privacy Act guards against disclosure of personal information and affords individuals opportunities to contest the accuracy of information in records on them. FAR requires contractors to accept potential criminal penalties for violations of the act.

Transparency

The final products produced by contractors are in many cases documents or electronic files that are turned over to the agency. Once a record is in an agency's possession, it usually becomes an agency record subject to FOIA. Information that is not considered an agency record is not subject to release through FOIA. The case law on the topic is extensive, but, basically, if a record is in the control of a federal agency, it is most likely an agency record. The FAR includes a section (section 4.700) on the document retention schedule of contractors. It focuses primarily on how long a contractor must keep documents to satisfy auditing requirements. It does not address the wider purposes of freedom of information. With this in mind, the Department of Energy (DOE) includes a clause regarding ownership of records and access in its Department of Energy Acquisition Regulation (DEAR):

> Government-owned records. Except [records on personnel, confidential financial matters, operations not related to DOE, legal matters, and some aspects of technology, intellectual property, and procurement], . . . all records acquired or generated by the contractor in its performance of this contract shall be the property of the Government and shall be delivered to the Government or otherwise disposed of by the contractor either as the contracting officer may from time to time direct during the progress of the work or, in any event, as the contracting officer shall direct upon completion or termination of the contract. (U.S. Department of Energy 2004)

Unlike the DOE's requirement, FAR does not include a general access and ownership of records clause. DEAR offers exact language that can be placed in contracts to specify which documents will become property of the federal government. Flexibly applied, some contracts could include extensive ownership of records and access clauses, whereas others would have few or none. The greater number of contractor records that are turned over to federal government the more accessible they are to the media and general public through FOIA. Alternatively, rather than leave discretion with the agencies, Congress could follow Connecticut's lead and amend the federal FOIA to cover certain classes of contractor records across the board.

Next Steps

These provisions of FAR and DEAR outsource constitutional and administrative law norms on a very limited scale. However, they illustrate that such outsourcing is feasible and salient to federal acquisitions professionals. Contractors can be asked to tolerate whistle-blowers, accept potential criminal punishment for violation of the Privacy Act, and supply their records to federal agencies for possible public release. A long historical view of how federal administrative agencies were subjected to constitutional constraints and administrative law regulations during the twentieth century (Rosenbloom 2000a, 2000b) suggests that further outsourcing of constitutional and administrative law norms to contractors is likely to be inevitable. A half-century struggle by judges and legislators to promote democratic-constitutional values over deep-seated interests in administrative economy, efficiency, effectiveness, and independence strongly suggests that, as the Supreme Court first held in 1880 and reiterated in 1995, ultimately "the Constitution constrains governmental action 'by whatever instruments or in whatever modes that action may be taken'" (*Lebron v. National Railroad Passenger Corporation* 1995, p. 392, quoting *Ex Parte Virginia* 1880, pp. 346–47). The question is less whether some constitutional and administrative law norms will be outsourced to contractors than when, how, and what role public administrative expertise will play in the process.

CONCLUSION: DEVELOPING A CALCULUS FOR DEMOCRATIC-CONSTITUTIONAL THIRD-PARTY GOVERNMENT

The scope of contemporary privatization and outsourcing is huge. As of 1996, Light (1999) estimated that the federal government had about 4.2 million civilian and military personnel and employed another 12.7 million workers on contracts, grants, and mandates (p. 37). To-day, the federal government is spending almost $28 billion annually on professional services contracts—a 57 percent jump from five years earlier (Adelsberger 2004, p. 1). As large as these numbers are, they are undoubtedly dwarfed by contracting at the state and local-government levels. Third-party government is clearly attractive to policy makers, but so are individual rights, governmental transparency, and other democratic-constitutional values.

Despite its expertise, the public administration community has not concertedly engaged the issues associated with outsourcing constitutional and administrative law norms. It may often be assumed that such outsourcing would be prohibitively expensive or otherwise impede third-party government. Yet, outsourcing the Constitution in incarceration, as the Supreme Court did in 1988 (*West v. Atkins* 1988), has not been a barrier to privatizing prisons. In fact, it may well have facilitated privatization by making privately managed prisons safer for prisoners and more palatable to legislators. Similarly, outsourcing these norms would not necessarily thrust burdensome red tape and litigation costs on to contractors. Following the DOE's approach, much of the third-party transparency issue could be resolved with minimal effort, litigation, and expense by the simple step of requiring contractors to supply specified documents to the agencies whose functions they perform. If necessary, liability could be capped in return.

Outsourcing constitutional and administrative law norms is necessarily selective. Except with regard to treatment of their own employees (which is regulated by employment law), these norms are probably irrelevant to the overwhelming number of contractors, who neither deal directly with the public nor possess significant information that would be available from public agencies under freedom of information and other transparency statutes. U.S. demo-cratic constitutionalism rests on a duality that protects private autonomy. Constitutional and administrative law norms need not be applied across the board to all contractors or to none at all. Their value and application should be systematically calculated when deciding which government functions to privatize and outsource. Largely by default, the guidelines available to the public administration community are being supplied by the courts: Is the contractor engaged in a public function, acting as a surrogate or adjunct for an agency in an area were constitutional rights are at risk, or so entwined with an agency as to be public in character? Are the funds involved so large that the endeavor would be of interest to taxpay-ers or to suggest that a contractor's employees ought to have whistle-blower protections? Is the contractor gathering or producing information that threatens personal privacy or speaks to the core purposes of freedom of information and other open government requirements? Is outsourcing a way of circumventing constitutional and administrative law constraints?

Such questions can be left to the judiciary. However, with observation, analysis, and thought, the public administration community should be able to bring its expertise to bear in refining, augmenting, and answering them. In the process, it could do what Savas (1987) explicitly and *Circular A-76* implicitly seek: to provide a "key to better government."

Rosenbloom, David H., and Suzanne J. Piotrowski. "Outsourcing the Constitution and Administrative Law Norms." *American Review of Public Administration* 35, no. 2 (2004): 103–21. Reprinted with permission of Sage Publications, Inc. Journals.

* * *

A Partial Revolution: The Diplomatic Ethos and Transparency in Intergovernmental Organizations

Alasdair Roberts

The crisis of legitimacy that now confronts intergovernmental organizations such as the World Trade Organization (WTO) has a precedent.[1] In the decades following the Great Depression, the responsibilities of governments in the advanced capitalist democracies grew substantially. This involved a rapid expansion in the number, size, and influence of administrative agencies that exercised discretion given to them through statutes, or that applied regulations made under authority of law but without close review by legislatures. Power seemed to shift from legislators to bureaucrats, provoking complaints that presaged those now made against the restructured public sector. Bureaucrats, it was said, exercised extraordinary influence—but did so secretively and often capriciously. Administrative agencies, said U.S. Supreme Court justice Robert Jackson, had formed a strange "fourth branch" of government that deranged traditional ideas about the division and control of political power (Rosenbloom 2000). In Britain, Lord Gordon Hewart complained about the "new despotism" of bureaucratic government (Hewart 1929).

Throughout the postwar years, the Western democracies constructed a new regime to regulate and legitimize bureaucratic power. New laws compelled administrative agencies to adopt more open procedures for rulemaking and established mechanisms by which citizens could appeal adverse decisions. Courts became more liberal in providing citizens with judicial remedies for administrative malfeasance. The construction of this new regime required a revision of the long-held belief that the control of administrative behavior should be the sole responsibility of political executives and legislators. Citizens acquired a new set of rights that could be asserted directly against the new fourth branch of government. One of these was the right of access to information held by departments and agencies—established first, and narrowly, in laws such as the U.S. Administrative Procedure Act of 1946, and later, and more broadly, in laws such as the Freedom of Information Act of 1966. Comparable legislation was adopted in other countries. By the end of the century, it was roughly accurate to say that a right to information had been recognized as a prerequisite for the legitimate exercise of public authority—a "constitutive principle" of governance within the nation state (Picciotto 2000).

However, the effectiveness of this new regulatory regime in legitimizing the exercise of public power was soon diminished because of another and equally profound shift in the structure of governmental authority. Influence over the content of public policy has moved from domestic authorities to intergovernmental organizations such as the International Monetary Fund (IMF), the World Bank, and the World Trade Organization, which are not bound by the old regulatory regime and do not seem to respect the "constitutive principles" of legitimate government. This has provoked a revival of complaints about "new despotism"—this time aimed at intergovernmental organizations rather than the administrative arms of national and subnational governments.

The World Trade Organization has been the object of much of this criticism. In 1996, Ralph Nader complained that important decisions on trade policy were now made by "a group of unelected bureaucrats sitting behind closed doors in Geneva" (Nader and Wallach 1996). Shortly after the WTO's Seattle ministerial meeting, Oxfam UK argued the organization confronted "a crisis of legitimacy" created as a result of "shadowy processes [that] are more medieval than millennial" (Oxfam UK 2000, 4). "The WTO operates in a secretive, exclusionary manner," said a manifesto circulated at the same time by a broad coalition of nongovernmental organizations. "People must have the right to self-determination and the right to know and decide on international commercial commitments. Among other things, this requires that decision-making processes be democratic, transparent and inclusive" (Raghavan 2000b).

Intergovernmental organizations have attempted reforms to rebut these criticisms. In 1996, the WTO's member states promised "the maximum possible level of transparency" in the organization (WTO 1996b). Former Secretary General Michael Moore said in July 2002 that the WTO had become "more transparent and accountable in the way we do things and the way we take [sic] decisions" (WTO 2002a). Stanley Fischer, former chief economist of the International Monetary Fund, says there has been a "transparency revolution"—a profound "culture change"—within that organization as well (Fischer 2001). "We used to publish nothing," said another IMF official. "Now we publish everything" (Dawson 2003). The World Bank has also undertaken reforms that it recently said would bring "greater transparency and accountability" to its operations (World Bank 2001).

Such claims must be treated skeptically. In fact, reforms aimed at promoting transparency within organizations such as the WTO have had limited reach. Such reform challenges deeply entrenched conventions about the confidentiality of intergovernmental communications and the right of states to retain control over the dissemination of information. Most often, reforms have carefully worked around such norms of confidentiality. Where clear disclosure requirements have been imposed on governments, they typically aim at a narrow range of information the disclosure of which is thought to be essential to the projects of trade and financial liberalization.

A true revolution in transparency would require more substantial steps to affirm a right to information relating to the activities of intergovernmental organizations and greater candor on the part of advanced economies about the limitations of the transparency agenda that is transmitted to the administrative apparatuses of other states through the WTO and IMF. More radical steps in transparency with regard to the operations of these organizations might be justified to protect basic human rights, such as the right to participate actively in the policy-making process.

THE "VICE OF PUBLICITY"

The effort to improve the transparency of intergovernmental organizations has not been easy because it challenges long-established norms of international relations. For centuries, executives have expected to conduct foreign relations with considerable autonomy. A strong code of secrecy about the conduct of intergovernmental affairs has been important in preserving this autonomy.

That there is a well-entrenched norm of diplomatic confidentiality is beyond dispute. G. R. Berridge (2002) suggests that secrecy is one of the main characteristics of the system of diplomacy constructed to manage relations among European states in the modern age. J. H. H. Weiler (2000) observes that the "ethos of confidentiality" continues to be a hallmark of modern diplomacy. In practice, the ethos of confidentiality is evidenced in two ways. The first is the unwillingness of executives to disclose their own views or plans relating to the conduct of intergovernmental relations. In the United States, for example, the right to keep such secrets is central to the doctrine of executive privilege (Rozell 1994). In Commonwealth countries, it is contained within the doctrine of crown privilege or public interest immunity.

The ethos of confidentiality is also manifest in the categorical refusal of governments to release information provided in confidence by other governments, even if the information is completely innocuous.[2] This is sometimes described as the rule of "originator control": The government that produced a document is given absolute discretion about its distribution.

The ethos of confidentiality is typically defended on realist grounds. The capacity of diplomats to resolve conflict is thought to hinge on their ability to manage the number and type of parties to the conflict (Schattschneider 1960; Elster 1995; Weiler 2000, 243). More open discussion of interstate conflicts may also increase pressure on government leaders to articulate basic principles or emphasize doctrinal differences, which may complicate the process of conflict resolution (Watson 1983, 136). Hans Morgenthau warned against the "vice of publicity" in diplomacy, observing, "It takes only common sense derived from daily experience to realize that it is impossible to negotiate in public on anything in which parties other than the negotiators are interested. . . . The degeneration of diplomatic intercourse into a propaganda match is . . . the inevitable concomitant of the publicity of the new diplomacy" (1954, 519–21). Realists also suggest the mass public is too shortsighted and ill informed to make sound decisions on foreign policy (Alterman 1998, 1–19). Furthermore, the costs of poor decision making in the field of international relations could be extraordinary, bearing as they do on matters of war and peace. The institutions and conventions of diplomacy emerged at a time when the state system was fragile, and "the risk of resort to force of arms was inevitably and always present" (Watson 1983, 104).

In the last half-century, profound social changes have challenged executive prerogatives in a range of policy fields. The franchise has broadened, and electorates have become better educated and more conscious of their political participation rights. Trust in government has declined precipitously. One result has been the adoption of several institutional innovations—stronger rules on administrative procedures, broader opportunities for judicial review, more extensive consultative procedures, funding for nongovernmental advocacy groups, rules on disclosure of information—intended to restrict the autonomy of political executives. However, the field of international relations is, to some degree, protected from efforts to check executive prerogatives. In the United States, Eric Alterman complains that foreign policy is still "deliberately shielded from the effects of democratic debate, with virtually no institutionalized democratic participation" (Alterman 1998, 4). Other commentators have suggested the preservation of executive prerogatives in this field has produced a form of bifurcated government.[3]

This incongruity in the treatment of executive power is evident in the drafting of national right-to-information laws. Many Western democracies have adopted such laws as electorates reacted against executive authority. However, these laws rarely impinge on executive prerogatives in the field of international relations. For example, Canada's Access to Information Act denies access to information when its disclosure could reasonably be expected to be injurious to international affairs,[4] and Canadian courts have made clear their reluctance to question the judgment of officials regarding the risk of injury. In the 1997 *Do-Ky* decision, the Federal Court of Canada suggested that fear of harm to Canada's reputation caused by breaching diplomatic norms of confidentiality would itself justify withholding information.[5]

A similar approach is taken in other established democracies. When the post-Watergate Congress attempted to strengthen the United States' Freedom of Information Act, it conceded the executive branch should continue to have broad authority to withhold information about foreign policy based on its "unique insights into what adverse effects might occur as a result of public disclosure."[6] In *United States v. Nixon* (418 U.S. 683 [1974]), the U.S. Supreme Court made clear that a president's decision to refuse access to "diplomatic secrets" should be treated with "utmost deference."

National right-to-information laws are even more careful in their treatment of information received in confidence from other governments. The rule of originator control is preserved: Final authority over the release of a document remains with the state that originally produced the document.[7] As the Canadian government observed during the debate over adoption of the Access to Information Act, domestic law acts on "the principle that the information is the other country's, not Canada's, to dispose of" (Fox 1980). This is a more severe rule than is applied to information provided to governments by domestic nonstate actors: Government institutions are more likely to have discretion to release personal information provided by individuals, or information provided in confidence by businesses, if disclosure is determined to be in the public interest.[8] In the *Do-Ky* case, Canadian diplomats made clear their reluctance to challenge the ethos of confidentiality: "Canada cannot afford to get too far in front of the expectations of those with whom we conduct business. We are not a great power. When we do not conform, or are seen not to conform, to their expectations of us, other countries do not change their practices to accommodate us. They simply adjust their expectations of us and react accordingly."[9]

Intergovernmental organizations such as the WTO, as products of diplomacy, are also imbued with this deeply rooted ethos of confidentiality (Weiler 2000). And yet the expanding role of such organizations has seemed, to many domestic observers, to create new reasons for questioning the ethos. In many cases, the disputes being resolved through intergovernmental processes do not relate directly to national security or the stability of the state system. On the contrary, they address problems of economic organization or social welfare that might otherwise have been addressed under the more liberal rules governing the "domestic" half of our bifurcated governments. The reallocation of these responsibilities to the sphere of intergovernmental relations has produced strong challenges to the more constrictive norms on transparency and participation that have traditionally prevailed in that sphere.

ACCESS TO INFORMATION WITHIN INTERGOVERNMENTAL ORGANIZATIONS

The fight for greater transparency in the WTO and other intergovernmental organizations challenges this convention of confidentiality, and the modest accomplishments of the last decade are evidence of this convention's durability. The WTO and other intergovernmental organizations may promise "the maximum possible level of transparency," but in practice improvements in policies on access to information have been cautious, and they have never directly challenged the convention of confidentiality in intergovernmental affairs. A brief review of the disclosure policies of the major intergovernmental organizations illustrates this point.

World Trade Organization

The WTO's policy on access to documents was laid down in a decision of its General Council six months before its 1996 Singapore conference. The 1996 decision modified the general rule that any document circulated to WTO members should be treated as restricted and not distributed publicly. In fact, the decision appeared to reverse this presumption entirely by proposing that WTO documents should generally circulate on an unrestricted basis (WTO 1996a).

As critics have pointed out,[10] the decision suffered from two substantial flaws. The first was the extensive list of documents that were exempted from the new presumption of immediate derestriction. Most documents were only to be considered for derestriction six months after circulation. These included timetables of meetings of WTO bodies and committees, draft agendas, Secretariat background notes, and other working documents that are essential for following the day-to-day operations of the WTO (Oxfam UK 2000, 27). Minutes of the meetings of all WTO bodies were also to be withheld for six months, as were some documents relating to overall reviews of national trade policies and the international trading environment. Furthermore, governments retained a general discretion to exempt from automatic disclosure any other documents submitted to the WTO Secretariat.

The second flaw of the 1996 decision related to the treatment of exempted documents. The policy stipulated they should be considered for derestriction six months after circulation. However, decision making within the WTO is based on consensus; as a result, derestriction could be blocked if only one government—for instance, the government that first circulated the document—objected. An articulation of reasons was not required. In 1999, for example, Mexico single-handedly blocked the derestriction of background papers relating to agricultural trade, despite arguments by the WTO Secretariat and many other nations that derestriction would enhance transparency (WTO, Agriculture Committee 1999, 9–10).

There were many proposals to reform the 1996 decision. In 1997, a major nongovernmental organization suggested the WTO should adopt a policy roughly comparable to that contained in national right-to-information laws, in which WTO documents would be accessible unless a denial of access could be shown to be essential to protect specified interests (Weiner and Van Dyke 1997). Canada and the United States made less radical proposals aimed at widening the class of documents that were automatically derestricted and shortening the period for which other documents could be withheld (United States and Canada 1998). In December 2001, the WTO Secretariat itself produced an ambitious proposal that would automatically derestrict almost all working documents and check the ability of governments to restrict their own documents (WTO 2001a). However, the need for consensus again stymied reform. Secretary General Michael Moore conceded in January 2002 that a formal review of the derestriction policy begun four years earlier has produced "little movement" on the subject (WTO 2002c).

A compromise reform of the 1996 policy was finally adopted by the WTO General Council in May 2002 (WTO 2002d). On two key points, the new policy retreated from the WTO Secretariat's proposal of December 2001. Member states preserved the right to block public access to documents produced by the Secretariat for WTO bodies for up to three months. This limited the power of individual states to block access indefinitely, as they could under the 1996 policy, but it also retreated from the Secretariat's bolder plan to eliminate this power entirely. With regard to documents actually provided by member states, the retreat was more substantial: Here, governments retained their power to block access indefinitely.

The European Community complained the 2001 proposals had been "considerably watered down"—a sentiment shared by the United States and Canada—but acceded to the proposed compromise. "If Members sought perfection on every point," said the General Council's chairman, "consultation would likely continue for another four years" (WTO 2002b, 5–8).

The debate over reform of the derestriction policy has been shaped by two considerations. Attempts to limit the circulation of restricted documents are acknowledged to be futile: The WTO has 142 members with sharply divergent interests, and it is inevitable that information will leak to well-connected nongovernmental organizations (WTO, General Council 2001, 19). However, there is an important distinction between discrete leaking to trusted allies and the automatic publication of documents on the WTO Web site. Some less influential states worry that automatic publication will discourage candor or lead to last-minute submissions designed to thwart publication requirements, undermining their ability to monitor activity within the WTO. "Radical derestriction," Bulgaria said in July 2001, could lead to a proliferation of "unofficial material which were of limited availability, did not remain in the records, [and] would never be derestricted" (WTO, General Council 2001, 19–20).

Whether the Bulgarian concern is reasonable is a matter of debate even among less advantaged states. However, it does highlight another significant limitation of WTO policy on access to documents. The policy does not provide access to "unofficial" documents such as the internal or administrative papers of the Secretariat itself, or other draft or working documents that are circulated to WTO members.[11] Neither does WTO policy provide a right of access to communications from one state to a limited number of other states outside WTO channels. (Indeed, it would be impossible for a WTO policy to establish a right to these documents. In such cases, access would be governed by national right-to-information laws, subject to the broad protection provided in those laws for intergovernmental communications.) As a consequence, the WTO derestriction policy is not in any way comparable to a national right-to-information law. On the contrary, it is what is known in the United Kingdom as a "publication scheme"[12]—a negotiated plan for the dissemination of certain kinds of official documents.

World Bank

The disclosure policies of other intergovernmental organizations have developed in a similarly cautious way. The World Bank first came under pressure to improve disclosure in the 1980s, when it was criticized by nongovernmental organizations for its support of dam-building projects whose social and environmental impacts had been ignored. The U.S. Congress played a key role in shaping Bank policy. The 1989 Pelosi Amendment led to disclosure of environmental assessments on Bank-financed projects (GAO 1998), and the Bank made further commitments to disclosure in anticipation of Congress's approval in 2000 of payments to the International Development Association, an arm of the Bank that provides assistance to the poorest countries (Chamberlain 1999). The Bank released an overhauled information disclosure policy in September 2001.

The new policy purports to establish a "presumption in favor of disclosure" of World Bank documents (World Bank 2002, 2). In fact, this is very far from the case. The policy is in fact another publication scheme, which specifies the conditions under which certain documents will be released and assumes confidentiality for the rest (Bank Information Center 2001). These excluded documents include all internal deliberative papers, communications with other intergovernmental organizations, draft documents not yet approved by the Bank's board, and minutes of board meetings. Some governments were reportedly worried that disclosure of further information about the Board's work "would invite external actors to become involved in the issues discussed by the board" (Bank Information Center 2001).

The Bank's 2001 policy expanded the list of documents that are routinely published. These include environmental assessments, still affected by the Pelosi Amendment, and documents relating to financing of projects or programs for the poorest countries, typically funded out of the International Development Association. In other circumstances, the Bank has simply moved from a categorical refusal of access to a policy of disclosure unless the affected government makes an objection. In other words, the convention of diplomatic confidentiality is wholly preserved. In addition, the policy preserves the right of governments to request the withholding of sensitive information contained in documents that are to be published, and the communication of sensitive material in separate and inaccessible memoranda (Bank Information Center 2001; World Bank 2002, 14–15).

The difficulties with the 2001 policy were illustrated by the controversy surrounding the World Bank's 2002 agreement to provide structural adjustment loans to the government of Uruguay. The Bank's disclosure policy states a "presumption" that Letters of Development Policy that are provided by borrowing governments to the Bank will be publicly disclosed. However, the Uruguayan government exercised its prerogative to block release of the letter relating to the 2002 loans. The letter was later leaked, and it showed the government had assured the Bank it had undertaken extensive consultations with nongovernmental organizations about its plans to cut public-sector salaries and social assistance payments. Critics complained the government's assurances were "completely untrue" (McIntosh 2002).

International Monetary Fund

The IMF has also responded to demands for improved transparency. Critics charged that secretiveness led to errors in the Fund's handling of the Asian financial crisis (Stiglitz 2000), and in October 1998, the U.S. Congress made the provision of $18 billion in support contingent on reform of the Fund's information disclosure policy.[13]

Despite such pressure, the reformed policy—adopted by the IMF in January 2001—has again been drafted as a publication scheme, designed to accommodate the principle of originator control (IMF 2001b). Like the WTO and World Bank policies, it does not establish a general right of access to documents held by the institution. The list of records covered by the policy excludes critical documents, such as the agendas and minutes of meetings of the IMF's Executive Board (Bretton Woods Project 2003). Furthermore, public access to almost all major documents relating to member states is contingent on the consent of their governments (IMF 2001b, table 1). A recent IMF study found that developing countries withhold consent to one of the most important of these documents—the so-called Article IV staff report on monetary, economic, and structural policies—about half the time (IMF 2003, table 3). The policy *presumes* that "policy intentions documents"[14] provided by governments receiving assistance from the Fund will be made public, but this still implies that nations reserve the right to block disclosure. Governments may also negotiate about the content of documents that are publicly released (Van Houtven 2002, 60).

While the IMF clearly discloses more information than it did a decade ago, it has also been candid about the limits of reform. Former managing director Michel Camdessus observed in 1998, "In these matters, the pace of change is largely in the hands of the IMF's members. . . . [W]e must recognize that the calls for more IMF transparency are, in many respects, calls on the member countries; after all, it is their policies that will be opened to scrutiny when documents are published. Once consensus is established, we will be enthusiastic to proceed with the necessary adaptation of procedures and policies."

In none of these three cases—the WTO, World Bank, or IMF—has there been a revolution in transparency that has overthrown conventions about diplomatic confidentiality. The notion that nonstate actors have a right to information held by these bodies is far from established. On the contrary, we are at a stage where reforms are halting and still required to conform to the principles that states must consent to the disclosure of information relating to their activities, and that changes in policy on transparency require consensus on the part of all participating states.

There are, furthermore, other policy domains where the ethos of diplomatic confidentiality is actually being reinforced. One of the little-noticed consequences of defense and intelligence integration among states following the end of the cold war has been an increase in the number of bilateral agreements that bind governments to respect the rule of originator control, use all available methods to resist disclosure of information received from other governments, and avoid the resolution of citizen complaints about denial of information by independent tribunals. These commitments wholly contradict the principles that underlie national right-to-information laws.[15] The Canadian government has recently signed such agreements with South Korea and Australia,[16] while the United States is now party to more than fifty such agreements.[17] Whether the consolidation of norms in this sector will affect other sectors remains an open question. It is conceivable that we are witnessing an elaboration of diplomatic conventions, with norms of confidentiality being reinforced in one policy field and loosened in another.

TRANSPARENCY IN THE WTO'S DISPUTE SETTLEMENT PROCESS

The WTO undertakes functions unlike those performed by the IMF or World Bank. It has also established processes for resolving interstate conflicts on trade matters. The creation of this new dispute settlement mechanism has led once again to calls for increased transparency. However, disagreement about transparency within the WTO's dispute settlement mechanism has proved even more intractable than the debate over access to documents.

Rules governing the dispute settlement mechanism are imbued with the ethos of diplomatic confidentiality and designed to limit the capacity of nongovernmental actors to monitor the process by which disputes are resolved. Expert panels appointed to resolve disputes meet in closed sessions. Only governments have the right to appear before a panel or have their submissions considered by it. All submissions are to be kept confidential, and so are the interim reports that are distributed by each panel for comment by interested governments. Comparable rules are used to preserve confidentiality for the appellate body that may be asked to take up complaints about a panel report.[18]

After their adoption in 1995, these confidentiality rules quickly became the object of protest by American nongovernmental organizations. In 1998, environmental groups complained about their inability to observe or submit briefs to the panel that was appointed to consider challenges to an American law mandating the use of turtle exclusion devices by foreign shrimp fishers. The U.S. government attempted to circumvent the ban on nongovernmental organization's briefs by including them in its own submission, a move that was unsuccessfully resisted by the four developing countries—Thailand, Pakistan, Malaysia, and India—that had initiated the case (WTO 1998). U.S. environmental groups also leaked a restricted copy of the panel's draft report upholding the complaint. Other American groups—such as steel producers threatened by a European challenge to U.S. antidumping laws—also called for a right to participate in the WTO's dispute settlement processes (Coalition for Open Trade 2000).

Nongovernmental organizations in other advanced economies also complained about the secretiveness of dispute settlement procedures,[19] but the impact on government policy was perhaps most obvious in the United States. Concern that the WTO's perceived secretiveness would undermine voters' willingness to accept further liberalization led the Clinton administration to make transparency in the dispute settlement mechanism a "priority issue" for the United States (USTR 1998, 37). The Clinton administration's proposals—open hearings, a right to submit nongovernmental organization briefs, and rapid release of draft decisions (Barshefsky 1999; United States 2000)—were said to be "critical . . . in ensuring the long-term credibility of the multilateral system" (U.S. Mission 1999). The proposals have been adopted by the Bush administration (United States 2002). Senator Max Baucus, chair of the U.S. Senate Finance Committee, said in April 2002 that these modifications and other reforms to the Dispute Settlement Understanding were essential to "defuse public mistrust" of the WTO and should be "the single most important goal for U.S. negotiators" in Geneva (Baucus 2002).

The United States has argued that its proposed reforms will help developing countries, who will be able to observe proceedings and "gain practical knowledge" about the dispute settlement system (USTR 2000). Nevertheless, many developing countries have strongly resisted the American proposals. In 1998, Mexico expressed the view of several governments that premature disclosure of draft panel reports encouraged "external pressures of a non-legal kind . . . [from] certain vested interests" (WTO, General Council 1998). Several developing countries have worried that transparency measures would be exploited by first-world nongovernmental organizations, to the detriment of their own national interests (Oxfam UK 2000, 25).

As a consequence of this profound "conceptual divide" (Raghavan 2000a) on the question of transparency, attempts to reform the Dispute Settlement Understanding have foundered. The WTO missed a deadline, set at the end of the Uruguay Round negotiations, to complete a review of the understanding by 1999. In current negotiations, developing countries have continued to resist measures that would open the dispute settlement mechanism to nongovernmental groups (ICSTD 2002b). In the fall of 2002, it was reported that a group of developing countries had protested that American proposals would result in "trials by media" that could cause "miscarriages of justice" (ICSTD 2002a).

The dimensions of this controversy were illustrated after a decision of the WTO's Appellate Body taken in November 2000. While preparing to hear the appeal of a dispute over restrictions the European Community had imposed on the importation of asbestos products, the Appellate Body announced it would exercise its discretion to accept briefs from nongovernmental groups or individuals (WTO 2001b, 18–23). The United States lauded the decision, but many developing countries protested strongly. In a special session of the General Council, Egypt complained that "the likely beneficiaries of such a decision were those individuals and NGOs who had the capacity in terms of resources and time. Those were entities which had more access to WTO work and documents, and were operating mainly in the developed world with few in developing countries" (WTO 2000, 5). India agreed the decision would "have the implication of putting the developing countries at an even greater disadvantage in view of the relative unpreparedness of their NGOs" (WTO 2000, 10), while Brazil worried that "the dispute settlement mechanism could soon be contaminated by political issues that did not belong to the WTO" (WTO 2000, 12). The Appellate Body subsequently finessed the dispute by rejecting every application to submit a brief it had received from nongovernmental actors (Mavroidis 2001).

The Canadian position in this debate appears to have been equivocal. As in the United States, concern about Canadians' support for liberalization has led the Canadian government to call for improved transparency of dispute settlement procedures (Clark and Morrison 1998, 34; Marchi 1998; Canada 2003). However, it has taken the view that "briefs [are] not a transparency issue" (WTO 2000, 19) and avoided a clear statement of the circumstances under which briefs should be permitted.

The premise underlying the Canadian position is at first plausible: The right to know about the state of discussions in dispute settlement procedures seems distinct from the right to participate directly in those discussions. On the other hand, improved transparency—in the narrow sense—is still likely to foster more extensive public discussion about disputes and more accountability of governments to nonstate actors for statements made in the context of dispute resolution. As a consequence, the risk that dispute settlement will be "contaminated by political issues" and that first-world nongovernmental organizations will garner disproportionate influence is still significant.

"TRANSMISSION BELTS" FOR TRANSPARENCY?

Norms of confidentiality have not been overturned with respect to the internal operations of intergovernmental organizations and the communications conducted through those organizations. However, there is another way in which these organizations, and the agreements upon which they are founded, may shape transparency: by influencing the domestic policies of member states on access to information. In a sense, intergovernmental organizations serve as "transmission belts" for the transfer of understandings about transparency that are already well established in the major trading nations.

In this area, progress toward transparency has been much more rapid. However, it is a distinctive kind of transparency that is being promoted, compelling the release of information that is immediately beneficial to commercial and financial interests and their home states. It is an open question as to whether the program of transparency reforms advocated by organizations such as the WTO and IMF will encourage other kinds of transparency that benefit domestic constituencies more directly.

In fact, information disclosure by member states is one of the main policy instruments relied upon by the IMF and WTO. In 1977, the IMF began a practice of completing regular reviews of the domestic policies of each member state that might affect exchange rates. Authorized by Article IV of the IMF's Articles of Agreement, the scope of these "surveillance" exercises (the IMF's own phrase) has broadened substantially in the past decade to include "much more detailed examination" of each country's financial sector, patterns of capital investment, and microeconomic policies (Pauly 1997, 42; IMF 2001c). Although some member states have resisted calls for public disclosure of surveillance reports produced by IMF staff, they have for some time been available on an informal basis to rating agencies, lenders, and investors (Group of Independent Experts 1999, 75–76). For small states in particular, the surveillance routine has become an important constraint on domestic policy (Group of Independent Experts 1999, 49), the principal aim of which is to create an international financial architecture that is "conducive to expanding world trade and investment" (Pauly 1997, 112).

The practice of surveillance begun by the IMF has been extended by the trade policy review mechanism that is now incorporated into the WTO agreement.[20] The mechanism's aim is to promote "greater transparency" in national trade policies, and thereby "contribute to improved adherence . . . to rules, disciplines and commitments" contained in trade agreements.[21] The mechanism is, as Asif Qureshi has noted, "an instrument of enforcement," intended to promote compliance with "a certain normative framework" (1995, 493–94). The reviews often provide other countries with evidence that can be used in later negotiations or disputes (Keesing 1998). The reviews may also be used to "boost investor confidence" by demonstrating that governments are honoring commitments made in trade agreements (Francois 1999, 6).

Other disclosure requirements are also imposed in WTO agreements. Disclosure rules were integral to the oldest component of the WTO agreements, the 1947 General Agreement on Tariffs and Trade. This agreement includes what is now a familiar provision in WTO agreements: a general obligation to publish laws, regulations, judicial decisions, and administrative rulings that would affect matters covered by the agreement—in this case, trade in goods. Intergovernmental agreements that affect trade policy must also be made available. As in domestic right-to-information laws, there are limitations: A government may withhold information if it would impede law enforcement, prejudice legitimate commercial interests, or otherwise harm the public interest.[22]

New right-to-information features were added in the more recent General Agreement on Trade in Services. The obligation to publish relevant documents is replicated; however, governments are also obligated to respond to requests from other governments for "specific information" about their policies affecting trade in services. Each government must designate "enquiry points" that are responsible for replying to such requests.[23]

The obligation to respond to governmental enquiries is contained in several other WTO agreements. The Agreement on the Application of Sanitary and Phytosanitary Measures—commonly known as the SPS Agreement—states that each government must respond to "all reasonable questions" from other governments about its SPS policies and practices.[24] Under the Agreement on Trade-Related Aspects of Intellectual Property Rights, governments must "be prepared to supply, in response to a written request" from another government, information about their policies and practices on intellectual property.[25] The Agreement on Trade-Related Investment Measures requires governments to "accord sympathetic consideration to requests for information" from other governments on matters relating to the agreement.[26] The European Union has proposed that a more strongly worded obligation to respond should be included in a proposed agreement on foreign direct investment (European Community 2002). Under the Agreement on Government Procurement, the government of an unsuccessful foreign supplier may also request information to determine whether a procurement decision has been made fairly and impartially.[27]

The Agreement on Government Procurement includes another innovation: It extends the right of information to nonstate actors. Under the agreement, governments must "promptly provide" foreign suppliers with an explanation of their procurement practices and procedures, as well as reasons for unfavorable decisions. Similarly, the 1997 Agreement on Basic Telecommunication Services is founded on the principle that foreign suppliers have a right to request information about unfavorable licensing decisions.[28] Under the Agreement on Technical Barriers to Trade, governments have an obligation to make information available to foreign producers—and other interested parties in other nations—about proposed changes to technical regulations. Governments must also answer "all reasonable questions" from foreign producers about the application of their technical regulations. This access-to-information code even includes rules about the price that may be charged for information and the language in which it must be provided.[29] The government of Japan has called this "an ideal model" for the proposed agreement on investment (Japan 2002).

The IMF has also become more active in encouraging disclosure of information by national governments. In 1999, the Fund began producing Reports on the Observance of Standards and Codes (ROSCs) that assess governments' compliance with principles of good practice in the design of economic and financial systems. These include principles on transparency in fiscal, monetary, and financial policy, as well as standards on securities regulation and corporate governance (IMF 2001a). It is hoped the disclosure of such information will reduce instability in international capital markets and avoid a reprise of the volatility in investment flows that precipitated the Asian financial crisis of 1997–1998 (Kuttner 2001, 150). In this context, transparency is a tool for facilitating the liberalization of capital flows, which the IMF's Interim Committee endorsed in 1997 as one of the central purposes of the Fund (Blustein 2001, 49).

Although participation in IMF reviews of compliance with standards and codes is voluntary, there are powerful pressures on weaker economies to conform. The IMF itself observed that ROSCs are increasingly being used to guide investment decisions in the private sector. In February 2002, one of the largest American pension funds said it relied on ROSCs to select countries in which they were prepared to invest (IMF 2002). Governments will find themselves under increasing pressure to conform these expectations to establish their credibility to foreign investors. Indeed, IMF officials have characterized the new emphasis on standards and policies as "a new kind of *réglementation*—a framework of rules for the conduct of policies and to guide financial policies . . . [that will] reduce the risk of abrupt changes in market sentiment through greater transparency" (Larsen 2002).

Such measures are intended to improve the transparency of national governments—but it is a certain kind of transparency, aimed at promoting the projects of trade and financial liberalization. Most immediately, it serves the states and corporations in a position to exploit the opportunities presented by such liberalization. As Ann Florini has observed,

> To date, most of the demands for transparency are coming from intergovernmental organizations in the form of new financial and macroeconomic disclosure standards. Their primary purposes are to improve global economic efficiency and to reduce the volatility of international capital flows. . . . [T]hey are aimed at improving efficiency and safeguarding international investors (although an additional benefit is said to be that citizens will more easily be able to assess the quality of their governments' macroeconomic policies). So far, calls for transparency are not aimed directly at improving equity and promoting the welfare of the poor. (1999, 2)

Similarly, Stephen Gill suggests the main aim of intergovernmental organizations is to pursue a project of "disciplinary neoliberalism"—"a world in which the discipline of capital . . . would operate along rationalist principles based on full access to relevant public and private information" (2000, 11).

It is a program for improving transparency that is distinct from that typically promoted by domestic advocates of open government, particularly in the developing world. These domestic advocates usually hope to improve access to information about the conduct of police or military forces; personal files collected by intelligence forces; information about the disbursement of public money for schools or local public works; information about decisions of government officials on entitlements to health care or education; or information about financial contributions to political parties (UNDP 2002, 82). For example, Kate Doyle writes that Mexico's new freedom of information law could improve access "to the most fundamental government information affecting their daily life," such as local school budgets, crime statistics, antipollution controls, and salaries of public officials (Doyle 2002). Many of these advocates also hope to improve access to information about the internal deliberations of public bodies about policy decisions. Overall, this is a program of reform that aims to improve access to information that is essential to protect an array of basic human rights, including the right to political participation.

Do these two transparency programs—one tied to the project of liberalization, the other tied to the protection of citizens' rights—complement one another, or are they essentially antithetical? To put it another way, does the active promotion of the liberalization-based transparency help or hinder the promotion of rights-based transparency?

Two arguments could be made in favor of the complementarity of the two transparency agendas: one diffuse, and the other more specific. The diffuse argument suggests the emphasis put on transparency by powerful states and intergovernmental organizations helps to build a zeitgeist of governmental openness, which may advantage domestic activists in unexpected ways. It is true, for example, that the last ten years have witnessed an extraordinary diffusion of national right-to-information laws, establishing broader entitlements to government documents. Almost thirty countries, most of them outside the club of industrialized democracies, have adopted such laws in the last decade (Blanton 2002). On the other hand, this phenomenon may be more directly attributable to the emphasis on democratization following the end of the cold war.

The second argument in favor of complementarity is similar but more specific. It suggests there is a parallel with the history of transparency policies within some industrialized democracies. In the United States and Canada, contemporary right-to-information laws were preceded by administrative procedure laws, which confirmed the obligation of government bodies to publish regulations and internal administrative guidelines and to provide reasons for adverse administrative decisions. These earlier administrative procedure laws have been described as tools used by conservative business interests to constrain the growing power of regulators in the middle decades of the last century (Horwitz 1992). These early laws provided a precedent for the adoption of broader right-to-information laws, which were again most heavily used by commercial interests. However, it is argued that the tools created by commercial interests also became available to other domestic actors, who used them for more progressive purposes (Arthurs 1997). Recently, for example, social activists have used disclosure laws to promote accountability of national security agencies and to obstruct efforts by conservative governments to dismantle the welfare state.

However, the historical analogy is imperfect. Although earlier reforms in the United States and Canada may have been intended as tools for constraining certain kinds of state activism, they were introduced as universal requirements, affecting all of the administrative activities of government. This quality of universality meant that rules introduced by conservative interests for one purpose could easily be adopted by other interests to control other components of the administrative apparatus of government. By contrast, the transparency rules now being imposed through intergovernmental organizations are limited to specific functions, such as sanitary and phytosanitary regulation or procurement. A general principle regarding transparency could be inferred, but universally applicable tools for achieving transparency have not been created.

In fact, there are reasons to doubt the complementarily of these two transparency programs. In many developing countries, the resources available for the administration of governmental services are highly limited. It is possible the transparency program that is imposed through WTO agreements will compel governments to divert these scarce resources into administrative agencies whose work is most directly related to trade obligations. Several developing countries have recently balked at the burden that might be created by transparency arrangements proposed for a new agreement on investment (ICSTD 2002c). The European Union concedes the difficulty:

It is objectively difficult for any country to identify and list all the domestic laws and regulations that may be relevant to the operation of foreign investors. . . . These laws and regulations are usually scattered in different legislative and regulatory texts (even where some of them are collected in an "investment code") and are the responsibility of different branches of government or, in many countries, of independent agencies or sub-national governments. A developing country could need help in financing and training the human resources to comb through such domestic laws and regulations, and to devise suitable, effective and non-cumbersome ways to disseminate the relevant information on its investment regime and to promote investment opportunities in its territory. (European Community 2002)

The European Union insists that such measures are essential to promote "the principle of fairness as well as economic efficiency and legal security" (European Community 2002). But it is obvious the immediate beneficiaries of such reforms are the states or investors who acquire rights to information under the proposed agreement. The effect may be to produce, within developing nations, administrative structures that are relatively robust in areas that are immediately relevant to WTO agreements but otherwise weak.

This tendency may be reinforced by the mechanisms available for enforcement of transparency requirements. States that are dissatisfied with compliance with transparency requirements under WTO obligations can pursue their complaints through the dispute settlement procedures established under WTO agreements. Domestic actors who are dissatisfied with their government's disclosure practices may have fewer resources with which to pursue their complaints, and less effective methods of recourse.

CONCLUSION

There has been no revolution in transparency in the WTO and other intergovernmental organizations. Although there have been advances in disclosure practices, the ethos of diplomatic confidentiality continues to be respected and remains a significant barrier to greater transparency. Where disclosure obligations are recognized by member states, they are typically tied to a narrow program of reform aimed at promoting trade and financial liberalization.

It is possible to imagine more demanding disclosure regimes for the WTO and IMF. Other intergovernmental organizations, such as the European Union and the United Nations Development Program, have adopted disclosure policies that begin to approximate the right-to-information laws regulating national governments (UNDP 1997; EU 2001). These include a general recognition of a right to information held by the organization, the specification of substantive reasons for nondisclosure, and some mechanism for independent enforcement of the right. This would be a revolution in practice—but would such a revolution be justified?

Arguably, yes. The material question is whether the denial of a right to information would damage the fundamental interests that undergird our conception of basic human rights (Roberts 2001). A strong case can be made that the political participation rights of citizens—such as their right to deliberate on and participate in policy choices that affect them in important ways—are constrained if a high level of transparency is not maintained. The countervailing considerations that have typically been used to justify secrecy—such as imminent threats to public order or the survival of the state—are not present.

The argument that national governments alone should be responsible for attending to these fundamental interests is not compelling. The right to information held by these intergovernmental organizations is inferred directly from basic human rights. The question of whether and how an individual should be informed about the work of an intergovernmental organization cannot be left entirely to national governments unless we have good reason to believe that governments will honor the right fully. In practice, of course, we know this is not the case. Governments do not have incentives to share information and influence, and they regard themselves as bound by norms that preclude the release of information they have received from other governments.

The more difficult argument against increased transparency is grounded in equity—that the right to information is more likely to be exploited by certain groups, and may actually diminish the influence of weaker groups. This is not a novel problem; the same predicament arises within states as well. In that situation, however, we would be leery about remedying the inequity by denying a right to the whole population. The more appropriate logic, equally applicable in the international context, would be to find methods of allowing weaker groups to exploit the opportunities created by the recognition of the right to information.

Equity can also be used to construct a case for a stronger disclosure policy. It is clear that in many cases, information relating to the work of intergovernmental organizations, although ostensibly restricted, is routinely circulated within a small elite of nonstate actors, including important financial and commercial interests and better-connected nongovernmental organizations. Even if inequities exist after a stronger disclosure policy is put into place, they may not be so severe as the inequities that persist under the status quo.

A revolution in transparency would also oblige us to be more candid about the pressures that are put upon smaller and weaker states by arrangements such as the WTO and IMF. It is fashionable for advanced economies to present their policies as the expression of universally acknowledged norms, such as transparency, nondiscrimination, and due process (Zoellick 2001). In reality, we are discriminate about the circumstances in which those norms should be applied. We care particularly about the application of such norms in those parts of the administrative apparatus of other states whose work most directly affects our economic interests.

Controversy over transparency in the WTO and other intergovernmental organizations illustrates a larger problem of contemporary governance. We are often said to be moving into an era of "network governance," in which goals are accomplished by the joint effort of many organizations who pool their resources or sovereignty. Collaborative efforts by states to coordinate economic activity could be construed as examples of network governance; there are many more examples of work that is undertaken by networks of subnational governments, or governmental and nongovernmental bodies.

The effectiveness of network governance appears to be contingent on a rich flow of information among constituents of the network. There is an understandable tendency to give a strong mutual assurance of confidentiality—such as that embodied in the rule of originator control—to promote the flow of information. The incentive to give strong assurances may actually increase with the size of network, as the risk of unauthorized disclosure increases, or it may diminish, as the realities of widespread unauthorized disclosure become apparent.

The tendency, at least in the early stages of network construction, to give strong assurances of confidentiality incurs inevitable costs. It undermines the capacity of actors who are not party to the network—such as legislators or domestic nonstate actors—to hold members of the network accountable for their conduct. The problem of accountability may be exacerbated as the flow of information within the network deepens, and the stock of information held by each member of the network is increasingly contaminated by information provided by other members and protected by the rule of originator control. The tendency over the last decade, at least, has been to give greater weight to the need for network effectiveness rather than external accountability. In the long run, this is an untenable position. A proper balancing of these two values will require an abandonment of the rule of absolute originator control.

Roberts, Alasdair. "A Partial Revolution: The Diplomatic Ethos and Transparency in Intergovernmental Organizations." *Public Administration Review* 64, no. 4 (2004): 410–24. Reproduced with permission of Blackwell Publishing Ltd.

4

Proactively Released Information

INTRODUCTION

USAspending.gov is the go-to website to find out which organizations are getting money from the U.S. federal government and how much they are receiving. The Federal Funding Accountability and Transparency Act of 2006 (Transparency Act) required the development of a free and searchable website that made available U.S. federal government spending data. The database that drives USASpending.gov includes the name and location of the entity that received the award, the amount of the award, the award transaction type, and funding agency (USASpending.gov 2009). Recently added to the website is the IT Dashboard that lets users monitor the more than $70 billion spent yearly by the federal government on information technology (Lohr 2009).

USASpending.gov is a classic example of the proactive dissemination of government information. The proactive dissemination of information is contrasted with the requestor model. The requestor model is when a person asks for public records from a government, usually by referring to a freedom of information act. In the simplest terms, a formal request for information is made, and the material is either released or it is withheld with an exemption cited. In the proactive model, governments release information either voluntarily, routinely, or because of statutory or regulatory requirements.

While websites are the most frequently cited avenue of proactive dissemination, they are by no means the only ways governments release information. Technology has enabled an increasingly wide array of tools. E-mail alerts, blogs, cable TV shows, and podcasts allow governments to relay information to the public. More traditional forms such as newsletters, media releases, physical bulletin boards, and depositing documents in archives allow for different segments of the population to gain access to government information. The articles included in this section deal with a small cross-section of these tools, specifically local government websites, the U.S. Federal Register, and agency spokespersons.

M. Jae Moon (2002) developed a five stage model of e-government for municipalities. These stages are (1) information dissemination/catalog, (2) two-way communication, (3) service and financial transactions, (4) vertical and horizontal integration, and (5) political participation. The first stage, information dissemination, most clearly aligns with the goal of transparency and access to government. Local governments even within the same political boundaries, such as city governments within a state, vary quite significantly with respect to website transparency (Piotrowski and Borry 2009).

Governments around the world are increasingly developing more sophisticated websites. Seoul, South Korea, scored the highest ranking in the Digital Governance in Municipalities Worldwide Survey every year the survey has been completed (2003, 2005, and 2007). Websites were evaluated on five components: (1) privacy/security, (2) usability, (3) content, (4) services, and (5) citizen participation. In the 2007 survey, only one of the top-ten cities was a U.S. city—New York City (Holzer and Kim 2007).

While having adequate access to government information is important, there is also the issue of information overload. At times governments release so much information that wading through the data to identify the relevant information is prohibitive. At other times, governments are highly selective in the type of information they release and are sometimes criticized for the choices they make. Cable TV programming that promotes elected officials has been accused of being propagandist. All levels of government employ spokespersons to act as liaisons with the media. Mordecai Lee (2001) surveyed chief public information officers in local government agencies in the United States. These spokespeople play an increasingly prominent role in government administration.

These different avenues of release are sometimes established by convention and other times by law or regulation. The U.S. Federal Register is published daily and is available in hard copy and online. Rules, proposed rules, notices of federal agencies and organizations, executive orders and other presidential documents are all published within the publication. Lotte Feinberg (2001) described the creation of the Federal Register and the surprising actors at play. Supreme Court Justice Louis D. Brandeis played a pivotal role in the 1935 passage of the Federal Register Act.

Assignments and Study Questions

1. Critically evaluate how e-governance initiatives are currently used and how they can enhance governmental transparency in the future.
2. Do you believe the proactive release of information model or the requester model is the most beneficial to transparency and the release of government information? Explain.
3. *Group Website Project*
   The class as a whole will research and write a report evaluating government websites with respect to transparency. While this assignment is presented as a review of local government websites, it can be done for any level of government or, with some modification, for nonprofit organizations. The first steps are to pick which websites will be reviewed, break the class into groups of two or three students, and assign groups two or three websites to evaluate.

   Each group needs to agree upon a set of criteria to evaluate the websites. The below table is an example of a form that includes evaluative criteria for a local government. Groups should review their assigned websites and fill out the agreed-upon form. One option is to do a test run to review the websites and bring questions to class before the official review.

   Once ambiguity is resolved, a specific range of dates should be identified, during which the content analysis of the websites will take place.

   Once the evaluation is complete, groups will write up a snapshot evaluating each website. Groups should bring to class the first draft of their one-page snapshots for each website. These snapshots can be photocopied and handed out to the other members of the class to read and give feedback. The snapshots should include an overall assessment by the group of how the municipal website did on the review. Groups should also include any other comments they have on the website's usability and the information the site conveys.

EXAMPLE OF EVALUATION FORM FOR GROUP WEBSITE PROJECT

City Website Reviewed: _____

Date Reviewed: _____

Reviewed By: _____

City Council Meetings Date/Time Information	
Date of upcoming meeting posted (Yes/No)	
Time of upcoming meeting posted (Yes/No)	
Calendar or other notice of meetings for year posted (Yes/No)	
Information on where meetings are held posted (Yes/No)	
Minutes	
Number of 2007 meeting minutes posted	
Number of 2008 meeting minutes posted	
Agendas	
Number of 2007 meeting agendas posted	
Number of 2008 meeting agendas posted	
2009 Budget	
Budget—summary or full document posted (Yes/No)	
General Contact Information	
Phone number (Yes/No)	
E-mail (Yes/No)	
Physical address or mailing address (Yes/No)	
Clerk Contact Information	
Phone number (Yes/No)	
E-mail (Yes/No)	
Physical address or mailing address (Yes/No)	

* * *

The Evolution of E-Government among Municipalities: Rhetoric or Reality?

M. Jae Moon

INTRODUCTION

Information Technology (IT) has become one of the core elements of managerial reform, and electronic government (e-government) may figure prominently in future governance. IT has opened up many possibilities for improving internal managerial efficiency and the quality of public service delivery to citizens. IT has contributed to dramatic changes in politics (Nye 1999; Norris 1999), government institutions (Fountain 2001), performance management (Brown 1999), red tape reduction (Moon and Bretschneider 2002), and re-engineering (Anderson 1999) during the last decade. The Clinton administration attempted to advance e-government, through which government overcomes the barriers of time and distance in providing public services (Gore 1993). Recently, some studies have found widespread diffusion of various IT innovations (mainframe and PC computers, geographical systems, networks, Web pages, etc.) in the public sector (Cats-Baril and Thompson 1995; Ventura 1995; Nedović-Budić and Godschalk 1996; Norris and Kraemer 1996; Weare, Musso, and Hale 1999; Musso, Weare, and Hale 2000; Landsbergen and Wolken 2001; Layne and Lee 2001; Nunn 2001; Peled 2001).

On June 24, 2000, President Clinton delivered his first Webcasted address to the public and announced a series of new e-government initiatives. One highlight of these new initiatives was to establish an integrated online service system that put all online resources offered by the federal government on a single Web site, *www.firstgov.gov*. The initiative also attempted to build one-stop access to roughly $500 billion in grants ($300 billion) and procurement ($200 billion) opportunities (White House Press Office 2000). Following the federal initiative, many local governments also adopted IT for local governance. For instance, they have created or improved their Web sites and provide Web-based services to promote better internal procedural management and external service provision.

Despite this continuing move toward e-government, the development, implementation, and effectiveness of e-government at the local level are not well understood.[1] This article is designed to conduct an empirical study of how the e-government initiative has been introduced and implemented effectively at the municipal level. The study will explore a basic conceptual framework for the evolution of e-government and will examine the effectiveness of e-government in municipal governments based on comprehensive survey data obtained from the 2000 Electronic Government Survey that was conducted by International City/County Management Association and Public Technology Inc. It will also discuss two primary institutional factors (size and type of government) that contribute to the development of e-government at the local level.

E-GOVERNMENT: THEORY AND PRACTICE

E-government is one of most interesting concepts introduced in the field of public administration in the late 1990s, though it has not been clearly defined and understood among scholars and practitioners of public administration. Like many managerial concepts and practices in public administration (TQM, strategic management, participative management, etc.), the idea of e-government followed private-sector adoption of so-called e-business and e-commerce. The Global Study of E-government, a recent joint research initiative for global e-government by the United Nations and the American Society for Public Administration, provides a broad definition of e-government:

> Broadly defined, e-government includes the use of all information and communication technologies, from fax machines to wireless palm pilots, to facilitate the daily administration of government. However, like e-commerce, the popular interpretation of e-government is one that defines it

exclusively as an Internet driven activity . . . to which it may be added "that improves citizen access to government information, services and expertise to ensure citizen participation in, and satisfaction with the government process . . . it is a permanent commitment by government to improving the relationship between the private citizen and the public sector through enhanced, cost-effective and efficient delivery of services, information and knowledge. It is the practical realization of the best that government has to offer. (UN and ASPA 2001, 1)

Similarly, e-government is narrowly defined as the production and delivery of government services through IT applications; however, it can be defined more broadly as any way IT is used to simplify and improve transactions between governments and other actors, such as constituents, businesses, and other governmental agencies (Sprecher 2000 21). In her recent book, Jane Fountain (2001) suggests the concept of the "virtual state," that is, a governmental entity organized with "virtual agencies, cross-agency and public-private networks whose structure and capacity depend on the Internet and web" (4).

Largely speaking, e-government includes four major internal and external aspects: (1) the establishment of a secure government intranet and central database for more efficient and co-operative interaction among governmental agencies; (2) Web-based service delivery; (3) the application of e-commerce for more efficient government transaction activities, such as procurement and contract; and (4) digital democracy for more transparent accountability of government (Government and the Internet Survey 2000). Various technologies have been applied to support these unique characteristics of e-government, including electronic data interchange, interactive voice response, voice mail, e-mail, Web service delivery, virtual reality, and public key infrastructure. For instance, by introducing electronic filing systems with custom-designed software that incorporates encryption technology, the U.S. Patent and Trademark Office has made a bold move toward substantially reducing the amount of paper it handles by allowing inventors or their agents to send documents over the Internet (Daukantas 2000). As a result of various Web technologies, 40 million U.S. taxpayers were able to file their 2000 returns over the Web, while 670,000 online applications were made for student loans using the Web-based system of the Department of Education (Preston 2000). Some governments also have promoted virtual democracy by pursuing Web-based political participation like online voting and online public forums.

The functionality and utility of Web technologies in public management can be broadly divided into two categories: internal and external. Internally, the Web and other technologies hold promise potential as effective and efficient managerial tools that collect, store, organize, and manage an enormous volume of data and information. By using the function of upload and download, the most up-to-date information and data can be displayed on the Internet on a real-time basis. Government also can transfer funds electronically to other governmental agencies or provide information to public employees through an intranet or Internet system. Government also can do many mundane and routine tasks more easily and quickly, such as responding to employees' requests for benefits statements.

Externally, Web technologies also facilitate government's linkages with citizens (for both services and political activities), other governmental units, and businesses. Government Web sites can serve as both a communication and a public relations tool for the general public. Information and data can easily be shared with and transferred to external stakeholders (businesses, nonprofit organizations, interest groups, or the public). In addition, some Web technologies (such as interactive bulletin boards) enable the government to promote public participation in policy-making processes by posting public notices and exchanging messages and ideas with the public.

. . . [T]here are various stages of e-government, which reflect the degree of technical sophistica-tion and interaction with users: (1) simple information dissemination (one-way communication); (2) two-way communication (request and response); (3) service and financial transactions; (4) integration (horizontal and vertical integration); and (5) political participation.[2] Stage 1 is the most basic form of e-government and uses IT for disseminating information, simply by posting information or data on the Web sites for constituents to view. Stage 2 is two-way communication characterized as an interactive mode between government and constituents. In this stage, the gov-ernment incorporates email systems as well as information and data-transfer technologies into its Web sites. A good example is the Social Security Administration's Web site, where the agency re-ceives new Medicare card applications and benefit statement requests, then processes and responds to service requests (Hiller and Bélanger 2001). In Stage 3, the government allows online service and financial transactions by completely replacing public servants with "web-based self-services" (Hiller and Bélanger 2001). This "transaction-based e-government" can be partially achieved by "putting live database links to on-line interfaces" (Layne and Lee 2001, 125). Through this online service and financial transaction, for example, constituents can renew licenses, pay fines, and ap-ply for financial aid (Hiller and Bélanger 2001; Layne and Lee 2001).

In Stage 4, the government attempts to integrate various government services vertically (in-tergovernmental integration) and horizontally (intragovernmental integration) for the enhance-ment of efficiency, user friendliness, and effectiveness. This stage is a highly challenging task for governments because it requires a tremendous amount of time and resources to integrate online and back-office systems (Hiller and Bélanger 2001). Hiller and Bélanger (2001) sug-gest three good examples: Australia's state of Victoria (*http://www.maxi.com.au*),[3] Singapore's e-Citizen Center (*http://www.ecitizen.gov.sg*),[4] and the U.S. government's portal site (*http:// www.firstgov.gov*). Both vertical and horizontal integrations push information and data sharing among different functional units and levels of governments for better online public services (Layne and Lee 2001). Stage 5 involves the promotion of Web-based political participation, in which government Web sites include online voting, online public forums, and online opinion surveys for more direct and wider interaction with the public. While the previous four stages are related to Web-based public services in the administrative arena, the fifth stage highlights Web-based political activities by citizens.

It should be noted that the five stages are just a conceptual tool to examine the evolution of e-government. The adoption of e-government practices may not follow a true linear pro-gression. Many studies of technological innovation also indicate the diffusion and adoption of technology may even follow a curvilinear path (that is, Cancian Dip).[5] For example, a government may initiate Stage 5 of e-government (political participation) without full practice of Stage 4 (integration). It is also possible that government can pursue various components of e-government simultaneously. Like other stage models of growth (Nolan 1979; Quinn and Cameron 1983),[6] the framework simply provides an exploratory conceptual tool that helps one understand the evolutionary nature of e-government.

. . . .

CONCLUSIONS AND FUTURE STUDIES

This study examined an emerging issue of e-government in municipal governments. The study surveyed the rhetoric and reality of municipal government by investigating the 2000

E-government Survey data collected by International City/County Management Association and Public Technology Inc. The assessment was based on the framework of e-government developmental stages. This study also evaluated the respondents' perception of the effectiveness of e-government initiatives in various functional areas.

The survey results show that municipality size and type of government are significant institutional factors in the implementation and development of e-government. As expected, larger governments are likely to be more proactive and strategic in advancing e-government, and council-manager governments seem to pursue e-government more actively than mayor-council governments. The study also finds that the lack of technical, personnel, and financial capacities are perceived to be major barriers to the development of e-government in many municipalities.

This study also suggests that many municipal governments are still in either Stage 1 or Stage 2 of e-government, where they simply post and disseminate government information over the Web or provide online channels for two-way communication, particularly for public service requests. Overall, the current state of the e-government initiative is still very primitive in many municipal governments, though the adoption rate for Web sites among municipalities is very high. Only half of the responding governments currently utilize an intranet, and only 8 percent of the responding governments have a comprehensive strategic plan for an e-government initiative. The study also finds that e-government has not been as effective as its rhetoric would suggest. Although many top city managers share the view that e-government has brought broadly defined changes in procedural practices and task environments, it seems that municipal e-government is still far from maturity and from contributing to cost savings, revenue generating, and downsizing. It echoes the conclusion of Musso, Weare, and Hale (2000) that the study only leads to "mild encouragement at best regarding the potential of Internet technologies to reinvigorate local governance" (16). In her recent book, Jane Fountain (2001) also gives a similar assessment of the current practice of virtual state: "The dot-coming of government is just beginning. . . . Agencies are still in the process of putting basic information on the web and institutionalizing secure methods and authentication so that web-based payments become possible and personal documents, such as social security benefit information and tax files, can be transmitted safely over the Internet" (201).

Despite seemingly limited practices and effectiveness of municipal e-government, the survey results also posit a positive and optimistic future by suggesting that many non-adopters of Web-based public services plan to offer those services in the near future. In order to enhance the effectiveness of their e-government practices, many municipal governments will need to move toward a higher level of e-government development, which will require more technical, personnel, and financial commitments. In particular, more continuing efforts should be made to advance Web-based participatory and democratic local governance. Municipal governments also need to establish systematic and comprehensive e-government plans, in which they assess available resources and address related legal issues like privacy and security as well (Fountain 2001). In the future, city governments should further promote horizontal (interagency relations at the municipal level) as well as vertical (intergovernmental relations with state and federal government) collaborations to advance e-government initiatives to Stage 4 (integration) and Stage 5 (political participation). These stages require a higher level of "interoperability" (Landsbergen and Wolken 2001) and demand further information sharing and interactive operations among various stakeholders and governmental agencies to deliver more efficient and effective online public services. They also demand more sophisticated technological solutions for encryption, information sharing, and interactive communication. Equipped with sustainable managerial support and resources, municipal governments should be prepared for legal and political challenges in order to accelerate the evolutionary process by which e-government can become reality, not just rhetoric in the near future.

As municipal governments continue their e-government march, future studies need to examine the progress and effectiveness of municipal governments in delivering Web-based public services and facilitating citizens' Web-based political participation. As addressed in Fountain's (2001) recent work, it should be further examined how IT and government institutions interplay through human actions and how actual e-government practices change the content and functions of governmental institutions and their interactions with other governments, business, and citizens. A comprehensive assessment of municipal e-government, along with federal and state e-government, should be followed in the future to address vertical/horizontal integration, public participation, citizen access/digital divide,[7] as well as other emerging regulatory and legal issues regarding e-government.

Moon, M. Jae. "The Evolution of E-Government among Municipalities: Rhetoric or Reality?" *Public Administration Review* 62, no. 4 (2002): 424–33. Reproduced with permission of Blackwell Publishing Ltd.

* * *

Mr. Justice Brandeis and the Creation of the *Federal Register*
Lotte E. Feinberg

Reasonable transparency of government and its accountability under law are enduring goals of American public administration. *The Federal Register,* created in 1935, is a historic institutional tool designed for these purposes, and it represented a seismic shift in the way government functions. Sixty-six years after its creation, as the "official public record of actions or revisions to the U.S. Code of Federal Regulations," it remains not only the daily compendium of almost all activities of the executive branch agencies, but also a principal mechanism for permitting citizens to know about and participate in agency decision making in a timely, uniform manner.

"I suppose no one person," wrote Felix Frankfurter in 1935, "is ultimately more responsible for the intellectual impetus that gave rise to the Federal Register Act than Mr. Justice Brandeis" (Frankfurter to Carr 1935b). In reality, Brandeis did far more than provide "intellectual impetus"—he played a pivotal but little known role in engineering the conditions necessary for the creation of the *Federal Register*.

The story of how the *Federal Register* came to be created is a fascinating study of the interplay of administrative, legislative, and judicial forces responding to the unprecedented expansion of federal regulatory activity under the Roosevelt administration. It was the product of efforts by key agency attorneys and administrators in the executive branch; public debate framed by the press and the American Bar Association; the willingness of one congressman to seize the moment; and, most importantly, the behind-the-scenes extrajudicial maneuvering of Justice Louis D. Brandeis.

This story provides new insight into the extraordinary influence that Brandeis exerted, in an extrajudicial capacity, to institutionalize his well-known belief in the importance of openness (publicity) and informed citizen participation in government. These, he believed, were key to safeguarding democracy (Strum 1995, 1-21ff). This study also provides a window into understanding how values, politics, law, administration, and theater mixed to produce a critical public policy decision that permanently changed the way the federal government handles executive branch records.

THE SUPREME COURT AS THEATER

It is Monday, December 10, 1934. The Supreme Court is in session. Chief Justice Charles Evans Hughes is presiding and will write the majority opinion (8-1). Two cases are being argued, *Amazon Petroleum Corporation v. Ryan* and *Panama Refining Company v. Ryan* (293 US388 [1935]). They are the first cases before the Court to challenge the constitutionality of the New Deal's centerpiece, the National Industrial Recovery Act (NIRA). Specifically, these two East Texas oil companies have challenged the right of the president, through regulations issued by his Secretary of the Interior (Harold Ickes), to set quotas limiting the production and transportation of "petroleum or petroleum products in interstate and foreign commerce" (Ruddy and Simmons 1944, 248–63). These are the "hot oil" cases, the term used for oil produced or transported in excess of the quotas; those who violate the quotas can be fined up to $1,000 or imprisoned for up to six months, or both.

Harold M. Stephens, assistant attorney general in the antitrust division, a man who prides himself on "always" trying to be "meticulously accurate in either oral or written statements made to a court" (Stephens to Griswold, January 7, 1935), is charged with presenting the government's case.

The place is the Old Senate Chamber, where the Supreme Court has sat, with two exceptions, since December 3, 1860. The room—a large, semicircular hall, 75 feet in diameter, with a 45-foot-high domed ceiling and circular apertures through which light filters—was modeled after a Greek theater. A screen of Grecian Ionic columns of native Potomac marble stretches behind the justices' chairs, with the chief justice's chair at the center, while an eagle, its wings spread in permanent flight, is mounted over an arched, curtained doorway directly behind his chair. Above the eagle is a large circular clock. Mahogany furnishings, deep sunken panels, and red drapes and carpets give "the impression . . . of a drawing room rather than a hall of justice." It is a room that encourages solemnity. By the fall of the following year, October 7, 1935, the Court would move to "the marble temple," its newly completed permanent home across from the Capitol, constructed at a cost of almost $10 million (Lavery 1941, 289).[1]

Outside, the temperature hovers just below 25 degrees; inside, Stephens is totally unprepared for the "vigorous" (Stephens to Griswold, January 7, 1935) questioning about the regulations governing oil production to which he is subjected by the justices.

> "Who promulgates these orders and codes that have the force of laws?" asked the justice [Brandeis].
>
> "They are promulgated by the President, and I assume they are on record at the State Department," he [Stephens] replied.
>
> "Is there any official or general publication of these executive orders?" Justice Brandeis continued.
>
> "Not that I know of," replied Mr. Stephens.
>
> "Well, is there any way by which one can find out what is in these executive orders when they are issued?"
>
> "I think it would be rather difficult, but it is possible to get certified copies of the executive orders and codes from the NRA," Mr. Stephens explained.
>
> "And that advantage is open to the staff of the Justice Department?" asked Justice Willis Van Devanter.

"Yes, sir, " Mr. Stephens replied as a titter swept the room.

"How many of these orders and codes have been issued in the last fifteen months—several thousand?" asked Justice James Clark McReynolds, who earlier had quizzed Mr. Stephens. . . .

"I am not certain, Your Honor, but I should say several hundred," the attorney [Stephens] replied. (Waltman 1934, 2)

The sharp questioning (described in some accounts as "critical and searching") is the Court's response, not to the constitutional issues posed, but to a problem with the *Amazon* case that is especially embarrassing to Mr. Stephens: the case arrived defective. The specific provision that the Amazon Petroleum Company is charged with violating, and whose constitutionality the company is now challenging (section 9(c) of Title I of the NIRA of June 16, 1933), was inadvertently omitted when it was sent to the printer.[2] This means that the company is charged with violating a provision that technically does not exist. More significantly, as the cases moved through the lower courts, almost no one knew about the omission—not the plaintiffs (Amazon Petroleum or Panama Refining), not the defendants (the Justice Department), and not the courts; instead, all believed "it in full force and effect."

It was not until the lawyers for *Amazon* petitioned the Supreme Court for certiorari that the Justice Department and Stephens became directly involved and discovered, to their distress, in August 1934 a problem with the regulations. The error was uncovered when M. S. Huberman, a Justice Department staff attorney assigned to the case, followed department practice and insisted on seeing the original executive order or a photostat held by the Petroleum Administration. Since the original could not be found, he settled for the copy and only then discovered the omission. Although copies of such orders were expected to be filed with the State Department when they were issued, this one was filed months later (December 1933), well after the case had been argued in the lower court. The Court was then notified and President Roosevelt promptly issued another executive order (September 25, 1934), replacing the omitted paragraph.

Stephens learned that the government lawyers from the Petroleum Administration, who had handled the case in the lower courts, had discovered the problem much earlier, shortly after the amendment of September 13, 1933. According to Stephens, these lawyers "had a theory," which he found "entirely untenable" (Stephens to Griswold, January 7, 1935). They believed "that because the error in amending the Code was inadvertent, the omitted paragraph was not legally omitted." Acting on this assumption, they did not raise the question of whether the Code was complete with either the lower courts or the Justice Department. And, Stephens said, although these lawyers were nominally special assistants to the attorney general, they "omitted in the large to consult with us concerning the details of the cases," leaving Stephens with the embarrassing task of notifying the Court (Stephens to Griswold, January 7, 1935).

What made Stephens and the Justice Department especially uncomfortable as he was "interrogated" by the justices was that he had notified the Court immediately upon discovering the defect when he wrote the government's response to the petition for the writ of certiorari and, because the Court had subsequently accepted the case without reservation, he "assumed, therefore, that the Court had taken the case as a whole" (Stephens to Griswold, January 7, 1935).[3]

Instead, as Stephens later plaintively wrote to a former colleague, Erwin N. Griswold, "notwithstanding this full disclosure in the response, and notwithstanding that the Court had taken the case . . . without reservation, Justices Brandeis, Van Devanter, McReynolds, and Butler, and particularly Justices Van Devanter and McReynolds, were most vigorous in their questions in reference to this matter." The result was that Stephens "was so occupied with questions by the Court" on issues surrounding publication of the codes "that a substantial amount of my time, as I remember about forty-five minutes, was exhausted before I got an opportunity to commence argument on the merits." In an unusual move, Chief Justice Hughes granted Stephens an additional three-quarters of an hour to make his arguments about what he considered the main points of his case, the commerce question (Stephens to Griswold, January 7, 1935).

Although the Court was focused on a critical constitutional question that went to the heart of Roosevelt's plans for economic recovery, an unintended outcome concerning government record keeping would have an enduring effect for the rest of the century.

In the short run, the *Amazon/Panama* decision against the president, along with three subsequent antiadministration Court decisions in May 1935 (Black Monday), set in motion Roosevelt's brief, unsuccessful, but turbulent attempt to pack the Court, followed by a general reversal in future Court rulings that were more supportive of his administration. The lasting effect, however, was that, as a result of Brandeis's skillful orchestration of conditions and events, these two cases led to the creation of *The Federal Register.*

SETTING THE SCENE: THE ACTORS

The story unfolds on two levels: the public record, and what Brandeis actually did behind the scenes, outside the awareness of even most of the key participants. The action took place between 1934 and 1935. The key actors, with Brandeis as the nexus, were Erwin N. Griswold, John Dickinson, H. Thomas Austern, and Harold M. Stephens; Felix Frankfurter played a small but important supporting role. Griswold, Dickinson, and Austern had all studied under Frankfurter at the Harvard Law School and had ties to Brandeis. Both Austern, who had clerked for Brandeis, and Dickinson wrote to the justice regularly about people, politics, and issues in Roosevelt's administration. Dickinson forwarded blind copies of letters exchanged with members of the administration, and he and Austern also sent the justice drafts of proposed *Federal Register* legislation.

In the spring of 1934, Griswold was completing his fifth year in the solicitor general's office and was, with some hesitation, about to assume a faculty position at the Harvard Law School that fall.[4] During his five years, he had often been frustrated in trying to find current regulations; shortly before leaving the position, he took the lead in a small group who sought, at first unsuccessfully, to formalize and regularize publication of these regulations.

Dickinson, who held a doctorate from Johns Hopkins and a Harvard law degree, was an assistant secretary of commerce and one of those assigned to help write the National Industrial Recovery Act. Roosevelt subsequently appointed him assistant attorney general (second in charge). His text on administrative law was required reading in Frankfurter's seminar.

It is Justice Brandeis, however, then seventy-eight years old, whose views, values, and actions are most central to understanding the establishment of a *Federal Register.* Brandeis held lifelong, almost implacable views on the dangers to democracy of "the curse of bigness"—big business and big government—views that eventually set him on a collision course with President Roosevelt. Long before his appointment to the bench, this concern for publicizing what government and business were doing was a recurrent theme in his writings, congressional testimony, and speeches. For example, speaking in 1914 he said, "The mere substitution of knowledge for ignorance—of publicity for secrecy—will go far toward preventing monopoly" (Mason 1946, 615).[5] Responsibility for making information available rested with government, he believed (Lief 1941, 86). In what has become one of his most-quoted perorations, he wrote:

"Publicity is justly commended as a remedy for social and industrial diseases. Sunlight is said to be the best of disinfectants; electric light the most efficient policeman" (Brandeis 1914).[6]

Brandeis, an ardent admirer of English political and legal institutions ("nearer civilization than any other country") (Goodhart 1949, 37), was also well aware of England's Rules Publication Act of 1893, which required systematic publication of all statutory rules and orders; it was this system of printing rules and orders that was used as a model for the *Federal Register*.[7] In 1935, after the "hot oil" decision, Frankfurter arranged for Brandeis and Justices Stone and Cardozo to meet with Cecil T. Carr, one of the founders of the field of administrative law in England, renowned for his work on delegated legislation, and long-time editor (1923–1943) of England's *Revised Statutes, Statutory Rules and Orders* (later called *Statutory Instruments).* Frankfurter, mentioning Brandeis's role in promoting the *Federal Register,* made a point of telling Carr that the justice "is especially alert to the deeper issues of the legislative and administrative processes" (Frankfurter to Carr, October 3, 1935b).[8]

Much has also been written about Brandeis's insistence that decisions incorporate not only the totality of relevant precedent, but also sociological, economic, and factual evidence, and he frequently proposed topics for articles to Frankfurter and other law professors that he then cited in his opinions or gave to other justices to use. In the case of the *Federal Register,* the record shows that Brandeis was highly interested in the prospect of creating this record, and he used the two hot oil cases to accomplish this goal.

THE CONTEXT: A CRITICAL NEED FOR CHANGE

Two factors combined to make the *Federal Register* happen. The first was the generally haphazard way in which federal government records had long been kept. The second was the stunning proliferation of regulations that had burst forth with the Roosevelt administration, dramatizing the need to bring order to the record keeping.

The struggle to ensure that government records would be kept and made available to "the public," however defined, in a consistent, neutral, timely way, began long before the middle or even the beginning of the twentieth century. However, it was by no means universally accepted as necessary. One of the first to comment on the abysmal state of record keeping and the problems this created for public administrators was Alexis de Tocqueville, during his memorable 1831 travels through the country. He found "Nothing is written, or if it is, the slightest gust of wind carries it off, like Sibylline leaves to vanish without recall. . . . Nobody bothers about what was done before his time. No method is adopted; no archives are formed; no documents are brought together, even when it would be easy to do so. . . . It is very difficult for American administrators to learn anything from each other" (de Tocqueville 1969, 207–8).

The one short-lived, contentious, effort to create an official gazette occurred in May 1917 with the publication of *The Official Bulletin of the United Sates* under the auspices of the Committee on Public Information, a wartime committee established by Woodrow Wilson through an executive order and chaired by the equally controversial journalist George Creel. Designed as the authoritative publication of the executive branch, the *Bulletin* was intended to provide the American people with "all the vital facts of national defense" and to publish agency rules, regulations, and orders; presidential proclamations and executive orders; and both "important foreign correspondence" and "statutes . . . relating to war matters of which the public should be informed" (Relyea 1996, 220-35; Walters 1992, 243-56). Although it was welcomed by agency officials, both Creel and the *Bulletin* quickly ran afoul of members of Congress. Members complained, not always correctly, of inaccuracies, of wasting taxpayers' dollars, and of not covering actions by Congress (never the intent), and increasingly they found reasons to criticize Creel on both partisan and personal grounds. The end of the *Bulletin* as a government publication came in an appropriations bill that ordered the publication to cease after April 1, 1919.

By the early 1930s, little had changed in the government's management of executive branch records, but the world was a vastly more complex and unsettled place, in which the lack of record keeping and systematic dissemination of official rules, regulations, and orders was far more problematic. The population was approaching 127 million (a tenfold increase over the century). The contours of the federal government were changing dramatically; the new "administrative state," one of the defining characteristics of twentieth-century American government, was beginning to take root. It was marked by the onset of what became a seemingly unstoppable deluge of administrative regulations and orders and the concomitant rise in power of government bureaucrats.[9] Much of the change came in response to the dire economic conditions: the October 29, 1929, stock market crash, followed by ruinous bank failures and catastrophic financial collapse. President Roosevelt's response to the Great Depression was to radically expand the federal government's role—a response that was immediately birthed in controversy. Banking and the gold standard were central problems to be solved; limiting oil production in western states was not far behind in importance. Within two weeks of his inauguration, FDR's cabinet was dealing with the problem of "curtailing the overproduction of oil" (Ickes 1933).

Regulation became the order of the day, and the federal government seemed to explode with new agencies and new regulations. In just four months, between March and June, thirteen major pieces of legislation were enacted, reaching into almost every corner of American life (Celler 1954, 20). Acceptance of government regulation, however, did not come without major political and constitutional fights. This was not some sedate academic debate, but a bare-knuckle fight that pitted the Supreme Court against the president. The lightening rod for all that was seen as good or evil in Roosevelt's plans quickly became the National Industrial Recovery Act (NIRA): Its unprecedented and staggering array of 546 codes and 185 supplemental codes regulated almost all aspects of business, industry, and commerce—everything from the age at which boys could deliver newspapers to the introduction of the minimum wage. More than 11,000 additional orders were issued that interpreted, granted exemptions from, and established classifications under the provisions of individual codes (Jaffe 1965, 61). The result, as one critic described, was an "ensemble of contradictions" (Roos 1937, 472).[10]

One fundamental problem—separate from the debate over constitutionality—was that, even for those working at the highest levels in government, it was often difficult or impossible to keep track of the codes. Erwin Griswold captured this sense of frustration when he wrote to Congressman David J. Lewis (D, Md.) about his own recent government experience and the congressman's proposal for some kind of gazette: "Frequently I could not find applicable rules and regulations in the library of the Department of Justice, and even application to the very bureau concerned was often fruitless. When that is the situation in Washington, it is obvious that lawyers throughout the country are confronted with a quite hopeless problem" (Griswold to Lewis, January 2, 1935).

It was against this unprecedented expansion of federal controls, and the great difficulty in tracking them, that the two hot oil cases made their way to the Supreme Court and became the vehicle that Brandeis would use, with a chess master's skill, to orchestrate the conditions for the *Federal Register*.

Prior to these cases, Roosevelt issued a total of five executive orders over a two-month period, between July 11 and September 13, 1933, as required by the NIRA. The first authorized
the Secretary of the Interior to develop the Code of Fair Competition; others modified some
of those regulations. The fifth and final executive order (EO 6284A), issued September 13,
1933, was extremely important because, when it was printed, it was the very section, which
had been challenged by Amazon Petroleum only one month later, that had inadvertently been
eliminated.

PUBLISHING AN OFFICIAL RECORD: EXECUTIVE BRANCH EFFORTS

Efforts to create the *Federal Register* started with a small group of men in the executive branch
who shared a sense of urgency about the need to bring order to regulatory morass. Their work
covered a four-month period (March to June 1934) before grinding to a halt. It began on a
Saturday night, when Griswold suggested to his friend John Dickinson and to Jerome Frank,
general counsel to the Agricultural Adjustment Administration, that the government publish
"an official gazette." At first, it seemed the proposal would be accepted quickly. Frank asked
for a memo, which Griswold promptly supplied one week later, sending a copy to Harold M.
Stephens. The plan was that Dickinson, Frank, and Stephens would present the proposal to
their respective cabinet secretaries (Daniel C. Roper, Henry Wallace, and Attorney General
Homer Cummings), who would then press the case with Roosevelt.

Griswold outlined the "pressing need for a publication to be known as the 'Official Gazette,' or 'Official Record,' or `Executive Record' or some similar title" (March 20). As he
envisioned it, "[T]his publication would be printed daily and it would be provided by law that
all executive orders, proclamations, regulations and codes should be published in it, and that
they should not be valid and effective until so published—with the qualification that the President alone should have power to suspend this latter provision in cases of need" (Griswold to
Stephens, March 20, 1934a).

In short order over the next month and a half, Griswold wrote a memo on "Why an Official
Gazette is necessary" (April 14), followed by a "Preliminary Draft of a Statute for an Official
Gazette" (April 18). By April 26, he was one of seven members of an informal committee,
chaired by Dickinson, set up within the National Emergency Council. Dickinson, Griswold,
Frank, and Stephens, were joined by representatives from the Treasury Department, the Library of Congress, and the State Department.[11] The committee went to work producing a report
and drafting a proposed statute with a due date of May 1, the next meeting of the National
Emergency Council. The title *Federal Register* replaced "Official Gazette." In April, Griswold
shared a copy with another friend, Charles Wyzanski (solicitor in the Department of Labor),
and in early May he sent a copy with a handwritten note, "this might interest you," to Felix
Frankfurter, then on leave at Oxford. By June, however, momentum had slowed.

ORCHESTRATING CHANGE: JUSTICE BRANDEIS SHAPES THE AGENDA

Justice Brandeis, on the sidelines, was very much interested in the progress of the proposed
statute; from the beginning, he was kept informed on a regular basis by former clerk, Tommy
Austern, who by this time had joined one of the most politically prominent Washington, D.C.,
law firms, Covington, Burling, Rublee, Acheson, and Shorb. Brandeis was also periodically

apprised by John Dickinson of both the draft report and the politics of the proposal. In mid-June 1934, Austern wrote a lengthy letter to the justice to "report on the matter of the Official Gazette for the publication of Executive Orders, Decrees, and the like." He noted that, although he and Griswold had reviewed the bill, the process had slowed because Dickinson "desired that each department submit a list of matters it would deem of sufficient importance to publish. He wanted to elaborate the obvious and crystalize [sic] in advance the precise scope of the official document to be published rather than to get out those orders which clearly needed definitive publication and determine empirically what else should be included" (Austern to Brandeis, June 14, 1934a). This meant that "the proposed bill will not be enacted in this Congress." However, Austern wrote, the committee was considering issuing an executive order as an alternative, and he promised that "if there is anything to report, I shall send it on."

Austern's next letter to Brandeis was sent a month later to the justice's summer home in Chatham, MA; he now informed the justice that "Professor John Dickinson is still conducting his researches on the necessity for and form of the proposed vehicle for the publication of Executive Orders and 'Administrative' orders and regulations. The matter has been passed (and undoubted responsibility conferred) on a man in the Library of Congress, presently on vacation. Those of us interested will follow the matter" (Austern to Brandeis, July 19, 1934b).

At about the same time, the *Panama* and *Amazon* cases were making their way to the Supreme Court and the second stage, guided by Brandeis, began to unfold. On June 20, 1934, the attorneys for *Panama* petitioned for certiorari, followed by those for *Amazon* on August 6. In September, Stephens wrote to inform the Court of the error in the code. In October, the justices, without making any specific reference to the error, granted certiorari.

By September, Griswold had left Washington for the Harvard Law School. It was a move applauded by Brandeis, who, when he learned of it, wrote to Frankfurter, "H.L.S. [Harvard Law School] did well to get Erwin Griswold" (Urofsky and Levy 1991, 543). His new office was "just down the hall" from Frankfurter. He was still much interested in the proposed *Federal Register,* but he was growing pessimistic. In late September, Griswold wrote to Charles Wyzanski that "The project for an Official Gazette was in a most quiescent state when I left Washington and I suspect that by now it is very nearly dead." He had not quite given up, however, and sent along a copy of England's Rules Publication Act of 1893 (with copies to Dickinson and J. G. Laylin, special assistant to the undersecretary of the Treasury and another member of the informal drafting committee) and asked that "If anything further develops along this line I would be very glad if you would let me know about it" (Griswold to Wyzanski, September 28, 1934).

Wyzanski, a bit more positive, wrote back, "The project for an official gazette is not quite so moribund as you suspect." He reported that the proposal had "bobbed up again," and that "[i]n recent weeks the Executive Council has been making a canvass of the various legal offices and legal problems of the government." He also hoped "that [Donald] Richberg (who has reached new and dizzy heights) will back the proposal" (Wyzanski to Griswold, October 1, 1934).[12]

Brandeis, still behind the scenes, began to set the stage for the next event, the argument of *Panama* and *Amazon* before the Supreme Court, scheduled for December. As he had done before, he moved to ensure the existence of a law review article articulating the need for a *Federal Register* when the cases were being considered. So it was that Frankfurter ambled down the hall to suggest that Griswold write for the *Harvard Law Review* what would become his much quoted article, "Government in Ignorance of the Law—A Plea for Better Publication of Executive Legislation," an assignment Griswold reluctantly assumed. Griswold remembered Frankfurter asking him to write on the need for "proper publication of administrative regulations, varying from Executive Orders at the highest level through regulations of executive departments and such things as notices of hearings or of other activities by an already burgeoning federal bureaucracy" (Griswold 1992, 115-19). In addition, "Frankfurter said the article had to be published right away." Only later did he learn that Frankfurter was actually relaying a request from Brandeis. What he did not know was that Brandeis had been fully aware of Griswold's interest in the subject and his prior work on a proposed statute. The suggestion and timing were anything but accidental.[13]

Although Griswold had not planned to start publishing so quickly, "a suggestion from Professor Frankfurter was, of course, not to be taken lightly," he recalled. Griswold's reluctance was understandable. "I was just 30 when I went to teach at Harvard. This was my first article. It had to be very thorough, very accurate, meet very high standards. And I had only a short time to write it" (interview with author, November 9, 1993). From his point of view, the resulting article was published, "[b]y pure coincidence . . . on almost the exact date" the Supreme Court considered the cases of *Panama Refining Co. v. Ryan* and *Amazon Petroleum Corporation v. Ryan.* In this case, "coincidence" was given a shove by Brandeis and Frankfurter, as Frankfurter later wrote to Brandeis, "Griswold . . . had to be pushed by me into writing and publishing [his article] promptly instead of letting it drag on" (Frankfurter to Brandeis, January 28, 1935).

Meanwhile, in October and November, there were new obstacles to the efforts to establish a *Federal Register* through executive branch action. Wyzanski, as it turned out, had been overly optimistic about Richberg's support. In October, Dickinson, trusting that he was not "overstepping the bounds of propriety" sent a copy of the draft report to Brandeis, "Knowing of your interest in the proposal to establish some regular publication of the administrative rules and regulations of the Federal Government, I thought you might be interested in the draft report of the Committee which has this matter under consideration" (Dickinson to Brandeis, October 8, 1934a). A month later, an angry Dickinson sent to Brandeis blind copies of a sharp exchange of letters between himself and Richberg. Dickinson once again referred to the Justice's interest: "In view of your expressed interest in the proposal to publish Federal administrative orders and regulations" (Dickinson to Brandeis, November 5, 1934b).

Richberg clearly did not support the proposal and, after he presented it to the president, neither did Roosevelt. Richberg told Dickinson that he had brought the proposal to Roosevelt's attention, "and I have just received a brief, emphatic message in writing which reads: 'I do not want any federal paper established.'" Word of Roosevelt's response quickly circulated among those who had worked on the project. Wyzanski wrote to Griswold, "the President had a rather peculiar reaction to the suggestion for an official gazette. . . . He seems to have thought it was something like a federal newspaper boosting the federal government" (Wyzanski to Griswold, November 23, 1934).

Richberg reported that he would kill the proposal by simply filing away the subcommittee's report and asked Dickinson, "Have you any other suggestions to make, or do you approve of my conclusion?" Dickinson very clearly did not approve. "I think if the President has gotten the idea that what was being proposed was the establishment of a 'Federal paper,' this must mean that he has not had an opportunity to become acquainted with the project in sufficient detail to visualize the type of publication intended, which is really no more like a 'paper' than is the periodical publication of Treasury decisions or the opinions of the courts." Instead, Dickinson asked that he, Stephens, and Laylin of the Treasury Department be given 10 minutes to meet with the president and to make their presentation (Richberg to Dickinson, November 3, 1934; Dickinson to Richberg, November 5, 1934; Dickinson to Brandeis, November 5, 1934b). The meeting, however, did not take place.

Frankfurter also seems to have gotten involved in lobbying the president at this time. Griswold told Wyzanski that "Felix seems to think that any difficulties . . . can easily be taken care of. I gather that he expects to take it up with the President personally" (Griswold to Wyzanski, November 26, 1934).

It was now November, and whatever else happened to the proposal in the executive branch, Griswold's article was nearing publication and the scene was set for the Supreme Court's theatrical handling of the *Panama* and *Amazon* cases in December.

And theater it was. Not only was Stephens challenged so that he could not initially present his carefully constructed arguments, but the lawyers for the defense supplied their own theatrics as well. At one point, James N. Saye, "a little known but very effective country lawyer from Texas," handling the Amazon Petroleum case, dramatically "pulled out of his pocket a bedraggled, lop-eared, old copy of the Petroleum Regulations published by the Petroleum Administration" (U.S. House 1936, 18). Then, "waving it in the eyes of an astonished court [he] said: 'There, Your Honor, is the law that I had to consult to defend my client's rights'" (Ruddy and Simons 1944, 248). He was followed by the lawyer for the Panama Refining Company, F. W. Fischer, a portly, red-haired man with a frontier manner of speech, who provided the humor, causing even the usually austere chief justice to smile *(The New York Times* 1934). Justice Brandeis was in the middle of questioning Stephens somewhat harshly about how one could find regulations. "Is there, then, no place where you can get them, or find out what the regulations are?" asked Brandeis. Before Stephens could answer, Fisher jumped in: "The only repository for the code is the pocket of some agent from the Department of the Interior sent down in Texas. But it would not make much difference if we had the code, or if we found one in the middle of the road. There are too many changes and amendments" *(The New York Times* 1934; Waltman 1934).[14]

Later, knowing the answer full well in advance, Brandeis, also asked whether Stephens knew if anything had been done to have the government publish these directives. Stephens explained that he had been a member of a "so-called 'Gazette Committee,'" which had made recommendations for publication, but they had not been approved" (Stephens to Griswold, January 7, 1935).

When privately recounting his public humiliation to Griswold, Stephens was somewhat bewildered by the unexpected intensity of the interrogation. He spelled out for his friend every step he had taken months earlier to inform the justices of the problem immediately after he had learned of it. He also noted, although he did not understand the significance of his observation, that "The Court seemed to have been prepared to go into this question of publication of codes, orders, and regulations in this way."

Stephens was not alone in his assessment. According to one astute observer, "[T]hose who heard and participated in the argument were struck by the almost gleeful eagerness with which the Court probed into the unsavory story (though it had previously been completely advised)" (Jaffe 1965, 63).

The Supreme Court handed down its decision quickly in the *Amazon* and *Panama* cases, focusing on the constitutional question but alluding to the problems of records. On January 7, 1935—just a week after Roosevelt's annual message to Congress—Hughes, writing for an eight-member majority, said "We see no escape from the conclusion that the Executive Orders of July 11, 1933 and June 14, 1933, and the Regulations issued by the Secretary of the Interior there under, are without constitutional authority" *(Panama Refining Company* 293 US 388 [1935]).

The Court, addressing *Amazon Petroleum,* also had particularly harsh words for the government about bringing a case that challenged a nonexistent regulation, "the controversy . . . was initiated and proceeded in the Courts below upon a false assumption . . . the fact is that the attack in this respect was upon a provision which did not exist" *(Panama Refining Company* 293 US 388 [1935]).

Sutherland and Brandeis were pleased with the result. On the back of the proof sheets circulated by Hughes, Sutherland wrote: "Clear, convincing and written with careful discrimination—am glad to agree." Brandeis was more succinct, writing: "Yes. . . . Complete and even the layman can understand." Privately he wrote to Frankfurter: "I was very glad that I was not asked to write the opinion, as I well might have been. . . . Chief (Hughes) came to me and said that in view of Johnson's (head of the National Recovery Administration) criticism earlier in the year he wondered whether I would not like to write opinion. I told him I would not object to writing it but I have no desire to do so. As a matter of fact I felt he was anxious to write it himself. . . . But I did have a great deal to do with 'hot oil' case . . . I had a good deal to do with shaping opinion and setting my brethren on either side to ask some of their questions" (Urofsky 1986, 315).

Clearly, this was not the end of the story. On the very day in December that Stephens was making his unsuccessful argument before the court and being subjected to the barrage of questions about where and how people could find administrative rules and regulations, Griswold's article was published in the *Harvard Law Review.* The article, which received wide coverage in the press and among lawyers and members of Congress, proposed that Congress create a *Federal Register* and included a model bill (interview with author, September 9, 1993).

THE MOMENTUM SHIFTS TO CONGRESS

The first result of the cases was a very public national airing of the problem of publishing government regulations, reported in news accounts and editorials around the country. Within days, "the answer" to this problem, in the form of Griswold's *Law Review* article, was circulated, and Griswold promptly sent copies to a large number of potentially influential people.

Dickinson suggested that Griswold meet Emanuel Celler, a savvy Congressman from Brooklyn, first elected in 1923. In 1934, he was chairman of Subcommittee No. II of the House Committee on the Judiciary and, according to Griswold, "was trying to find some way to make himself known. I went up and called on him. Left him with a copy of my law review article. He was immediately much interested" (interview with author, September 9, 1993). According to Celler, it was reading this "very illuminating article" on the urgent need to establish a consistent, uniform published source of federal rules and regulations that "caused me to file the . . . Federal Register bill" (U.S. House 1936). It was not a matter of chance that Celler read the article.

Publicly, while Brandeis was given credit for "a canny move to impress on the Administration the need for an official gazette," the fiction spread that Brandeis was moved to action *because* of Griswold's article. On January 1, 1935 (before the Supreme Court issued its *Panama* and *Amazon* decision), Drew Pearson, in his widely circulated column, "The Washington Merry-Go-Round," highlighted Griswold's article and wrote that "Justice Brandeis is a regular reader of this distinguished legal publication, and it was shortly after this that he gently prodded Attorney General Stephens . . . on the failure of the Administration to create a readily accessible file of its great volume of "hip pocket" laws. Brandeis's remarks received wide publicity and probably will bear fruit" (Pearson and Allen 1935). Pearson's column did not note that the "prodding" actually occurred shortly before Brandeis could have read the article.

Frankfurter again stepped in behind the scenes. Just three days after the cases were heard, on December 13, he telegrammed Roosevelt's secretary, Marguerite (Missy) LeHand, to ask that Roosevelt hold off on making any "final decision regarding form and procedure for systematic publication of executive orders until I have had opportunity for talk with you. It happens to be a particular subject of mine and I am bringing a detailed scheme and draft for necessary legislation" (Freedman 1967, 248).

Whatever Roosevelt's response to Frankfurter, once the Supreme Court had so publicly castigated the executive branch for its sloppiness in making regulations available, it was probably inevitable that direct control over "form and procedure," would shift to the legislative branch. Even before the Supreme Court handed down its decision (January 7, 1935), Griswold and Celler were exchanging letters about establishing a *Federal Register* (Celler to Griswold, December 27, 1934; Griswold to Celler, January 2, 1935; Celler to Griswold, January 4, 1935).

By December 27, 1934, Celler had written that he wished to introduce Griswold's bill (included in the appendix to his article) and Griswold, pleased, responded modestly that "it was simply a mark to shoot at. I have no doubt that it can be greatly improved by those who are more experienced in legislation than I am." Within days (by January 4), Celler had introduced the bill with a modification. The attorney general, not the librarian of Congress, would be responsible for compiling and publishing the complete record of all statutory rules and regulations, with aid from the librarian.

Once the issue was opened for discussion by news articles and editorials, broad-based support was quickly marshaled. The administrative law section of the American Bar Association had been studying this problem of obtaining agency rules and regulations, concerned as it was with both the difficulties of finding executive orders and regulations and the imposition of criminal penalties for violating these hard-to-find orders. As part of the solution, it had recommended in 1934 some form of publication, particularly for those rules and regulations with criminal or civil penalties or liabilities. It had supported a 1934 House bill to this effect and members were ready to testify before Celler's subcommittee (Griswold 1934; Ruddy and Simmons 1944, 252; U.S. House 1936, 6).[15]

Although other legislative efforts had occurred along similar lines, Celler's bill (reworked several times as it moved through committee) was more comprehensive and rapidly gained broad support. Celler quickly scheduled hearings to consider its enactment. Griswold contributed, first with his own testimony, and second, by suggesting others to Celler who should testify before the subcommittee. Griswold, drawing on both his experiences in the solicitor general's office and his research after leaving that office, forcefully made the point that "for some regulations, it is not so hard to find them as it is awfully hard to be sure you have got the latest thing. The dangers are from the regulations you do not know about, and as the situation now stands, it is almost hopeless to find out whether that is the regulation on any certain particular matter" (U.S. House 1936, 19).

The bill passed the House on April 1, 1935, and the Senate on July 11 (after several delays by Senator Alben Barkley), with the Senate insisting on a number of changes in language and punctuation. The House agreed to the Conference Report on July 22, and it became law on July 26, 1935. Publication, however, was still more than half a year away. It was not until February 18, 1936, that Roosevelt, taking his time while Celler and others waited impatiently, signed Executive Order No. 7298, which set forth the regulations governing publication. Finally, on March 14, 1936, the first issue of *The Federal Register* was published.

PUBLISHING REGULATIONS: SUBSTANCE, FORM, AND STATUTORY GUIDANCE

The decision to publish the *Federal Register* was only the first step. Almost immediately, even before the first issue had been printed, Missouri Congressman John J. Cochran introduced a bill to repeal the act, claiming he wanted to protect the taxpayer and avoid creating a "useless" agency; his views appeared to be gaining support. Celler, however, quickly and successfully marshaled his forces again, with Griswold, Dickinson, and Stephens among those who presented statements against Cochran's bill.

Administratively, decisions had to be made as to the frequency of publication (daily or weekly), size, style, pagination, indexing, and quality of paper. Although Roosevelt's executive order spelled out in great and precise detail the form, page size, and writing style to be followed for preparing, presenting, filing, and distributing executive orders and proclamations, a large number of other issues were left to negotiation. Griswold urged daily publication, "but with the provision, if there wasn't anything on a particular day, they could skip a day; of course, this didn't happen. . . . When we were starting this thing, we figured [it would run] 400 or 500 pages a year" (interview with author, September 9, 1993). That guess, it turns out, never envisioned the 2000 total of 83,294 pages (averaging 333 pages per day).

Griswold also had such concerns as staffing costs of the new office (too high) and quality of paper used in printing the *Register* (so poor that it was likely to disintegrate over time). Pages of single-spaced correspondence and memoranda exchanged among Griswold, Dickinson (now assistant attorney general) and the director of the *Federal Register* Division at the National Archives, Major Kennedy, attest to Griswold's continuing close attention to detail and the sharp policy disagreements that remained. These were clearly administrative issues in which Brandeis took no part.

THE *FEDERAL REGISTER:* MECHANISM FOR TRANSPARENCY

In many ways, the *Federal Register* has transformed participation in American government into the twenty-first century as it documents "both the substance of, and the reasoning behind, regulatory actions." While the *Federal Register* continues as a paper record, the Government Printing Office Electronic Information Access Enhancement Act of 1993 requires free online availability. With a click of a mouse, readers can learn about the *Federal Register* and how to use it and are provided (in print and on the web) with detailed "reader aids." A detailed guide to Freedom of Information indexes, agency-by-agency, and guidance to help comply with President Clinton's memorandum for "Plain Language in Government Writing" *(Code of Federal Regulations* 1998) are also provided, as required by statute.

ASSESSING THE ROLE OF JUSTICE BRANDEIS

So integral is the *Federal Register* to the activities of the federal government that it is hard to imagine "doing business" with the government without it. Assessment of Brandeis's role in its creation is more complex and, like the story itself, must take place on two levels. His extrajudicial intervention in this, as in other well-documented areas,[16] raises some important questions about the separation of powers and acceptable actions of members of the bench. It also provides important insights for today's scholars who embrace "new institutionalism" to enhance understanding of governmental structures and decision making.

It is reasonable to assume that Brandeis's intervention was a decisive factor in the time and form of creation of the *Federal Register*. He was perhaps the one person uniquely positioned to take action, having the values, vision, knowledge of all the players, and the means to orchestrate the necessary conditions to lead to its creation. Brandeis was said to have a "special genius" to "devise institutional arrangements designed to salvage moral values in a modern technological age," according to legal scholar Paul Freund, a former law clerk to the Justice (Freund 1977/78, 7).

This single issue drew together most of Brandeis's lifelong concerns about transparency, knowledge, and accountability. He distrusted "bigness" in business and in government, believed government overregulation to be dangerous, watched with growing alarm the extraordinary proliferation of federal regulations, and feared that "difficulties of bigness are being realized in governmental matters." He believed with equal fervor that private interests had to yield to the public good, that "knowledge is the first essential of wise and just actions," and above all that government had an obligation to ensure that information about its actions be widely available.

As Brandeis well knew, consensus about need and form for routine publication of federal regulations had not coalesced by 1934 in either the executive or the legislative branch, and it was unlikely to do so in the short term. President Roosevelt was getting conflicting advice from various trusted members of his administration, and even those who supported publication had yet to agree on details. Efforts to propose legislation or to issue an executive order had fallen victim to disagreements in the administration and the press of other matters. Several legislative efforts had also failed. Some members of Congress believed such a publication entirely unnecessary, arguing that lawyers who needed to know regulations could get them from agencies or individual congressmen. There was the strong likelihood that legislation aimed at controlling the executive branch and broadening public access to government records would lead to years of debate before a statute would be enacted, as was the case with the Administrative Procedure Act and the Freedom of Information Act. The *Amazon* and *Panama* cases were the ideal vehicle to illustrate the dangers of big government and the proliferation of federal regulatory powers. These cases spoke to widespread national fears of an overarching, out-of-control government that could assess criminal penalties against people who had no way of knowing their behavior was prohibited.

To improve the chances for creating a *Federal Register,* it was necessary to have both a cogent scholarly argument and a model bill. Griswold, although he had not seen himself in this role, was perfectly positioned to provide both. Brandeis was the person who not only had followed Griswold's work, but was also the only one to be able (through Frankfurter) to get Griswold to write the article in time for maximum exposure; he knew exactly when the cases would be argued and when the article would be needed. Griswold would not have undertaken to write the article then had anyone but Frankfurter asked him (interview with author, September 9, 1993).

Brandeis also knew the stance of the Court. He could (and did) work with his fellow justices to see that they asked key questions in the two cases. Thus, he was able to link actions in the three branches of government, capitalizing on the strengths of each, to produce what has become one of the most important, ongoing records of government regulatory activity.

In the end, the study speaks also to the vagaries of time. While the *Panama* and *Amazon* cases have become a footnote in history, the legacy for which they paved the way is alive and well, testimony to the vision of such leaders as Griswold, Dickinson, Frankfurter, and Celler, and to the unique skill and dedication to the commonweal of Justice Brandeis.

Feinberg, Lotte E. "Mr. Justice Brandeis and the Creation of the *Federal Register.*" *Public Administration Review* 61, no. 3 (2001): 359–70. Reproduced with permission of Blackwell Publishing Ltd.

* * *

At the Intersection of Bureaucracy, Democracy, and the Media: The Effective Agency Spokesperson

Mordecai Lee

CONTEXT

At the close of the first decade of the twenty-first century, bureaucracy found itself in what could be called a geometrical dilemma. Bureaucracy is an inherently hierarchical and pyramidal entity that needs to adapt to what Friedman calls a flat world (2006). This contemporary paradox can be seen as the modern manifestation of the traditional problem of democracy relying on an inherently non-democratic bureaucracy to organize the delivery of public goods and services (Blau and Meyer, 1993).

Bureaucracy's placement in the public sector has always meant that it operates in a fishbowl. Yet, the twenty-first century has redesigned the fishbowl to put unprecedented pressures on public administration (Roberts, 2006). Demands by the news media, advocacy organizations, politicians, legislative auditors and reformers constantly push the envelope for greater transparency, increased freedom of information, more openness in drafting of policies and regulations, enhanced whistle blower protections (and, subtly, encouragement of it), and expanded citizen involvement in agency decision-making. Simultaneously—if not hypocritically—those same social forces often push for greater privacy protections regarding agency data and personal information.

A bureaucracy has many different ways it can respond to these contemporary pressures for increased external communications, including specialized training for its staff, development of policies, pursuit of alternative channels to reach the public, use of e-government technology to interact with the citizenry directly, public reporting and specialized operations during crises and disasters (Lee, 2007; 2008a; 2008b).

Still, the in-house professional who faces the greatest pressures to communicate on a daily basis is the agency's spokesperson. This person is the voice and face of the agency on a daily, even hourly, basis in dealing with the news media in all of its variegated twenty-first century manifestations: daily newspapers, wire services, specialized publications and magazines, cable news channels, TV networks and radio reporters, along with bloggers, websites and other emerging social media. The agency spokesperson is at the crucial and important intersection of bureaucracy and democracy, trying to serve several clamoring and, sometimes, contradictory stakeholders. But, surprisingly, "Few positions in government are as misunderstood as the public information official" (Willis-Kistler, 2003, p. 15).

OVERVIEW

Bureaucracy's antecedents extend to the early Middle Eastern and Mediterranean societies. By Biblical times, bureaucracy was an essential component of advanced civilizations (Lee, 2002a).

Yet it was not until the nineteenth and twentieth centuries, with the parallel emergence of mass democracy and the independent daily newspaper, that a new reality of public administration set in (Starr, 2004, pp. 395–402). Government agencies were expected to engage in symmetrical two-way communications with the citizenry-at-large (Grunig, 1997). Outwards, they needed to be explaining, advertising, reporting, promoting, encouraging and interpreting. Simultaneously, inwards, they sought to be initiating, listening, responding, adjusting, changing and terminating. This was public relations in the plainest and best meaning of the term, before the initials PR took on the manipulative, insincere and superficial meaning of contemporary usage. Such public relations programs were sometimes conducted indirectly via the news media and sometimes through direct contact with the public-at-large. Either way, modern bureaucracy needed to learn how to engage in public relations. The nexus for bureaucratic PR is the agency spokesperson and his/her home base in the agency's public information office.

The subtlety and nuance involved in the practice of the public information profession is illustrated by a story told of Robert McCloskey, the near legendary spokesman for the US State Department in the 1970s:

> McCloskey has three distinct ways of saying, "I would not speculate": spoken without accent, it means the department doesn't know for sure; emphasis on the "I" means "I wouldn't but you may–and with some assurance"; accent on "speculate" indicates that the questioner's premise is probably wrong (Crisis Spokesman, 1970).

McCloskey himself, after retirement, acknowledged one technique of his mastery of the profession: "After a while, an official's *gesture* may be all that a reporter needs to confirm a lead" (1990, p. 117, emphasis added).

This chapter presents the role of, and best practices for, government public information officers (PIOs) as identified from research by academicians and practitioners. This has been a somewhat neglected subject in public administration, an odd omission given that the central tenet of the discipline is that management in the public sector is inherently different from the business sector. One key aspect of that difference is a news media that is a Constitutionally based instrument of democracy with government managers having an absolute obligation to cooperate with it. Virtually total transparency is the premise imposed on American public administration. This is a wholly different dynamic than that faced by executives in the corporate or nonprofit sectors (Lee, 2002b). Furthermore, using the prism of bureaucratic politics, the conduct of external communications is a vital aspect of any public agency's struggle for survival, stability, and security.

(*Note to the reader*: If only for variety in the text, the terms spokesperson and PIO are used as synonyms in this chapter, even though they are slightly different.)

EFFECTIVENESS AS A PERFORMANCE STANDARD

As academic disciplines, public administration and public relations have paid attention to the role of government public relations (in contradistinction to media relations by *elected* officials) sporadically (Lee, 1998). Book-length and major contributions from academicians and independent researchers that focused in whole or in part on the broad subject of external communications in the public sector have included McCamy (1939), Mosher (1941), Pimlott (1972 [1951]), Lindsey (1956), Rubin (1958), Rourke (1961), Nimmo (1964), Hiebert and Spitzer

(1968), Dunn (1969), Chittick (1970), Sigal (1973), Helm et al. (1981), Schachter (1983), Hess (1984), Morgan (1986), Garnett (1992), and Graber (2003). This broader literature naturally includes some attention to the work of PIOs.

Academic literature that focuses more directly on spokespersons in public administration is sparser, largely limited to articles in refereed journals. Some of it is quite dated. Major examples include Stephens (1981), Dunwoody and Ryan (1983), Fletcher and Soucy (1983), Swartz (1983), and Motschall and Cao (2002). This author has surveyed spokespersons for local governments to document their roles and work (Lee, 2001a), examined the film image of government PIOs (Lee, 2001b), identified strategies by government agencies for dealing with new trends in media coverage (Lee, 1999), and presented a comprehensive typology of the purposes of public relations in public administration (Lee, 2000).

Paralleling the academic literature, personal memoirs by PIOs working for administrative (rather than elected) officials constitute a significant, if anecdotal, ground-level view of the difficulties of speaking for a bureaucracy. While there is a relatively plentiful literature of spokespersons for elected officials, such from former White House press secretaries, that category of spokespersonship must necessarily be excluded from this inquiry. The extant literature of senior PIOs in public administration has included books by two former Assistant Secretaries of State for Public Affairs (Barrett, 1953; Berding, 1962), a former Assistant Secretary of Defense for Public Affairs (Goulding, 1970), the US government spokesman in Saigon during the early years of the Vietnam war (Mecklin, 1965), an Army PIO (Oldfield, 1956), the Deputy Commissioner of Public Affairs of the New York City Police Department (Daley, 1978), and a guidebook from an association of PIOs (Krey, 2000). A non-US source is the memoir of the Chief Information Officer of the British Ministry of Supply (Williams-Thompson, 1951). Some contemporary examples of articles by practitioners have been authored by the official State Department spokesman (a position sometimes separated from the role of assistant secretary for public affairs) (McCloskey, 1990), a housing agency spokeswoman (Arnette, 1995), a health and human services PIO (Denning, 1997), the PIO for the Los Angeles Fire Department (Ruda, 1998), the spokesman for the Maryland Fire Marshall (Gosnell, 2000), an FBI communications trainer (Staszak, 2001), the PIO of a California city (Willis-Kistler, 2003), and a public affairs officer for the American reconstruction agency in Iraq (Krohn, 2004). A non-US source was written by the PIO for an international organization in post-Communist Eastern Europe (Édes, 2000). Earlier articles and published lectures by practitioners, now mostly of historical value, include a Marine Corps publicity specialist (Proctor, 1920), two more Assistant Secretaries of State for Public Affairs (Manning, 1966; Carter, 1984), a Foreign Service officer (Zorthian, 1971), PIOs of two state social service agencies (Courter, 1974; Goldstein, 1981), and the head of an association of federal PIOs (Brown, 1976).

What lessons can be learned from this relatively modest academic and practitioner literature? A consistent theme is the contemporary focus of public administration and public relations on organizational effectiveness (Wise, 2002-03). The performance standard of effectiveness helps identify the Holy Grail of successfully connecting bureaucracy with democracy in general and to the news media in particular. The components of effectiveness are those that relate to the multiple—and usually conflicting—perspectives of the news media, the agency head, the agency's staff and, finally, the profession's own code of standards.

Defining the effectiveness the spokesperson for a bureaucracy, of course, is a reflection of who is making the observation. Certainly, where you stand depends on where you sit. Reporters are seeking a spokesperson who is well informed, truthful, volunteers information, helpful, willing to act as a fact-finder, and has unlimited access to the highest level of officials in the agency. On the other hand, the head of the agency may want the spokesperson to advance his/her short-term career interests, such as providing positive publicity and suppressing negative coverage. Meanwhile, the careerists in the agency may want the PIO to emphasize or downgrade issues that will advance the long term interests of the agency itself, which may or may not correlate with the short term interests of the appointed head of the agency. Finally, the spokesperson has his/her own professional standards and ethics, derived from a conception of an accountable public administration that serves the citizenry, the public interest and democracy. Yet this professional code of conduct may at times conflict with the tugs and pulls of other constituencies.

These cross-cutting currents suggest that a PIO works in an unusually precarious environment in public administration. They also raise the question of what or where spokespersons consider themselves to be? Are they loyal members of a bureaucracy? Paid by a bureaucracy, but loyal to the professional standards of journalism? Or somewhere in-between?

EFFECTIVENESS FROM THE MEDIA'S PERSPECTIVE

Reflecting on his two years as the State Department's spokesman and acting Assistant Secretary for Public Affairs, Nicholas Burns identified three key factors that the media used to measure the effectiveness of a bureaucracy's spokesman:

- Credibility: "he or she must speak, and be seen to speak, clearly and authoritatively" for the agency
- Knowledge: "Always try to be better prepared than the press corps"
- Responsiveness: "understand the often Byzantine nature of the modern press corps" (Burns, 1996, pp. 10–11).

When possessing this trifecta, a bureaucracy's PIO can be effective in the eyes of the news media. If Burns had lacked even one of the three it would have been fatal, because reporters would quickly turn against him. For example, if Burns had been credible and informed, but he didn't cater to the technical needs of reporters (such as deadlines and connectivity) to do their jobs, then his effectiveness would have sharply dropped.

More crucially, in a different incomplete combination of the trifecta, Burns could have been well informed and responsive, but he would not have the respect of journalists covering the agency if they perceived a lack of credibility when speaking on behalf of the Department's senior leadership. In this kind of situation, it was not enough for reporters to know that Burns was fully informed of developments within the State Department. For them to trust him, they needed to have the confidence that the information he was dispensing was not only technically accurate, but credible. For example, if Burns had said, "The Secretary has no plans to meet today with the Governor of California," but then the two met the next day as perhaps had been previously arranged, then Burns would have lost his credibility. While he had been literally correct in what he said, he was misleading by parsing the meaning of his words to be misleading. If he claimed that he was providing all the information that had been given to him, then he'd be implicitly confessing to not being truly in the know. The prompt response from reporters would be, "In that case, give us someone who is."

Even though the professional role the spokesperson is playing is, strictly speaking, only that of an amplifier and conveyer of information, but because it was coming from Burns the reporters gauged the credibility of the information on Burns' own authority and reputation. The press corps wants someone who is an objective conveyer of information and doesn't add spin; doesn't withhold information, lie, deceive or mislead; withstands intra-agency pressures to withhold information; and, when needed, acts as a reporter and fact finder within the agency to be sure he/she knows what's really going on.

Credibility and knowledge are gained when the spokesperson has the confidence and trust of the senior leaders of the agency. When that happens, then the PIO knows what the agency head is thinking about or leaning towards, long before a matter is ready to become public. He/she is included in preliminary policy decisions and trusted to be discrete about such information. The spokesperson is well informed of the agency head's activities and preferences, even if that information cannot be released to the media. The PIO is always kept in the know, if only for background purposes, and is trusted to use his/her best judgment and skills not to share such information inadvertently with the press. There are several indicators of credibility and knowledge-ableness, measures used by reporters and outside observers to identify how close the spokesperson actually is to the head of the agency, and in turn, how "in the know" the spokesperson is.

Access: How much personal and direct access does the spokesperson have to the boss? How frequently do they see each other? Can the PIO see the agency head on very short notice, leaving it up to the spokesperson to decide whether the topic is important enough to bring up, even interrupt a meeting?

Physical proximity: How close is the PIO's office to that of the agency head? Is it within earshot, at least on the same floor? Or, is it outside hailing distance, even on a different floor of the agency's headquarters building? For example, during the Nixon administration, State Department spokesman Robert McCloskey had the title of Deputy Assistant Secretary for Public Affairs, clearly hierarchically a subordinate to the Assistant Secretary for Public Affairs. However, McCloskey's office was on the seventh floor of Foggy Bottom (a nickname for the State Department's headquarters in Washington, DC, in a low-lying neighborhood near the Potomac River that often was shrouded in fog), near the office of the Secretary, while McCloskey's bureaucratic superior, the Assistant Secretary, was one floor below with all the other assistant secretaries.

Invited to daily senior staff meetings: Is the spokesperson a regular attendee of the start-of-the-day senior staff meeting? While these sessions cover mostly routine business, they are vital for keeping the PIO aware of the diurnal agenda that all subunits of the agency are working on. For example, when Caspar Weinberger was Secretary of Defense during the Reagan administration, the department's spokesperson was a regular participant in the secretary's 8:00 a.m. daily staff meeting (Weinberger, 2001, p. 290). Or, perhaps the spokesperson is only invited during media crises?

Participates in policy discussions: Besides the morning staff meeting, is the spokesperson routinely invited to major policy-making meetings? At a minimum, such participation should be as an observer, so that the PIO will be well informed about agency developments. Signals of stronger standing in the agency would be if at such meetings the spokesperson would be asked to evaluate the potential public relations and media relations aspects of the idea or invited to suggest revisions to the nascent policy to improve probable external reaction.

Title: In a bureaucracy, a person's power is not constant. Rather, it depends on exactly how much the superior wants the staffer to have. The successful spokesperson needs to have the full backing and support of the agency head, which can only emanate from a personal relationship of trust. No formal title can obscure or overcome the lack of this personal relationship. Formal titles cannot confer power in organizations the way a personal relationship can. Certainly, a formal title has some importance in any bureaucracy, especially in hierarchy-sensitive organizations, such as the military. The title can confer some amount of bureaucratic clout to the spokesperson when he/she engages in in-house politics. For example, there have been proposals that all federal cabinet departments have an assistant secretary for public affairs, a position that only about half the departments had at the time of writing (Lee, 2008c, pp. 191–2). The argument is that the title strengthens the hand of the spokesperson in occasional battles with lower ranked program officials for releasing information. However, this emphasis on titles can be misguided. An assistant secretary is not automatically a powerful person, rather only as powerful as the secretary would want.

When a PIO has, and is also perceived to have, credibility and knowledge, then the journalists covering the agency can themselves develop a relationship of trust with the spokesperson. They would concede to themselves that even if they were to prowl the corridors of the agency headquarters building or pound the pavement for external sources they would not be likely to get any more key information than already provided by the spokesperson. When that perception is achieved, then the phrase used by all cautious PIOs, "to the best of my knowledge," becomes synonymous with "here's the maximum amount of information you'll be able to get one way or the other." (McCloskey used the phrase, "I am informed," to signal to the press the opposite meaning.)

The third factor that Burns listed for an effective PIO was responsiveness to the media. This means that the spokesperson can see the world through the eyes of the press corps and thereby know what reporters need to be able to do their job. Whether a former journalist or not, the PIO can identify enough with the journalistic profession to be understanding of the sine qua non of being a media correspondent. Some components of responsiveness overlap with the preceding discussion of credibility and knowledge, while others relate more to the technical, physical, and professional needs of the news media to be able to do its work. Regarding the latter category, from journalists' perspective, the ideal PIO demonstrates responsiveness by being helpful and of assistance to them; understanding and acting on their different needs, interests, deadlines, timing, technical infrastructure and span of attention of the disparate press corps; and by not taking personally the adversarial tone of reporters' inquiries, not becoming defensive or insulted, and not carrying a grudge.

As soon as the media senses that the spokesperson is no longer fulfilling Burns' three factors of credibility, knowledge, and responsiveness, they will then treat the PIO in an increasingly hostile manner and demand access to someone who *is* effective and has the power to fulfill Burns' typology. This usually means the head of the agency. Hence, the rational and pragmatic agency head does well to evaluate the consequences of keeping the agency's spokesperson uninformed and ineffective, for this inevitably leads to having to cope directly with the press which can be, amongst other things, an extremely time consuming activity.

CONFLICTING CONSTITUENCY: THE AGENCY

Based on the preceding discussion, the PIO would simply need to have a self-identification with the press and work at accomplishing effectiveness from its perspective. Some press officers indeed have the philosophy that their role is exclusively to serve the press, even though they are on the government's payroll.

However, the difficulties inherent in being an effective spokesperson immediately become clear when identifying the other constituencies that the PIO must work with. While reporters might be the most vocal publicly about what they want, the interests of internal stakeholders often conflict with, or are diametrically opposed to, those of the press corps. In-house constituencies include the agency head and the agency staff. They have their own conflicting interests that can lead them to wonder about the spokesperson, "Whose side are you on?" In this multi-player game, all participants are trying to decide who is friend or and who is foe—for today's policy issue.

What the media wants to know might be precisely what the agency doesn't want it to know. Conversely, a press release extolling the successes of the agency or activities of its CEO might prompt a ho-hum reaction from the media. Reporters want to focus on what's new, controversial and unprecedented. They want to pry the secrets of the organization out of it. Simultaneously, public administrators often want to focus on such matters as the agency's performance, the continuity and expansion of its programs, indicators of accomplishment, and lowering expectations relating to modest experiments with alternate approaches. Journalists want to talk about people, whether victims or heroes, and who gets the credit or the blame. On the other hand, the agency wants to talk about the organization, its teamwork and cooperation. Reporters and bureaucrats can be ships passing in the night.

In some circumstances, an agency official might leak some confidential information on a proposed policy as a trial balloon or as a way to generate opposition. Whatever the motive, the leaking official has interests at odds from the agency's PIO. State Department spokesman Robert McCloskey, in criticizing leaking, articulated the benefits of relying on the PIO to present policy developments. Official spokespersons, he wrote,

> work hard to prevent leaks, partly out of self-interest (because they want to be the recognized authoritative voice) but, more important, also because they believe that the public interest is best served on-the-record, where policy can gain the respect that comes with clarity and consistency. (1990, p. 119)

The inherent conflict-filled environment of the PIO had been identified early by researchers. Beginning in the 1960s, the academic and practitioner literature has been consistent and replete with efforts to describe the conflicting constituencies of the spokesperson, including:

- an intermediary and go-between who tries to balance conflicting needs and requirements (Nimmo, 1964, pp. 24–25)
- "in an administrative no-man's land . . . not quite trusted by either the public or the agency" (Moss, 1968, p. 30)
- "a step-child of the bureaucracy" (Cutlip, 1976, p. 15)
- in a relationship with reporters as "allies and adversaries" simultaneously (Morgan, 1978, p. 34)
- a mediator between the media and the agency (Dunwoody and Ryan, 1983)
- on the margin, between journalist and agency (Swartz, 1983)
- a boundary spanner (Fletcher and Soucy, 1983)
- "in the bureaucracy but not truly of it" (Hess, 1984, p. 37)
- "are expected to be all things to all people" (Willis-Kistler, 2003, p. 15)

Therefore, hypothetically, an alternative scenario to the PIO who chooses to concentrate solely on being effective with the media could be to resolve the issue of trust by focusing exclusively on loyalty to the agency head or to the agency as an organization. After all, the citizenry pays his/her salary. If selecting this path, the PIO is a promoter, advocate, and publicist for the government agency. But a spokesperson cannot simply resolve any dilemmas regarding a proper role by asserting loyalty solely to the agency whose name appears on one's paycheck (let alone deal with the concomitant loss of effectiveness with reporters). Since the PIO deals constantly with the press, it is inevitable that people within the agency view him/her as being tainted by this. When trying to respond to a request for information held by an agency staffer, the reflexive answer might be, "You and *your* press corps can go to hell."

These kinds of conflicts can arise in the daily work of a bureaucracy. The agency head, probably a political appointee, is there for only a few years and may have career ambitions that are different from the careerists in the agency (Peters, 1988, p. 147). Coverage that benefits the agency head may not be welcome by the civil servants. When the PIO successfully blunts the impact of negative coverage, the benefits might accrue only to the agency head, not to the careerists. The conflicting interests of the CEO and organizational staff can manifest themselves when the latter want to hold information closely and when asked by the PIO for information might respond, "*Why* do you want to know?" In those situations information is, indeed, power. Yet when the agency head has to intervene too often with staff to release information to the spokesperson, then the CEO's own political capital can become depleted, leading the agency head to wonder if the PIO is more trouble than is worth.

Hence, the spokesperson must accept the inevitable tugs and pulls of being a person with a foot in two (or three) different camps, each sometimes the adversary of the other(s). This adversarial relationship is often described in combat metaphors, such as entering a battle zone, being on the firing line, or "surviving" a media gaggle. These, of course, are extreme examples that occur only in some situations. They are useful because they help identify the important elements of the environment that a PIO works in, whether those factors are on the surface at any given moment or not. However, it is also important to emphasize that many of the daily contacts with the press on the outside and agency staff on the inside are routine and without conflicting pressures. Cooperation is more common in day-to-day interactions that the spokesperson has with the media, on one hand, and agency staff on the other.

RESOLVING CONSTITUENCY CONFLICTS: PIO PROFESSIONALISM

Given the built-in conflicts of public spokespersonship, the literature has identified some best practices for navigating the minefield located at the intersection of bureaucracy, democracy and the news media. Most important, one needs to transcend the parochial demands for loyalty, whether coming from the media, the agency head or the agency staff. A spokesperson can define his/her loyalty to the public interest and democracy itself. Using this as a permanent professional North Star, the actions and decisions of the PIO might in any particular instance be viewed as pro-media and anti-agency or the opposite.

How can a spokesperson's commitment to professional standards as the resolution to constituency conflicts be operationalized? Research has identified several practices that strengthen the professionalism of public agency spokespersons:

- has full responsibility and authority for all public communications of the agency
- has budget control over all information activities
- views self as an agent of the public
- depending on circumstances, is a direct source of information to the media or the facilitator of information, by connecting a reporter to the appropriate agency official

- willingness to act as the conscience of the agency, an ever-present goad and reminder of the agency's public role and civic responsibilities
- willingness to acting as a gadfly, calling managerial attention to sources of actual and potential criticism affecting the agency
- serves as a feedback loop from the public to the agency, making sure that important outside information is brought to the attention and consideration of the decision-makers

A great deal of empirical research still needs to be done regarding the work of public information officers. As is clear from this synthesis, the literature has too few contemporary contributions, whether from academic or practitioner authors. In the meantime, until additional theoretical and applied research is published, the last word appropriately belongs to a statement of professional values developed by six practitioners in the 1990s. They zeroed in on the conflicting constituencies and pressures that face the public spokesperson. In that context, they suggested a professional's orientation as a way out of the morass of contradictory loyalties that occurs at the intersection of bureaucracy, democracy and the news media:

> While they [PIOs] must satisfy their current masters, they also are duty bound to always keep the public interest, however defined, as their overriding obligation and concern. In the final analysis, allegiance to the national or public interest is the full measure of their performance and professionalism. (Avery et al., 1996, p. 175)

Lee, Mordecai. "At the Intersection of Bureaucracy, Democracy, and the Media: The Effective Agency Spokesperson." Pp. 351–62 in *Bureaucracy and Administration,* edited by Ali Farazmand. New York: CRC Press, 2009. Reprinted with permission of Taylor & Francis Group.

5

Open Public Meetings

INTRODUCTION

A famous visual of an open meeting is Norman Rockwell's lithograph *Freedom of Speech*. In the image a man is speaking at a town hall meeting. He is dressed in casual clothes while the men sitting around him are all in suits—presumably businessmen. The businessmen appear to disagree with the speaker but are not interrupting him. This poignant image of a local government meeting shows a town resident voicing his opinion on an issue and participating in the political process. Public participation is typically an integral part of an open public meeting.

While open meetings are commonly thought of as a tool to allow for greater citizen participation, they also play a major role in information dissemination. Government information at all levels is disseminated to the public through open meetings. For example, at local government meetings the public can learn about contracts that are going to be awarded, ordinances to be passed, and resolutions that are proposed. By receiving this information, residents can better understand how their government is fulfilling basic functions such as water supply, refuse removal, and public safety.

The general arguments for transparency differ slightly from the specific ones for and against open meetings. A 1962 seminal *Harvard Law Review* article ("Open Meeting Statutes: The Press Fights for the 'Right to Know'" 1962) presents six specific reasons why public meetings should be open. The first is that open meetings provide public knowledge that is essential to a democratic process. Even though the actual number of people who attend a meeting may be small, the information concerning the meeting can be disseminated by these few individuals to a wider audience. The second reason is so that the public can observe decisions regarding public expenditures being made and become aware of how public money is spent. The hope is that openness will deter misappropriations and conflicts of interest. The third is that government officials will be more responsive to the public if there is an opportunity for public participation. Fourth, meetings as a whole are a way for elected officials to gain information. Factual errors or misconceptions can be corrected by members of the public who may know more about a specific local issue. Fifth, if citizens gain a better understanding of complex and difficult decisions, they may be more understanding about accepting initially undesirable policy outcomes. And lastly, open meetings promote better reporting of governmental activities ("Open Meeting Statutes 1962, pp. 1200–1201).

The article then presents reasons against holding all meetings in the open. Firstly, in some cases, freedom from public pressure is desirable during deliberation and decision-making. An example is the secrecy surrounding the Constitutional Convention. Second, public officials are less likely to make long, time-wasting speeches during a closed meeting without an audience. Third, open meetings may be to the disadvantage of lower-level government employees who may object to a program and voice those objections in public but who, in the end, have to administer the objectionable program or policy. Fourth, an elected official may be hesitant to change her position publicly on a policy issue during the course of the deliberative process. And the fifth objection is the tendency of the press to sensationalize stories and emphasize only controversial topics brought up at meetings ("Open Meeting Statutes" 1962, p. 1202).

Open meetings take place at all levels of government. At the U.S. national level, the Federal Advisory Committee Act requires the relevant U.S. bodies to hold open meetings. The extent to which the European Union committee system is open and accountable was researched by Mark Rhinard (2002). Rhinard offers suggestions for the EU committee system in the areas of openness and transparency, consistency and standardization, and strengthening accountability.

Much of the discussion and literature on open meetings focuses on participation. If you have ever been to a public meeting that allows for public comment, you may start questioning if participation is productive or even necessary. It is not unusual for gadflies—very vocal public activists—to speak at public meetings with more enthusiasm than focus. This seems even more likely to happen if the public meeting is being videotaped or shown on a local cable TV channel. Bryan Adams (2004) asks the question: Do public meetings play a role in fostering citizen participation in policy-making? He considers not only how participation directly affects immediate policy outcomes but also how participation plays a role in agenda setting and informing public officials.

Factors have been identified that contribute to successful public meetings (McComas 2001; Baker, Addams, and Davis 2005). Critical factors for a successful public hearing are "effectively notifying and educating the public before the hearing; carefully planning the meeting; giving a clear, media-rich presentation of the issues; properly facilitating the meeting; and conducting appropriate follow-up" (Baker, Addams, and Davis 2005, p. 490). Notifying the public of the meeting using multiple media types is essential. See Box 5.1 for an announcement of a public meeting posted in the U.S. Federal Register.

Box 5.1 Public Meeting Announcement in the U.S. Federal Register

DEPARTMENT OF COMMERCE
National Oceanic and Atmospheric Administration
RIN 0648-XN62
Western Pacific Fishery Management Council; Public Meetings

AGENCY: National Marine Fisheries Service (NMFS), National Oceanic and Atmospheric Administration (NOAA), Commerce.

ACTION: Notice of public meetings and hearings.

SUMMARY: The Western Pacific Fishery Management Council (Council) will hold meetings of its Scientific and Statistical Committee (SSC), American Samoa Archipelago

Fishery Ecosystem Plan Regional Ecosystem Advisory Committee (REAC), Advisory Panel (AP), and Plan Team (PT). The Council will also hold its 144th meeting to consider advisory group recommendations and take actions on fishery management issues in the Western Pacific Region.

DATES: The 100th SSC Meeting will be held on March 17–19, 2009, and the American Samoa REAC will be held on March 20, 2009. The Advisory Panel and Plan Team will meet on March 23, 2009. The 144th Council meeting will be held on March 23–26, 2009. All meetings will be held in Pago Pago, American Samoa. For specific times and agendas, see SUPPLEMENTARY INFORMATION.

ADDRESSES: The 100th SSC, REAC, PT, and 144th Council meetings will be held at the Governor H. Rex Lee Auditorium (Fale Laumei), Department of Commerce Government of American Samoa, Pago Pago, American Samoa. . . . The Council Standing Committee and AP meetings will be held at Sadie's by the Sea, Pago Pago, American Samoa. . . .

Source: U.S. Federal Register, vol. 74, no. 392, 2 March 2009. <edocket.access.gpo .gov/2009/pdf/E9-4302.pdf> (10 July 2009).

Assignments and Study Questions

1. Discuss the advantages and limitations of public meetings. Do these differ by level of government?
2. What do you think are the most important aspects of an open public meeting? What are the limitations of open meetings?
3. Attend a public meeting in your town or city. Was there time allotted for public participation? If so, do you feel that the type and level of participation was productive?

* * *

Open Meeting Statutes: The Press Fights for the "Right To Know"

Harvard Law Review

I. A CRITIQUE OF THE OPEN MEETING PRINCIPAL

The basic argument for open meetings is that public knowledge of the considerations upon which governmental action is based is essential to the democratic process.[1] The people must be able to "go beyond and behind" the decisions reached and be apprised of the "pros and cons" involved if they are to make sound judgments on questions of policy and to select their representatives intelligently.[2] The presence of outside observers is an invaluable aid in making such information available, for official reports, even if issued, will seldom furnish a complete summary of the discussion leading to a particular course of action.[3] Even though only newspaper reporters and a few interested citizens actually are present, the benefit of granting access to governmental meetings will inure to a far larger segment of the population, because those who do attend will pass on the information obtained. It is further argued that decisions which result in the expenditure of public funds ought to be made openly so that the people can see how their money is being spent;[4] publicity of expenditures further serves to deter misappropriations, conflicts of interest, and all other forms of official misbehavior."[5] Several other considerations support the principle of open meetings. Government will be more responsive to the governed if officials are able to ascertain public reaction to proposed measures. Public meetings also may operate to provide officials with more accurate information; individual citizens will be able to correct factual misconceptions, particularly in local government where the public is apt to have greater knowledge of the issues involved. Then too, as people better understand the demands of government and the significance of particular issues, they will be better prepared "to accept necessary, and perhaps difficult and unpalatable, measures essential to the public good."[6] Finally, open meetings foster more accurate reporting of governmental activities. Even when meetings are closed, some hint of what occurs generally reaches the press; but such reports are often incomplete and slanted according to the views of the informant.[7] To restrict the press to such sources of information is a disservice both to the public, which is misled, and to the officials, who may be judged on the basis of these distorted reports.[8]

Granting the virtue of open meetings in general, substantial objections can be made to enacting the principle as a legal requirement. Publicizing proposed governmental action may benefit citizens whose interests are adverse to the general community or harm individual reputations. In some cases, particularly when sharply conflicting interests must be accommodated, freedom from the pressure of public opinion may be desirable; the delegates to the Constitutional Convention, for example, felt constrained to work in secrecy.[9] Even in less unique circumstances "there is something to be said for open covenants, unopenly arrived at."[10] One public official has remarked that "there are many details, ramifications and opinions that no sound administrator . . . would care to express in public,"[11] and it appears that officials are often reluctant to request information at open meetings lest they create a public image of ignorance.[12] In addition, public officials are prone to waste time making speeches for the benefit of an audience, while in a closed meeting they "are less on their dignity, less inclined to oratory."[13] If the meeting is for preliminary consideration of action, there are additional objections. An open meeting requirement will tend to disadvantage subordinate officials by publicizing their disagreement with policies that they must administer. And publicity of proposals put forth during preliminary discussions may frustrate ultimate agreement, for an official hesitates to abandon a view that he has publicly advocated.[14] A final objection to an open meeting requirement arises from the tendency of the press toward "sensational" reporting. All too frequently newspaper stories are distorted by the bias of the reporter or his paper. Even when there is no bias, newspapers prefer to emphasize as "newsworthy" only "controversial matters about which there is some conflict or . . . those items which tend to make legislators appear substantially less than bright."[15] It has even been contended that the need for "right to know" laws has been exaggerated, as "editorials and news articles on star chamber sessions and the like have long been an easy, inevitably irrefutable, and popularly accepted part of every experienced, and frequently cynical, news editor's bag of tricks."[16] Although these arguments cannot be ignored, they do not compel the conclusion that a legal requirement of open meetings is untenable. Some have urged that the benefits of requiring that all governmental activity be done openly outweighs any disadvantages that may result;[17] perhaps a more rational approach would be to seek to devise a legal standard affording the fullest possible degree of openness while recognizing the interests promoted by governmental secrecy.

"Open Meeting Statutes: The Press Fights for the 'Right To Know.'" *Harvard Law Review* 75, no. 6 (1962): 1199–1221. Reprinted with permission of Harvard Law Review Association.

* * *

The Democratic Legitimacy of the European Union Committee System

Mark Rhinard

THE DEMOCRATIC LEGITIMACY OF THE EUROPEAN UNION COMMITTEE SYSTEM

Introduction[1]

This article assesses the operation and democratic legitimacy of the European Union (EU) committee system, an important site of European governance. Committees make a critical contribution to the effectiveness of the EU policy-making system. As an institutional feature of the EU, committees are responsible for the vast majority of policy preparation and are omnipresent at all stages of the decision-making process. As a manifestation of broader strategies chosen to pursue integration, committees provide essential arenas for specialized problem-solving, consensual styles of bargaining, and mutual learning among an array of multilevel actors. Perhaps a victim of the EU's success as a policy system, committee governance has recently come under public attack. European citizens, now directly affected by the laws and regulations developed within committees, seek clarification of the democratic credentials of this form of governance. From the bovine spongiform encephalopathy (BSE) scandal to the dioxin scares, and from bank fees to trading rules, criticism of "faceless bureaucrats," "hidden committees," and "the private processing of public issues" is growing stronger. It is not difficult to recognize that the public's once permissive attitude toward supranational decision-making is eroding (see, for example, Black 2001).

In essence, the state of the EU committee system throws an enduring dilemma into sharp relief: the trade-off between system effectiveness and democratic politics (Dahl 1994). On the one hand, a policy-making system must have the capacity to effectively solve problems requiring collective solutions. On the other hand, citizens must ultimately be able to exercise democratic control over the operation of that system. The proper and sustainable balance between these oft-conflicting values is, of course, a subjective, long-debated, and contextually dependent question. With growing public disapproval of European-level governance threatening to stall the "European project," an urgent return to this question seems in order. In his 1994 article, Robert Dahl voices grave concern over the expansion of transnational political systems such as the EU. Such expansion represents a "third transformation" of democracy, following earlier moves in history from city-state to nation-state. "The danger," Dahl (1994, 33) argues, "is that the third transformation will not lead to an extension of the democratic idea beyond the national state, but to the victory in that domain of de facto guardianship." As such, "[T]he burden of proof should be placed squarely on the advocates to show that the trade-offs definitely support the values of a majority of its citizens" (Dahl 1994, 34).

The main argument of this article is that the EU committee system does not represent an appropriate balance between system effectiveness and democratic legitimacy: the former has been emphasized at the expense of the latter.[2] The next section begins with a description of the pivotal role played by committees over the course of European integration and their contribution to the EU's policy-making capacity. Since the object of the article is to find ways to strike a better balance between effectiveness and democracy, existing approaches to "democratizing" the EU are reviewed briefly. Finding such approaches unsatisfactory, the third section outlines three fundamental democratic principles that allow us to assess committee governance in context while also offering operational standards of democratic legitimacy. The fourth section presents the evidence through a descriptive overview of Commission advisory committees, Council working groups, and "comitology" committees,[3] giving the reader a glimpse into the trade-offs inherent in the current EU committee system. An in-depth assessment follows in the fifth section, in which the three democratic principles are applied to the evidence on committees. The analysis concludes that the EU committee system indeed suffers from a lack of democratic legitimacy, but suggests that it can be remedied by the implementation of a number of reforms. The final section offers some suggestions for change and encourages further reform in the interest of sustaining committee governance and the future of an effective, democratic EU.

Effectiveness

The dilemma between system effectiveness and democratic politics was a formative theme in early debates over European integration. While the proponents of a federal future for the EU repeatedly emphasized the importance of familiar democratic institutions, it was the pragmatists—or, as Wallace and Smith (1995, 140) describe them, advocates of an "elite-led gradualism"—who stressed the immediate need for effective and efficient policy-making. Prioritizing the problem-solving capacity of European governance, the pragmatists believed, would allow the founders to avoid awkward constitutional issues and thus win the support of stubborn national governments. The bruising defeat of proposals for a federalist European Political Community (EPC) appeared to vindicate the pragmatists' strategies; it was this approach, therefore, that strongly influenced the development of a mode of supranational governance unique to Europe (Cardozo 1987, 72).

The European mode of governance rested upon the Monnet method, or "integration by stealth" (Hayward 1996, 255). Substantial policy-making authority would be transferred to the European level but in strictly limited fields. There, policy would be developed and decided among national experts working intimately with European civil servants and other directly affected interests. In his memoirs, Jean Monnet (1978, 373) voiced the hope that a few hundred European civil servants would be enough to set thousands of national experts to work. Governance was a process of consensus building amongst national administrators and concerned interests, coming to agreement on common policies through the processes of mutual learning and group socialization ("engrenage," to integration theorists). The intention was to downplay broader political issues by splitting decisions into functional administrative divisions, "thus replacing a public clash among national interests, as far as possible, by a private reconciliation of limited differences" (Wallace 1996, 243). Clearly, the Monnet method was not the only element of European integration. Intergovernmental bargains set the broad parameters of integration, and individual actors like de Gaulle presented periodic obstacles. However, the strategies of functional differentiation and technocratic administration, and the mode of governance that these entail, have been "an essential element" of the process of integration, "driving it relentlessly forward, so that in its absence, European integration would not have reached the point it has today" (Weale 2000, 161).

From this perspective, committee-style governance is a logical result of the overall strategy of supranational problem-solving. Committees are a highly suitable institutional mechanism for consensual and depoliticized decision-making: small, insulated groups allow for extensive, ongoing consultation in an intimate atmosphere among actors from multiple levels of government and society. Not surprisingly, committee governance evolved into a key feature of European decision-making. In 1968, Walter Hallstein reported that the European Commission convened some 1,450 meetings with civil servants and experts from the member states, involving some 16,000 national officials. At that time, that meant some six meetings per working day, linking between 2,000 and 3,000 officials from within each government to the European Community process (in Wallace 1996, 243). By 1971, Commission Secretary General Emile Noel remarked that "[B]eing based on a dialogue," the Community system

> bears little resemblance to the concept of government in the traditional sense of the word. The Community does not have a single head or single leader. Decisions are collective and taken only after much confrontation of viewpoints. The Communities have in fact been transformed into a vast convention. They are a meeting place for experts, ambassadors and ministers at hundreds, even thousands, of meetings (Noel 1971 in Wallace 1996, 243).

More recently, the important contribution made by committees to effective European governance has been bolstered by two factors. First, the Single European Act (1986), Treaty of European Union (1992), and Amsterdam Intergovernmental Conference (1996) represented a dramatic shift toward European action and increased competencies in the areas of environmental policy, social cohesion, and consumer protection. The agreement settled at Nice, France (2001) proposes to consolidate further the EU role in military, security, and immigration matters, drawing each of these areas closer to the "Community Method" of governance. Committees have been called upon to absorb much of the administrative and procedural burden of these shifts in the absence of a significant expansion of the permanent European civil service. Second, frequent treaty reforms concerning institutional matters and ad hoc interinstitutional agreements have required institutional means of reconciliation and coordination. Since formal mechanisms for coordination amongst the EU's institutional structures are sparse, committees substitute for this role and provide fora to ease the evolving and fitful power relations amongst institutions (Christiansen and Kirchner 2000, 2–4). Thus committees have taken an increasingly conspicuous role in the EU's policy process and in its institutional politics.

Committees endow the European Union governance system with the capacity to fulfill its basic problem-solving remit. Yet increasing criticism of this type of governance begs the question: has the prioritization of system effectiveness come at the expense of democratic mechanisms which secure legitimacy and sustain public consent? In this regard, it is useful to remember that "Jean Monnet and those who supported the technocratic strategy believed that the problem of popular consent could be postponed: that the creation of effective administrative government in discrete areas would provide the economic welfare which would in turn generate public support" (Wallace and Smith 1995, 144). Not only has explicit public support failed to materialize, but the implicit "permissive consensus" once underpinning moves toward European integration appears to be unraveling (see, for example, *The Economist* 2001, 15). Now more than ever there is a call to readdress the classic debate between system effectiveness and democratic legitimacy.

While this call has not gone unheeded in scholarly circles, academic proposals for reform tend to veer to one side of the debate at the expense of the other. This asymmetry is largely the result of differing conceptions of what constitutes democratic politics. Majoritarian-style conceptions of democracy, for example, emphasize the importance of democratic *inputs* to a political system: the ability of citizens to choose, through regular elections, between rival elites and political agendas (Schumpeter 1943; Weber 1942). Scholars adhering to this approach believe that only this process can lead to a true mobilization of bias, where every individual, regardless of economic and political resources, can participate equally in setting the boundaries of political action. Not surprisingly, this approach privileges familiar, parliamentary-style institutions as the only proper mechanism of democratic legitimacy. Reform proposals usually envision the creation of a dual-chamber European Parliament representing both nations and peoples (Hermann 1994), the strengthening of European political parties to reflect explicit cleavages (Mancini 1998), the parliamentary selection of the Commission to replicate a "formation of government" (King 1981), or the need to convene a constitutional convention tantamount to that held in the United States of America in 1787 (Siedentop 2000). Not only do proponents of majoritarian democracy overestimate the ability of parliaments to secure legitimacy and assure accountability, they also offer solutions with very little utility in the short-to-medium term.

Nonmajoritarian conceptions of democracy imply a vastly different perspective on the democratic legitimacy of the EU. According to this approach, any set of reform proposals must contend with the fact that because the EU is not a nation-state, it does not have a demos, a citizenry with the collective sense of identity required to form majoritarian-style government (Weiler, Haltern, and Mayer 1995, 5). Therefore, European governance can only be legitimate if it is "nonmajoritarian," concentrating on *output* forms of democratic legitimacy (Dehousse 1995; Joerges and Neyer 1997b; Scharpf 1999). Policy-makers must strive for positive-sum and pareto-optimal policy outputs in order to secure the public's consent. Corresponding to this approach is the belief that the EU should develop along the lines of a "regulatory state" (Majone 1994, 1996). In this model, efficiency-oriented independent regulatory agencies shielded from strict political oversight would be better positioned than elected officials to satisfy the problem-solving needs of today's Europe (Majone 1996, 299). While the nonmajoritarian approach to EU democracy has much to recommend it—including its recognition of committee governance and effective outputs (Joerges and Neyer 1997b)—it, too, offers unacceptable solutions. Defenders of independent regulatory authorities in the EU ignore the fact that, in most democratic systems, regulators are connected to majoritarian institutions (see, for example, Rose-Ackerman 1992, 187–193; Shapiro 1988, 107–128). Moreover, a narrow attention to shielded yet efficient problem-solving has characterized the EU policy process since its inception, leading to the democratic issues with which we must now grapple.

A more balanced approach to the democratization of EU committees should take into account the insights of several recent studies on transnational democracy. John Dryzek (1996), for example, urges us to avoid the implicit or explicit connection of democratic principles with familiar institutional forms. Analysis must proceed based on the application of general principles, not the glib comparison of familiar institutions. Dahl (1994) also writes that just as democracy required new and unique structures when political organization moved from the city-state to national-state levels, so the third transformation from the nation-state to international order might require a fresh look at how democratic politics is constructed. Yet while broad principles, unencumbered by the specifics of institutional arrangements, are important, they must also be applied in context. Thus, in his study on democratizing EU politics, Lord (1998, 13) writes that "democracies may often be shaped more by constraints, trade-offs, and legitimate contention as to how best to make those trade-offs than by democratic values themselves" (see also Dahl 1998). Given the unique nature of committee governance—and its historical effectiveness in the EU—any reform proposals must "face the peculiarities of the

EU political system" (Radaelli 1999, 771). The following section develops a set of democratic principles suitable to this task.

Democracy

A useful way of assessing the democratic credentials of EU committees rigorously but in context is by focusing the light of democratization through a liberal individualist lens. The pertinent question stemming from such an approach is this: what rights should European citizens have over a governance system that influences their lives? Phrasing the question this way allows us to return to some "first principles" of citizen engagement with government, irrespective of how this interaction is typically institutionalized at national levels. The following principles of democratic governance thus focus, in turn, on citizens' perceptions of, participation in, and control over policy-making systems.

The first democratic principle, and in many ways a precondition for subsequent criteria, is an *intelligible system of decision-making*. This criterion does not mean that the political process itself cannot be a complex, technical, and "messy" affair. Indeed, these are characteristics shared by most democratic policy-making systems. However, politics must be intelligible on two accounts, both procedurally and substantively. First, the individuals and infrastructure behind policy-making should be identifiable. Citizens have the right to see what interests are represented in the processing of policy, which actors are making decisions, and what procedural steps are taken to arrive at those decisions. Second, the political process should illuminate the societal issues at stake and make the multiplicity of alternative solutions clear. Policy-making systems that adhere to these standards offer citizens an equal opportunity to access information of crucial importance and to provide input which may differ from "internally" decided solutions. As Schattschneider (1960, 135) notes, "Democracy was made for the people, not people for democracy."

A second democratic principle by which to judge committees concerns the *deliberative nature of political processes*. A "deliberative democracy," at its most basic, is one in which preferences are not just aggregated but deliberated at the level of political decision-making (Weale 1996, 607; see also Habermas 1995 in Joerges and Neyer 1997b). This presupposes a system in which, first, differing conceptions of the public interest are allowed into the policy process, and, second, those conceptions are given a fair and thoughtful hearing. The former criterion was an explicit part of early constitutional debates in the U.S.: emphasis was placed on the need to create a "marketplace of ideas" in which a wide diversity of interests and opinions could be vetted. The conveyance of alternative preferences was encouraged through public meetings, instructed representatives, and public debate—what de Tocqueville described as "schools of civic virtue" (see also Lipset, Trow, and Coleman 1956). The latter criterion emphasizes that once in the "marketplace," differing conceptions must be considered fairly, unimpeded by closed agendas or a monopoly of dominant interests (Dahl 1998). John Stuart Mill (1972, 239–40) captures the essence of adequate deliberation when he states that government should form "an arena not only of opinions but of that of every section," in which points of view can "present themselves in full light and challenge discussion to be tested by adverse controversy . . . where those whose opinion is overruled feel satisfied that it is heard, and set aside not by a mere act of will, but for what are thought to be superior reasons."

Finally, citizens must have an element of *control over a policy-making system*, with the opportunity to hold officials accountable for their conduct and the system responsible for the decisions it ultimately produces. This principle of democracy derives from the fundamental notion that government serves at the will of its citizens; if displeased, the public should be able to "throw the rascals out" (Weiler 1997, 275; see also Plamenatz 1973; Schumpeter 1943; Weber 1942). Accountability allows citizens to entrust government to specialists, while retaining rights of access and participatory deliberation (discussed above) and "ultimate controlling power" (Mill 1972, 239). Of course, the "nuclear" option of sweeping officials out of office is, alone, a crude and imperfect mechanism (Lord 1998). However, other mechanisms of accountability can be found in legislative investigations, judicial oversight, and electoral threats toward politicians responsible for policy-making bureaucracies. By whichever means accountability is derived, citizens should have ways to ensure that political power will be exercised responsibly. In this way, we build support for policy-making institutions over time because blame and condemnation are heaped not onto the structures themselves, but onto the fallible individuals who temporarily occupy them (Beetham 1991).

Of course, the principles of clarity, deliberation, and accountability represent a stylized and incomplete portrayal of democracy and democratic theory. This approach conflates rights-based democracy and procedure-based democracy. But it does so knowingly, with the intent of drawing out the principles most critical to engaging a citizenry and to revitalizing public support. The principles thus derived imply a set of serviceable standards by which we can measure the democratic credentials of the EU committee system in light of its diverse and peculiar form. That form is described below.

EU Committees

In presenting a general typology of European committees, the analyst must contend with the incredibly diverse and famously obscure nature of committee governance. Some scholars begin by distinguishing committees by legal status (Christiansen and Kirchner 2000; Joerges and Vos 1999; Pedler and Schaefer 1996). Among the committees based on primary law are the oft-cited "grand" committees, such as the Committee of the Regions, the Economic and Social Committee, and the high-level advisory and regulatory committees set up in specific policy areas. Examples of the latter include the K.8 committee on justice and immigration issues, the Monetary Committee, the Article 133 committee in the area of external trade, and the Special Committee on Agriculture. However, analysis based on the legal moorings of committees tells us little about the actual power they yield and neglects the broader influence of more informal and less publicized groups.

The following section breaks committees into three divisions based on the stage of policy-making with which they are most closely associated: policy formation (Commission advisory committees), policy decision (Council working groups), and policy implementation (comitology committees). Clearly, this approach ignores the frequent blurring of the EU decision-making stages. For example, comitology committees may be involved in policy formation, and advisory committees may be convened to discuss implementation issues. Nonetheless, this typology offers a suitable simplification that preserves the attempt at comprehensive analysis. Moreover, we can interpret exceptions to the "three-stages" approach as compelling evidence of the range of committee influence over Commission law-making.

Commission Advisory Committees

EU scholars often emphasize the policy formation process as a critically influential stage of European policy-making (Nugent 1999; Peters 1996; Richardson 1996). Here, the Commission, exercising its exclusive right of initiative, has the responsibility for developing legislation that is not only technically sound but also politically palatable to the Council and Parliament. The Commission is, by and large, free to choose whatever channel of information and advice it deems necessary. While bilateral contacts with relevant actors and ad hoc hearings on a specific legislative proposal take place at this stage, the overwhelming tendency is to form a group capable of providing sustained input. For simplicity's sake, we call these types of groups Commission advisory committees, although they are subject to an array of various labels: "expert groups" (Schaefer 1996, 6), "coordination committees" (Christiansen and Kirchner, 7), or even "thinkers' groups" (interview, Commission DG Agri, May 2001). These committees have a wide remit, may include a diverse array of members, and operate according to informal and flexible procedures. According to a 1999 internal Commission list (European Commission 1999), almost 800 of these committees exist—the immense number and diversity of groups attesting to their functionally segmented and unregulated functions.

The function of Commission advisory committees is to assist the Commission in forming arguments for action, developing solutions for existing problems, and maximizing support for legislation. A conventional academic distinction is made here between ad hoc committees, intended to provide short-term input, and well-established standing committees. Ad hoc committees are formed as and when the Commission desires to form a position on an issue, even if an actual legislative proposal is a distant priority. These committees, however, will lose their ad hoc prefix when technical or political progress illuminates further issues and problems. For example, in 1988, after the Commission decided to develop a proposal for a "Council Directive concerning Common Rules for the Internal Market in Electricity," it established two ostensibly ad hoc advisory committees. The first committee was comprised of member-state officials with necessary expertise, while the second consisted mainly of interest groups, industrial electricity producers, environmental groups, and consumer representatives capable of providing additional political support. These committees met both separately and together for over three years, and provided significant input in shaping the Commission proposal for the directive, which it submitted in 1991 (European Commission 1991). The two groups continued to advise the Commission on follow-up and peripheral legislation concerning the directive long after their initial work was completed, thus taking on the likeness of permanent committees. Some Commission advisory committees are established based on the Commission's desire to have a lasting "standing" group that can advise on a wide variety of legislative proposals. For instance, in order to obtain advice on all issues relating to dangerous substances, the Commission formed the Scientific Committee on Toxicity, Ecotoxicity, and the Environment. The self-imposed mandate of the Commission states that this committee must be consulted before any relevant proposals go to the Council. Made up of Commission-selected academics and researchers, the standing group was formed explicitly to address criticisms that the Commission was producing poor policy decisions in this area (European Commission 1997).

The membership of a Commission advisory committee depends on the piece of legislation at hand. It can include industry representatives, research scientists, national civil servants, nongovernmental organization (NGO) staff members, academic experts, or even third-country experts. Whatever their status, participants gain entry if they have a credential to offer, a resource perceived as valuable by the Commission. As a small bureaucracy with a sizable mandate, the Commission relies heavily on the resources of these external actors. When asked what qualities are valued in committee members, committee chairmen within the Commission typically emphasize such traits as "functionally useful," "technical competence," "strong players in the field," those "involved in the past," and actors "well-connected with folks back home [in national capitals]" (interviews, European Commission, October–November 1999). This last comment is particularly revealing. Commission officials maintain that membership of Commission advisory committees stems primarily from an individual's specialist expertise and technical know-how. In addition, experts from national ministries offer the added benefit of supplying the Commission with politically sensitive information:

> Member-state reps attend [this committee] because we need their scientific knowledge and expertise. That is clear. However, we have no qualms about asking that person, maybe out in the hallway if not in the meeting itself, "How will this fly in your capital?" (Interview, Commission DG Info Soc, November 1999)

In terms of membership of Committee advisory groups, then, the Commission is the sole authority in determining what resource credentials are important, and thus who gets into the committees.

Given the Commission's independent role as convener and mediator of these types of groups, Commission advisory committee procedures and functions are kept very informal. Rarely do "rules of procedure" exist, nor are any records of proceedings kept for use beyond that of the Commission officials concerned. This is largely intentional: one official argued vehemently that formal rules would hamper the valued "free exchange of ideas and information" between committee members (interview, Commission DG Enterprise, November 1999). The regular attendance at meetings and the shared backgrounds of representatives undoubtedly contribute to the camaraderie and familiarity felt amongst members, each of whom may also interact with others in broader networks within science, academia, or civil services (van Schendelen 1996). Formal decision rules, voting procedures, and record-keeping are not given a high priority: "Anyone who has to ask about procedural rules clearly has not participated in our committee," said a chairwoman overseeing a committee on business contracts for industrial waste clean-up work (interview, Commission DG Enterprise, October 1999), alluding strongly to the shared, informal norms which guide committee action. In addition, there is little desire to expose or clarify the work of the committees; not only because the subject matter can be highly technical, but also because of an insulated approach to committee work. When asked how members of the public might participate in such committees, one respondent said only half-jokingly, "I doubt the general public would even want to know we existed, much less participate in our meetings" (interview, Commission DG Energy and Transport, November 1999, speaker's emphasis).

Council Working Groups

If a Commission proposal—once formulated through the above committees and approved in a meeting of the twenty Commissioners—requires a Council or Council/Parliament decision, it is sent to the Secretariat-General of that institution. The Parliament committee structure carries the major burden of legislation voted in plenary sessions and can, in this way, be compared to Commission committees and Council working groups. However, the Parliamentary committees are the laudable exception to problems of democratic accountability within the rest of the EU committee system. They are open to the public, relatively transparent, and procedurally comprehensible. Thus in the interest of addressing the EU's most pressing democratic issues first, Parliamentary committees are excluded from this analysis.

Once sent to the Council Secretariat-General, the Commission proposal enters a new decision-making process. Sectorally divided Council meetings, composed of national ministers taking the final decisions on Commission proposals, are the main decision-taking centers in the EU. Ministers in Council are assisted by the Committee of Permanent Representatives (COREPER)—consisting of two separate committees of national ambassadors seconded to Brussels—which prepares the agendas and manages the process. In turn, COREPER has delegated these time-consuming tasks to a broad host of working groups. Council documents reveal that during the recent Swedish presidency of the Council, over 300 working groups operated at ostensibly "low levels" (internal document, Council of the EU, 2001; see also Swedish Presidency Web Site). This is where the hard work of examining, discussing, and negotiating consensus on specific Commission proposals is performed by low-ranking national administrators before the legislation is pushed "upward" through the Council hierarchy. Formally speaking, working groups are charged with preparing decisions on behalf of member-state governments, but by most estimates, the final texts of legislation and other actions are decided at this level approximately 90 percent of the time and simply rubber-stamped at higher levels (Rometsch and Wessels 1994, 213). This de facto decision-making authority is surprising in light of the fact that Council committees are not mentioned in the treaties and are only referred to once in the Council's institution-wide rules of procedure (Council of the European Union 2000).

The membership of Council working groups appears clear enough, but several nuances need to be exposed. First, many of the smaller member states lack official representatives comfortable with negotiating highly technical and complex issues. Denmark, the Netherlands, and Finland, for instance, are well known for allowing private industry representatives and contracted experts to attend on behalf of their governments. Second, it is likely that the same individuals who participate in the Commission advisory committees also represent their government in the decision-taking exercises of the Council working groups. Thus, from providing personal, expert opinions in one committee to acting under government instructions in the next, an interesting phenomenon can be observed: "Representatives of Member States who have participated in advisory committees, thus advising the Commission in developing its policy proposal, are naturally also participating—and often playing a crucial role as their country's 'expert' on the subject matter—in shaping their own government's position on such an issue" (Schaefer 1996, 11). When asked for the Council's view of this unmistakable dynamic, one official said, "It certainly helps the process work. That is the nature of European decision-making" (interview, COREPER member, November 1999). Far from provoking any uneasy feelings among participants, these informal and unregulated features of Council working groups are viewed as crucial lubricants of EU policy-making effectiveness.

Procedures and rules in Council working groups are more explicit than in Commission committees, largely because the function of the committees is obvious and modeled on COREPER and Council negotiations. However, unlike the fierce, adversarial bargaining which can characterize high-level Council negotiations, working groups tend to operate under much more consensual conditions. Two factors offer possible explanations. First, working groups tackle the "easy" agenda items first, whereas the more difficult "political" decisions are sent upward to COREPER for decisions (Hayes-Renshaw and Wallace 1997). Secondly, close working relationships foster a strong sense of camaraderie within the Council working groups, with a process of socialization influencing how national interests are determined and defended. Shared frames of reference lead to a negotiation process characterized far more by consensus than by competition (Beyers and Dierickx 1998; Lewis 1998). Whatever the case, the decision-making influence wielded by committee members wearing multiple "hats" and deciding issues in consensual, insulated policy fora is considerable.

Comitology Committees

"Comitology" has become the accepted term for a widely known but poorly understood set of committees within the broader EU committee system. These committees are established by the Council in order to advise, assist, and control the Commission when implementing Council decisions (Docksey and Williams 1994; Dogan 2000; Joerges and Neyer 1997a, 1997b). The need for comitology derives from the fact that the Council, along with the Parliament in some cases, is the sole legislator in the Union's institutional infrastructure. Because the Council does not have the resources to enact its own legislation or to adjust existing rules to changing conditions, it must delegate this responsibility to the Commission. To oversee and control the Commission's delegated implementation powers, the Council has established three different types of comitology committees—advisory, management, and regulatory—composed of member-state officials. Each committee type affords a different level of procedural control by the national members over the Commission chairman when an implementation proposal is tabled. For example, the advisory committee procedures only require the Commission to *consider* the committee's opinion, while the regulatory procedure requires the Commission to secure the approval of a majority of the members. The number of comitology committees has risen dramatically since the 1960s to almost 300 today, a further indication of their critical role in administrative policy-making (see, for example, Dogan 2000; Franchino 2000; Joerges and Vos 1999; Vos 1997; Wessels 1998).

Not only are comitology committees rising in number, they are also taking on a greater number of functions. We might differentiate between the rule-interpreting, fund-approving, and rule-setting functions of the committees (Schaefer 1996, 16). The rule-interpreting function occurs where legal acts adopted at Council level are often general and abstract in nature, requiring specification within comitology committees. In interpreting the intention of the Council, comitology committee members have considerable room for maneuver. The fund-approving function can be found in policy areas such as structural development and research. For example, the Fifth Framework Program for Research and Development includes seventeen comitology committees charged with overseeing the distribution of ECU1.5 billion of research funding amongst different priorities. Finally, these committees are involved in influential rule-setting when, for instance, they change environmental quality limits (such as the amount of lead permissible in drinking water) or make certain chemicals illegal in the EU. All three functions thus expand the remit of simple policy implementation and illustrate the substantial influence comitology can have over different areas of the economy and society.

The influence of comitology on the EU policy process is bolstered by the procedural realities of comitology decision-making. Legalistic approaches typically focus on comitology membership stipulations, procedures, and voting rules—all fixed in statute—to explain the formal role of comitology committees in the EU policy process (Haibach 1999; van der Knaap 1996). Indeed, a formal approach to comitology would examine the powers of the chair of the meeting (a Commission official presenting implementation proposals) and committee members (national civil servants responsible for carrying out the proposals). The member-state representatives will, in all likelihood, attempt to water down Commission propositions, although only in the case of regulatory committees are the decision rules structured to give these representatives the upper hand.

A behavioral approach to comitology, however, sheds light on the *actual* operation of comitology committees, and thus offers some insight into their influence. Comitology committees are well known for eschewing formal rules in favor of informal and consensual procedures. One rule often overlooked concerns access for nonauthorized actors. Some committees, for instance, regularly allow non-member-state participants entry to the proceedings and participation rights when appropriate. When asked whether the participation of environmental NGOs in comitology procedures changes the dynamic of the meeting, one official responded, "It is not as if we have never seen these people before; what is important is that they know how to adapt to our working methods and play a helpful role in our work" (interview, Commission DG Enterprise, November 1999). Thus, a camaraderie and informality similar to those of other committee types exists in comitology as well, often amongst actors who actually have no official participation rights. When pressed on the issue, another official responded with a surprisingly perfunctory air: "Of course we ask non-member-state reps to leave the room at the time of the vote" (interview, Commission DG Enterprise, November 1999). A disregard for membership rules does not *always* lead to inclusive outcomes, however. In 1998, the efforts of two members of the European Parliament to join a critical comitology committee meeting discussing dioxins in poultry were rebuffed following two hours of frantic research on comitology rules (personal communication, European Commission official, November 1999).

The laxity in enforcing the rules of comitology is associated closely with the fact that, again, membership plays a determining role in the camaraderie and consensual policy-making style. Often comitology members may be the same as those found in Commission advisory committees and Council working groups, simply changing "hats"—if not rooms—when a comitology decision needs to be made.

Assessment

How do EU committees stand up to the three principles of democracy outlined earlier in this article?

The first, and perhaps the clearest, finding of the above evidence is the lack of *intelligible politics and procedures* in the EU committee system. Committee governance is both structurally confusing and procedurally obscure. Commission advisory committees are most heavily implicated in this indictment. No rules restrict the creation, functioning, or decision procedures of advisory committees: they are born (and multiply) unrestrained by internal regulation and operate unrestricted by standard rules of procedure.[4] Only a few Commission officials—those concerned directly with the issue at hand—control participant access to a committee. Once in the committee, members enjoy the explicit efforts of the Commission to insulate committee members from external exposure, ostensibly for the sake of securing "independent" opinions and avoiding "public" confrontations.

The second requirement of intelligible politics—clarity of issues at stake and potential solutions—is also much too rigorous for Commission groups. Evidence suggests that far from clearly defining issues and alternatives, these groups work from a fixed set of shared assumptions regarding the nature of policy problems and the "right" solution. Based on past experience and personal capabilities, these assumptions guide action and make clarification to any broader audience unnecessary. Moreover, the vast array of Commission groups, functionally specialized into detailed policy areas yet operating under sweeping and often overlapping remits, makes it virtually impossible to comprehend where an issue will be processed. As Renaud Dehousse (1995, 124) laments: "Who can say with exactitude the number of committees of experts in existence at the European level? Who can vaunt their knowledge of the rules which govern their composition and mode of functioning? At best, a handful of people."

Do Council working groups or comitology committees offer some hope for intelligible politics? The remit of Council groups is, in formal terms, relatively clear: the preparation of issues for decisions by higher levels of COREPER or Council. Committee apologists thus argue that committees process more legislation than they actually decide: eventually decisions must leave Council groups for debate and discussion in the wider EU and national political processes. Yet the procedural steps in Council decision-making are blurred by the realities exposed by empirical evidence. Two powerful incentives operate to ensure that decisions "upstairs" do not depart too far from positions favored by committees. First, these positions usually come recommended by an interinstitutional consensus determined in the course of committee work. Second, highly technical solutions are known to have been addressed in committee settings where complexities are jointly addressed, interlocutors fairly stable, and preferences collectively developed. More senior authorities are loath to change positions adopted at working-group level for fear of uncovering dissent, exposing uncertainties, or, worse, drawing public attention. Therefore, decision-making authority, as well as the processing of the critical issues, is spread throughout the Council chain of command at the expense of procedural clarity.

Comitology committees also offer only an illusion of intelligible politics. As the most formal type of committee, legally authorized comitology committees are governed by a complex set of statutory rules. An extra layer of regulation was added in 2001, when pressure from the European Parliament led the Commission to issue a template to all comitology committees in order to standardize rules of procedure (Council of the European Union 2001). The effects of this endeavor have been slow to materialize, leaving even the keenest observer frustrated by the complexity of comitology. In fact, comitology committees exhibit the ironic trait of having too many rules, thus repelling both EU scholars and practitioners alike. This situation hides the actual implementation and rule-making authority of comitology behind a veil of complex rules and procedures. For comitology committees, as well as Council groups and Commission advisory committees, the system appears to be declining in comprehensibility as quickly as it is increasing in legislative importance.

As presented earlier, a *deliberative policy-making system* is one in which divergent views have access to decision-making and in which those views receive an adequate hearing. The first requirement reflects a normative belief that democratic decision-making should be capable of conveying a variety of conceptions of the public interest into the policy process. Conventional wisdom holds that the EU is an exceptionally open political system, actively encouraging the regular participation of interests in Community processes (Mazey and Richardson 2001; see also Mazey and Richardson 1993). In terms of openness to the participation of new interests, it is certainly the case that the steep increase in new committees correlates with the growth of organized interests in Brussels and a desire by the Commission to draw in a variety of actors. In this way, such committees contribute towards the formation of a "marketplace of ideas," where the EU is arguably more open than national-level governments. Yet when we turn to the second component of deliberative politics—whether issues are considered fairly and thoughtfully— Commission advisory committees are often found lacking. Commission officials act as gatekeepers to committees and determine with impunity what resources and voices are important to Union decision-making. The logic here is one of functional appropriateness, not reflection of the public interest. Thus, while EU committees have proliferated, it is questionable whether a diversity of views has been secured. In this regard, Philippe Schmitter (1989) warns us not to confuse the presence of more actors with an actual increase in the diversity of conceptions of public interest. And, as one official put it, "there is access, and then there is *influence*. Don't confuse the two" (interview, Commission DG Agriculture, December 1999, speaker's emphasis).

To illustrate the point briefly, research revealed that on at least one occasion, Commission officials were upset with their own committee members for harboring a fundamental intolerance towards new participants. In one instance, an effort to widen the membership of a committee charged with classifying dangerous substances evoked hostile reactions: existing participants objected to new challenges that might derail the existing consensus. In that particular case, tempers subsided only when the Commission agreed to consult committee members on the admission of new actors (interviews, Commission DG Enterprise, November 1999). In effect, then, a genuine effort by the Commission to go outside of an established network simply resulted in a more targeted effort to attract the "right" type of actor. Rather than constituting an active effort to reflect the public interest, committee structures may in fact be said to foster an active deflection of the public interest.

Are Council working groups and comitology committees any more deliberative than Commission committees? Here, the interaction and discussion amongst actors representing member states can be held up as a laudable indication of a "bargaining democracy" (Héritier 1999, 275) or as an opportunity for "mutual reflection of preferences and social integration by means of discourse" (Joerges and Neyer 1997b, 621). Indeed, the diversity of opinion amongst member-state representatives can be quite broad, and the close-knit, interactive style of working groups and comitology committees helps to upgrade the "Community interest" (Lewis 1998).

Yet the evidence presented above reveals a darker side to this ostensibly positive perspective. Traits such as low procedural formality, actors wearing many "hats," and disincentives to examine shared frames of reference all may lead to more efficient and consensual outcomes, but they also "mask ideological choices which are not debated and subject to public scrutiny beyond the immediate interests related to the regulatory or management area" (Weiler, Haltern, and Mayer 1995, 33). Moreover, a worrying trend can be found in the Commission's growing number of scientific committees that are intent on drawing deliberation out of the realm of political conflict and into a world of "scientific universalism" immune to political, legal, and regulatory division (Joerges 1997). Evidence suggests that scientific arguments simply become another element in the strategic deployment of resources, not a method to discover new, "enlightened" preferences.

Committee processes and procedures may actually damage deliberation by aggravating existing sources of deliberative democracy. The Council, for example, stands as arguably the strongest reserve of democratic legitimacy in the EU and the arena where national and societal viewpoints can be aired and debated. Yet the vast array of comitology committees offer the attractive opportunity to defer politically difficult questions to the implementation stages, where they can then be processed in lower, less public arenas. Council working groups, too, can be easily criticized for processing a vast amount of Council legislation that never sees the light of high-level political discussion owing to the pro forma approval of much of the Council's agenda.

The third and final principle of democratic governance set forth for committee evaluation was *citizen control over politics*. As described earlier, the notion of accountability concerns the ability to monitor power and to sanction it when used inappropriately. In any political system, administrative activities need to be linked—at some level—with accountable politics. Clearly, bureaucratic accountability, in the form of sanctioning elected officials in charge of bureaucracies, does not yet fully exist in the EU. While this is a democratic weakness, it would not be such a serious problem if other accountability mechanisms could be found. Unfortunately, political or administrative accountability of committees, their members, and those members' actions is little more than illusory. Again, the worst culprits are Commission advisory committees, but the fault here lies largely in the position of such committees within the broader institutional hierarchy. The structure of the European Commission, for instance, is such that the college of Commissioners—the twenty European ministers nominated by national governments every five years—is the only body with defensible democratic qualifications. Below this level, political and administrative hierarchies tend to dissolve (Christiansen 1996). Therein lies a primary reason behind the failure of committee accountability: the average Commission committee is answerable to no one but the handful of officials directly responsible for—and reliant on—its operation. A telling sign of the uncontrollable nature of committee governance is the fact that, in the Commission, no central lists of advisory groups exist. Information is now being collected and collated, but it is a difficult process (interview, Commission Secretariat-General, May 2001).

If we subscribe to the notion that responsibility should flow from individual members of committees, rather than the committee system in abstract, Council working groups and comitology committees appear slightly more accountable. National representatives are ostensibly just that: emissaries of a particular government, responsible for voicing the opinion of, and negotiating for, their political masters. In reality, however, working-party representatives are several steps removed from links with national governments. One reason for this is that committee members are drawn largely from the ranks of middle- to low-level specialists residing in Brussels as part of permanent representations or from specialist units within national ministries. Research shows that their actions in Brussels may go unreported (or even falsely reported) at higher ministerial levels (interviews, national civil servants, October–November 1999).[5] For a member state sending industry representatives on behalf of the government, the problem of accountability may be compounded.

The structural and procedural elements of comitology also point to a disturbing lack of accountability. When new Council laws assign implementation authority to a comitology committee, no specification is made of which committee shall be responsible (see also Dogan 2000, 47). Thus the creation, delegation of authority, and management of comitology are driven "underground," beneath the level of political accountability. Procedural barriers also exist to committee accountability. EU committees are characterized by consensual decision-making and informal voting practices, where individual differences and conflicts are glossed over. More specifically, committees exhibit procedural tendencies toward "creative ambiguity," where decisions are designed to allow actors to put different interpretations on outcomes, and "log-rolling," where decisions are crafted to obscure winners and losers on any given issue (Lord 1998, 91).

Combined or alone, these features tend to obscure responsibilities and make it difficult to hold committees to task for decisions taken. To complete our conceptualization of democratic committee governance, a simple nine-cell matrix is both helpful and applicable to future research (see table 5.1). On the horizontal axis, the three different types of committee are listed; on the vertical axis, the three principles of democracy appear. Committee types are assessed on a scale ranging from "low" to "high" depending on how well each type adheres to the democratic standards set out earlier.

Conclusion: The Future of Committees in the EU

The preceding analysis provided a manageable set of democratic principles applicable to committee governance, offered a broad-brush typology of committees, and then applied the democratic principles to the committee evidence at hand. The obvious conclusion to be drawn is that while European committees contribute substantially to the effectiveness of European policy-making, they are also a democratic liability. The next step for future research should involve using the typology and principles as an analytical framework for more specific research involving case studies. Unfortunately, in this article there is little space to delve into such detail. Even though continued research is crucial, a few practical thoughts on how to improve the democratic credentials of the EU committee system are in order. The aim, of course, is to

Table 5.1 Assessing the Democratic Credentials of EU Committees

Democratic Principles	Committee Types		
	Commission Council Advisory Committees	**Working Groups**	**Comitology Committees**
Intelligible Politics			
Clear procedures and identifiable actors?	*Low*	*Low*	*Middle*
Clear issues at stake?	*Low*	*Low*	*Middle*
Deliberative Politics			
Access for diverging views?	*Middle*	*Low*	*Low*
Issues considered fairly?	*Low*	*Low*	*Low*
Accountable Politics			
Individuals held accountable?	*Low*	*Middle*	*Middle*
System held accountable?	*Low*	*Middle*	*Middle*

provide suggestions for democratic improvement that do not incapacitate the policy-making capacities of EU committees. Therefore, the following proposals adhere to the wise advice that "Reform policies should be formulated in small, clearly stated stages so that their premises can be scrutinized and their implications are transparent" (Höreth 1999, 264).

1. *Openness and Transparency:* Since a vast majority of public complaints about European decision-making emanate from a lack of understanding of EU-level governance, any attempt to reactivate public support must face this challenge. A critical first step is the creation of an open list of committees, including committee names, respective remits, and participant lists. A systematic procedure for making agendas and minutes available to the public is another simple but crucial reform. Prioritizing the education of the public by mobilizing the EU's information services, even if only to offer clear descriptions of EU policy sector competencies and the status of legislation, would be both a symbolic and a significant move in the right direction. Opening meetings to observers could provide a crucial element of accountability to committee proceedings and provide an identification of the most relevant actors. There is no reason why comitology committees, for example, should not be open to members of the European Parliament. Of course, some efficiency may be sacrificed, but the benefits gained from oversight—or at least the potential for oversight—would be immeasurable. The office of the EU ombudsman should be strengthened and encouraged to become a "citizens' advocate" by overseeing and mandating public notices, the publications of documents, and transparent working practices. Finally, public hearings should become a standard part of the EU policy process, much as they are in some national systems. Here, the European Parliament could play a constructive role in this regard by hosting the public hearings through their committee system.

2. *Consistency and Standardization:* Another basic problem of the EU committee system can be found in its structural informality. On the one hand, a broad diversity of committees exists in the EU; on the other hand, their roles and functions sometimes blur. In order to

alleviate the surreptitious creation of committees and to prevent committees performing unauthorized Community functions, an institutionalization of the EU committee system is necessary. First, the distinction between Commission advisory committees, Council working groups, and comitology committees should be formally recognized. Second, following a Community-wide discussion of the role of these committees in the Community process, legislation should establish the general remits of each and their expected function. Third, there should be an agreed-upon template for committee rules of internal procedure, and this model should form the basis for the approved rules of each committee. The Commission initiated this reform recently in the case of comitology (see Council of the European Union 2001); similar measures should now be applied equally to other committee categories. Not only would this reform provide a necessary consistency in operational principles, it would also create a more level playing field for those wishing to understand—and to participate in—committee procedures. The intent of any effort to standardize committee governance should be to strengthen and to centralize internal oversight procedures—in essence, to encourage each Community institution to "get its house in order."

3. *Strengthening Accountability:* A fundamental weakness of the EU committee system concerns the absence of structural oversight. The creation, constitution, and functioning—and even the very existence—of committees often goes unnoticed by actors in other institutions. Since the Commission, Council, and Parliament already interact in institutionalized patterns of cooperation and competition, each institution should have committee-monitoring rights over the others. A system of checks and balances could be developed by which an institution wishing to create a committee and to assign it a certain remit would have to make this information available for scrutiny by the others. The workload involved with implementing this reform would not be prohibitive, because it would operate primarily on the basis of notification. In fact, some moves have already been made in this direction. In 2000, an interinstitutional agreement stipulated that the Parliament would receive agendas, minutes, and action summaries in the area of comitology.[6] This procedure should now be expanded to include all committees, and particularly to include committee formation and membership. Furthermore, the Parliament holds much promise as a mechanism of accountability. The Parliament's role in the downfall of the scandal-struck Santer Commission in 1999 shows not only its growing institutional muscle, but also its seriousness about enforcing accountability in the European policy process. This trend should be encouraged, with parliamentary scrutiny reaching as far as possible into the EU committee system.

Ultimately, improving committee openness and accountability will not incapacitate the effectiveness of committee governance. It may put pressure on committees to open their proceedings to external observers and to publish more thoroughly their actions—but this would be an acceptable trade-off to secure more solid democratic foundations. Some committees may not object; the ones that do should have to justify why closed proceedings are an integral part of policy-making. Thus the proposals would have an immediate effect on committee governance. They may also have longer-term influence, however, if they encourage a change of thinking amongst European policy makers. The conventional paradigm of European governance, oriented as it has been toward the creation of effective policy and "integration by stealth," requires urgent adjustment. The notion of enlightened administrators working on behalf of uninformed publics has always been an arrogant approach to European policy-making. In today's world, it may very well be dangerous, too. We have already seen the mobilization of public support in defense of national interests rather than supranational solutions (Hayward 1996, 225). Without immediate attention to European governance and a meaningful effort to rebalance system effectiveness and democratic legitimacy, the EU faces an uncertain future.

Rhinard, Mark. "The Democratic Legitimacy of the European Union Committee System." *Governance* 15, no. 2 (2002): 185–210. http://www.nrc.nl/redactie/Doc/weblog/europa/rhinard.pdf (20 July 2009). Reproduced with permission of Blackwell Publishing Ltd.

* * *

Critical Factors for Enhancing Municipal Public Hearings

William H. Baker, H. Lon Addams, and Brian Davis

Public participation has long been a fundamental element of local and national governmental processes in the United States. Conceptually, public participation empowers citizens to influence government actions through various means of involvement. Burby (2003, 35) summarizes four arguments for citizen involvement that go beyond the obvious goal of producing better decisions:

1. The principle of fairness or equity.
2. The right of citizens to be informed and to express their views on governmental decisions.
3. The need to represent the interests of disadvantaged and powerless groups.
4. The need to capture the insights of citizens.

Burby states that citizen involvement can "generate information, understanding, and agreement on problems and ways of solving them. It can give stakeholders a sense of ownership . . . and ease the formation of coalitions who will work hard for their realization." Burby's empirical research on municipal planning shows that citizen involvement in the municipal planning process does indeed result in better plans and greater public acceptance of those plans, and it reduces the likelihood that latent opposition groups will arise unexpectedly at the last moment. King, Feltey, and Susel cite a "growing recognition on the part of administrators that decision making without public participation is ineffective" (1998, 319), and Young's article on political activism summarizes a number of governmental entities that have recently undertaken proactive measures to increase public participation in their decision making (2001, 677–79).

The public participation literature identifies at least six useful standards for evaluating public input methods (Crosby, Kelly, and Schaefer 1986, 171; Fiorino 1990, 229; Lowndes et al. 1998, 43; Rowe and Frewer 2000, 11–16; Smith, Nell, and Prystupa 1997, 143):

- Participants should be representative of the broad public.
- Proceedings should be fair, cost-effective, and flexible.
- Proceedings should increase the public's understanding.
- Proceedings should enable citizen participation and influence in discussion and decision making.
- Proceedings should promote improved decision making.
- The public should have at least some degree of satisfaction with the outcome, resulting in subsequent sustained public participation.

Although public participation makes good theoretical sense, many problems are encountered in actual practice. Participants in research conducted by King, Feltey, and Susel (1998, 320) indicated they agreed with the concept of public participation, but found the way it is currently practiced and framed problematic. Further, confrontational relationships may occur because many citizens feel they cannot trust the government (Pew Research Center 2000). Additional reasons relate to the attitudes of public officials. Walters, Aydelotte, and Miller (2000, 349–50) summarize six reasons for these attitudes:

1. Today's problems are too complex for the lay public to comprehend.
2. Democratic decision making is irrational.
3. The public is either disinterested or self-serving.
4. Democratic decision making and rational decision making have different goals.
5. Officials don't want to share power in making decisions.
6. Citizen participation means slower, more expensive, more complicated, and more emotionally draining processes.

In Great Britain, Lowndes et al. (1998, 17) cite a growing interest in more innovative public participation techniques, although traditional methods (such as public meetings) are still the dominant method. The same can be said of the United States: Public administrators have expressed an interest in alternative participation methods, but public hearings are still the most pervasive form of public participation (Fiorino 1990, 228). Hearings are mandated by law in most states and in many communities across the country, and Nalbandian (1999, 189) suggests that public hearings, discussions, deliberations, and other means of fostering citizen participation are important ways for municipal managers to strengthen needed community-building efforts.

In spite of the widespread use of public hearings, relatively little research has been conducted to refine this communication event. Our research attempts to address that void. This article, based on nationwide survey research, offers guidelines that can help public managers to maximize the potential of this widely used communication genre. We first review the public hearing literature and describe the study design, and then we analyze and discuss the survey's qualitative and quantitative data.

PUBLIC HEARING LITERATURE

Despite their popularity, public hearings often fail to achieve their intended goals, frustrating both agencies and communities. After analyzing various public participation methods, King, Feltey, and Susel (1998, 323) concluded that "the most ineffective technique is the public hearing." One reason is that administrators may comply minimally with laws requiring a public hearing, simply going through the motions without real intent (Burby 2003, 36). Walters, Aydelotte, and Miller (2000, 357) point out, however, that laws requiring public hearings are usually only minimum standards, and additional input methods can be used to great advantage. For example, if a law requires hearings, public administrators can employ other input methods earlier in the decision process. Regarding balancing the need for public input and the need for technical input on difficult decisions, Thomas (1995, 93) states that decision makers should seek more public input when acceptance of a decision is more important and less public input when technical knowledge is more important.

Additional problems are that hearings are sometimes held at difficult times and locations and too late in the decision-making process. The public hearing is "ineffective and conflictual, and it happens too late in the process. . . . Therefore, rather than cooperating to decide how best to address issues, citizens are reactive and judgmental, often sabotaging administrators' best efforts" (King, Feltey, and Susel 1998, 320). Middendorf and Busch (1997, 50) point out that public hearing communication is often one way—a monologue rather than a dialogue—and input from the public is too tightly controlled. Lowndes et al. (1998, 83) cite a lack of awareness about participation opportunities as a limitation. Another problem is that many hearings attract very small crowds, perhaps because of citizens' lack of trust in government officials and assumptions their input does not make a difference—for example, a belief that the government does not truly care what people think (Ebdon 2002, 289).

Adding to this credibility problem is citizens' lack of interest concerning public issues (Davis 2000, 43). Attracting and involving younger citizens and ethnic minorities has also proven to be challenging (Lowndes et al. 1998, 47). Midden's (1995, 316) research in Europe identified participation differences on the bases of gender (more men than women participate), age (less involvement by the very young and the very old), education (more participation by the well educated), and political persuasion (overrepresentation by left-wing citizens). Even on critical health-related issues that were widely publicized by government or by private firms, Golding, Krimsky, and Plough (1992, 32) concluded that citizens didn't participate because they were alienated by "media sensationalism," as well as by mitigation companies (firms whose services help clients minimize risk or achieve compliance) out to make a fast buck. Government officials thus face a media dilemma—on the one hand trying to communicate in an objective and nonsensational way, while on the other hand trying to highlight the critical nature of the subject to build public interest (Chipman et al. 1996, 138).

Although the literature highlights numerous challenges facing administrators as they attempt to hold effective public hearings, this meeting format continues to be the most pervasive type of public participation method. Thus, research is needed to identify best practices and to assist administrators in improving the effectiveness of their public hearings.

Table 5.2   Factors Contributing to the Success or Failure of Public Hearings

Phase	Rank	N	Success/failure factors
Prehearing	7	37	—Good planning (clear goals, good timing, accessible location, prepared officials, reports, procedures, and agenda)/poor planning (vague goals, poor timing, poor location, unprepared people, reports, procedures, and agenda)
	6	42	—Effective notification/ineffective notification
	4	49	—High public interest in topic/limited public interest in topic
	3	69	—Effective prehearing education (including refuting false information)/inadequate prehearing education
Hearing	1	73	—Good meeting conductor, facilitator/ineffective meeting conductor, facilitator
	2	71	—Clear, complete presentation at beginning of the hearing, with visual aids, graphics, handout materials/unclear, incomplete message at beginning of hearing, with inadequate handouts and graphics
	5	43	—Adequate opportunity for public input/inadequate time or opportunity for public input
	8	35	—Open, receptive attitude of city officials/closed, unreceptive attitude of city officials
	10	26	—Open-minded citizens/narrow-minded, emotionally charged citizens who are unwilling to listen or talk rationally
Posthearing	9	32	—Effective action and follow-up on citizens' input/untimely, inadequate action and follow-up on citizens' input

STUDY DESIGN

This research study employed survey methodology to study public hearings in U.S. cities with populations of 25,000 to 99,999. The membership database of the International City/County Management Association, the nation's largest local public management organization, included 1,031 cities in this population range. From this list of cities, we used systematic random sampling to select 500 cities for inclusion in the study. After numbering the managers of these cities from 1 to 500, we sent the 250 odd-numbered managers a questionnaire asking about the *most*-successful recent public hearing in their community, and we sent the 250 even-numbered managers a questionnaire relating to their recent *least*-successful public hearing. Our study examined city managers' perceptions of success; we did not survey citizens who attended the hearings. However, as our results show, these city managers' definitions of success reflect balanced sensitivity to citizen and government concerns.

The survey instrument was first pilot tested with city managers and then refined and prepared for mailing. The final questionnaire contained one open (qualitative) question and 14 closed (quantitative) questions. The open question asked the respondents to list the three most significant factors they felt had contributed to the success of their most-successful public hearings or to the failure of their least-successful public hearings. The closed questions requested information on more detailed aspects of the hearings. Two mailings of the questionnaire generated 256 usable responses, a 51.2 percent return rate. Forty-six of the 50 United States were represented in the responses. Of the 256 city managers who responded, 121 (47.3 percent) answered a questionnaire focusing on their least-successful hearing; 135 (52.7 percent) responded to the questionnaire regarding their most-successful hearing.

ANALYSIS OF QUALITATIVE DATA

The city managers were asked to consider all of the public hearings in which they had participated and to indicate three factors that contributed most to the success or failure of those public hearings. Respondents focused on either success or failure factors according to the group in which they were placed. To process the qualitative data, we individually read the detailed responses and inductively developed a list of categories into which all of the comments could be classified. We then compared our individual results and consolidated them into a final category list. Using the final list, we classified all of the comments, eliminating items with a frequency of 10 or less. Table 5.2 shows the final 10 critical factors, along with their frequencies (n = 477) and rankings.

ANALYSIS OF QUANTITATIVE DATA

The quantitative data came from city managers' reflections on one recent public hearing their city had held. The managers answered according to the "successful" or "unsuccessful" perspective they had been assigned. We analyzed these data to determine whether any public hearing planning or execution factors correlated with managers' perceived success. Only five of the closed questions generated statistically significant differences between more- and less-successful hearings (see table 5.3). Specifically, more successful hearings had (1) a greater number and mix of prehearing educational methods, (2) more media types and greater media

Table 5.3   Statistical Results of Quantitative Data Analysis

Prehearing	Most successful	Least successful
Notification methods	NS*	NS
Education	More methods	Fewer methods
Location	NS	NS
Hearing		
Topic		
Format		
Communication media	More media used	Fewer media used
Audience management	More speaker control	Less speaker control
Ratio of presenter/audience input	NS	NS
Length of hearing	NS	NS
Participation by public officials	NS	NS
Posthearing		
Open follow-up meeting	Yes	No
Number of media used in communicating final decision	More media	Fewer media

*NS = No statistically significant difference at the .05 level of confidence.

Table 5.4   Methods and Media Used to Educate the Public

Method	Most	Least	Overall	p value
Newspaper	70.4	65.3	68.0	.384
Direct mail	43.0	35.5	39.5	.225
Oral presentations	42.2	31.4	37.1	.074
Television	25.9	19.8	23.0	.248
Documents in public places	23.0	19.8	21.5	.543
Website	20.0	14.0	17.2	.208
Radio	11.1	9.1	10.2	.593
Other	17.0	14.0	15.6	.511
Number of methods used	2.32	2.09		.019

frequency used in the informational presentation, (3) more control over speakers' presentation time, (4) greater usage of an open follow-up meeting, and (5) more use of newspaper and direct mail to communicate posthearing decisions to the public. Detailed analyses of the quantitative data follow.

Prehearing Factors

We gathered information about three prehearing factors: notification, education, and location.

Notification Methods and Media. Cities employed an average of three notification methods to advertise public hearings, and the ranking was the same for most- and least-successful public hearings. The following methods were used: newspaper, 97 percent; direct mail, 51.2 percent; posted public notices, 48.8 percent; television, 34.8 percent; and Web sites, 28.5 percent. Oral announcements, community organizations, and radio announcements all had frequencies of less than 25 percent. Analyzing most- and least-successful public hearing data, we found no significant difference in either the total number of methods used or the mix of methods.

Educational Methods. Our next question went beyond mere notification and focused on how the cities educated citizens about public hearing issues. Table 5.4 shows no significant difference in the mix of methods used, but it indicates a consistent and statistically significant difference in the total number of methods used ($p = .019$), meaning that the most-successful hearings were accompanied by a greater number of educational methods than were the least-successful hearings. Although this finding does not prove a causal relationship between educational efforts and meeting success, it does suggest the possibility of such a relationship. Providing better prehearing education enables the audience to be more well informed about the hearing.

Location of Hearings. The overwhelming majority of the hearings were held in a city or county building (93 percent of the least-successful and 89 percent of the most-successful hearings were held in these facilities). The difference between the most- and least-successful public hearings was not statistically significant ($p = .666$). Because the large majority of hearings were held in city or county buildings, this study was unable to analyze the effect of holding hearings in other locations. Additional research is needed to analyze the impact of location on public hearing participation.

Hearing Factors

Seven survey questions dealt with the actual hearing, including the (1) meeting topic, (2) meeting format, (3) communication media used, (4) audience management, (5) meeting structure, (6) length of hearing, and (7) participation by elected and appointed city officials.

Topic of Hearing. Regarding the topic of the public hearing that each manager used as the basis for answering the questionnaire, our analysis showed no statistically significant difference between the most- and least-successful hearings. Thus, the public hearing topic does not appear to be a good predictor of success or failure. Zoning changes, land development, and budget matters constituted about three-fourths of all of the public hearings—72.5 percent for the most successful and 74.2 for the least successful. Other hearing types mentioned by at least 5 percent of the respondents included land-use changes; roads, streets, parking; and water and utility issues.

Meeting Format. Respondents indicated great similarity in how the most- and least-successful public hearings were structured. Overall, 90 percent of the hearings employed an initial presentation to a large group, followed by an opportunity for the audience to give input and ask questions. Thus, we found no statistically significant difference in the structure of the most- and least-successful public hearings ($p = .135$).

Communication Media. Cities used a variety of technologies in their presentations to the public. Table 5.5 shows that charts, maps, and handouts were used by more than 50 percent of the cities. Compared with the least-successful hearings, the most-successful hearings used a greater number of communication media ($p = .008$), with statistically significant differences for photographs ($p = .026$) and projected noncomputerized media, such as slides and video ($p = .004$). Although the current study did not determine how such usage actually affected hearing success, the greater media richness in the most successful hearings may have contributed to greater message clarity by capitalizing on the audiences' visual and aural senses.

Audience Management. In the least-successful hearings, 51.3 percent employed a time limit on each person's input; 46.9 percent allowed each individual to speak as long as desired. Conversely, 61 percent of the most-successful hearings employed a time limit on audience input; only 34.7 percent allowed individuals to speak as long as desired. The difference between the least- and most-successful hearings was statistically significant ($p = .031$), with the most-successful

Table 5.5 Usage of Communication Media

Technology	Most	Least	Overall	p value
Charts	71.1	64.5	68.0	.255
Maps	70.4	64.5	67.6	.313
Handouts	61.5	57.0	59.4	.469
Reports and position papers	51.9	38.0	45.3	.026*
Photographs	51.9	44.6	48.4	.248
Computerized media	40.0	31.4	35.9	.152
Lecture	32.6	28.9	30.9	.526
Noncomputerized media	34.1	18.2	26.6	.004*
3-D models	6.7	5.0	5.9	.561
Other	5.9	3.3	4.7	.322

*$p < .05$.

hearings exerting more control over audience members' speaking time. Given the heightened emotions in many public hearings, audience management appears to be an important factor.

Meeting Structure. This study analyzed the ratio of municipal and audience input. Overall, municipal presenters occupied the floor most of the time in the first quarter of the meeting, the audience occupied the majority of the time in the second and third quarters of the meeting, and the presenter and audience shared meeting time relatively equally during the fourth quarter. Thus, the meetings became more interactive as time passed. No statistically significant differences between the least- and most-successful meetings were found (p values for the four quarters were .619, .604, .563, and .150, respectively).

Length of Hearing. Our statistics revealed that the length of public hearings varied widely, probably because of the issues being discussed or the audience-management methods used. Overall, roughly one-third of the meetings lasted less than one hour; another one-third lasted one to two hours. Only about 10 percent lasted more than three hours. We found no statistically significant difference in length between the most- and least-successful hearings ($p = .668$).

Participation by Elected and Appointed Officials. Survey responses indicated that approximately a dozen city officials attended the hearings, with slightly more elected than appointed city officials attending. The difference in attendance of elected officials between the most- and least-successful hearings, however, was not statistically significant ($p = .307$). An average of 6.65 elected and 5.43 appointed representatives attended the most-successful meetings; an average of 6.38 elected and 4.23 appointed officials attended the least-successful hearings. The *p* values for elected and appointed officials were .448 and .092, respectively.

Posthearing Factors

We questioned city managers about two posthearing factors: (1) what follow-up actions were taken after the hearing, and (2) how city officials communicated their final decisions to the public.

Follow-up Actions. Citizens obviously want public officials to consider their input seriously. Therefore, we gathered information about follow-up actions taken after the public hearing. Table 5.6 shows the actions taken, with more than 90 percent of the respondents indicating some type of follow-up action. Compared with the profile of the least-successful hearings, the most-successful hearings showed a higher percentage of open follow-up meetings ($p = .032$).

Communication of Final Decisions to the Public. After the public hearings, final decisions were communicated to the public in a variety of ways (see table 5.7). Compared with the least-

Table 5.6   Follow-up Action Taken on Audience Input

Action Taken	Most	Least	Overall	p value
Took no action	6.7	10.7	8.6	.245
Reviewed in closed meeting	8.9	5.0	7.0	.219
Reviewed in open meeting	36.3	24.0	30.5	.032*
Reviewed by individuals outside of meetings	55.6	43.8	50.0	.060
Other	17.8	17.4	17.6	.929

*p < .05.

Table 5.7   Methods Used to Communicate Final Decisions to the Public

Method	Most	Least	Overall	p value
Newspaper (city-authored)	34.1	20.7	27.7	.017*
Newspaper (independent)	74.8	62.8	69.1	.038*
Radio	14.8	16.5	15.6	.706
Television	30.4	30.6	30.5	.971
Public notices	9.6	10.7	10.2	.768
Direct mail	27.4	9.1	18.8	.000*
Website	19.3	16.5	18.0	.570
Oral announcements	15.6	17.4	16.4	.698
Other	17.0	10.7	14.1	.148

successful hearings, the most-successful hearings employed significantly more city-authored newspaper articles ($p = .017$), independently authored newspaper articles ($p = .038$), and direct mail ($p = .000$).

DISCUSSION

The city managers participating in this study identified 10 factors that exert a critical influence on public hearings. First, the prehearing elements emphasize planning and the important, but difficult, tasks of notifying and educating the public and building interest in the issue to be discussed at the public hearing. Also important is the need to orient officials, prepare information, and develop procedures. Second, the hearing factors highlight the crucial initial presentation and the skillful facilitation of audience input. Further, adequate time must be provided for individuals' comments, but the facilitator also must effectively carry out crowd control and manage people's emotions. Third, effective follow-up is essential to inform citizens of the city officials' final decisions. The following sections discuss the research findings and offer prescriptive guidelines for improving public hearings.

Prehearing Factors

The first critical prehearing factor reflects the importance of planning, including clarifying goals, deciding when and where to hold the hearing, orienting city officials, developing an effective agenda and procedures, and preparing effective written and oral reports. Typical negative responses from surveyed city managers concerning the lack of meeting preparation included "staff reports not complete," "poor preparation by staff and presenter," "lack of understanding of facts by elected officials," and "inadequate research on overall effect of proposed issue."

Concerning goals, officials need to decide whether the purpose of the hearing is primarily to inform or to invite public comment that can influence their decision. Walters, Aydelotte, and Miller state, "It is crucial to the success of citizen involvement that decision makers determine in advance how the results will be used" (2000, 354). This study highlights the fact that public hearings should be just one part of an overall public participation strategy. Our literature review reveals that probably the most frequently cited criticisms of public hearings relate to when they are held in the decision-making process (timing) and how the public input is utilized (impact). Consequently, public hearings often become a combative encounter. Citizens become frustrated because they want to influence the outcome, whereas government wants only decision acceptance. If citizen stakeholders are appropriately involved from the problem definition through the decision, the decision often will be better and citizen buy-in will be greater.

Everyone involved in planning and executing the hearing needs a solid knowledge of all of the relevant issues and facts. The person giving the initial presentation must be especially prepared to launch the meeting and give the presentation. How an issue is framed is critical. Procedural matters also must be well planned to ensure that hearings run smoothly. For example, how will citizen input be managed and captured? Will everyone meet in large groups or break into small groups? Finally, officials may need to be reminded to keep an open and receptive mind.

Of the four prehearing factors cited as critical, three pertain to the difficult task of getting people to attend. Obviously, if few people attend, a public hearing cannot obtain broad public input, a critical factor in effective public participation. Regarding attendance problems, survey respondents cited "lack of interest," "lack of interest: no tax increase, no public [attendance]," and "insufficient press coverage." King, Feltey, and Susel (1998, 322) emphasize that it is especially difficult to get younger people to public hearings. Two other comments provide possible causes of attendance problems. The first, a positive comment about public officials, states that the "public [does have] faith in good government decisions," suggesting that some citizens feel their input would not improve decision quality. The second comment reflects negatively on public officials: "Participants feel [the] decision has already been made [and that] their input will not matter." Holding meetings earlier in the process, as previously stated, would help to overcome this problem. In addition, public officials must work to build trust during every interaction with the public (Frewer et al. 1996, 484). They must solicit, listen to, and genuinely act on public input, demonstrating that this input is valued and does indeed make a difference. British research shows that citizens were most likely to participate in "issues that mattered." The list included such problems as the environment, crime, housing, and health issues (Lowndes et al. 1998, 71). Other research also shows that people who stand to gain or lose from proposed governmental programs often will become more involved (Balla 2000, 636).

Prehearing communication relies almost completely on the effective use of media, such as newsletters, newspapers, public notices, radio, television, and the Internet. Research by the Pew Research Center (1998) shows changes in readership trends for newspapers, television, radio, and the Internet, with Internet usage up and nightly network news down. Print audiences seem to be holding steady. Studies reveal a positive correlation between mass communication's coverage of a public issue and public awareness and opinion (McCombs, 1997, 437; Sei-Hill, Scheufele, and Shanahan 2002, 7). Thus, municipalities should work closely with the media to get good coverage of the issues. However, because all of these media may be ignored by the citizenry, cities have an ongoing challenge to get people to notice, read, and respond appropriately to the messages.

Cities also should consider using multiple public participation methods and approach public participation from a strategic standpoint, rather than considering any one method or agency in isolation (Walters, Aydelotte, and Miller 2000, 357). Lando (2003, 80) states that local governmental decisions fall into two categories: (1) those that provide basic municipal direction and have a large impact on citizens, and (2) those that are largely irrelevant to citizens in general. Public hearings that are used mainly to disseminate information are more effective for the latter purpose; hearings that capture citizen input to influence decisions are more appropriate for the former.

For maximum effectiveness, city administrators should employ a multifaceted approach to media and communication. Research by McLeod, Scheufele, and Moy (1999, 329) included a study of the impact of newspaper, television, and interpersonal discussion on a person's likelihood of involvement in a civic forum. Their findings suggest that television seems to make people aware of a public issue but gives limited details about the issue. For more information, citizens then often turn to newspapers. Of the three factors studied, however, interpersonal discussion of an issue was most highly correlated with a person's actual participation in a civic forum. British research recommends that public officials work through both informal and formal leaders and actively recruit participants rather than wait for citizens to come forward (Lowndes et al. 1998, 73). Neighborhood groups can be tremendously influential at the interpersonal discussion level. Carson (1999, 40) highlights the benefits that ordinary telephone calls from city hall can provide. Citing the use of phone calls to citizens as a form of "deliberative democracy," Carson observes that she is "constantly surprised by the extent to which people . . . divulge quite personal information to a stranger over the phone."

Nearly all of the public hearings reported in this study were held in a municipal building rather than a more geographically distributed format. King, Feltey, and Susel (1998, 323) emphasize that distributing meeting locations can help, such as holding hearings in elementary schools throughout the city rather than requiring everyone to come to city hall. As Young reminds us, "Even when a series of public hearings are announced for an issue, people who might wish to speak at them need to know about them, be able to arrange their work and child care schedule to be able to attend, be able to get to them, and have enough understanding of the hearing process to participate. Each of these abilities is unevenly present among members of a society" (2001, 681). Taking hearings to the citizens helps to address this area of inequality in our society.

In spite of the best efforts by public officials, however, Davis (2000, 43) suggests that most of the population, because they are less politically interested, will refuse to take an active interest in public issues, regardless of what information is provided or how it is provided to them. Further, Davis states that the majority of American adults don't watch television news regularly, nor do they read newspapers daily—and those who do read newspapers do so mainly for nonpolitical news. If Davis's assertions are true, it appears that public officials must simply do the best they can, using multiple notification methods and multiple strategies and realizing there is no magic solution to the problem.

Along with effective notification, cities must also educate the public during the prehearing phase, including combating false information. Reporting on how a lack of good prehearing education affects public hearings, city managers commented, "the majority of residents were ignorant," "incomplete information available," and "misinformation distributed by interest groups prior to meeting." To combat these problems, cities can use a variety of methods including articles in newspapers and newsletters, explanations on the city's Web site, presentations at neighborhood groups and other public meetings, and public service announcements aired on public radio and television.

There was a statistically significant, positive relationship between the richness of the media mix and public hearing success. Thus, cities should cultivate a positive relationship with local mass media. Several studies highlight the major agenda-setting role that newspapers play. Thus, newspapers should be used to both notify and educate the public. Also, to overcome the frequent problem of subject complexity (Ebdon 2002, 289), municipalities must learn to effectively communicate in the language of lay persons. How an issue is framed is critical in informing and educating the public, both before and during public hearings.

Hearing Factors

Unlike the mediated communications with the public during the prehearing phase, communication during the actual hearing is face to face and involves all of the dynamics of human interaction: spoken messages, nonverbal messages, listening, human emotions, defensiveness, turf protection, individual agendas, and more. Table 5.2 reveals that the two most frequently mentioned critical success factors at this phase are giving a good initial presentation and facilitating the communication exchange effectively.

Selecting an effective presenter is critical in launching the meeting and laying the groundwork for the meeting. Regarding the initial presentation, numerous city managers mentioned poor presentations as a major cause of public hearing failure: "poor presentation," "not preparing and presenting a thorough, understandable outline of the issues to be discussed," and "not enough graphics, visual aids, etc." Often the person who knows the most about the issue is not the best person to present. This person may have poor communication skills, may be too close to the subject to be objective, or may be unable to articulate technical topics to a lay public. It is vital for the presenter to be able to frame the issue from the public's point of view and to clearly communicate technical information in lay terms. Rehearsing the presentation in front of a pilot audience can refine the presenter's delivery.

Commenting on critical factors helping to achieve success, many city managers made comments such as "having good, simple-to-understand information to hand out" and "good staff presentations; e.g., written, PowerPoint, handouts, drawings." An oral presentation with no accompanying visuals is difficult for an audience to follow, especially for technical, complex subject matter. Providing information that can be seen and not just heard can be a tremendous help. Examples include printed executive summaries and PowerPoint slides, but even these can be used ineffectively if they aren't well designed. For example, many presenters use too many bulleted text slides with no visual augmentation. Photographs, line drawings, process charts, and visual models can greatly enrich the clarity and visual appeal.

City managers also point out the importance of clarifying the purpose to the participants. If participants don't understand the purpose, they will infer their own. One administrator stated, "The first step is to make it clear that you're going to be receptive to their comments. But also . . . a critical second step to maintaining their trust is to demonstrate to them that they're being heard" (King, Feltey, and Susel 1998, 320).

Following the initial presentation, meeting facilitation becomes critical. In fact, facilitation was the most frequently mentioned factor contributing to the success or failure of public hearings. City managers commented on "lack of leadership in running meetings," "lack of capabilities of [the] person chairing the hearing," and "failure of chair to control [the] meeting." Effectively facilitating the discussion and sensitively managing audience emotion require the meeting conductor to have highly polished human and communication skills. Facilitators must be incredibly patient and thick-skinned. As Nalbandian points out, "facilitative work is not designed to 'make people feel better.' It is designed to help promote a problem-solving orientation and to develop consensus among diverse interests" (1999, 195). Crewson and Fisher (1997, 384) also emphasize the importance of learning these critical interpersonal and community-building skills for today's public managers.

Respondents identified two frequent problems exhibited by hearing facilitators: failure to manage time and failure to manage audience emotions. Typical respondent comments were as follows:

Time management:

- "Weak chair's failure to move agenda along"
- "Too much repetition of statements by audience"
- "Unlimited public input"
- "Lack of fair way to control speaking time"

Emotion management:

- "Disruption by a small minority"
- "Failure of both sides to respect the others' point of view"
- "Inability of elected officials to control audience"

Bryson and Anderson (2000, 144–45) state that for large-group planning and implementation meetings, the facilitator should be more of a process expert than a content expert. Table 5.2 cites three critical factors the facilitator must address. First, provide adequate time for citizen comments, which is a central reason for hearings in the first place. The meeting, however, should not drag. Obviously, citizens want to fully disclose their comments and feelings, but uncontrolled input by a few long-winded individuals can monopolize the time, resulting in limited or no opportunity for others and long meetings that generate feelings of frustration. To manage time well, the facilitator can place time limits on citizens' comments and stick to the time limit. As our study discovered, there was a statistically significant relationship between limiting the length of participants' comments and perceived hearing success. One way to effectively manage public input with large crowds is to break them into smaller groups, each managed by a separate facilitator, and give individuals longer periods of time for comment. As one city manager commented, "Small groups work well."

Second, the facilitator must control citizen emotions, keeping the comments focused on the topic and preventing angry outbursts. To assist in controlling emotion, the facilitator may reply by paraphrasing comments to assure speakers their comments were understood. Perhaps the most underutilized technique in information-gathering or problem-solving meetings is to capture and display participants' comments on a large display device such as a chalk board, computer projection screen, or flip chart. Although most cities captured citizen input with a tape recorder (81 percent) or a legal secretary (27 percent), citizens cannot "see" their comments, contributing to the tendency of most people to keep stating and restating their points to ensure they have been understood. Publicly displaying citizen comments can achieve several key benefits. This technique (1) records citizen comments for later use, (2) helps to clarify critical concerns, (3) validates citizens and their concerns, (4) assists in controlling emotions, and (5) reduces discussion time.

Third, along with managing time and controlling emotion, meeting facilitators, as well as all governmental officials in attendance, must demonstrate a listening and understanding attitude. Comments such as, "A listening attitude on the part of staff and elected officials" and "Listen, listen, listen" were made by many of the city managers regarding one of the keys to successful public hearings. If public officials project an attitude of closed-mindedness or defensiveness, probably nothing else can save the meeting from disaster. Covey observes that "the root cause of almost all people problems is the basic communication problem—people do not listen with empathy" (1991, 45).

Posthearing Factors

One frequently mentioned critical factor related to the posthearing phase of public hearings is effective follow-up. This factor includes appropriately using public hearing information in making final decisions and then communicating final decisions to the public. The public hearing literature states that citizen input should have a real and positive impact on decision outcomes. Further, the public should have at least some degree of satisfaction with the output. Our statistical analysis showed a high relationship between hearing success and subsequent open meetings to discuss the hearing's findings and conclusions, supporting the idea that hearings should be held early enough in the decision process to make a difference. Citizens want to hold government accountable to its constituents and to know that public input matters, and effective postmeeting communication can fulfill these citizen desires. Handled effectively, the posthearing feedback can help to build critical citizen trust and foster ongoing citizen participation.

SUMMARY AND CONCLUSION

This study suggests that an effective public hearing results from successfully executing a series of steps. These steps are summarized in the following list and in figure 5.1. Failure to execute any point along the way can have a negative impact on the entire process.

1. Carefully prepare for the hearing. Clarify goals, hold the hearing or alternative public participation events early in the decision process, select an appropriate site, and select an effective facilitator. Be sure the meeting facilitator possesses critical communication skills (for instance, he or she is open, unbiased, patient, nondefensive, and adaptable). Prepare government officials, develop detailed procedures, and prepare clear written and oral reports.
2. Effectively publicize the hearing using multiple media. Create public interest and educate citizens about what is involved and how they will be affected. Use multiple communication channels to notify, educate, and build interest.
3. Launch the meeting well. Clearly frame the key issues and use multiple media to help achieve understanding. Clarify the procedures to be used during the meeting.
4. Ensure the facilitator guides and moves the discussion along, clarifying and summarizing main points, assuring citizens of the value of their input, and managing citizens' emotions.
5. Make sure that attending government officials carefully listen to and value citizens' comments, remembering that they are stewards rather than owners. Help officials to be honest and forthright yet respectful and sensitive in their responses.

6. Follow up effectively after the meeting, carefully considering and using applicable input and reporting back to the citizenry.

In addition to these recommendations, public administrators should consider public hearings only one part of an overall public communication strategy. For example, because of the inherent limitations of public hearings, city officials should consider multiple participation methods, and they should not view convening a public hearing as full spirit-of-the-law compliance with public participation requirements.

Although the participants in this research included only city administrators, we believe many of the conclusions and recommendations can be adapted to other governmental entities. All levels and units of government face similar public participation challenges, and we believe the principles highlighted in this study are applicable in many settings. The study results can also provide a useful basis for public management classroom instruction and for further research on government communication.

Figure 5.1 Summary of Public Hearing Guidelines

Prepare		**Publicize**		**Launch**		**Facilitate**		**Listen**		**Follow Up**
• Clarify goals • Involve citizens • Select good site • Choose facilitator	➡	• Use multiple channels • Create interest • Educate citizens	➡	• Explain procedures • Clarify issues • Use multiple media	➡	• Guide discussion • Summarize input • Validate concerns • Manage emotions	➡	• Be respectful • Be sensitive • Be honest	➡	• Consider input in finalizing decision • Report back to Citizens

Baker, William H., H. Lon Addams, and Brian Davis. "Critical Factors for Enhancing Municipal Public Hearings." *Public Administration Review* 65, no. 4 (2005): 490–99. Reproduced with permission of Blackwell Publishing Ltd.

6

Whistleblowing and Leaked Information

INTRODUCTION

The Watergate scandal, which led to the eventual resignation of President Richard Nixon, came to light after Mark Felt, a high-ranking government official at the FBI, leaked information to two *Washington Post* reporters (Weiner 2008; Woodward and Bernstein 2005). Daniel Ellsberg authored part of the Pentagon Papers, an official, classified history of the United States' involvement in Vietnam, and then subsequently worked covertly to have them published in the *New York Times* and the *Washington Post*. The Pentagon Papers showed that the U.S. government was lying to the public about decisions surrounding the war and what was actually taking place in Vietnam (Ellsberg 2003; Prados and Porter 2004).

Most cases of whistleblowing and leaking information are not as high profile or well known. In 2009, a twin-engine turboprop plane crashed outside of Buffalo, New York. The year prior, a Federal Aviation Administration (FAA) inspector noted problems with that type of airplane, which was flown by the airline Colgan Air (Wald 2009). When these issues were reported to superiors, the inspector was relieved of important components of his job. The FAA subsequently put him on paid leave, saying he menaced a lawyer. For its part, the FAA insists that it did take the inspector's concerns seriously.

Conflicting issues like this are common with whistleblowers. The individual and the organization are frequently at odds. Whistleblowers face various forms of retaliation, including loss of job, responsibilities or salary reduction, harassment or transfer, or having their work more closely monitored (Jos, Tompkins, and Hays 1989). Because of the fear of retaliation, many government employees choose not to whistleblow or leak information (Lovell 2003).

Whistleblowing and leaking are not unique to the United States. Ad Bos blew the whistle on corruption and bribery of public officials in the Dutch construction industry in the 1990s (Heuvel 2005). Before he blew the whistle he had taken part in corrupt, illegal activities. He was convicted based on the information he brought forward, though the judge did not give him a penalty. He suffered retaliation and was just recently awarded compensation ("Nuclear Whistleblower Wins Compensation" 2009).

When whistleblowing takes place, it typically is associated with the individual's name. The release may be done through formal organization channels or directly to the press or a public interest group. Conversely, leaking is at times illegal and is usually associated with an anonymous source and potentially classified information. Sissela Bok wrote a classic chapter on "Whistleblowing and Leaks" in her book *Secret: On the Ethics of Concealment and Revelation*. Bok offers definitions of whistleblowing and leaks and discusses how to decide if either is the appropriate course of action (Bok 1989).

Assignments and Study Questions

1. Research a case of a recent whistleblower or leaked information in the news. Did the release of the information add to great transparency? Explain.
2. When do you think it is appropriate to whistleblow? When is it appropriate to leak? What criteria would you use to help you decide?
3. Watch the movie *The Insider* about a whistleblower in the tobacco industry. Would you have gone public with the information? Why or why not?

* * *

Whistleblowing and Leaks
Sissela Bok

REVELATION FROM WITHIN

> All that pollution up at Mølledal—all that reeking waste from the mill—it's seeped into the pipes feeding from the pump-room; and the same damn poisonous slop's been draining out on the beach as well. . . . I've investigated the facts as scrupulously as possible. . . . There's irrefutable proof of the presence of decayed organic matter in the water—millions of bacteria. It's positively injurious to health, for either internal or external use. Ah, what a blessing it is to feel that you've done some service for your home town and your fellow citizens.
>
> Dr. Thomas Stockman, in HENRIK IBSEN,
> *An Enemy of the People*, Act 1

Such was Dr. Stockman's elation, in Ibsen's play, after having written a report on the contamination of the town's newly installed mineral baths. As the spa's medical director, he took it for granted that everyone would be eager to learn why so many who had come to the baths for health purposes the previous summer had been taken ill; and he assumed that the board of directors and the taxpayers would gladly pay for the extensive repairs that he recommended. By the fifth act of the play, he had been labeled an "enemy of the people" at a public meeting, lost his position as the spa's medical director, and suffered through the stoning of his house by an angry crowd. But he held his ground: "Should I let myself be whipped from the field by public opinion and the solid majority and other such barbarities? No thank you!"[1]

"Whistleblower" is a recent label for those who, like Dr. Stockman, make revelations meant to call attention to negligence, abuses, or dangers that threaten the public interest. They sound an alarm based on their expertise or inside knowledge, often from within the very organization in which they work. With as much resonance as they can muster, they strive to breach secrecy, or else arouse an apathetic public to dangers everyone knows about but does not fully acknowledge.[2]

Few whistleblowers, however, share Dr. Stockman's initial belief that it will be enough to make their message public, and that people who learn of the danger will hasten to counter it. Most know, rather, that their alarms pose a threat to anyone who benefits from the ongoing practice and that their own careers and livelihood may be at risk. The lawyer who breaches confidentiality in reporting bribery by corporate clients knows the risk, as does the nurse who reports on slovenly patient care in a hospital, the engineer who discloses safety defects in the braking systems of a fleet of new rapid-transit vehicles, or the industrial worker who speaks out about hazardous chemicals seeping into a playground near the factory dump.

For each of the rationales of shared secrecy that I have discussed—confidentiality, trade secrecy, secrecy for research, and administrative and military secrecy—concealment of negligence and abuses creates strong tensions for insiders. They must confront questions of loyalty, conscience, and truthfulness, and personal concerns about careers and peace of mind. What should they consider revealing? And which secrets must they at all costs bring to public attention?

Would-be whistleblowers also face conflicting pressures from without. In many professions, the prevailing ethic requires above all else loyalty to colleagues and to clients; yet the formal codes of professional ethics stress responsibility to the public in cases of conflict with such loyalties. Thus the largest professional engineering society asks members to speak out against abuses threatening the safety, health, and welfare of the public.[3] A number of business firms have codes making similar requirements; and the United States Code of Ethics for government servants asks them to "expose corruption wherever uncovered" and to "put loyalty to the highest moral principles and to country above loyalty to persons, party, or Government department."[4] Regardless of such exhortations, would-be whistleblowers have reason to fear the results of carrying out the duty to reveal corruption and neglect. However strong this duty may seem in principle, they know that in practice, retaliation is likely. They fear for their careers and for their ability to support themselves and their families.

Government service in the United States offers insight into the variety of forms that retaliation can take. A handbook issued during the Nixon era recommends reassigning "undesirables" to places so remote that they would prefer to resign. Whistleblowers may also be downgraded or given work without responsibility or work for which they are not qualified; or else they may be given more tasks than they can possibly perform.

Another risk to outspoken civil servants—devastating to their careers—is that they may be ordered to undergo a psychiatric "fitness for duty" examination. Congressional hearings in 1978 uncovered a growing tendency to resort to such mandatory examinations, and found that it frequently results from conflicts between supervisors and employees. A person declared unfit for service can then be "separated" and his assertions discredited. The chairman of the investigating subcommittee, Senator Edward Kennedy, concluded that "there was general agreement . . . that involuntary psychiatric examinations were not helpful to the Government, unfair to employees, and that the agencies placed psychiatrists in an impossible situation."[5]

Outright firing, finally, is the most direct institutional response to whistleblowers. Those who bring suit incur heavy legal expenses and have little assurance of prevailing in court. One civil servant, reflecting on her experience and on that of others, stated that their reactions, after speaking out about the agency in which they worked, had "ranged from humiliation, frustration, and helpless rage to complete despair about our democratic process."[6]

The plight of whistleblowers has been documented in the last decade by the press and by a growing number of books and scholarly articles.[7] Evidence of the hardships imposed on those who chose to act in the public interest has combined with a heightened awareness of professional malfeasance and corruption to produce a shift toward greater public support of whistleblowers. Public-service law firms and consumer groups have taken up their cause; institutional reforms and legislation have been enacted to combat illegitimate reprisals. Some would encourage ever greater numbers of employees to ferret out and publicize improprieties in the agencies and organizations where they work.

Given the indispensable services performed by so many whistleblowers—as during the Watergate period and after—strong public support is often merited. But the new climate of acceptance makes it easy to overlook the dangers of whistleblowing: of work and reputations unjustly lost for those falsely accused, of privacy invaded and trust undermined. There comes a level of internal prying and mutual suspicion at which no institution can function. And it is a fact that the disappointed, the incompetent, the malicious, and the paranoid all too often make groundless accusations. Worst of all, ideological persecution throughout the world tradition-ally relies on insiders willing to inform on their colleagues or even on their family members, often through staged public denunciations or press campaigns.

The very societies that encourage such revelation from within of political or religious deviation are often least tolerant of whistleblowing concerning abuse or neglect in ruling circles. Such messages require some larger context where secrecy, corruption, and coercion are less solidly entrenched, some forum where an appeal to justice can still be made. They also require an avenue of concerted public response; for if the audience is not free to receive or to act on the information—as when censorship or fear of retribution stifles response—then the message only rebounds to injure the whistleblower. If protest within a nation is thus blocked, international appeals may be the only remaining possibility. Depending on the severity of the repression, only the most striking injustices may then filter through with sufficient strength to alert ordinarily indifferent foreigners. Alarms, like ripples in the water, weaken as they move away from their point of origin; if forced to go below the surface, they may be further attenuated.

No society can count itself immune from the risk that individuals or groups in power might use whistleblowing for their own purposes, and crush it when they see fit. A society that fails to protect the right to speak out even on the part of those whose warnings turn out to be spurious obviously opens the door to political repression. Given such protection, however, we still need to weigh the uses and the costs of whistleblowing, and to try to distinguish between its more and its less justifiable forms. From the moral point of view, there are important differences between the aims, messages, and methods of dissenters from within.

BLOWING THE WHISTLE

The alarm of the whistleblower is meant to disrupt the status quo: to pierce the background noise, perhaps the false harmony, or the imposed silence of "business as usual." Three ele-ments, each jarring, and triply jarring when conjoined, lend acts of whistleblowing special urgency and bitterness: dissent, breach of loyalty, and accusation.*

---

* Consider the differences and the overlap between whistleblowing and civil disobedience with respect to these three ele-ments. First, whistleblowing resembles civil disobedience in its openness and its intent to act in the public interest. But the dissent in whistleblowing, unlike that in civil disobedience, usually does not represent a breach of law; it is, on the contrary, protected by the right of free speech and often encouraged in codes of ethics and other statements of principle. Second, whistle-blowing violates loyalty, since it dissents from within and breaches secrecy, whereas civil disobedience need not and can as easily challenge from without. Whistleblowing, finally, accuses specific individuals, whereas civil disobedience need not. A combination of the two occurs, for instance, when former CIA agents publish books to alert the public about what they regard as unlawful and dangerous practices, and in so doing openly violate, and thereby test, the oath of secrecy that they have sworn.

Like all *dissent*, first of all, whistleblowing makes public a disagreement with an authority or a majority view. But whereas dissent can arise from all forms of disagreement with, say, religious dogma or government policy or court decisions, whistleblowing has the narrower aim of casting light on negligence or abuse, of alerting the public to a risk and of assigning responsibility for that risk.

It is important, in this respect, to see the shadings between the revelations of neglect and abuse which are central to whistleblowing, and dissent on grounds of policy. In practice, however, the two often come together. Coercive regimes or employers may regard dissent of any form as evidence of abuse or of corruption that calls for public exposure. And in all societies, persons may blow the whistle on abuses in order to signal policy dissent. Thus Daniel Ellsberg, in making his revelations about government deceit and manipulation in the Pentagon Papers, obviously aimed not only to expose misconduct and assign responsibility but also to influence the nation's policy toward Southeast Asia.

In the second place, the message of the whistleblower is seen as a *breach of loyalty* because it comes from within. The whistleblower, though he is neither referee nor coach, blows the whistle on his own team. His insider's position carries with it certain obligations to colleagues and clients. He may have signed a promise of confidentiality or a loyalty oath. When he steps out of routine channels to level accusations, he is going against these obligations. Loyalty to colleagues and to clients comes to be pitted against concern for the public interest and for those who may be injured unless someone speaks out. Because the whistleblower criticizes from within, his act differs from muckraking and other forms of exposure by outsiders. Their acts may arouse anger, but not the sense of betrayal that whistleblowers so often encounter.

The conflict is strongest for those who take their responsibilities to the public seriously, yet have close bonds of collegiality and of duty to clients as well. They know the price of betrayal. They know, too, how organizations protect and enlarge the area of what is concealed, as failures multiply and vested interests encroach. And they are aware that they violate, by speaking out, not only loyalty but usually hierarchy as well.

It is the third element of *accusation*, of calling a "foul" from within that arouses the strongest reactions on the part of the hierarchy. The charge may be one of unethical or unlawful conduct on the part of colleagues or superiors. Explicitly or implicitly, it singles out specific groups or persons as responsible: as those who knew or should have known what was wrong and what the dangers were, and who had the capacity to make different choices. If no one could be held thus responsible—as in the case of an impending avalanche or a volcanic eruption—the warning would not constitute whistleblowing. At times the whistleblower's greatest effort is expended on trying to show that someone is responsible for danger or suffering: that the collapse of a building, the derailment of a train, or a famine that the public may have attributed to bad luck or natural causes was in reality brought about by specific individuals, and that they can be held responsible, perhaps made to repair the damage or at least to avoid compounding it.

The whistleblower's accusation, moreover, concerns a present or an imminent threat. Past errors or misdeeds occasion such an alarm only if they still affect current practices. And risks far in the future usually lack the immediacy needed to render the alarm compelling, as well as the close connection to particular individuals that would justify accusations. Thus an alarm can be sounded about safety defects in a rapid-transit system that threaten or will shortly threaten passengers; but the revelation of safety defects in a system no longer in use, while of historical interest, would not constitute whistleblowing. Nor would the disclosure of potential problems in a system not yet fully designed and far from being implemented.

Not only immediacy but also specificity is needed for the whistleblower to assign responsibility. A concrete risk must be at issue rather than a vague foreboding or a somber prediction. The act of whistleblowing differs in this respect from the lamentation or the dire prophecy.

Such immediate and specific threats would normally be acted upon by those at risk. But the whistleblower assumes that his message will alert listeners to a threat of which they are ignorant, or whose significance they have not grasped. It may have been kept secret by members within the organization, or by all who are familiar with it. Or it may be an "open secret," seemingly in need only of being pointed out in order to have its effect. In either case, because of the elements of dissent, breach of loyalty, and accusation, the tension between concealing and revealing is great. It may be intensified by an urge to throw off the sense of complicity that comes from sharing secrets one believes to be unjustly concealed, and to achieve peace of mind by setting the record straight at last. Sometimes a desire for publicity enters in, or a hope for revenge for past slights or injustices. Colleagues of the whistleblower often suspect just such motives; they may regard him as a crank, publicity-hungry, eager for scandal and discord, or driven to indiscretion by his personal biases and shortcomings.[8]

On the continuum of more or less justifiable acts of whistleblowing, the whistleblower tends to see more such acts as justified and even necessary than his colleagues. Bias can affect each side in drawing the line, so that each takes only some of the factors into account—the more so if the action comes at the end of a long buildup of acrimony and suspicion.

THE LEAK

When Otto Otepka sent classified documents and names of persons he considered security risks to "Red-hunter" Julian Sourwine of the Senate Internal Subcommittee in the early 1960s, or when "Deep Throat" revealed facts about Watergate in deepest secrecy, each was engaged in a practice that has come to be called "leaking."[9] Each meant to disclose information from within but to do so covertly, unlike the whistleblower or the official who resigns in protest.*

Any kind of information can be leaked; but the word "leak" is most often used in connection with administrative secrets, such as the anonymous revelations in 1980 from within the Department of Justice concerning the ABSCAM investigations of members of Congress, or with classified military secrets."[10] The originator of a leak is usually unknown to the public and sometimes even to the journalist or other intermediary. Anonymous messages may be sent by mail, dropped at doorsteps, transmitted in coded form on computers.

Leaking has a symbiotic relationship with secrecy. Without secrecy there would be no need to leak information. As government secrecy grows and comes to involve more people, the opportunities to leak from within expand; and with increased leaking, governments intensify their efforts to shore up secrecy.

At the same time as they combat leaking, however, executives use it selectively to further their own policies. With modern governments guarding vast amounts of information, much of it inaccessible to the public or actively kept secret, and with the media eager to circulate newsworthy revelations to vast audiences, the leak, unlike acts of whistleblowing, has become

---

* The two cases differ in that Otepka's actions come much closer to informing than most efforts to leak. Leaks are generally directed to the public via an intermediary, whereas informing is meant for the authorities. But Otepka considered those in charge of federal appointments to be overly lenient, and so chose a different outlet for his revelations.

an important tool of governing.* Administrators may leak stories as trial balloons, to deflect attention from recent failures, or to smear political opponents. And civil servants who want to combat policies or particular decisions may leak selected compromising facts. If a secret plan is sufficiently sensitive, those who learn about it may, in this way, exercise a veto power over its execution. Thus the members of congressional committees overseeing CIA activities know that they need only leak details concerning any one of them to destroy its effectiveness.

Press and television reporters cooperate in bringing many of these leaks to public attention. They may discard pieces of information that cannot be verified or that seem of little interest; but at times they publish the flimsiest of rumors. Whether knowingly or not, they are also often the conduits for leaked disinformation. Because of their eagerness for news and "scoops," reporters become, as Francis Rourke has pointed out, "willing if not enthusiastic collaborators" with those who engage in leaking to influence public opinion.[11]

Unlike whistleblowing, leaking need not concern danger, negligence, or abuse, though both bring something that is secret or unnoticed into the open from within an organization. Thus a civil servant may leak secret documents in his agency's possession concerning another nation's military preparedness, or specifying steps in fragile diplomatic talks. But when a leak from within does concern misconduct, it is a variant of whistleblowing, undertaken surreptitiously because the revealer cannot or does not want to be known as its source.

Whether as a surreptitious form of whistleblowing, a tool for news management by administrators, or a means of bureaucratic maneuvering, leaking has become one of the main forms of communication about matters of public interest. But it is far from ideal from the point of view of the media or the public. For while it is preferable to complete secrecy, and offers one of the few ways of learning about risky policies and mismanagement otherwise shrouded in secrecy, it does so haphazardly and is ceaselessly used to manipulate public opinion.

Both leaking and whistleblowing can be used to challenge corrupt or cumbersome systems of secrecy—in government as in the professions, the sciences, and business. Both may convey urgently needed warnings, but they may also peddle false information and vicious personal attacks. How, then, can one distinguish the many acts of revelation from within that are genuinely in the public interest from all the petty, biased, or lurid tales that pervade our querulous and gossip-ridden societies? Can we draw distinctions between different messages, different methods, and motivations?

We clearly can, in a number of cases. Whistleblowing and leaks may be starkly inappropriate when used in malice or in error, or when they lay bare legitimately private matters such as those having to do with political belief or sexual life. They may, just as clearly, offer the only way to shed light on an ongoing practice such as fraudulent scientific research or intimidation of political adversaries; and they may be the last resort for alerting the public to a possible disaster. Consider, for example, the action taken by three engineers to alert the public to defects in the braking mechanisms of the Bay Area Rapid Transit System (BART):

The San Francisco Bay Area Rapid Transit System opened in 1972. It was heralded as the first major breakthrough toward a safe, reliable, and sophisticated method of mass transportation. A public agency had been set up in 1952 to plan and carry out the project; and the task of developing its major new component, a fully automatic train control system, was allocated to Westinghouse.

---

* Leaks are often seen as related to national, state, or local government affairs. But there is no reason not to use the word for analogous revelations from international government bodies such as UN agencies or OPEC circles, or from nongovernmental ones such as IBM or Nestle.

In 1969, three of the engineers who worked on this system became increasingly concerned over its safety. They spotted problems independently, and spoke to their supervisors, but to no avail. They later said they might well have given up their effort to go farther had they not found out about one another. They made numerous efforts to speak to BART's management. But those in charge were already troubled by costs that had exceeded all projections, and by numerous unforeseen delays. They were not disposed to investigate the charges that the control system might be unsafe. Each appeal by the three engineers failed.

Finally, the engineers interested a member of BART's board of trustees, who brought the matter up at a board meeting. Once again, the effort failed. But in March 1973, the three were fired once the complaint had been traced to them. When they wrote to ask why they had been dismissed, they received no answer.

Meanwhile, the BART system had begun to roll. The control system worked erratically, and at times dangerously. A month after the opening, one train overshot the last station and crashed into a parking lot for commuters. Claiming that some bugs still had to be worked out, BART began to use old-fashioned flagmen in order to avoid collisions.

The three engineers had turned, in 1972, to the California Society of Professional Engineers for support. The society, after investigating the complaint, agreed with their views, and reported to the California State legislature. It too had launched an investigation, and arrived at conclusions quite critical of BART's management.

The engineers filed a damage suit against BART in 1974, but settled out of court in 1975. They had difficulties finding new employment, and suffered considerable financial and emotional hardship in spite of their public vindication.[12]

The three engineers were acting in accordance with the law and with engineering codes of ethics in calling attention to the defects in the train control system. Because of their expertise, they had a special responsibility to alert the company, and if need be its board of directors and the public, to the risks that concerned them. If we take such a clear-cut case of legitimate whistleblowing as a benchmark, and reflect on what it is about it that weighs so heavily in favor of disclosure, we can then examine more complex cases in which speaking out in public is not so clearly the right choice or the only choice.

INDIVIDUAL MORAL CHOICE

What questions might individuals consider, as they wonder whether to sound an alarm? How might they articulate the problem they see, and weigh its seriousness before deciding whether or not to reveal it? Can they make sure that their choice is the right one? And what about the choices confronting journalists or others asked to serve as intermediaries?

In thinking about these questions, it helps to keep in mind the three elements mentioned earlier: dissent, breach of loyalty, and accusation. They impose certain requirements: of judgment and accuracy in dissent, of exploring alternative ways to cope with improprieties that minimize the breach of loyalty, and of fairness in accusation. The judgment expressed by whistleblowers concerns a problem that should matter to the public. Certain outrages are so blatant and certain dangers so great, that all who are in a position to warn of them have a *prima facie* obligation to do so. Conversely, other problems are so minor that to blow the whistle would be a disproportionate response. And still others are so hard to pin down that whistleblowing is premature. In between lie a great many of the problems troubling whistleblowers. Consider, for example, the following situation:

An attorney for a large company manufacturing medical supplies begins to suspect that some of the machinery sold by the company to hospitals for use in kidney dialysis is unsafe, and that management has made attempts to influence federal regulatory personnel to overlook these deficiencies.

The attorney brings these matters up with a junior executive, who assures her that he will look into the matter, and convey them to the chief executive if necessary. When she questions him a few weeks later, however, he tells her that all the problems have been taken care of, but offers no evidence, and seems irritated at her desire to learn exactly where the issues stand. She does not know how much further she can press her concern without jeopardizing her position in the firm.

The lawyer in this case has reason to be troubled, but does not yet possess sufficient evidence to blow the whistle. She is far from being as sure of her case as was Ibsen's Dr. Stockman, who had received laboratory analyses of the water used in the town spa, or as the engineers in the BART case, whose professional expertise allowed them to evaluate the risks of the faulty braking system. Dr. Stockman and the engineers would be justified in assuming that they had an obligation to draw attention to the dangers they saw, and that anyone who shared their knowledge would be wrong to remain silent or to suppress evidence of the danger. But if the attorney blew the whistle about her company's sales of machinery to hospitals merely on the basis of her suspicions, she would be doing so prematurely. At the same time, the risks to hospital patients from the machinery, should she prove correct in her suspicions, are sufficiently great so that she has good reason to seek help in looking into the problem, to feel complicitous if she chooses to do nothing, and to take action if she verifies her suspicions.

Her difficulty is shared by many who suspect, without being sure, that their companies are concealing the defective or dangerous nature of their products—automobiles that are firetraps, for instance, or canned foods with carcinogenic additives. They may sense that merely to acknowledge that they don't know for sure is too often a weak excuse for inaction, but recognize also that the destructive power of adverse publicity can be great. If the warning turns out to have been inaccurate, it may take a long time to undo the damage to individuals and organizations. As a result, potential whistleblowers must first try to specify the degree to which there is genuine impropriety, and consider how imminent and how serious the threat is which they perceive.

If the facts turn out to warrant disclosure and if the would-be whistleblower has decided to act upon them in spite of the possibilities of reprisal, then how can the second element—breach of loyalty—be overcome or minimized? Here, as in the Pentagon Papers case, the problem is one of which set of loyalties to uphold. Several professional codes of ethics, such as those of engineers and public servants, facilitate such a choice at least in theory, by requiring that loyalty to the public interest should override allegiance to colleagues, employers, or clients whenever there is a genuine conflict. Accordingly, those who have assumed a professional responsibility to serve the public interest—as had both Dr. Stockman in Ibsen's play and the engineers in the BART case—have a special obligation not to remain silent about dangers to the public.

Before deciding whether to speak out publicly, however, it is important for them to consider whether the existing avenues for change within the organization have been sufficiently explored. By turning first to insiders for help, one can often uphold both sets of loyalties and settle the problem without going outside the organization. The engineers in the BART case clearly tried to resolve the problem they saw in this manner, and only reluctantly allowed it to come to public attention as a last resort. Dr. Stockman, on the other hand, acted much more impetuously and with little concern for discretion. Before the directors of the mineral baths had even received his report, he talked freely about it, and welcomed a journalist's request to publicize the matter. While he had every reason to try to remedy the danger he had discovered, he was not justified in the methods he chose; on the contrary, they were singularly unlikely to bring about corrective action.

It *is* disloyal to colleagues and employers, as well as a waste of time for the public, to sound the loudest alarm first. Whistleblowing has to remain a last alternative because of its destructive side effects. It must be chosen only when other alternatives have been considered and rejected. They may be rejected if they simply do not apply to the problem at hand, or when there is not time to go through routine channels, or when the institution is so corrupt or coercive that steps will be taken to silence the whistleblower should he try the regular channels first.

What weight should an oath or a promise of silence have in the conflict of loyalties? There is no doubt that one sworn to silence is under a stronger obligation because of the oath he has taken, unless it was obtained under duress or through deceit, or else binds him to something in itself wrong or unlawful. In taking an oath, one assumes specific obligations beyond those assumed in accepting employment. But even such an oath can be overridden when the public interest at issue is sufficiently strong. The fact that one has promised silence is no excuse for complicity in covering up a crime or violating the public trust.

The third element in whistleblowing—accusation—is strongest whenever efforts to correct a problem without going outside the organization have failed, or seem likely to fail. Such an outcome is especially likely whenever those in charge take part in the questionable practices, or have too much at stake in maintaining them. The following story relates the difficulties one government employee experienced in trying to decide whether to go public with accusations against superiors in his agency:

As a construction inspector for a federal agency, John Samuels (not his real name) had personal knowledge of shoddy and deficient construction practices by private contractors. He knew his superiors received free vacations and entertainment, had their homes remodeled, found jobs for their relatives—all courtesy of a private contractor. These superiors later approved a multimillion no-bid contract with the same "generous" firm.

Samuels also had evidence that other firms were hiring nonunion laborers at a low wage while receiving substantially higher payments from the government for labor costs. A former superior, unaware of an office dictaphone, had incautiously instructed Samuels on how to accept bribes for overlooking sub-par performance.

As he prepared to volunteer this information to various members of Congress, he became tense and uneasy. His family was scared and the fears were valid. It might cost Samuels thousands of dollars to protect his job. Those who had freely provided him with information would probably recant or withdraw their friendship. A number of people might object to his using a dictaphone to gather information. His agency would start covering up and vent its collective wrath upon him. As for reporters and writers, they would gather for a few days, then move on to the next story. He would be left without a job, with fewer friends, with massive battles looming, and without the financial means of fighting them. Samuels decided to remain silent.[13]

Samuels could be sure of his facts, and fairly sure that it would not help to explore avenues within the agency in trying to remedy the situation. But was the method he envisaged—of volunteering his information to members of Congress and to the press—the one most likely to do so, and to provide a fair hearing for those he was charging with corruption and crime? Could he have gone first to the police? If he had been concerned to proceed in the fairest possible manner, he should at least have considered alternative methods of investigating and reporting the abuses he had witnessed.

These abuses were clearly such as to warrant attention. At other times, potential whistleblowers must also ask themselves whether their message, however accurate, is one to which the public is entitled in the first place or whether it infringes on personal and private matters that no one should invade. Here, the very notion of what is in the public interest is at issue: allegations regarding an official's unusual sexual or religious practices may well appeal to the public's interest without therefore being relevant to "the public interest." Those who regard such private matters as threats to the public voice their own religious and political prejudices in the language of accusation. Such a danger is never stronger than when the accusation is delivered surreptitiously; the anonymous allegations made during the McCarthy period regarding political beliefs and associations often injured persons who did not even know their accusers or the exact nature of the charges.

In fairness to those criticized, openly accepted responsibility for blowing the whistle should therefore be preferred to the secret denunciation or the leaked rumor—the more so, the more derogatory and accusatory the information. What is openly stated can be more easily checked, its source's motives challenged, and the underlying information examined. Those under attack may otherwise be hard put to it to defend themselves against nameless adversaries. Often they do not even know that they are threatened until it is too late to respond.

The choice between open and surreptitious revelation from within is admittedly less easy for the persons who intend to make them. Leaking information anonymously is safer, and can be kept up indefinitely; the whistleblower, on the contrary, shoots his bolt by going public. At the same time, those who leak know that their message may be taken less seriously, precisely because its source remains concealed. And because these messages go through several intermediaries before they appear in print, they may undergo changes along the way. At times, they are so adulterated that they lose their point altogether.

Journalists and other intermediaries must make choices of their own with respect to a leaked message. Should they use it at all, even if they doubt its accuracy? Should they pass it on verbatim or interpret it? Or should they seek to "plug" the leak? Newspaper and television bureaus receive innumerable leaks but act on only some of them. Unless the information is accompanied by indications of how the evidence can be checked, the source's anonymity, however safe, diminishes the value of the message.

In order to assure transmission of their message, yet be safe from retaliation, leakers often resort to a compromise: by making themselves known to a journalist or other intermediary, they make it possible to verify their credibility; by asking that their identity be concealed, they still protect themselves from the consequences they fear.

If anonymous sources can point to independent evidence of genuine risk or wrongdoing, the need for them to step forward is reduced and their motives are less important. For this reason, the toll-free numbers that citizens can use to report on government fraud, tax evasion, or police abuse serve an important purpose in protecting critics both from inside and from outside an organization. Without such evidence, accusations openly made by identifiable persons are preferable. The open charge is fairer to the accused, and allows listeners to weigh the motives and the trustworthiness of the whistleblowers.

Must the whistleblower who speaks out openly also resign? Only if staying on means being forced to participate in the objectionable activity, and thus to take on partial responsibility for its consequences. Otherwise, there should be no burden on whistleblowers to resign in voicing their alarm. In principle, at least, it is often their duty to speak out, and their positions ought not thereby to be at issue. In practice, however, they know that retaliation, forced departure, perhaps blacklisting, may be sufficient risks at times so that it may be wise to resign before sounding the alarm: to resign in protest, or to leave quietly, secure another post, and only then blow the whistle.[14] In each case, those who speak out can then do so with the authority and knowledge of insiders, but without their vulnerability.

It is not easy to weigh all these factors, nor to compensate for the degree of bias, rationalization, and denial that inevitably influences one's judgment. By speaking out, whistleblowers may spark a re-examination of these forces among colleagues and others who had ignored or learned to live with shoddy or corrupt practices. Because they have this power to dramatize moral conflict, would-be whistleblowers have a special responsibility to ask themselves about biases in deciding whether or not to speak out: a desire for self-defense in a difficult bureaucratic situation, perhaps, or unrealistic expectations regarding the likely effects of speaking out.*

As they weigh the reasons for sounding the alarm, or on the contrary for remaining silent, they may find it helpful to ask about the legitimacy of the rationale for collective secrecy in the particular problem they face. If they are wondering whether or not to blow the whistle on the unnecessary surgery they have witnessed, for example, or on the manufacture of unsafe machinery, what weight should they place on claims to professional confidentiality or corporate secrecy?

Reducing bias and error in moral choice often requires consultation, even open debate; such methods force us to articulate the arguments at stake and to challenge privately held assumptions. But choices about whether or not to blow the whistle present special problems for such consultation. On the one hand, once whistleblowers sound their alarm publicly, their judgment *will* be subjected to open scrutiny; they will have to articulate their reasons for speaking out and substantiate their charges. On the other hand, it will then be too late to retract their charges should they turn out to have been unfounded.

For those who are concerned about a situation within their organization, it is therefore preferable to seek advice *before* deciding either to go public or to remain silent. But the more corrupt the circumstances, the more dangerous it may be to consult colleagues, and the more likely it is that those responsible for the abuse or neglect will destroy the evidence linking them to it. And yet, with no one to consult, the would-be whistleblowers themselves may have a biased view of the state of affairs; they may see corruption and conspiracy where none exists, and choose not to consult others when in fact it would have been not only safe but advantageous to do so.

Given these difficulties, it is especially important to seek more general means of weighing the arguments for and against whistleblowing; to take them up in public debate and in teaching; and to consider changes in organizations, law, and work practices that could reduce the need for individuals to choose between blowing and "swallowing" the whistle.[15]

ORGANIZATIONAL CHANGE AND SOCIAL POLICY

What changes inside and outside organizations might protect the rights of dissenters and critics, and assure the public of needed information, while cutting down on undue reaches of loyalty and on false accusations?

An organization can reduce the need to resort to whistleblowing by providing mechanisms for evaluating criticism before it reaches the press or the courtroom. These mechanisms must

---

* If, for example, a government employee stands to make large profits from a book exposing the iniquities in his agency, there is danger that he might slant his report in order to cause more of a sensation. Sometimes a warning is so clearly justifiable and substantiated that it carries weight no matter what the motives of the speaker. But scandal can pay; and the whistleblower's motives ought ideally to be above suspicion, for his own sake as well as for the sake of the respect he desires for his warning. Personal gain from speaking out increases the need to check the accuracy of the speaker.

work to counteract the blockages of information within an organization and the perennial pressures to filter out negative information before it reaches those who make decisions.[16] The filtering process may be simple or intricate, well-in-intentioned or malevolent, more or less consciously manipulated. Some abuses are covered up at the source; others are sidelined en route to department heads; still others are kept from reaching review boards or trustees.

Surveying the damage from such failures of communication, David Ewing has argued that managers have much to gain by not discouraging internal criticism.[17] In a recent survey, he found that over 60 percent of the business firms responding to a questionnaire claimed that a senior executive's door is always open to anyone with a grievance.[18] A number of managers have other ways of encouraging the views of dissenters, and promise that no one will be unfairly dismissed or disciplined.

Such an "open-door" policy may suffice at times. When the policy is taken seriously by management, and its results are publicized, employees learn that they have nothing to lose from speaking out. But such policies are frequently inadequate. In the first place, the promises of protection given by top management cannot always be fulfilled. Though employees may keep their jobs, there are countless ways of making their position difficult, to the point where they may be brought to resign of their own volition or to stay while bitterly regretting that they had spoken out. Second, it would be naive to think that abuses in industry or in government are always unknown to top management and perpetrated against their will by subordinates. If those in charge knowingly manufacture unsafe products or engage in corporate bribery, then the open-door policy is but a trap for the outspoken; even when employees suffer no reprisal for having voiced a criticism to management, they will usually find that it has simply been ignored.

For these reasons, proposals have been made to ensure independent internal consideration of the criticisms, while protecting those who voice them more formally. Internal review boards, ombudsmen, consumer or citizen representatives on boards of trustees, bills of rights for employees: these methods of protection spring up and die away with great rapidity. When they work, their usefulness is undeniable. They allow for criticism with much less need for heroism; give a way to deflect the crank or the witch-hunter *before* his message gains publicity, and a process of checking its accuracy; make it easier to distinguish between urgent alarms and long-range worries; and provide an arena for debating the moral questions of motive, loyalty, and responsibility to the public.

The methods fail when they are but window-dressing from the outset, meant only to please or exhaust dissenters; or when they change, no matter how independent at the start, into management tools. Such is the fate of many a patient representative in hospitals: their growing loyalty to co-workers and to the management and their distance from the patients they are meant to represent once again leave critics little choice between submission and open revolt. Still another reason for the failure of such intermediaries is that they often lack credibility. No matter how well-meaning, they will not be sought out if they cannot protect from retaliation those who turn to them for help. Even if they can give such protection, but cannot inspire confidence in their independence, their role will be largely ceremonial. Finally, they may protect the outspoken but not succeed in correcting the problem brought up; once again, they will quickly lose credence.

In the last decade, a growing number of laws have been enacted to protect employees against reprisals. First to be passed were laws covering federal and state employees; these, however, still work slowly and unevenly. In April 1981, Michigan became the first state to enact a "Whistleblowers Protection Act" covering corporate employees.[19] It allows courts to grant back pay, reinstatement in the job, and costs of litigation to employees who can demonstrate improper treatment.

Alan Westin points out that citizens of Michigan had special reason to support such leg-islation.[20] In the mid-1970s, a chemical company mistakenly shipped PBBs (polybrominated biphenyls) to state feed-grain cooperatives instead of their regular nutritional supplement. As a result, the health of residents was seriously injured, and a great many cattle died. The spon-sor of the law stated that an official inquiry was begun when the farm animals began to die in large numbers. But it was seriously hampered by the reluctance of employees of the chemical company to come forth with information that might have given a clue to the link between the deaths of the animals and the accidental delivery of PBBs. Employees later testified that they had been threatened with dismissal if they told investigators that the PBB accident might have been the cause.

It is too early to tell whether laws such as that enacted in Michigan will become the rule rather than the exception, and whether they will succeed in protecting whistleblowers. The problem with such laws is that there are so many other ways to penalize employees without detection; and that it is not always easy for courts to tell the difference between legitimate and spurious complaints.* Nevertheless, such laws will continue to be needed to protect whistle-blowers against the most egregious reprisals, and to encourage firms to set up more workable internal mechanisms for complaint.[21]

A different method for reducing the tension and risk of whistleblowing can complement laws that protect those who voice criticism. It is to state clear conditions under which those who learn about a certain kind of danger *must* report it. If such requirements to report are properly limited and if they succeed in deflecting reprisals, they can lessen the conflict of loyalties felt by would-be whistleblowers and strengthen their resolve. Such laws already exist in a number of places. One is the Toxic Substances Control Act, enacted in 1977, which requires companies to instruct employees that any person must report information about a chemical they take to present "a substantial risk of injury to health or to the environment.[22]

This type of law, like that protecting whistleblowers, can be undercut and circumvented in a number of ways; it is nevertheless useful insofar as it facilitates reporting of serious and docu-mented dangers. Such laws must, however, be limited to clear-cut improprieties; and the lines must be firmly drawn against requiring reporting on political dissent or on purely personal matters. In many societies, citizens are asked to report "deviations," fellow workers encour-aged to spy on one another, and students asked to expose the subversive views of their teachers and vice versa. No matter how great the need to eradicate unlawfulness and corruption, such parallels should not be ignored.

The alarms of whistleblowers would be unnecessary were it not for the many threats to the public interest shielded by practices of secrecy in such domains as law, medicine, commerce, in-dustry, science, and government. Given these practices, whistleblowers perform an indispensable public service; but they do so at great human cost, and without any assurance that they uncover most, or even the worst, abuses. While they deserve strong support in their endeavors, every ef-fort should therefore be made to combat the problems they signal by other means.

The most important task is to reduce the various practices of collective secrecy in order to permit the normal channels of public inquiry to take the place of whistleblowing and of leak-ing. The more encrusted a society becomes with unnecessary secrecy, confidential procedures,

* In watching the evolution of such laws, their broader effect must also be kept in mind. To what extent might they contribute to making institutions more litigious? And to what extent will protection in one place put increased pressure on another? Is it not possible, for example, that the increasing difficulty in firing incompetent federal employees led to the growing resort to psychiatric fitness-for-duty examinations, and that these, in turn, have become a new weapon with which to fight outspoken critics within a bureaucracy?

systems of classification, and means of corporate, professional, and administrative self-protection, the harder it is for the public to learn in time about risks and wrongdoing.

As I have argued, all secrecy cannot and should not be discarded. But even where limited secrecy fulfills an important function, as in protecting certain military secrets, controls are needed in order to reduce the dangers that arise when power and secrecy combine. And whatever the assumed benefits of secrecy, its role in damming up the usual alternatives to whistleblowing is a cost all too often forgotten.

* * *

The Enduring Phenomenon of Moral Muteness
Alan Lovell

Much is made of the need for individual employees, and organizations as a whole, to act ethically. In the United States, federal and state laws make illegal certain types of environmental abuse, while other laws provide protection for government employees who disclose government waste or misuse of funds. In the United Kingdom, the Public Interest Disclosure Act moved onto the statute books in 1999. It relates to all employees in the public sector and private sector, offering protection to anyone who reveals evidence of an organizational malpractice as long as certain conditions are satisfied, including a judgment that the revelation is in the public interest.

The issue of conscience objectors at work (Beardshaw 1981), principled dissenters (Winfield 1989), or whistleblowers, as others prefer to call them (e.g., Jos, Tomkins, and Hays 1989; Miceli and Near 1992; Soeken and Soeken 1987; Hunt 1995 and 1997; Vinten 1994) has received considerable attention over the years. Although the original objectives of the study upon which this paper draws (Fisher and Lovell 2000) did not include an investigation of whistleblowing scenarios, revelations of potential whistleblowing situations arose spontaneously. The fact that none of the interviewees actually chose to object to the practices that concerned them is a particular aspect that this article explores.

THE RESEARCH DESIGN

The project described in this paper arose out of a competition organized by a professional accountancy body in the United Kingdom, the Chartered Institute of Management Accountants (CIMA), with the researchers ultimately being successful with the research design outlined below. The work focused upon members of two significant professional groupings: accountants and human resource specialists. The representation of these groups in so many organizational and economic sectors makes their experiences especially relevant. However, another factor is that they are often referred to as the two ends of the organizational spectrum, reflecting the stereotypical "hard" and "soft" approaches to managerial issues.

The primary objectives of the study were to:

- explore the types of issues that gave the interviewees "ethical twinges"[1]
- determine why they regarded these issues as ethically problematic
- see how they handled or coped with the situations they identified

Many studies have sought the views of managers and surrogate managers (e.g., students) on a series of hypothetical ethical scenarios (e.g., Waters, Bird, and Chant 1986). Others have considered differences arising from gender influences (e.g., Tsaliki and Ortiz-Buonafina 1990; Prasad, Marlow, and Hattwick 1998) or the impact of cultural and educational systems on ethical reasoning (e.g., Franke, Crown, and Spake 1997; Stevenson and Bodkin 1998). From these responses, levels of ethical reasoning have been interpreted that are then debated in terms of what they might say about managerial, professional, gender, or cultural groupings.

As much as such studies might reveal about levels of ethical reasoning, the distance between this reasoning and actual behavior can be considerable and filled with contextual factors that can inhibit, distort, frustrate, and finally overwhelm the initial reactions and reasoning of an individual in a given situation (see, e.g., Bartels et al. 1998; Sims and Keenan 1998; Fritzsche 2000). Straughan (1984, 151), while generally supportive of Kohlberg's theory of moral development, took issue with Kohlberg's reliance upon verbal responses to hypothetical dilemmas "as a way of understanding what might be called a person's moral principles . . . direct emotional experience of a situation is a necessary precondition of participating in it as a moral agent." Schroeder (2001, 128) also observes that "empirical research using 'real whistleblowers' is uncommon and the investigation of groups of employees who have taken a decision *not* to report their concerns is even more difficult to undertake" (emphasis added).

Once the researchers obtained access to an organization, the initial interview was usually with the chief executive, director of finance, or director of human resources. From there, it was a question of getting agreement to be allowed to talk to other accounting and HR managers. The interviewees were asked, among other things, whether there were any issues that were causing them ethical concerns. As the cases illustrate, the interviewees took the opportunity to raise critical issues. Although the incidents were causing them great angst (sufficient for some to consider resigning), none of the respondents felt able to fully reveal their concerns either within or without their employing organization.

Three instruments were employed at different points during the research. Initially a series of semi-structured interviews was conducted. Of the forty-five interviewees who took part, twenty-eight were accountants and seventeen were HR specialists. Two focus groups were held to explore some of the themes from the interviews. The third instrument was a mail questionnaire involving an organizational simulation that contained a series of sequential decision points.[2] The analysis which follows concentrates upon a particular feature arising from the semi-structured interviews and focus groups.

The average length of interviews was seventy-five minutes (none was less than one hour and a number exceeded two hours). Some cases involved a series of sessions, either multiple interviews with the principal individual or confirmatory interviews with people privy to the complexities of the case. One case (Exhibit 4) involved three interviews with the accountant in question and interviews with four other "witnesses."

All the interviews were conducted around broadly similar questions, but as the interviewees responded to the request to reflect upon any issues in the recent past (within four years), the subsequent questioning and discussion reflected the nature of the responses. The reason for choosing the four-year cut-off point was to defend the study from the accusation that interviewees were invited to trawl their memories in search of any incident that might be construed as an ethical dilemma irrespective of its vintage. The constraint was intended to underline the contemporary nature of the findings. In fact, of the nine cases, only one was four years old, two were ongoing, and the rest had arisen within the previous twelve to twenty-four months.

Of the seven organizations studied, none was known to have been the subject of negative publicity regarding ethical issues. The intent of the study was to avoid easy targets, that is, organizations that had recently experienced notable ethical problems. Not only would access to such organizations have been difficult, but the outputs from such research could have been dismissed as examples of practices from organizations with known problems. The goal, instead, was to concentrate upon the ordinary, the everyday, and the unexceptional, however that might be defined. A mix of profit-seeking and non-profit-seeking organizations was requested by the sponsoring body, as well as the inclusion of companies operating in the manufacturing and service sectors. To these characteristics, organizations with a public profile to protect and a lack of any known unethical practices or incidents were added.

Thirteen of the forty-five interviewees reported fifteen instances in which they had been or were in a position that challenged their personal ethical stance to such an extent that they were forced to consider whether they could continue working in the employing organization. Of the fifteen cases, eight involved public sector or non-profit organizations. An additional case (Exhibit 1) concerned an organization now in the private sector (until the mid-1990s, it had been state owned, and those interviewed claimed that the practices reported had existed many years prior to privatization).

A further ten cases posed significant ethical challenges for the individuals concerned, but the proximity of the interviewees to the practices and behaviors that caused disquiet was too removed for them to be counted as potential whistleblowing cases. The significance of these numbers, relative to the overall number of people interviewed, surprised the researchers in that it had not been anticipated that whistleblowing matters would be encountered.

RAISING ETHICAL CONCERNS IN PUBLIC ORGANIZATIONS

Bird and Waters (1989) observed the reluctance of managers to air concerns in front of colleagues. The character of the discussions in their management seminars changed when the participants were asked to switch from discussing hypothetical scenarios to ethical challenges they were experiencing at work.

> When managers begin to consider problems that they actually face in their organizations, the character of the discussions often changes. Moral expressions recede and are replaced by discussions of organizational politics, technical qualifications, competitive advantages, as well as costs and benefits measured solely in economic terms. In the midst of these kinds of practical considerations, moral terms are abandoned because they seem to lack robustness. (Bird and Waters 1989, 78)

Harrison (1988, 52, 55) makes a similar point about his workshops on managerial integrity.

> Often power issues and concerns blocked the trust building and opening programs, so that the group did not achieve its objectives. . . . I think we were learning that most organizations are not very good places to try and develop personal integrity. It took me, like many others, quite a while to get that point. I find little discussion of business ethics in the organizations I work with and even less discussion of personal integrity.

Although the interviewees stated that certain situations caused them ethical problems, it is surprising that none felt able to raise their concerns at a formal level within their organizations, let alone reveal any of the incidents to an external agency. While Exhibit 3 possesses an element of internal whistleblowing, it cannot be categorized as an example of full-blown whistleblowing.

Bird and Waters (1989) identified three factors that appeared to explain this moral muteness. The first of these was the need to maintain good relations in the employing organization—what they describe as the need for "harmony." The second was a potential threat to efficiency. Moral talk was seen to be anti-problem-solving, a form of obfuscation in the face of difficult ethical choices, but choices that nonetheless had to be made. The final factor was that displaying uneasiness about particular organizational practices could or would threaten personal advancement (all of these factors were in evidence here, as well as others).

Nonetheless, Srivastva and Cooperrider (1988, 2, 14), citing Dewey, argue that organizations have to nurture integrity for their own enlightened self-interest.

> Integrity . . . is one of the key *life-sustaining* properties involved in the *relational* nature of organizational existence. [It] speaks of a unifying process leading to a state of wholeness, completeness, or undividedness. . . . In a critical sense . . . *organization is impossible without integrity, for by definition, organization is differentiation integrated.* . . . All organizations are morally educative in the sense of providing arenas of interaction and learning that shape and mould every participant. In this sense, the enactment of executive integrity cannot be understood apart from the experiential context in which it operates and is shaped.

Based on these observations, Srivastva and Cooperrider (1988, 7) offer a definition of integrity that speaks to the process side of integrity—that is, not a fixed state of being, but a state of continuous dialogue and transformation:

> Executive integrity is dialogical. Executive integrity is more than the presence of morality or the appropriation of values; integrity involves the process of seeing or creating values. Whereas ethical moralism is blindly obedient, integrity represents the "insightful assent" to the construction of human values. In this sense, organization is not viewed as a closed, determined structure but is seen as in a perpetual state of becoming. . . . Dialogue is the transformation of mere interaction into participation, communication, and mutual empathy. Executive integrity is, therefore, a breaking out of a narrow individualism and is based on a fearless trust in what true dialogue and understanding might bring, both new responsibilities and new forms of responsiveness to the other.

Notwithstanding the high ideals set for managers by such writers, a number of major disasters in the United Kingdom during the very late 1980s and the 1990s led to much public disquiet over safety processes, governance practices, management culpability in the disasters, and the moral climate within organizations in general.[3] The enactment of the Public Interest Disclosure Act was a reflection of the concern over organizational practices and the need to protect those who wished to reveal evidence of organizational malpractices. CIMA's decision to hold a competition to study ethical issues within organizations can also be seen as reflecting the wider concern over ethical practices within organizations. This is the context within which the research study commenced.

With the pressure of financial markets removed, with the need to "hit the financials" (in the conventional sense of the term) not apparently an issue, it might seem unlikely that ethically charged incidents would occur in public sector organizations. Without such pressures, one might ask what would stimulate the sort of behavior outlined in the cases featured below. The suggestion that financial pressures exist only in profit-seeking organizations, however, is clearly misplaced. Organizations outside the profit-seeking world invariably operate in environments that are extremely resource-constrained. When an organization also operates in the overtly political world of local or central government,[4] the complexities become many-layered. Add to these elements the complexities brought about by non-financial factors (e.g., cover-ups of mistakes [innocent but significant], errors of judgment, fraud, negligence, deceit), then the sector of the economy in which an organization operates becomes less of an issue in understanding the cause of ethical problems. What gives added poignancy to unethical practices in public service, however, is when the service in question is life-saving, life-sustaining, or life-changing (i.e., its primary aim is to achieve the well-being of individual citizens). In such circumstances, any demurring from the organization's goals is likely to have a direct and deleterious impact upon the quality of life of those dependent upon the service.

THE CASES

This section presents nine case examples of suppressed whistleblowing—evidence that is extremely difficult to obtain (Schroeder 2001). It must be stressed that the observations concerning the silence, or muteness, of the interviewees are not criticisms of the individuals concerned. It is not suggested that they should have revealed their knowledge to internal or external publics. The observations are merely statements concerning the probability (i.e., from a group of fifteen incidents, some twenty-five if one adds the other difficult situations) that at least one case would have led to some form of internal or external whistleblowing. A combination of considerations (loyalty to the organization, loyalty to managerial colleagues/superiors, and most particularly, fear for their position should they refuse to "keep their head below the parapet") led in each case to a decision to "do nothing." Given that these incidents involved individuals who were not known to have experienced difficult ethical situations, and who were working in organizations that were comfortable with the researchers' presence, it is argued that these cases are not an over-representation of unethical/illegal practices. Indeed, as noted, the reverse might be true.

Table 6.1 reflects the types of behaviors that were cited to explain the interviewees' muteness in the cases: efficiency, fear, harmony, loyalty, floating responsibility, cynicism. In four instances, double Xs are used to emphasize the depth of the beliefs expressed in these particular cases (this is not to suggest that single Xs represent examples of only mild emotional disturbance; rather, they are suggestive of deeply felt emotions, whereas double checks are indicative of expressions of concerns that it would be very difficult to overstate). A particular feature is the widespread and quite profound cynicism displayed by the interviewees. Whatever the claims of organizations regarding the ethicality of corporate practices, the attitude of many of the interviewees who had actually been faced with challenges to their ethical principles displayed deep cynicism toward management. This is exemplified by what Titmuss (1970, 199) said in comparing the different approaches in the United States and the United Kingdom to the collecting of blood donations, with specific reference to the notion of "gift" which is central to the blood donor service in the UK:

> There is nothing permanent about the expression of reciprocity. If the bonds of community giving are broken the result is not a state of value neutralism. The vacuum is likely to be filled by hostility and social conflict . . . the myth of maximising growth can supplant the growth of social relations.

TABLE 6.1   Reasons for Managers' Moral Muteness

Case Number and Title	Efficiency	Fear	Harmony/ Loyalty	Floating Responsibility	Cynicism
1. Consequences of a moral vacuum	xx	xx		x	xx
2. Expressing concern but we're not whistleblowers (a)		x	x	x	x
3. Expressing concern but we're not whistleblowers (b)			x	x	xx
4. The revealing of an individual's organizational impotency		x		x	xx
5. Doing wrong to do right	x		x	x	x
6. Moral concerns, but a climate of fear		xx			xx
7. Abuses of power and unwritten organizational understandings (a)		x		x	x
8. Abuses of power and unwritten organizational understandings (b)		x	x	x	x
9. Abuses of power and unwritten organizational understandings (c)		x	x	x	xx

Key:

Efficiency: To raise, let alone discuss, moral issues was perceived as a sign of not prioritizing the economic/ financial performance of the organization.

Fear: Suppression of expression caused by fear for one's present employment or future career prospects.

Harmony/loyalty: Suppression of expression to achieve continued good relations with other managers or to protect the reputation of the employing organization.

Floating responsibility: The continual shifting of moral responsibility for an act or decision to others, with no final resting place for the responsibility to be located; obfuscation in behavior compounded by poorly defined roles and responsibilities.

Cynicism: The expressed view that no good would come of a whistleblowing act as a result of the immorality or lack of courage of others.

The case presented as Exhibit 1, illustrating four of the five factors, is a powerful example of what can develop in the absence of a positive moral climate, the vacuum referred to by Titmuss. In this organization, the moral vacuum left by the absence of moral debate and behavior became filled with an anarchic approach to values and a cancer-like growth of profound cynicism. The void had drawn in ethical cynicism, with the tendency towards anarchy.

In relation to the "arrangements" with overseas agents, it was revealed that the practice had come to the attention of foreign governments and that the major operators in this market (including the British engineering company) were making provisions for substantial repayments of undeclared import taxes. There was also the possibility that a number of the operators could be barred from selling in the overseas market. This development did not suddenly make the decision-making procedures employed invalid, when previously they could be justified on a means-ends basis. An action does not acquire the status of being ethical/unethical merely because its existence is publicly either known or unknown.

The issue that concerned the three accountants involved in the cases in Exhibits 2 and 3 might be described as a technical matter in which there was only one of two possible explanations. Either the budget was being balanced fairly or it was not, but this is too simplistic. Despite national rules covering the development of local authority budgets, considerable discretion remains over the numbers included in forecasts. The accountants felt reasonably sure that the politicians and senior officers were "playing games with the numbers" and, as a consequence, that the electorate and the central government were being misled. However, to make a public stand on this issue could have (1) invoked a great deal of publicity that, irrespective of the outcome, would have been deleterious to the accountants' career prospects and (2) involved the accountants in making accusations of misconduct which could have been difficult to prove, given the subjective nature of forecasts. Allowing the problem to be the responsibility of someone else echoes Bauman's (1994) notion of "floating responsibility." That is, the continual shifting of moral responsibility for an act or decision to others, without locating a final resting place for the responsibility. Obfuscation in behavior compounded by poorly defined roles and responsibilities makes floating responsibility a recurring issue in some organizations, particularly highly bureaucratized ones.

Exhibit 1: Consequences of a Moral Vacuum

This example illustrates both the shallowness of the allegiance of some organizations to ethical behavior and also how the principle of moral agency can be so eroded that what would otherwise be judged unacceptable, nay illegal, practices become tolerated. As one manager (D) observed, "It is the way things are done around here."

A large engineering company operated in a range of domestic (UK) and overseas markets. In at least one of the overseas markets, "arrangements" sometimes had to be negotiated with overseas agents that involved exported goods being artificially reclassified to reduce the level of import duties in the overseas country.[5] The engineering company did not suffer because of the reclassification, but the importing agents acquired the goods at a lower cost (taking import taxes into account) than they would otherwise have had to pay. The only losers were the governments of the countries concerned. When these situations arose, the unofficial but well understood procedure within the engineering company was for the requested "arrangement" to be passed directly to the sales director and managing director. This ultimate decision-making unit would weigh the risks, the returns, and the implications of the decision and then decree whether the proposed deal with the agent would be sanctioned. This was clearly illegal, yet it was argued to the researcher that such behavior was necessary in order to stay in the markets concerned and to protect jobs in the United Kingdom. Other operators in these markets, it was claimed, offer similar "arrangements." Here the consequentialist argument that all the implications of a decision should be weighed in order to identify the decision that offers the greatest good to the greatest number might be tabled. The waters were further muddied when the management of the engineering company argued that the government of the overseas country operated a repressive regime, employing punitive import taxes in order to shore up excessive governmental expenditure on military equipment and governmental largesse.

None of the claims about the foreign government could be validated, but even if they were accurate, what did the actions of the senior management of the company say to the rest of the employees of the engineering company? Whatever the rights and wrongs of the situation, the engineering company was employing criteria and a decision process that allowed a decision to be reached that sanctioned law-breaking activity. If the argument is raised that business is not a precise and neat ethical practice, and that one has to accept that in certain cases ends justify the means, one is accepting a situation where different rules apply in different contexts. No part of a code of behavior can be seen to be inviolate, and every organizational value has its price. This is not to suggest that all laws have to be respected however repressive and immoral, but the behavior of the engineering executives was not law-breaking born from high ideals. The law-breaking was related to organizational and possibly personal gain.

It was also recounted that travel expenses were consistently manipulated by most staff involved in selling (this information was provided by a middle-ranking finance manager). Another manager suggested that the composition of the administrative staff (which was in excess of 2,000) should be looked at in order to identify how many ethnic people and people over fifty years of age could be observed. These "anomalies" did not exist on the shop floor, where the employee profile represented the full range and weightings of ethnic, gender, and chronological categories. Thus, company-wide statistics of racial, gender, and chronological composition masked the disparity of practices within the organization. There were clearly very different cultures and practices in evidence in this organization, and although most of the rules were unwritten, they were well understood. This picture might conjure up images of a little-known engineering company languishing in nineteenth-century management practices. However, this was a very large, high-profile company with an international reputation to protect.

Gifts from overseas clients are an issue for many organizations. In the engineering company, the official practice was for the gifts to be accepted but deposited with the engineering company. They would subsequently be auctioned and the resulting monies donated to charities. However, when a senior manager was given a lavish wedding gift (a vacation worth $16,000) by an overseas agent, he followed the procedure of disclosing the present to a fellow director but then retained it. The case was well known among the senior management of this company. The nature of the incident and its currency meant that it not only left a sour taste in the mouths of some of the management, but the sense of discomfort was still high at the time of the interviews.

Exhibit 2: Expressing Concern, But "We're Not Whistleblowers" (a)

A local authority was preparing its coming year's budget and experiencing problems in producing a balanced budget. Accountant C became concerned when a number of senior managers predicted revenue streams for particular council activities and ventures that were not supported by past experience or anything known about the immediate future. Accountant C did not do anything on his own because he saw it as the responsibility of "those higher up" to make the decision, although he was concerned that the budget was becoming "illegal." Political promises had been made to the local electorate and the use of "optimistic" forecasts relating to particular council activities was the only way left for the Council to "legitimately" fulfill the promises.

The suggestion that the act described in Exhibit 3 could be tantamount to a declaration to whistleblow was received with concern by the interviewees. They perceived whistleblowing as a pejorative term, in the sense of being a nomenclature to avoid for fear of damaging future career prospects and because it implied the negative connotations of 'snitch" or "grass" (i.e., informing), behaviors they frowned upon. The pejorative connotations are underscored by Schroeder's (2001) observation that the British police often conflate the term "whistleblower" with "informer." As he remarks, whistleblowers regard themselves as in a quite distinct category from informers. They regard the latter as wrongdoers who become evidence-providers—a police informer is a villain who provides evidence against other villains. Whistleblowers, in contrast, are invariably innocent of wrongdoing, unless the revelation of malpractices or criminal activities by others is itself considered a crime. However, police officers hold their informers in very low esteem, and police officers who blow the whistle on the wrongdoings of other police officers are invariably excluded and ostracized by their colleagues. The experiences of non-police whistleblowers appear little different.

The fact that G, in Exhibit 4, had no intention to whistleblow was not sufficient for the directors of the charity. Potentially he could, and therefore he was perceived as a threat, to both the charity and, more particularly, to themselves. Thus, having the potential to whistleblow can be as problematic as whistleblowing itself.

Exhibit 3: Expressing Concern, But "We're Not Whistleblowers" (b)

This case relates to the previous one, but occurred a year later. The practices that had concerned Accountant C the year before were being perpetuated, and two other accountants discussed the issues with C. Without the allegedly overstated revenue streams, planned expenditure on a wide variety of local services in the authority would have projected an overspending situation and would have been highlighted by local authority auditors and rejected. The concern was that accounting information was being used to square political circles. As a result of discussions between the accountants, a letter expressing their concerns was sent to the treasurer (the most senior accounting and finance position in the authority). Following receipt of the letter and further discussions, some adjustments were made to the budget, but the changes did not address the main points raised by the accountants. Nonetheless, they felt they had done all they could within the procedures of the organization and they would now progress with the wishes of the local politicians. This local authority now has a process for handling the concerns of troubled employees. However, the administrator of the "whistleblowing system" is the secretary of the chief executive. and anything coming before the investigations committee will undoubtedly be brought to the attention of the chief executive. How confident will the employees (including the accountants) of the local authority be in complaining about a matter such as the one described in this case when they know that the chief executive must be a party to any "illegal" budget? The mere existence of ethical hotlines guarantees nothing if they are constructed as they were in this local government organization.

The accountant in Exhibit 5 summed up his dilemma with the words, "I'm damned if I do and damned if I don't." He did not delight in his dilemma—indeed, he was depressed about it. He was berated by the doctors and consultant clinicians for being a representative of the accounting mentality that was perceived to be corrupting the National Health Service (NHS) and other public services. He was also troubled both by the hospital's inability to deliver the breadth of medical care that was needed and by the types of abuses of power that Exhibits 7, 8, and 9 illustrate. He felt trapped in a difficult situation.

In Exhibit 6, W's fear of loss of employment was not merely a potential outcome; it became a reality. He was first interviewed while still employed by the hospital in question. Subsequent interviews took place after he left, the last one being seven months after he had departed. Even then, his fear for his future career prospects was palpable. His departure did not relate to a single incident but to a litany of alleged unscrupulous behavior on the part of the hospital's chief executive and the regime of fear imposed by this individual upon everyone employed at the hospital.

In the public service sector, senior personnel are often known throughout their region, not just their local organization. All the interviewees testified that W was a person who enjoyed a high reputation, both within his own hospital and within the region in which he worked. However, the situation experienced by W had a direct and telling impact upon their perceptions of how they would react if faced by a situation such as W's. The profound cynicism displayed by these interviewees, resulting from observing W's plight, is itself testimony to the test-case principle. Had W, or others, felt able to reveal the practices that permeated life at the hospital, and had the chief executive's behavior been addressed by NHS senior management, then W (and the others who suffered during the chief executive's reign) might have established the principle that moral agency would be respected. As it was, W and others suffered and/or lost their self-respect in the process. The absence of moral agency allowed profound cynicism to flourish among those who remained or who observed the hospital's plight from the health region.

The cases in Exhibits 7, 8, and 9 all reflect concealment of practices by clinicians and hospital executives that if widely known would have created a furor. The power of the clinicians exposed the culpability, born of weakness, of the chief executives. They also displayed their preparedness to collude with, nay encourage, the executives to do private deals with themselves, at the expense of their clinician colleagues. The suppression of knowledge apparently did not result from any individual act of intimidation but from unwritten, although well-understood, local practices.

Each case reflects a decision on the part of the interviewees to adopt a wringing-of-the-hands approach, expressing feelings of great angst at the problems they described, but in none of the cases feeling able to do anything to raise the issues for managerial discussion or concern.

Exhibit 4: The Revealing of an Individual's Organizational Impotency

G works for a very well known and large charitable organization whose raison d'etre is love, understanding, tolerance, and forgiveness. During the initial interview with G, he revealed that he had an interesting example of principle going on at the time of the interview. Having recently attended a national seminar on the value-added, or sales, taxes (VAT), G had realized that a practice operated by the charity was liable to VAT but had never been declared for VAT purposes. On returning from the seminar, G had brought the matter to the attention of the directors, believing that the correct approach would be to notify the tax authority and discuss the issue with it. G was very aware that the charity could not afford to repay the sums that were now clearly owing, but believed that the tax authority would agree that the VAT rules were never intended to apply to charities like his own, and at worst the charity would need to lobby Parliament and the Treasury to get the rules changed—including retrospectively.

At the next meeting G was clearly less buoyant. He described how the charity's lawyers had been contacted to obtain a legal ruling on the practice in question, and they had confirmed G's assessment. However, the attitude of the senior management toward G was not one of gratitude, but rather coolness, even a degree of wariness. At the third meeting G revealed that the affair had been a sickening experience for him. The legal advice had been that the practice should be terminated immediately, but that no mention should be made to the tax authority. The lawyers thought it unlikely that the tax authority would waive their rights to the unpaid taxes and that the Treasury would change its rules to exclude the charity from future liability, with no chance of retrospective [same question as above] legislation. G's wishes to be honest and "up front" with the tax authority were dismissed as naive. In G's view the coolness displayed by the directors was not impelled by the threat that he would expose the charity to a devastating tax liability (which he had given assurances not to do) but by unwillingness to reveal the directors' error in setting up the practice in the first place.

Whatever the source of the tension, G was now regarded as a potential whistle blower and increasingly treated with coolness and wariness. His position as senior accountant had turned from one that had given him great satisfaction (believing wholeheartedly as he did in the work of the charity) to one that brought him face-to-face with his own organizational impotency. He had thought that he and his work were valued, but now he was seen as something of a risk by the board of the charity. He had no intention of whistleblowing, but it hurt to be treated as if he would. He did not wish to leave the charity, as his family commitments were very constraining, and he still believed in the work of the charity. He viewed his future with sadness and unease.

Exhibit 5: Doing Wrong to Do Right

J was the finance director of a large hospital with significant financial problems. Very recently, a deficit budget had been negotiated with the regional health authority for the hospital to move from a deficit-funding situation to break even within two years. To even get close to this budgetary requirement J needed to consider breaking both Department of

Health rules and national accountancy guidelines on cross-subsidization and the classification of expenditure. If J reclassified certain operating costs as capital costs (the hospital was engaged in a lot of capital expenditure), then some semblance of operational normality could be maintained, although if discovered (by external auditors) he risked losing his job. As a consequence of reclassifying the operating costs, the level of genuine capital expenditure would be much less than recorded. J estimated that the cumulative amount of operating costs that had needed to be reclassified in recent years as capital costs was in the region of £20 million, but without this manipulation the hospital would have been in more trouble than it was and patients would have suffered. J also had his internal audit department demanding replacement staff. J considered this an entirely reasonable request, because the internal audit department was significantly understaffed. It would take £50,000 of recurring annual expenditure to raise the number of internal auditors to the appropriate number. However, J explained that there were more demanding medical needs desperate for an additional £50,000 per year. What should J do? What he actually did was to cross-subsidize and reclassify the operating costs, endeavoring to keep this practice from the prying eyes of the external auditors. The internal audit department continued to operate at 50 percent of its required staffing level.

Exhibit 6: Multiple Causes for Concern, But Set in a Climate of Fear

This case relates to an accountant (W). To obtain verification of W's case, four "witnesses" were interviewed to provide corroboration. All had either worked in W's organization with W (but subsequently left) or were aware of W's circumstances by virtue of working in organizations that had very close working relationships with W's employers over many years. Without exception, all of W's assertions were supported by the four witnesses. The assessment of W by the other interviewees was of an extremely conscientious, able, and trustworthy accountant and colleague, "one of the rising stars."

W had worked in the organization for twelve years and had risen to a position two steps below the director of finance. The current chief executive had been in office for five years, and the initial reaction of staff (including W) to the appointment had been one of relief, for he offered leadership, a quality that had been missing from the organization for a number of years. Gradually, however, management by fear via firings began to reveal itself. Managerial employment contracts were moved from permanent positions to twelve-month rolling contracts. W had accepted one such contract as a condition of being promoted to his last position. The first sign that a member of the management team had fallen out of favor would be that the chief executive would humiliate the manager at an important meeting. Several examples of these humiliations were recounted by the witnesses. W also became concerned at some of the accounting techniques he was asked to employ in order to make the books balance, but he was also concerned at the rise of a then-unqualified member of the finance department (P), who appeared to have a special relationship with the chief executive.

Although W enjoyed working for his employing organization, in that he fervently believed in the services it provided, he was becoming extremely uncomfortable at the callous way employees (managerial and non-managerial) were treated. As one of the witnesses observed, "The HR director had not had a good week unless half-a-dozen manual staff had been sacked." The atmosphere at the organization had turned sour, and W began to feel that his own position had become vulnerable when he returned from a period of absence caused by illness. P had been promoted over W in his absence, even though P was still at this stage only a partially qualified accountant (W had qualified some seven years before). Even though W's performance had been very good in the previous twelve months (as evidenced by his performance review), he was now informed by the chief executive that his performance was no longer acceptable and had not been for some time. The chief executive had decided that W was not able to perform his current position satisfactorily and was terminating his contract. The finance director had objected to the decision but had been overruled.

Although the final interview with W took place seven months after he had left the organization, he displayed considerable anxiety during the interview. His response when asked to explain the basis of his continued anxiety is worth recalling. "Because they drag you down to such an extent that your confidence is absolutely rock bottom. You have no confidence in your own ability, and it takes you a long time to realize that you didn't deserve this. You hadn't done anything wrong . . . in the back of your mind you're thinking, did I do something wrong to deserve this? Until now, I have not said anything about my case. . . . You want a career and you're not quite sure what influence they have in the rest of the public sector—I still haven't got a permanent position. But, I thought, no, I don't want to work for that organization anymore. I'm doing things I don't want to do. I'm being compromised professionally and I don't like the attitude of the whole place. I've got a wife who works. If I don't get a job straightaway, we can manage although there were not many jobs around at the time. I was lucky, I could walk away other people can't walk away."

Exhibit 7: Abuses of Power and Unwritten Organizational Understandings (a)

In NHS hospitals, consultants have their working week analyzed into eleven "sessions." Consultants whose private-practice income exceeds 10 percent of their basic salary over a three-year period are required to declare this and lose payment for one of their eleven NHS sessions, that is, they move to a NHS salary equivalent to ten-elevenths of the full salary. There is no retrospective adjustment associated with this change, and the maximum adjustment is to lose one-eleventh of the basic salary, irrespective of the size of the private-practice income.

A personnel manager at a large hospital was required to write to all the consultants and ask them to complete a standard questionnaire. Six consultants indicated that their respective private-practice incomes had indeed exceeded the 10 percent rule. Three of the consultants accepted, without any rancor, the loss of one-eleventh of their NHS salary for the coming year. However, the other three consultants resisted any such change and individually took issue with the hospital's chief executive. At the time of the research interviews, the three resisting consultants had not had their pay adjusted. From the personnel manager's perspective, two issues were troubling. The first was the sheer inequity and brazen display of power on the part of the resisting consultants. The second was the problems it would create when other consultants became aware of the situation. At the time of the interviews, she did not intend to take the issue further, as it was a decision of senior management and not hers. She had voiced her feelings to the HR director, but no further. She was satisfied that she had done as much as she could and as much as she was going to do, but the morality of the situation troubled her. There is a sense of floating moral responsibility in this "solution," although the personnel manager remained troubled by the situation.

Exhibit 8: Abuses of Power and Unwritten Organizational Understandings (b)

This situation involved drugs distribution on a hospital's wards. M (a personnel manager) described it as "another Bristol." By this is meant the suppression of information concerning clinical malpractice. This was clearly not an issue that was privy only to M, but this ward was part of his area of responsibility and he felt quite deeply about it. However, he was too scared to say anything. "Although it wasn't right, at the end of the day I didn't have the bottle to do anything about it."

In M's defense, and without exception, all the National Health Service managers who took part in the study displayed a sense of identity with, and loyalty to, their hospital, the nature of its work, and the constraints under which it existed, which was far greater than any other organization the researchers experienced. This is not offered as either an excuse or a justification of the actions of these individuals. It is mentioned to recognize that in the process of weighing the issues contained in a case, the interviewees do appear to have been sincerely concerned about the adverse effects any disclosure of their cases would have had on their hospitals.

Exhibit 9: Abuses of Power and Unwritten Organizational Understandings (c)

This case was recounted by a range of middle-ranking HR managers and accountants in a hospital, as well as the deputy director of finance (H), although other senior management did not comment on the case. It was clearly a situation that troubled many in the hospital. Subsequent interviews by the researcher at other hospitals indicated that the following situation prevailed beyond the hospital in question.

The case relates to the waiting list initiative instigated by the Department of Health in 1998. The intention of the initiative was to provide additional funds to hospitals to allow them to reduce hospital waiting lists in key areas. This was a pledge of the incoming Labour government in 1997. The following are the words of the deputy director of finance: "The government has just put all this money into the waiting list initiative, to treat patients and get them off the waiting list. It's taxpayers' money—the spirit of that money was not to line consultants' pockets. In theory, it's NHS money, health sector money. A number of the specialties reacted as one would hope. However, the ophthalmologists said, 'Yes, we will do this, if you pay me something like $1,200 per case. We will pay the nurses time and a half. . . . And if you don't pay us that rate, we won't do the list.' So ophthalmologists got their way—a very dirty deal—nurses get a bit and porters and cleaners get nothing. The ophthalmologists are getting about $24,000 extra per list." In addition to the ophthalmologists, ENT specialists and anesthetists at this hospital also negotiated their own special deals with regard to the waiting list initiatives. When asked how particular specialties could drive through such arrangements, the response was, "They confronted the organization. The chief executive is frightened of the power of these groups, so he is prepared to do deals, rather than risk not getting patients done."

When asked to describe her own feelings toward this situation, H replied, "Perhaps I am naive, but I wouldn't have let it happen. I think all staff should be treated equally, and I would have waged war with the consultants and said, I am sorry—we are not playing."

Had H ever been tempted to blow the whistle at any time? The answer was yes, and the above situation was such a time. She had not, because "I have to respect the chief executive's decision. My loyalty to him, my accountability—I haven't done anything wrong." Once again, the notion of floating moral responsibility is in evidence.

DISCUSSION

The fear of impairing one's future career prospects was a significant factor shaping the muteness of many of the managers about their respective ethical dilemmas. Different notions of managing will need to hold sway if the forms of change necessary to minimize the profound cynicism exemplified in the cases are ever to be approached, let alone addressed.

There is very limited evidence of internal whistleblowing processes being employed by organizations in the United Kingdom, certainly with external membership. Where they are required (e.g., in local government), there is no evidence of any local authority employing an external, independent voice on its investigative panel. Cynicism was supported by the paucity of the commitment to instituting, facilitating, and nurturing sincere attempts to enhance the exercise and expression of moral agency in the organizations studied.

As a number of the cases reflect, the concerned employee's angst focused on senior management. In such situations, internal whistleblower procedures have to possess strong independent and external representation. Otherwise, revealing one's concerns can be tantamount to signing one's career's death warrant, not just within the organization concerned but possibly within the public sector as a whole. The observation of O'Connor (1984), a former head of the U.S. Office of Special Counsel (an agency of the executive branch of the federal government charged with handling complaints of waste, fraud, and abuse of public funds), remains apposite. He offered the following advice to anyone contemplating whistleblowing. "I'd say that unless you're independently wealthy, don't do it. Don't put your head up, because it will get blown off" (Jos, Tomkins, and Hays 1989).

This might be realistic advice to offer troubled employees, but it begs the question as to why it might be so, and whether it is satisfactory that such an expression retains currency today. Doubts of the effectiveness of corporate hotlines and the wisdom of whistleblowing are supported by Arthur Anderson (1999, 33), who reports that 60 percent of the responding companies that had hotlines reported no usage of them: "The low usage may reflect an aversion to whistleblowing on colleagues, lack of a need, or lack of awareness of or confidence in the mechanism."

Not only do the cases present examples of behavior that appears to be both immoral and illegal, but also they suppress moral agency, personal autonomy, and commitment to seeing staff as an important corporate resource. Instead of perceiving their concerns as acts of good corporate practice, the interviewees saw them as at best heroic or, more likely, suicidal. As Bird and Waters (1989, 82) observe,

> moral muteness eliminates any opportunity that might exist for creative, collaborative problem solving that would be best for the manager, as well as for the organization and its stakeholders . . . what could and should be ordinary practice—i.e. questioning of the propriety of specific decisions and actions—tends to require an act of heroism and thus is less likely to occur.

If a form of ethical schizophrenia is allowed to exist between the values and ethics of personal and business life, the individual's ability to keep these two spheres of practice separate will be severely tested as the influence of the economic gains ever more dominance in organizations.

Ways to move forward from this somewhat depressing set of images are not difficult to identify, but the evidence suggests that they will be difficult to operationalize. Mechanisms that genuinely allow dissent to be expressed, listened to, responded to, and, if appropriate, acted upon are crucial. These mechanisms must be more than organizational vents that allow personal angst to be expelled but do not address the cause for concern. Talking is not enough. Training programs are, on their own, insufficient. Listening, if unconnected to, or not followed by, a response that is considered and well thought through is likely to lead to further cynicism. Where situations cry out for action, then criticism must be accepted, dissent must be tolerated, and responsibilities identified, acknowledged, and acted upon.

This requires a vision that itself demands patience. Existing power blocs, particularly those represented by professional groups, will have to accept far greater public scrutiny. However, litigation should not be the primary lever through which to effect change. It is an extremely blunt, lengthy, expensive, and problematic instrument of change.

That the ways forward are neither new nor little more than commonsensical begs profound questions about the recurring evidence of the driving out of moral agency from organizational life. This calls to mind the observation of Legge (1998, 166) that if management does have a moral base, then moral agency, both individual and corporate, has to be possible. In this respect, professional associations have an important role to play in supporting the rights of their members to exercise agency. If, however, the principles of management and moral agency are such as to render any rapprochement between the two sets of principles impossible, then accountants and HR professionals, like all other employees and their professional associations, are faced with a fundamental dilemma, a profound contradiction.

The type of evidence reported here does not indicate that all managers are immoral. However, the cases should not be dismissed as associated with rogue organizations or inherently immoral individuals. What this study reveals is the vulnerability and susceptibility of moral agency in contexts where there are power asymmetries and inadequate accountability mechanisms, where whistleblowing is regarded as a more serious problem than the crime it reports, and where managerial imperatives allow organizational loyalty to be treated as more important than personal integrity and societal interests.

Lovell, Alan. "The Enduring Phenomenon of Moral Muteness." Public Integrity 5, no. 3 (2003): 187–204.
Reprinted with permission from The American Society for Public Administration.

Notes

CHAPTER 1: WHAT IS TRANSPARENCY?

The Power Position of the Bureaucracy (Pp. 3–5)

1. This is directed, among others, at Robert Michels, to whom Weber wrote in November 1906:

> Indispensability in the economic process means nothing, absolutely nothing for the power position and power chances of a class. At a time when no "citizen worked, the slaves were ten times, nay a thousand times as necessary as is the proletariat today. What does that matter? The medieval peasant, the Negro of the American South, they were all absolutely "indispensable." . . . The phrase contains a dangerous illusion. . . . Political democratization is the only thing which can perhaps be achieved in the foreseeable future, and that would be no mean achievement. . . . I cannot prevent you from believing in more, but I cannot force myself to do so.

Quoted in Wolfgang Mommsen, *Max Weber und die deutsche Politick. 1890–1920* (Tübingen: Mohr, 1959), 97 and 121.

2. *Katholikentag:* An annual conference established in 1858, under the direction of a central committee, to discuss ecclesiastical, political and social welfare issues and to represent German Catholicism before the public which was then largely Protestant. Discontinued during the Nazi period, the Congress has been meeting biannually since 1950.

3. *Enquêterecht.* Weber assigned great significance to this right of parliamentary investigation, which the Reichstag was substantially lacking.

4. See Anatole Leroy-Beaulieu, *The Empire of the Tsars and the Russians* (New York: Putnam, 1894). Vol. II, pp. 69–86. Weber seems to have used the German translation by L. Pezold (3 vols., 1884–1890).

5. Weber refers here to *monarchic* constitutionalism, the form of government that Bismarck gave to Imperial Germany: the prime minister remained responsible to the king, not parliament, and the army also remained under the king's control. In practice, this arrangement gave extraordinary power first to Bismarck, then to the Prussian and Imperial bureaucracy, both vis-à-vis the monarch and the parliament. Weber attacked this system in a sensational series of articles in the midst of the First World War. A brilliant comparative analysis of monarchic constitutionalism was written by the historian who came closest to Weber's sociological (but not his political) approach: Otto Hintze, "Das monarchische Prinzip und die konstitutionelle Verfassung," *Preussische Jahrbücher,* vol. 144, 1911, 381–412; reprinted in Hintze's collected writings, ed. By Gerhard Oestreich: *Staat und Verfassung* (Göttingen: Vandenhoeck and Ruprecht, 1962), 359–89.

6. This passage is an addition to the older manuscript; however, it is not clear how many changes Weber actually made. Weber wrote the passage not only after the downfall of William II and the monarchic

bureaucracy, but after he had attacked them in the *Frankfurter Zeitung* in 1917. Hence, whereas Weber draws in "Parliament and Government in a Reconstructed Germany: on the earlier part of the chapter he also seems to draw on that essay in the present section.

In referring to 1076, Weber compares the downfall of William II with the desertion of Henry IV by most of his great nobles in the face of the emperor's spectacular excommunication by Gregory VII; Henry's dramatic submission at Canossa helped him to recoup his political fortunes and began Gregory's decline. The incident was one of the high points in the conflict between papacy and empire, which determined much of the course of European history with all its eventual consequences for rationalism, capitalism and democracy. Weber's comparison can also be seen in the context of Bismarck's famous dictum at the height of his conflict with the Catholic church that "we will not go to Canossa" (1872). A few years later, Bismarck did go, and in 1919 Weber went with the German peace delegation to another Canossa: Versailles.

7. When in 1899 the German Reichstag discussed a bill for the construction of the Mittelland Kanal the conservative Junker party fought the project. Among the conservative members of the parliamentary party were a number of Junker officials who stood up to the Kaiser when he ordered them to vote for the bill. The disobedient officials were dubbed *Kanalrebellen* and temporarily suspended from office. Cf. Chancellor Bülow's *Denkwürdigkeiten* (Berlin 1930), vol. I, pp. 293ff.; H. Horn, "Der Kampf um die Mittelland-Kanal Vorlage aus dem Jahre 1899," in K. E. Born (ed.), *Moderne deutsche Wirtschaftsgeschichte* (Cologne 1966). (G/M)

Administrative Secrecy: A Congressional Dilemma (Pp. 5–9)

1. For a description of some of the principal episodes in this conflict see Wilfred Binkley, *The President and Congress* (New York, 1947). A recent tabulation of controversies in this area from the time of Washington to the present day may be found in *The Power of the President to Withhold Information from the Congress,* Memorandums of the Attorney General, Compiled by the Subcommittee on Constitutional Rights of the Senate Committee on the Judiciary, 85th Cong., 2d Sess., Feb. 6 and Oct. 31, 1958.

2. The House Subcommittee has held hearings periodically since November 7, 1955, and has issued interim reports since that time. The work of the Committee up to July, 1958, is summarized in two progress reports, *Twenty-Fifth Intermediate Report of the Committee on Government Operations,* 84th Cong., 2d. sess., H. Rept. No. 2947, July 27, 1956; and *Thirty-Fifth Report by the Committee on Government Operations,* 85th Cong., 2d. sess., H. Rept. No. 2578, Aug. 13, 1958.

3. Under the chairmanship of Senator Thomas Hennings of Missouri, the Subcommittee on Constitutional Rights of the Senate Committee on the Judiciary has also carried on investigations in this area.

4. Many of the principal issues that have arisen over defense policy are discussed in an interim report by the Moss subcommittee. *Twenty-Seventh Report by the Committee on Government Operations,* 85th Cong., 2d Sess., H. Rept. No. 1884, June 16, 1958.

5. As the AEC itself was subsequently to admit when it held the contract invalid on the grounds of Wenzell's conflicting private interest. As the agency put it: "The matters on which Wenzell was advising the contractor (Dixon) were the same on which he had been employed to advise the government." However, in a decision reimbursing Dixon-Yates for out-of-pocket costs before the contract was cancelled, the Court of Claims ruled that Wenzell's actions did not represent a genuine conflict of interest. *Mississippi Valley Generating Co. v. U. S.,* 175 F. Supp. 505 (1959).

6. For a summary of the Dixon-Yates dispute, see the *Congressional Quarterly Almanac,* Vol. 11 (1955), pp. 533–38.

7. See *New York Times,* June 20, 1959, p. 8.

8. See the memorandum from Attorney General Brownell to President Eisenhower, as printed in *Replies from Federal Agencies to Questionnaire Submitted by the Special Subcommittee on Government Information,* 84th Cong., 1st sess., Nov. 1, 1955, pp. 546–52.

9. *Thirty-Fifth Report by the Committee on Government Operations,* 85th Cong., 2d Sess., H. Rept. No. 2578, Aug. 13, 1958, p. 243.

10. See *New York Times,* June 23 and July 12, 1957.

11. *Twenty-Third Report by the Committee on Government Operations,* 85th Cong. 2d Sess., H. Rept. No. 1619, April 22, 1958, p. 21.

12. See *Hearings,* House Subcommittee on Government Information, 84th Cong., 2d Sess., Mar.7, 8, 9, 1956, p. 756.

Claude Reyes et al. v. Chile (Pp. 9–15)

1. *Cf.* Letter dated May 7, 1998, from the Executive Director of the Terram Foundation to the Executive Vice President of the Foreign Investment Committee (file of appendixes to the application, appendix 1(1), folios 40 and 41); testimony given by Marcel Claude Reyes before the Inter-American Court during the public hearing held on April 3, 2006; and print-out of some links on the Terram Foundation web page of August 9, 2000 (file before the Commission, volume II, folio 429).

2. *Cf.* Letter dated May 7, 1998, from the Executive Director of the Terram Foundation to the Executive Vice President of the Foreign Investment Committee (file of appendixes to the application, appendix 1(1), folios 40 and 41); and testimony given by Marcel Claude Reyes before the Inter-American Court during the public hearing held on April 3, 2006.

3. *Cf.* Letter dated May 7, 1998, from the Executive Director of the Terram Foundation to the Executive Vice President of the Foreign Investment Committee (file of appendixes to the application, appendix 1(1), folios 40 and 41).

4. *Cf.* Request for information of May 7, 1998, from the Executive Director of the Terram Foundation to the Executive Vice President of the Foreign Investment Committee (file of appendixes to the application, appendix 1(1), folios 40 and 41).

5. *Cf.* Testimony given by Marcel Claude Reyes before the Inter-American Court during the public hearing held on April 3, 2006; testimony given by Eduardo Moyano Berríos before the Inter-American Court during the public hearing held on April 3, 2006; and written statement made by the witness, Arturo Longton Guerrero of March 2006 (file on merits, reparations, and costs, volume III, folio 915).

6. *Cf.* Testimony given by Marcel Claude Reyes before the Inter-American Court during the public hearing held on April 3, 2006.

7. *Cf.* Written statement made by the witness, Liliana Guiditta Macchiavello Martini on March 10, 2006 (file on merits, volume III, folio 828); and testimony given by Eduardo Moyano Berríos before the Inter-American Court during the public hearing held on April 3, 2006.

8. *Cf.* Copy of the facsimile letter of May 19, 1998, from the Executive Vice President of the Foreign Investment Committee to Marcel Claude Reyes (file of appendixes to the application, appendix 2, folio 48); and testimony given by Marcel Claude Reyes before the Inter-American Court during the public hearing held on April 3, 2006.

9. *Cf.* Letters of June 3 and July 2, 1998, from Marcel Claude Reyes to the Executive Vice President of the Foreign Investment Committee (appendixes to the application, appendixes 1(2) and 1(3), folios 43 and 46); testimony given by Marcel Claude Reyes before the Inter-American Court during the public hearing held on April 3, 2006; and testimony given by Eduardo Moyano Berríos before the Inter-American Court during the public hearing held on April 3, 2006.

10. *Cf.* Testimony given by Marcel Claude Reyes before the Inter-American Court during the public hearing held on April 3, 2006; testimony given by Eduardo Moyano Berríos before the Inter-American Court during the public hearing held on April 3, 2006; and brief of August 13, 1999, presented by the State of Chile during the proceedings before the Inter-American Commission on Human Rights (file before the Inter-American Commission on Human Rights (file before the Inter-American Commission on Human Rights, volume II, folios 908 to 910).

11. *Cf.* Report presented by the State to the Inter-American Commission on June 30, 2005 (file before the Commission, volume I, folio 221); and final arguments brief submitted to the Court by the State on May 18, 2006 (file on merits, reparations, and costs, volume IV, folio 1264).

12. *Cf.* Facsimile letter of May 19, 1998, from the Executive Vice President of the Foreign Investment Committee to Marcel Claude Reyes (file of appendixes to the application, appendix 2, folio 48); testimony given by Marcel Claude Reyes before the Inter-American Court during the public hearing held on April 3, 2006; testimony given by Eduardo Moyano Berríos before the Inter-American Court during the public hearing held on April 3, 2006; and application brief presented by the Inter-American Commission (file on merits, reparations, and costs, volume I, folio 54).

13. *Cf.* Testimony given by Eduardo Moyano Berríos before the Inter-American Court during the public hearing held on April 3, 2006.

CHAPTER 2: TRANSPARENCY AND COMPETING VALUES: PRIVACY, SECURITY, AND EFFICIENCY

The Right to Privacy (Pp. 19–21)

1. Year Book, Lib. Ass., folio 99, pl. 60 (1348 or 1349), appears to be the first reported case where damages *were* recovered for a civil assault.

2. These nuisances are technically injuries to property; but the recognition of the right to have property free from interference by such nuisances involves also a recognition of the value of human sensations.

3. Year Book, Lib. Ass., folio 177, pl. 19 (1356), (2 Finl. Reeves Eng. Law, 395) seems to be the earliest reported *case* of an *action* for slander.

4. Winsmore v. Greenbank, Willes, 577 (1745).

5. Loss of service is the gist of the action; but it has been said that "we are not aware of any reported case brought by a parent where the value of such services was held to be the measure of damages." Cassoday, J., in Lavery v. Crooke, 52 Wis. 612, 623 (1880). First the fiction of constructive service was invented; Martin v. Payne, 9 John. 387 (1812). Then the feelings of the parent, the dishonor to himself and his family, were accepted as the most important element of damage. Bedford v. McKowl, 3 Esp. 119 (t800); Andrews v. Askey, 8 C. & P. 7 (1837); Phillips *v.* Hoyle, 4 Gray, 568 (1855); Phelin v. Kenderdine, 20 *Pa.* St. 354 (1853). The allowance of these damages would seem to be a recognition that the invasion upon the honor of the family is an injury to the parent's person, for ordinarily mere injury to parental feelings is not an element of damage, e.g., the suffering of the parent in case of physical injury to the child. Flemington v. Smithers, 2 C. & P. 292 (1827); Black *7.1.* Carrolton R. R. Co., to La. Ann. 33 (1855); Covington Street Ry. Co. v. Packer, 9 Bush, 455 (1872).

6. "The notion of Mr. Justice Yates that nothing is property which cannot be earmarked and recovered in detinue or trover, may be true in an early stage of society, when property is in its simple form, and the remedies for violation of it also simple, but is not true in a *more* civilized state, when the *relations of* life and the interests arising therefrom are complicated." Erle, J., in Jefferys v. Boosey, 4 H. L. C. 815, 869 (1854).

7. Copyright appears to have been first recognized as a species of private property in England in 1558. Drone on Copyright, 54, 61.

8. Gibblett v. Read, 9 Mod. 459 (1743), is probably the first recognition of goodwill as property.

9. Hogg v. Kirby, 8 Ves. 215 (1803). As late as 1742 Lord Hardwicke refused to treat a trademark as property for infringement upon which an injunction could be granted. Blanchard v. Hill, 2 Atk. 484.

10. Cooley on Torts, 2d ed., p. 29.

11. Amer. Law Reg. N. S. I (1869); 12 Wash. Law Rep. 353 (1884); 24 Sol. 5. & Rep. 4 (1879).

12. Scribner's Magazine, July, 1890. "The Rights of the Citizen: To his Reputation," by E. L. Godkin, Esq., pp. 65, 67.

13. Manola v. Stevens & Myers, N. Y. Supreme Court, "New York Times "of June 15, 18, 21, 1890. There the complainant alleged that while she was playing in the Broadway Theatre, in a role which required her appearance in tights, she was, by means of a flash light, photographed surreptitiously and without her

consent, from one of the boxes by defendant Stevens, the manager of the "Castle in the Air" company, and defendant Myers, a photographer, and prayed that the defendants might be restrained from making use of the photograph taken. A preliminary injunction issued *ex parte,* and a tune was set for argument of the motion that the injunction should be made permanent, but no one then appeared in opposition.

Privacy Rights and Protection: Foreign Values in Modern Thai Context (Pp. 21–25)

1. B. Moore. *Privacy: Studies in Social and Cultural History.* Almonde, New York, 1984.

2. P. Ramasoota. Privacy: A Philosophical Sketch and a Search for a Thai Perception. *MANUSYA: Journal of Humanities,* 4 (2: September 2001), 89–107, p. 98.

3. N. Mudler. *Inside Thai Society.* Silkworm Books, Chiengmai, 2000. Generations. According to Holmes and Tangtongtavy, the two cornerstones of Thai culture are conflict avoidance and the hierarchical.

4. H. Holmes and S. Tangtingtavy. *Working With the Thais.* White Lotus Press, Bangkok, 1997.

5. H. Irwin. *Communicating With Asia: Understanding People and Customs.* Allen & Unwin, Malaysia, 1996.

6. S. Piker. *The Psychological Study of Theravada Societies.* Contributions to Asian Studies 8. Brill, Leiden, 1997.

7. C. Engholm. *When Business East Meets Business West: The Guide to Practice and Protocol in the Pacific Rim.* John Wiley & Sons, New York, 1991.

8. *The Nation.* "Thaksin Dismisses Concerns," May 8, 2003. www.nationalmultimedia.com/search/page.acrview.php?clid=2&cli=78393& usrsess.

9. Phra Dhammapitaka (P. A. Payutto). *Buddhist Approach to Law.* Buddha-Dhamma Foundation, Bangkok, 1998.

10. Phra Dhammapitaka (P. A. Payutto). *A Constitution for Living: A Handbook for Living.* Buddha-Dhamma Foundation, Bangkok, 2004.

11. In their book *Working With the Thais* [see note 4], variations of *kreng-jai* can be differentiated in terms of *kreng-jai* towards junior people and towards government officials.

National Security and Open Government in the United States: Beyond the Balancing Test (Pp. 25–29)

1. See Arnold Wolfers, "'National Security' As An Ambiguous Symbol," *Political Science Quarterly* 67 (December 1952), pp. 481–502.

2. Vannevar Bush, *Science—the Endless Frontier: A Report to the President on a Program for Postwar Scientific Research* (Washington D.C.: Office of Scientific Research and Development, July 1945), quoted by Arvin Quist, *Security Classification of Information,* p. 96.

3. R. C. Tolman, R. F. Bacher, A. H. Compton, E. O. Lawrence, J. R. Oppenheimer, F. H. Spedding, and H. C. Urey, *Report of Committee on Declassification,* Memorandum to Maj. Gen. L. R. Groves, November 17, 1945, P. 3, quoted in Arvin Quist, *Security Classification of Information,* p. 97.

4. Edward Teller, Letter to the Editor, *The New York Times,* May 27, 1973, quoted in Stephen Dycus, et al., eds., National Security Law—Third Edition, p. 1047.

5. "Lost Chance on Terrorists Cited: INS, FAA Might Have Found 2 of 19 Hijackers, Officials Say," *The Washington Post,* October 2, 2002, p. A1.

6. Vernon Loeb, "When Hoarding Secrets Threaten National Security," washingtonpost.com, January 26, 2003.

7. Eleanor Hill, Staff Director, "Joint Inquiry Staff Statement," October 17, 2002, p. 5, see www.fas.org/irp/congress/2002_hr/101702hill.html.

8. For extensive detail on the Bay of Pigs 40th anniversary conference, see the National Security Archive website at www.gwu.edu/~nsarchiv/bayofpigs/index.html.

9. See the September 19, 1995 special section of *The Washington Post*, and the joint statement by the publishers of the *Post* and the *Times*.

10. For the most thorough report of the Ressam arrest, see Josh Meyer, "Border Arrest Stirs Fear of Terrorist Cells in U.S.," *Los Angeles Times*, March 11, 2001, p. A-1.

11. *Brown v. Glines*, 444 U.S. 348, 369 (1980) (Justice William Brennan, dissenting).

Governmental Transparency in the Path of Administrative Reform (Pp. 29–34)

1. The U.S. Department of Justice will be abbreviated U.S. DOJ for parenthetical citations.

2. Don Kettl places the management reforms of the 1990s at the tail end of a series of reforms. He argues: "From the late 1970s through the mid-1990s, a remarkable revolution swept much of the world. Governments around the globe adopted management reforms to squeeze extra efficiency out of the public sectors—to produce more goods and services for lower taxes" (Kettl 1997, 446).

CHAPTER 3: FREEDOM OF INFORMATION

Outsourcing the Constitution and Administrative Law Norms (Pp. 38–52)

1. Kettl (2002, pp. 507–8) lists "a commitment to public values" under a section entitled, "Lessons for Managing Indirect Government." He suggests that "rotation of government employees through nongovernmental partners" (p. 508) might alert contractors to "public-sector norms" such as "responsiveness to citizens" and "equity" (p. 507). Perhaps because he focuses on public administration's service rather than regulatory activities, Kettl does not mention the constitutional and administrative law constraints that largely define—and enforce—"public-sector norms" in the public sector itself.

2. Since 1969, dismissals of federal employees covered by civil service protections against adverse actions have been guided by the principle that "a finding that an employee has done something immoral or indecent could support a dismissal without further inquiry only if all immoral or indecent acts of an employee have some ascertainable deleterious effect on the efficiency of the service" (*Norton v. Macy*, 1969, p. 1165).

3. Light's (1999) use of the term *formal rulemaking* is probably technically incorrect. Most federal rulemaking, including that of the EPA, is in accordance with the Administrative Procedure Act's procedures for informal (*notice and comment*) rulemaking as opposed to those for formal (*on the record*) rulemaking.

4. U.S. Office of Management and Budget (OMB, 2003a). A list appears in the section on "Acronyms and Definitions"; the terms are used throughout the document.

5. OMB (2001), *The President's Management Agenda*, reports "The President's vision for government reform is guided by three principles. Government should be: Citizen-centered . . . ; Results-oriented; Market-based" (p. 4).

6. See also *Pennsylvania v. Board of Directors of City Trusts of Philadelphia* (1957).

7. After releasing them from jail, a deputy sheriff tailed their vehicle, stopped it, put the three in the sheriff's car, and took them to a place on an unpaved road where they were assaulted and killed by three law enforcement agents and the 15 private individuals.

8. See New (2004) and Strohm (2004). With the approval of the Transportation Security Administration (TSA), JetBlue transferred passenger data to the Department of Defense. The TSA's Computer-Assisted Passenger Pre-screening System (known as CAPPS II) envisioned relying on commercial databases to identify passengers who present security threats. The Fourth Amendment question would begin with consideration of whether individuals have a reasonable expectation of privacy in the information in these databases, which they may not. At the federal level, private organizations engaged in state action cannot be sued for constitutional torts, whereas their employees are subject to such suits (see *Correctional Services Corporation v. Malesko*, 2001).

9. In dissent, Justice Clarence Thomas, joined by Chief Justice William Rehnquist and Justices Anthony Kennedy and Antonin Scalia, argued that "we have never found state action based upon mere 'entwinement'" (*Brentwood Academy v. Tennessee Secondary School Athletic Association*, 2001, p. 305).

10. Defined in *Black's Law Dictionary* (Black, 1979) as "an action whereby the owner or person entitled to repossession of goods or chattels may recover those goods or chattels from one who has wrongfully distrained or taken or who wrongfully detains such goods or chattels" (p. 1168).

11. Executive Order 8802 (1941).

12. The program does not prohibit discrimination or the teaching of hatred based on sex or sexual orientation.

13. Under the 1998 "Shelby Amendment" (Public Law 105-277), data gathered pursuant to federal grants (although not contracts) are subject to the Freedom of Information Act. According to OMB's guidance, the amendment applies only to data used as a basis for federal regulation (see Bass & Hammitt, 2002, p. 608).

14. To learn more about federal contracting practices, we e-mailed all 34 members, alternate members, and liaisons of the Federal Acquisitions Council seeking information about compelling contractors to turn over records to the agencies, discrepancies between Federal Acquisition Regulation's (FAR) language and actual practice, and how FAR might be improved. Although we received only five responses, these were factual and helped inform our discussion in this section.

A Partial Revolution: The Diplomatic Ethos and Transparency in Intergovernmental Organizations (Pp. 53–68)

1. For a survey of the criteria that might be used to define the set of intergovernmental organizations, see Archer (2001, 30–34). Key attributes include a multilateral membership, a permanent and autonomous structure, and an avowed aim of advancing the common interests of members.

2. It is "longstanding custom and accepted practice in international relations," the U.S. Justice Department recently insisted, "to treat as confidential and not subject to public disclosure information and documents exchanged between governments and their officials" (DOJ 1999).

3. This is an amendment of Theodore Draper's notion of a "bifurcated presidency" (Draper 1991, 580–98). In a similar vein, Aaron Wildavsky wrote about the emergence of "two presidencies" (Wildavsky 1969, 230–45).

4. Section 15 of the Access to Information Act.

5. *Hien Do-Ky v. Minister of Foreign Affairs and International Trade*, Federal Court of Canada (T-2366-95, February 6, 1997). The decision was subsequently upheld by the Federal Court's Appeal Division.

6. Conference Committee Report of 1974, Amendments to the Freedom of Information Act, H. Rept. 93-13 80, September 25, 1974; also published as S. Rept. 93-1200, October 1, 1974.

7. Section 13 of the Access to Information Act.

8. The rules on treatment of state-to-state communications are specified in section 13 of the Access to Information Act. For the comparable rules on treatment of personal information, see section 19(1)(c) of the Access to Information Act and section 8(2)(m)(i) of the Privacy Act. For business information, see section 20(6) of the Access to Information Act.

9. Statement of the Department of Foreign Affairs and International Trade, quoted in the *Do-Ky* case.

10. See the complaints of the International Centre for Sustainable Trade and Development (1999), ActionAid (2000), and Oxfam UK (2000).

11. Some internal or administrative papers of the Secretariat are contained in the OFFICE collection, and draft documents in the JOBS collection. Neither collection is affected by the derestriction policy.

12. The phrase is used in the United Kingdom's new Freedom of Information Act, 2000.

13. Omnibus Appropriations Bill, H.R. 4328 (PL105-277), section 601.

14. Such as letters of intent or memoranda of economic and financial policies, documents prepared by borrowers that describe the policies that a country intends to implement in the context of its request for financial support from the IMF.

15. For example, section 2(1) of Canada's Access to Information Act says that its purpose is "to provide a right of access to information in records under the control of a government institution in accordance with the principles that government information should be available to the public, that necessary exceptions to the right of access should be limited and specific and that decisions on the disclosure of government information should be reviewed independently of government."

16. The treaty with South Korea (Canada Treaty Series 1999/28) was signed in 1999, the treaty with Australia (Canada Treaty Series 1996/31), in 1996.

17. Response by the U.S. Department of Defense, Freedom of Information Directorate to Request 02-F-1850, September 30, 2002.

18. The operation of the dispute settlement mechanism is governed by the Dispute Settlement Understanding, Annex 2 to the WTO Agreement. See in particular Articles 10, 17.10, and 18 of the understanding and its Appendix 3.3. See also Article VII of the rules of conduct for the understanding on rules and procedures governing the settlement of disputes, December 11, 1996, WTO Document WT/DSB/RC/1. In addition, other documents—such as agendas for meetings of the Dispute Settlement Body and requests from governments to that body for establishment of a panel—are subject to the delayed derestriction rules contained in the derestriction policy (Debevoise 1998, 3).

19. For example, Oxfam UK observed the WTO's policy regarding the role of nongovernmental organizations was more restrictive than that of other intergovernmental organizations.

20. The trade policy review mechanism was actually begun on an interim basis in 1989 and later included in the 1995 agreement establishing the WTO.

21. Marrakesh Agreement Establishing the WTO, Annex III(A).

22. General Agreement on Tariffs and Trade, Article X.

23. General Agreement on Trade in Services, Articles III and III bis.

24. A general obligation to provide information on SPS measures is established in Article 7 of the SPS Agreement. Detailed provisions on access to information are contained in Articles 1, 3, and 5 of Annex B of the Agreement. The agreement is intended to ensure that domestic rules on food safety, and animal and plant health standards, are not used to discriminate against foreign producers.

25. Agreement on Trade-Related Aspects of Intellectual Property Rights, Article 63.

26. Agreement on Trade-Related Investment Measures, Article 6.

27. Agreement on Government Procurement, Articles XVIII and XIX. The agreement also contains the usual obligation to publish laws, regulations, and decisions relating to procurement practices, as well as an obligation to provide statistics on procurement.

28. Reference paper on principles on the regulatory framework for basic telecommunications services, April 1996, Article 4.

29. Agreement on Technical Barriers to Trade, Articles 2.9 and 10. The agreement is intended to ensure that technical regulations such as rules on packaging, marking, and labeling are not used to discriminate against foreign producers.

CHAPTER 4: PROACTIVELY RELEASED INFORMATION

The Evolution of E-Government among Municipalities: Rhetoric or Reality? (Pp. 71–76)

1. Some studies were conducted with the sample collected in a specific geographic boundary (California). Musso, Weare, and Hale (2000) examine the applications of Web technologies for local governance based on data collected from a structured content analysis of 270 Californian municipal governments' Web sites. The study concluded that many municipal Web sites are not well designed and do not make substantial contributions to better local governance.

2. The five-stage framework is adapted from Hiller and Bélanger (2001). The United Nations and the American Society for Public Administration (2001) also suggest a similar framework for the Global Study of E-government: (1) emerging Web presence; (2) enhanced Web presence; (3) interactive Web presence; (4) transactional Web presence; and (5) fully integrated Web presence. These proposed stages of e-government seem to focus on Web-based public services (information provision and public service delivery) and do not include Web-based political participation and virtual democracy (online voting and public forums). Layne and Lee's study (2001) also proposes a similar stage-growth model of e-government that presents a general progress of e-government based on technical, organizational, and managerial feasibilities. The stage model includes the cataloguing stage, transaction stage, vertical integration stage, and horizontal integration stage. While this model does not include the political participation stage, it distinguishes vertical integration (integration of similar functionalities among different levels of government) from the horizontal integration (systems integration across different functions).

3. The "maxi" system enables citizens to obtain government information, request permits, and make various transactions, such as bill payment.

4. Singapore's "e-citizen" includes various public services such as birth registration, education, employment search, business-related government services, and retirement.

5. Cancian, an anthropologist, rebuked the positive and linear relationship between socioeconomic status and innovativeness and suggested a nonlinear relationship between the two variables. For more information, see Rogers (1995, 270–72). Nolan's (1979) model of advanced data processing systems posits six stages of growth in companies, including initiation, contagion, control, integration, data administration, and maturity. The model has been widely applied for the adoption and growth of various IT innovations. In their study of organizational life cycle and effectiveness, Quinn and Cameron (1983) posit four stages of organizational growth, including the entrepreneurial stage, collectivity stage, formalization/control stage, and structural elaboration stage.

6. Nolan's (1979) model of advanced data processing systems posits six stages of growth in companies, including initiation, contagion, control, integration, data administration, and maturity. The model has been widely applied for the adoption and growth of various IT innovations. In their study of organizational life cycle and effectiveness, Quinn and Cameron (1983) posit four stages of organizational growth, including the entrepreneurial stage, collectivity stage, formalization/control stage, and structural elaboration stage.

7. Some municipal governments indicated that they have implemented various programs such as establishing pubic access terminals in city facilities (729 municipalities), working with local schools (392 municipalities), and providing training and technical support for citizens (201).

Mr. Justice Brandeis and the Creation of the *Federal Register* (Pp. 76–89)

1. A number of the justices were uncomfortable with the new building's opulence. Frankfurter (still a professor), in a 1935 letter to Justice Harlan Stone, referred to the new Court even 10. more irreverently as "the Temple of Karnak." October 16, 1935. Harvard Law School, Manuscript Division.

Added descriptions are from: Senate Documents, 71st Cong., 3rd sess., December 1, 1930–March 4, 1931, vol. II. Washington, DC: Government Printing Office, 1932, 181; Glenn Brown (1900) *History of the United States Capitol,* vol. I, The *Old Capitol.* LVI Cong., 1st sess., Senate Document Number 60. Washington, DC: Government Printing Office, 69 and photos from the U.S. Supreme Court, Office of the Curator. The phrase "marble temple" is from Merlo J. Pusey, *Charles Evans Hughes,* vol. II. New York: Columbia University Press, 1963, 690.

2. The Panama Refining Company attacked the "validity" of a number of regulations issued by the Code and argued that section 9(c) was "an unconstitutional delegation to the President of legislative power" and transcended "the authority of the Congress under the commerce clause."

3. Stephens wrote in this letter that he "was much pained over the error both from the Department standpoint and personally."

4. Griswold was dean of the Law School from 1946 to 1967, 11, then solicitor general from 1967 to 1973, under Presidents Johnson and Nixon. He argued the Pentagon Papers case before the Supreme Court.

5. The 1914 quote is found in two sources cited by Mason: Sherman E. Mittell, ed., *Brandeis and the Modern State.* Washington, DC: National Home Library Foundation, cites Brandeis's testimony before the U.S. Congress, House Committee on Interstate and Foreign Commerce, 63rd Cong., 2nd sess., January 30, 1914, 4. It is also cited as part of an address before the National Rivers and Harbors Congress, December 9, 1914, "Constructive Co-operation v. Cutthroat Competition."

6. Brandeis published a series of 10 articles on the "money trust" in *Harpers' Weekly,* the first on August 13, 1913, and the remainder between November 22, 1913, and December 17, 1914. The articles were then compiled in a book, published by Frederick A. Stokes Company.

7. These rules and orders were initially published in the *London Gazette,* a twice-weekly document dating from the mid-1600s (under Charles II), and were mixed among a voluminous assortment of official notices and advertisements. Later they were published in the *Revised Statutes, Statutory Rules and Orders*.

8. One purpose of Carr's visit to the United States was to advise on setting up the *Federal Register.* He also spoke about delegated legislation to law school students in seminars at Harvard and Yale.

9. John Fairlie, in an early discussion highlighting the problem, wrote, "Notwithstanding the variety and volume of administrative regulations, and their importance in the work of government, comparatively little attention has thus far been given to the methods of their preparation and publication" (828).

10. The code drafting process varied widely. In some industries, such as textile, iron and steel, and lumber, leaders of management and labor, after much government pressure and considerable bargaining, drafted codes for their operations. In other industries, such as bituminous coal and crude oil production, this was not the case. In 1933, the oil industry was among the first to seek federal controls, although there was disagreement over the extent of control needed.

Initially, beginning with Oklahoma in 1927, efforts to control oil production had been a state matter. When this failed to stem the flow of "hot oil," states and major producers turned to the federal government with the NIRA seen, correctly, as offering a solution. Only later, when the crisis had receded, were there industry objections to federal controls. The "hot oil" issue was also very high on President Roosevelt's agenda. It was discussed in his second cabinet meeting, March 14, 1933, at which time Interior Secretary Ickes was authorized to invite the governors of Oklahoma, Texas, and California (or their representatives) to a meeting in Washington, D.C. to try to set policy. See Hawley (1966), Ickes (1933), and Roos (1937).

11. The other members of this group were J. G. Laylin, special assistant to the undersecretary of the Treasury; D. J. Haykin, chief, division of documents for the Library of Congress; and Cyril Wynn, chief of the division of research and applications at the State Department.

12. Richberg, a labor expert and early advisor to Roosevelt, was chief assistant to the head of the National Recovery Administration, General Hugh Johnson, and later (1935) temporary chairman of the National Industrial Recovery Board.

13. This was not an unusual practice for Brandeis and Frankfurter. For example, in 1926, James Landis, a former Frankfurter student and Brandeis clerk, was completing his doctoral dissertation on congressional rights under the Constitution in investigations as the Supreme Court was considering this question in a case before it. Brandeis pushed him to finish and publish his work before the Court reached a decision; the dissertation was published in the *Harvard Law Review* and Van Devanter, writing for the majority, used Landis's arguments (though, to Landis's disappointment he did not cite him). See Ritchie (1980, 31).

14. Fischer's response was quoted in many papers. The lengthy quote is found in *America,* December 29, 1934, 275, a copy of which is in the Brandeis papers at Louisville, Reel 65. A shortened version in *The New York Times* is slightly different; here the copy was "in the hip pocket of the agent."

15. There was an exchange of letters between Erwin Griswold and H. T. Newcomb, vice president and general counselor for the Delaware and Hudson Railroad, about the Lewis bill and Griswold's ob-

jections to that bill because it was too narrow in focus. December 1934b, Griswold, Box 23-6. Harvard Law Library, Manuscript Division.

16. See, for example, Murphy (1982).

CHAPTER 5. OPEN PUBLIC MEETINGS

Open Meeting Statutes: The Press Fights for the "Right To Know" (Pp. 101–2)

1. "A popular Government, without popular information, or the means of acquiring it, is but a Prologue to a Farce or Tragedy; or, perhaps both." 9 WRITINGS OF JAMES MADISON 103 (Hunt ed. 1910) (letter to W. T. Barry, Aug. 4, 1822).

2. A Memorandum on Open Meetings From J. R. Wiggins to the Board of Commissioners of the District of Columbia, March 27, 1951, p. 7, on file in the office of the American Society of Newspaper Editors, Wilmington, Delaware.

3. Even the reports of congressional debates published in *The Congressional Record* are frequently revisions of the actual remarks, although the debates are open and alterations thus subject to contradiction. See Neuberger, *The Congressional Record Is Not a Record,* N.Y. Times, April 20, 1958, § 6 (Magazine), p. 14.

4. The governor of one state attempted to defend closed sessions for investigating the spending practices of state institutions by commenting: "You would discuss your personal finances around the dinner table, not out in the street or at your next-door neighbors"; one newspaper editorially replied: "Whose dinner table does . . . [the governor] think he's sitting at? . . . The public business is the public's business. Open up those dining room doors, governor! Let's all have a seat at the table." Material Enclosed in Letter From Chief Editorial Writer of the Chicago Sun-Times to the Harvard Law Review, Nov. 28, 1961.

5. See Yankwich, *Legal Implications of and Barriers to the Right To Know,* 40 MARQ. L. REV. 3, 35 (1956)

6. WIGGINS, FREEDOM OR SECRECY 20 (1956) [hereinafter cited as WIGGINS].

7. "I do not remember a single executive session but that there was a report in the newspaper. . . . [T]he report was tinged and slanted by the personal opinion and desires of the person who had revealed what had transpired." Chamberlain, *Let's Take the Hush! Hush! Out of Local Government,* reprinted in part in Bull. of the American Soc'y of Newspaper Editors, March 1, 1958, p. 10.

8. See WIGGINS 22.

9. "The debates were secret, and fortunately so, for criticism from without might have imperilled . . . [the] work . . . so great were the difficulties encountered from the divergent sentiments and interests of different parts of the country . . . ." I BRYCE, THE AMERICAN COMMONWEALTH 24 (2d ed. 1908). It has been observed, however, that because of the secrecy of the convention *The Federalist* had to be written to achieve acceptance of the Constitution. WIGGINS 9.

10. Sommers, *Kick Against the Goad,* 48 NAT'L CIVIC REV. 15, 19 (1959).

11. *Ibid.*

12. A Letter From Chief Editorial Writer of the *Chicago Sun-Times* to the *Harvard Law Review,* Nov. 28, 1961, states:

   [I]t is not so much an unwillingness to express public views that accounts for the desire for secrecy as it is the need to cover up just plain ignorance that so many public officials have. That is the basis for the one argument for secret meetings that might have some validity. . . . In a secret meeting a public official can honestly confess ignorance of a subject and seek enlightenment from his fellow committee members and witnesses. He would not be able to bring himself to do this in a public meeting and such reluctance might have an adverse effect on the proceedings.

13. The International City Managers' Ass'n, The Technique of Municipal Administration 23 (4th ed. 1958).

14. See Pickerell & Feder, Open Public Meetings of Legislative Bodies—California's Brown Act 26 (1957) [hereinafter cited as Pickerell & Feder]; Peterson, *The Legislatures and the Press,* 27 STATE GOV'T 223, 224 (1954).

15. Letter From Richard Carpenter, Executive Director & General Counsel of the League of California Cities, to the *Harvard Law Review,* Nov. 16, 1961.

16. Western Governmental Research Ass'n, Conference Proceedings 30–31 (1956).

17. See, e.g., Advancement of Freedom of Information Comm. of Sigma Delta Chi, Annual Reports 1957–1961.

The Democratic Legitimacy of the European Union Committee System (Pp. 103–19)

1. This article is based on original research carried out while the author was employed as a trainee in the Secretariat-General of the European Commission from October 1999 to February 2000. The evidence presented is drawn from twenty-seven semistructured interviews conducted in five Commission Directorates-General (DG Information Society, DG Enterprise, DG Health and Consumer Protection, DG Agriculture, and DG Energy and Transport), the Council Secretariat-General, two permanent representations (Denmark and the United Kingdom), and three private-sector organizations. Extensive documentary collection and analysis, along with personal participation in several different types of committees, provided further evidence.

2. This article recognizes, firstly, that democracy can have many meanings, and secondly, that legitimacy does not necessarily translate into democratic governance. Yet a connection can be made along the lines of Markus Jachtenfuchs's effort. He (6) writes: "*Democracy* is understood here as the institutionalization of a set of procedures for the control of governance which guarantees the participation of those who are governed in the adoption of collectively binding decisions" (emphasis added). *Legitimacy* is connected to democracy in this regard because citizens recognize such a "democratic" system: "Legitimacy means a generalized degree of trust of the addressees of these decisions towards the political system" (Jachtenfuchs, 6, emphasis added). Jachtenfuchs (6) continues: "From this definition it follows that democracy does not necessarily and exclusively have to be synonymous with parliamentary government."

3. For reasons made apparent later in the article (in the subsection entitled "Council Working Groups"), European Parliamentary committees are excluded from this analysis.

4. However, if the creation of a Commission advisory committee requires financial expenditure (to cover the participants' travel and accommodations costs, for example), it must be reported to the Secretariat-General of the Commission. In these cases, a line item to cover the cost of the committee is added to the Commission budget.

5. Of course, the accountability of national representatives to their "home" capitals varies widely. Some governments have designed efficient oversight mechanisms meant to keep tabs on national representatives attending meetings in Brussels (cf. Kassim, Peters, and Wright).

6. This agreement was formed as the result of commitments made by the Commission—and codified in the new comitology decision of 28 June 1999 (Council of the European Union 1999)—to make comitology agendas and minutes more accessible to both the European Parliament and the general public. For a discussion regarding the Comitology Decision of 1999, see Lenaerts and Verhoeven, and Haibach.

CHAPTER 6: WHISTLEBLOWING AND LEAKED INFORMATION

Whistleblowing and Leaks (Pp. 134–47)

1. Henrik Ibsen, *An Enemy of the People,* (1982), in *Henrik Ibsen: The Complete Major Prose Plays,* trans, and ed. Rolf Fjelde (New York: New American Library, 1965), pp. 281–386; passage quoted on p. 384.

2. I draw, for this chapter, on my earlier essays on whistleblowing: "Whistleblowing and Professional Responsibilities," in Daniel Callahan and Sissela Bok, eds., *Ethics Teaching in Higher Education* (New York: Plenum Press, 1980), pp. 277–95 (reprinted, slightly altered, in *New York University Education Quarterly 11* (Summer 1980): 2–10; "Blowing the Whistle," in Joel Fleishman, Lance Liebman, and Mark Moore, eds., *Public Duties: The Moral Obligations of Officials* (Cambridge, Mass.: Harvard University Press, 1981), pp. 204–21.

3. Institute of Electrical and Electronics Engineers, Code of Ethics for Engineers, art. 4, *IEEE Spectrum*, 12 (February 1975): 65.

4. Code of Ethics for Government Service, passed by the US House of Representatives in the 85th Congress, 1958, and applying to all government employees and office holders.

5. US, Congress, House of Representatives, Committee on Post Office and Civil Service, Subcommittee on Compensation and Employee Benefits, *Forced Retirement/Psychiatric Fitness of Duty Exams*, 95th Cong, 2d sess., November 3, 1978, pp. 2–4. See also Subcommittee Hearings, February 28, 1978. Psychiatric referral for whistleblowers has become institutionalized in government service, but it is not uncommon in private employment. Even persons who take accusations without being employed in the organization they accuse, moreover, have been classified as unstable and thus as unreliable witnesses. See, for example, Jonas Robitscher, "Stigmatization and Stone-walling: The Ordeal of Martha Mitchell," *Journal of Psychohistory* 6 (Winter 1979): 393–407.

6. Carol S. Kennedy, "Whistle-blowing: Contribution or Catastrophe?" Address to the American Association for the Advancement of Science, February 15, 1978, p. 8.

7. For analyses and descriptions of whistleblowing, see: Rosemary Chalk and Frank von Hippel, "Due Process for Dissembling 'Whistle-Blowers,'" *Technology Review* 81 (June–July 1979): 49–55; Louis Clark, "The Sound of Professional Suicide," *The Barrister* 5 (Summer 1978): 10–19; Helen Dudar, "The Price of Blowing the Whistle," *New York Times Magazine*, October 30, 1977, pp. 41–54; John Edsall, *Scientific Freedom and Responsibility*; David W. Ewing, *Freedom Inside the Organization* (New York: E. P. Dutton & Co., 1977); Nader, Petkas, and Blackwell, Whistle Blowing; Charles Peters and Taylor Branch, *Blowing the Whistle* (New York: Praeger Publishers, 1972); Alan F. Westin and Stephen Salisbury, eds., *Individual Rights in the Corporation* (New York: Pantheon Books, 1980); Alan F. Westin, *Whistle Blowing! Loyalty and Dissent in the Corporation* (New York: McGraw-Hill Books Co., 1980).

8. Judith P. Swazey and Stephen R. Scheer suggest that when the whistleblowers expose fraud in clinical research, colleagues respond *more* negatively to the whistleblowers who report the fraudulent research that to the person whose conduct has been reported. See "The Whistleblower as a Deviant Professional: Professional Norms and Responses to Fraud in Clinical Research," Workshop on Whistleblowing in Biomedical Research, Washington, D.C., September 1981, to be published.

9. See Peters and Branch, *Blowing the Whistle*; Carl Bernstein and Robert Woodward, *All the President's Men* (New York: Simon & Schuster, 1974).

10. On leaking, see Bernstein and Woodward, *All the President's Men*; Douglass Cater, *The Fourth Branch of Government* (Boston: Houghton Mifflin Co., 1959); Rourke, *Secrecy and Publicity*; David Wise, "The President Leaks a Document," *The Politics of Lying* (New York: Random House, 1973), pp. 117–33; Halperin and Hoffman, Top Secret; and the works cited above on whistleblowing and in note 14 on resignation in protest.

11. Rourke, *Secrecy and Publicity*, p. 198.

12. See Robert J. Baum and Albert Flores, ed., *Ethical Problems in Engineering* (Troy, N.Y.: Center for the Study of Human Dimensions of Science and Technology, 1978), pp. 227–47; Chalk and von Hippel, "Due Process for Dissenting 'Whistle-Blowers,'" pp. 4–55.

13. The case is adapted from Clark, "The Sound of Professional Suicide."

14. On resignation in protest, see Albert Hirschman, *Exit, Voice, and Loyalty* (Cambridge, Mass.: Harvard University Press, 1970); Brian Barry, in a review of Hirschman's book in *British Journal of Political Science* 4 (1974): 79–104, has pointed out that "exit" and "voice" are not alternatives but independent variations that may occur separately or together. Both leaking and whistleblowing represent "voice." They can be undertaken while staying on at work, or before one's voluntary exit, or simultaneously with it, or

after it; they can also have the consequence of involuntary or forced "exit" through dismissal or being "frozen out" even though retained at work. See also Edward Weisband and Thomas M. Franck, *Resignation in Protest* (New York: Viking Press, 1975); James Thomson, "Getting Out and Speaking Out," Foreign Policy, no. 13 (Winter 1973–1974), pp. 49–69; Joel L. Fleishman and Bruce L. Payne, *Ethical Dilemmas and the Education of Policymakers* (Hastings-on-Hudson, NY: Hastings Center, 1980).

15. Alan Westin discusses "swallowing" the whistle in the *Whistle Blowing!*, pp. 10–13. For a discussion of debate concerning whistleblowing, see Rosemary Chalk, "The Miner's Canary," *Bulletin of the Atomic Scientists* 38 (February 1982): pp. 16–22.

16. John C. Coffee, in "Beyond the Shut-eyed Sentry: Toward a Theoretical View of Corporate Misconduct and an Effective Legal Response," *Virginia Law Review* 63 (1977): 1099–1278, gives an informed and closely reasoned account of such "information blockages," such "filtering out," and possible remedies. See also Christopher Stone, *Where the Law Ends: The Social Control of Corporate Behavior* (New York: Harper & Row, 1975), pp. 201–16.

17. David W. Ewing, "The Employee's Right to Speak Out: The Management Perspective," *Civil Liberties Review* 5 (September–October 1978): 10–15.

18. David W. Ewing, "What Business Thinks About Employees Rights," *Harvard Business Review* 55 (September–October 1978): 81–94.

19. Alan Westin, "Michigan's Law to Protect the Whistle Blowers," *Wall Street Journal*, April 31, 1981, p. 81.

20. Ibid.

21. For a discussion of legal approaches, see Alfred G. Feliu, "Discharge of Professional Employees: Protecting Against Dismissal for Acts Within a Professional Code of Ethics," *Columbia Human Rights Law Review* 11 (1979–1980): 149–87; Westin, Whistle Blowing!

22. Environmental Protection Agency, "Toxic Substance Control Act," *Federal Register*, Thursday, March 16, 1978, pt.5.

The Enduring Phenomenon of Moral Muteness (Pp. 147–62)

1. The term "ethical twinge" was used by an early interviewee and captured nicely the type of issue examined by the research.

2. The simulation was sent to 1,500 members of CIMA, and the findings have been featured elsewhere (Fisher and Lovell 2000).

3. The *Herald of Free Enterprise* disaster in which 192 people lost their lives, the Lyme Bay canoeing tragedy in which seven schoolchildren lost their lives, and the rail crashes at Clapham, Southall, Paddington, and Hatfield, in which many lives were lost. In all of these cases, management failures appear to have been significant contributory factors to the disasters.

4. There are several layers of government in the United Kingdom. At the center is the national government, with its administrative support based principally in London, although the administrative centers of ministries are sometimes located outside of London. The next layer is local government, principally counties and cities. Some cities, such as Manchester and Birmingham, are extremely large, and these are known as metropolitan authorities. Below the county and city authorities come borough councils, and then the smallest of all administrative political institutions, parish councils.

Each layer of political authority has tax-raising powers, but as one moves down through the layers (with the national government as the first layer) the money-raising power becomes increasingly limited. County and city authorities have caps placed upon their money-raising powers by the central government. This is because all the monies raised by local and central governments are aggregated together to make up the Public Sector Borrowing Requirement, which is judged a major indicator of the central government's financial well-being.

Politicians are elected to each of the political layers on a cyclical basis, although nonparty political administrators are permanently in office. In the past three years, regional governments with certain tax-raising powers have been established in Scotland and Wales. Additional regional governments that would sit between the national government and the county/city authorities in the North-East and the Midlands are under discussion. In May 2002, the government brought forward proposals to activate this development.

5. For example, a £1 million order for engineered products would be reclassified for invoice purposes as £700,000 engineered products and £300,000 consultancy services. In this particular overseas country, consultancy services (and many other service industry "products") were not subject to import duty.

Bibliography

INTRODUCTION

BBC. "Q&A: MP expenses row explained." 18 June 2009. http://news.bbc.co.uk/2/hi/uk_news/ politics/7840678.stm (11 July 2009).

Rosenbaum, M. "Open Secrets: The state of FOI." 20 May 2009. http://www.bbc.co.uk/blogs/ opensecrets/2009/05/the_state_of_foi.html (11 July 2009).

The Daily Telegraph. "MPs' expenses: Bizarre claims part ii." http://www.telegraph.co.uk/news/ newstopics/mps-expenses/5388279/MPs-expenses-Bizarre-claims-part-ii.html?image=1 (11 July 2009).

UK Parliament. "Allowances by MP." http://mpsallowances.parliament.uk/mpslordsandoffices/ hocallowances/allowances-by-mp/ (10 July 2009).

CHAPTER 1: WHAT IS TRANSPARENCY?

Introduction (Pp. 1–2)

Associated Press. "Word of the Year Named." *The World* (Oregon), 16 Dec. 2003. http://www .theworldlink.com/articles/2003/12/16/news/news08.txt (15 Feb. 2009).

Birkinshaw, P. "Freedom of Information and Openness: Fundamental Human Rights?" [commentary]. *Administrative Law Review* 58, no. 1 (2006): 177–218.

Heald, D. "Varieties of Transparency." Pp. 25–43 in *Transparency: The Key to Better Governance?*, edited by C. Hood and D. Heald. New York: Oxford University Press, 2006.

Hood, C. "Transparency in Historical Perspective." Pp. 3–22 in *Transparency: The Key to Better Governance?*, edited by C. Hood and D. Heald. New York: Oxford University Press, 2006.

Hood, C., and D. Heald, eds. *Transparency: The Key to Better Governance?* New York: Oxford University Press, 2006.

Inter-American Court of Human Rights. *Order of the Inter-American Court of Human Rights Case of Claude Reyes et al. v. Chile Judgement of September 19, 2006.* http://www.elaw.org/node/2546 (18 Feb. 2009).

Moynihan, D. P. *Secrecy: The American Experience.* New Haven, CT: Yale University Press, 1998.

Obama, B. Memorandum for the Heads of Executive Departments and Agencies Subject: Transparency and Open Government. 2009. http://www.whitehouse.gov/the_press_office/TransparencyandOpenGovernment/ (2 May 2009).

Rourke, F. E. "Administrative Secrecy: A Congressional Dilemma." *American Political Science Review* 54, no. 3 (1960): 684–94.

Weber, M. *Economy and Society: An Outline of Interpretive Sociology.* New York: Bedminster Press, 1968.

CHAPTER 2: TRANSPARENCY AND COMPETING VALUES: PRIVACY, SECURITY, AND EFFICIENCY

Introduction (Pp. 17–19)

Birkinshaw, P. "Freedom of Information and Openness: Fundamental Human Rights?" [commentary]. *Administrative Law Review* 58, no. 1 (2006.): 177–218.

Blanton, T. "National Security and Open Government in the United States: Beyond the Balancing Test." Pp. 31–71 in *National Security and Open Government: Striking the Right Balance*, edited by A. Roberts and H. Darbishire. Syracuse, NY: Campbell Public Affairs Institute, The Maxwell School of Syracuse University, 2003.

Davis, C. N. "Reconciling Privacy and Access Interests in E-Government. *International Journal of Public Administration* 28 (2005): 567–80.

Kitiyadisai, K. "Privacy Rights and Protection: Foreign Values in Modern Thai Context. *Ethics and Information Technology* 7, no. 1 (2005): 17–26.

Markman, S. "Excerpts from Justice Testimony." *FOIA Update* IX, no. 3 (1988). http://www.usdoj.gov/oip/foia_updates/Vol_IX_3/ix_3page2.htm (2 May 2009).

Piotrowski, S. J. *Governmental Transparency in the Path of Administrative Reform.* Albany, NY: State University of New York Press, 2007.

Governmental Transparency in the Path of Administrative Reform (Pp. 29–34)

Cha, Arian Eunjung. 2002. Risks Prompt U.S. to Limit Access to Data: Security, Rights Advocate Clash Over Need to Know. *The Washington Post* (February 24). A1, A10.

Gore, Al. 1993. *Creating a Government that Works Better and Costs Less: Report of the National Performance Review:* Washington, D.C.: U.S. Government Printing Office.

Hamilton, Alexander. 1788. Federalist No. 70 in C. Rossiter, ed., *The Federalist Papers,* 423–31. New York: New American Library, 1961.

Kettl, Donald F. 1997. The Global Revolution in Public Management: Drives Theses, Missing Links. *Journal of Policy Analysis and Management* 16(3): 446–62.

Kettl, Donald F. 2005. *The Global Public Management Revolution,* 2nd ed. Washington, D.C.: Brookings Institution.

Lynn, Laurence E. 2001. The Myth of Bureaucratic Paradigm: What Traditional Public Administration Really Stood For. *Public Administration Review* (March/April) 61(2): 144–60.

Madison, James. 1822. Letter to William T. Barry, August 4, 1822, in *James Madison: Writings.* 1999. New York Literary Classics of the United States.

Osborne, David, and Ted Gaebler. 1992. *Reinventing Government.* Reading, Ma.: Addison-Wesley.

Osborne, Stephen, and Kate McLaughlin. 2002. The New Public Management in Context in Kate McLaughlin, Stephen P. Osborne, and Ewan Ferlie, eds., *New Public Management: Current Trends and Future Prospects.* New York: Routledge.

Overbye, Dennis. 2002. New Details Emerge from the Einstein Files. *New York Times* (May 7). Downloaded on 5/7/02 from http://www.nytimes.com/2002/05/07/science/physical/07EINS/html.

Pollitt, Christopher, and Geert Bouckaert. 2000. *Public Management Reform: A Comparative Analysis.* New York: Oxford University Press.

Riccucci, Norma M. 2001. The "Old" Public Management Versus the "New" Public Management: Where Does Public Administration Fit In? *Public Administration Review* (March/April 2001) 61(2): 172–75.

Rohr, John. 2002. *Civil Servants and Their Constitutions.* Lawrence: University Press of Kansas.

Rosenfield, Seth. 2002. Secret FBI Files Reveal Covert Activities at UC Bureau's Campus Operations Involved Reagan, CIA, *San Francisco Chronicle.* June 9. Downloaded on 9/24/02 from http://www .sfgate.com/cgi-bin/article.cgi?file=/chronicle/archive/2002/06/09MNCFLEADIN.DTL.

Tapscott, Mark, and Nicole Taylor. 2001. *Few Journalists Use the Federal Freedom of Information Act: A Study by the Center for Media and Public Policy.* The Heritage Foundation. Washington, D.C.

U.S. Congress. 1940. *Congressional Record.* Vol. 86, 76th Cong., 3rd sess. Washington, D.C.: U.S. Government Printing Office.

U.S. Department of Justice. 2003. Summary of Annual FOIA Reports for Fiscal Year 2002. *FOIA Post.* www.usdoj.gov/oip/foiapost/2003foiapost31.htm.

U.S. Senate. 1974. *Freedom of Information Act Source Book: Legislative Materials, Cases, Articles.* U.S. Washington, D.C.: Government Printing Office.

Zifcak, Spencer, 1998. Freedom of Information (FOI), pp. 941–44 in Jay Shafritz, ed., *International Encyclopedia of Public Policy and Administration.* Boulder: Westview.

CHAPTER 3: FREEDOM OF INFORMATION

Introduction (Pp. 35–37)

Article 6 of Mexican Constitution [English Translation]. 2007. http://www.gwu.edu/~nsarchiv/mexico/ article6%20_english.pdf (2 May 2009).

Bookman, Z. Secrecy Makes a Comeback in Mexico. *Los Angeles Times.* 22 April 2008. http://articles .latimes.com/2008/apr/22/opinion/oe-bookman22 (16 Feb. 2009).

freedominfo.org. Country Pages: Mexico. 27 March 2009. http://freedominfo.org/countries/mexico.htm (30 March 2009).

Leaf, D., and J. Scheinfeld. *The U.S. vs. John Lennon.* Lion Gate Films, 2006.

Mendel, T. *Freedom of Information: A Comparative Legal Survey.* 2nd ed., revised and updated. Paris: United Nations Educational Scientific and Cultural Organisation, 2008.

Neuman, L., and R. Calland. "Making the Law Work: The Challenges of Implementation." Pp. 179–213 in *The Right to Know: Transparency for an Open World,* edited by A. Florini. New York: Columbia University Press, 2007.

Piotrowski, S. J. *Governmental Transparency in the Path of Administrative Reform.* Albany, NY: State University of New York Press, 2007.

Rosenbloom, D. H., and S. J. Piotrowski. "Outsourcing the Constitution and Administrative Law Norms." *American Review of Public Administration* 35, no. 2 (2005): 103–21.

Roberts, A. "A Partial Revolution: The Diplomatic Ethos and Transparency in Intergovernmental Organizations." *Public Administration Review,* 64, no. 4 (2004): 410–24.

Wiener, J. *Gimme Some Truth: The John Lennon FBI Files.* Berkeley, CA: University of California Press, 1999.

Outsourcing the Constitution and Administrative Law Norms (Pp. 38–52)

Adelsberger, B. (2004, March). Top 50 contractors. *Federal Times,* p. 1.

American Correctional Association. (2004). *Accreditation and standards.* Retrieved from http://www. aca.org/ standards/index.html.

Asimow, M., Bonfield, A., and Levin, R. (1998). *State and federal administrative law* (2nd ed.). St. Paul, MN: West.

Bass, G., and Hammitt, H. (2002). Freedom of Information Act access to documents of private contractors doing the public's business. *Journal of Poverty Law and Policy,* *9,* 607–14.

Brentwood Academy v. Tennessee Secondary School Athletic Association, 531 U.S. 288 (2001).

Burton v. Wilmington Parking Authority, 365 U.S. 715 (1961).

Caiden, G. (1991). *Administrative reform comes of age.* New York: Walter de Gruyter.

Chemerinsky, E. (2002). The rhetoric of constitutional law. *Michigan Law Review, 100,* 2008–35.

City of Ladue v. Gilleo, 512 U.S. 43 (1994).

CNN.com/U.S. (2003, March 6). *"Peace" T-shirt gets man arrested.* Retrieved from http://www.cnn
.com/2003/US/ Northeast/03/05/offbeat.peace.arrest.reut/

Columbia Accident Investigation Board. (2003). *Final report.* Retrieved from http://www.caib.us._

Correctional Services Corporation v. Malesko, 534 U.S. 61 (2001).

Crawley, V., and Adelsberger, B. (2004, August 30). Abu Ghraib reports fault contracting, leadership.
Federal Times, p. 12.

Dolan v. City of Tigard, 512 U.S. 374 (1994).

Executive Order 8802. (1941, June 25). Reaffirming policy of full participation in the defense program
by all persons regardless of race, creed, color, or national origin, and directing certain actions in fur-
therance of said policy. *Federal Register, 6,* 3109.

Ex Parte Virginia, 100 U.S. 339 (1880).

Federal Acquisition Regulation. (2004). *Federal acquisition regulation.* Retrieved from http://www.
amet.gov/far/ authorityframe.html.

Feiser, C. (1999). Privatization and the Freedom of Information Act: An analysis of public access to
private entities under federal law. *Federal Communications Law Journal, 52,* 21–62.

Feiser, C. (2000). Protecting the public's right to know: The debate over privatization and access to
government information under state law. *Florida State University Law Review, 27,* 825–64.

Freeman, J. (2003). Extending public law norms through privatization. *Harvard Law Review, 116,*
1285–1352.

Friel, B. (2003, May 13). *IRS plan to outsource tax collection panned.* Retrieved from http://www
.GovExec.com

Gillette, C., and Stephan, P. (1998). Constitutional limitations on privatization. *American Journal of
Comparative Law, 46* (Suppl., section IV), 48 1-502.

Gilmour, R., and Jensen, L. (1998). Reinventing government accountability: Public functions, privatization, and the meaning of "state action." *Public Administration Review, 58,* 247–57.

Gore, A. (1993). *From red tape to results: Creating a government that works better and costs less.*
Washington, DC: U.S. Government Printing Office.

Gruber, A. (2004, September 15). *House votes to bar IRS from outsourcing tax collection.* Retrieved
from http://www.GovExec.com.

Guttman, D. (2000a). Public purpose and private service: The twentieth century culture of contracting
out and the evolving law of diffused sovereignty. *Administrative Law Review, 52,* 859–926.

Guttman, D. (2000b). Public purpose and private service: The twentieth century culture of contracting
out and the evolving law of diffused sovereignty (electronic insert between pp. 890-89 1). *Administrative Law Review, 52,* 859–926.

Harris, S. (2004a, July 16). *GSA canceled Guantanamo interrogator contract.* Retrieved from http://
www.GovExec.com.

Harris, S. (2004b, June 22). *GSA establishes new contract policy office.* Retrieved from http://www
.GovExec.com.

Hudgens v. National Labor Relations Board, 424 U.S. 507 (1976).

Lawrence v. Texas, No. 02-102 (2003).

Lebron v. National Railroad Passenger Corporation, 513 U.S. 374 (1995).

Light, P. (1999). *The true size of government.* Washington, DC: Brookings Institution.

Lloyd Corp. v. Tanner, 407 U.S. 551 (1972).

Lynn, L. E., Jr. (2001). The myth of the bureaucratic paradigm: What traditional public administration
really stood for. *Public Administration Review, 61,* 144–60.

Marsh v. Alabama, 326 U.S. 501 (1946).

Mays, S. (1995). Privatization of municipal services: A contagion in the body politic. *Duquesne Law Review, 34*, 41–70.

Moe, R. (1987). Exploring the limits of privatization. *Public Administration Review, 47*, 453–60.

Moe, R. (2001). The emerging federal quasi government: Issues of management and accountability. *Public Administration Review, 61*, 290–312.

Moe, R., and Gilmour, R. (1995). Rediscovering principles of public administration: The neglected foundation of public law. *Public Administration Review, 55*, 135–46.

NASA. (2003). *Freedom of Information Act (FOIA): Summary of requests currently being processed related to STS- 107 Columbia.* Retrieved from http://www.nasa.gov/pdf/2239main_Col_FOIA_Summary030221.pdf.

National Collegiate Athletic Association v. Tarkanian, 488 U.S. 179 (1988).

National Performance Review. (1995, April 7). *Reinvention roundtable.* Washington, DC: Author.

Peckenpaugh, J. (2004, June 3). *Army contractor count stymied by red tape.* Retrieved from http://www.GovExec.com.

Piotrowski, S. J., and Rosenbloom, D. H. (2002). Nonmission-based values in results-oriented public management: The case of freedom of information. *Public Administration Review, 62*(6), 643–57.

Posner, P. (2002). Accountability challenges of third-party government. In L. Salamon (Ed.), *The tools of government* (pp. 523–51). New York: Oxford University Press.

Press, E. (2003). Faith based furor. In J. Dolan and D. H. Rosenbloom (eds.), *Representative bureaucracy: Classic readings and continuing controversies* (pp. 185–88). Armonk, NY: M. E. Sharpe.

Reinert, P. (2004, January 24). Contractor to lose $45 million in fees for Columbia loss. *Houston Chronicle.* Retrieved from http://www.chron.com/cs/CDA/ssistory.mpl/space/2369033.

Richardson v. McKnight, 521 U.S. 399 (1997).

Roberts, A. (2000). Less government, more secrecy: Reinvention and the weakening of Freedom of Information Law. *Public Administration Review, 60*, 308–20.

Rosenbloom, D. H. (2000a). *Building a legislative-centered public administration: Congress and the administrative state, 1946–1999.* Tuscaloosa: University of Alabama Press.

Rosenbloom, D. H. (2000b). Retrofitting the administrative state to the Constitution: Congress and the judiciary's twentieth century progress. *Public Administration Review, 60*, 39–46.

Rosenbloom, D. H. (2003). *Administrative law for public managers.* Boulder, CO: Westview.

Rosenbloom, D. H., and O'Leary, R. (1997). *Public administration and law* (2nd ed.). New York: Marcel Dekker.

Savas, E. S. (1987). *Privatization: The key to better government.* Chatham, NJ: Chatham House.

Shafritz, J. M., Rosenbloom, D. H., Riccucci, N. M., Naff, K. C., and Hyde, A. C. (2001). *Personnel management in government* (5th ed.). New York: Marcel Dekker.

Terry v. Adams, 345 U.S. 461 (1953).

United States v. Price, 383 U.S. 787 (1966).

U.S. Congress. (1989, February 3). *Examination of the use of consultants and contractors by the Environmental Protection Agency and the Department of Energy* (hearings before the Subcommittee on Federal Services, Post Office, and Civil Service of the Senate Committee on Governmental Affairs, 101st Congress, 1st session). Washington, DC: U.S. Government Printing Office.

U.S. Department of Defense v. Federal Labor Relations Authority, 510 U.S. 487 (1994).

U.S. Department of Energy. (2004). *Department of Energy Acquisition Regulation 970.520-3: Access to and ownership of records.* Retrieved from http://professionals.pr.doe.gov/MA-5Web.nsf/Procurement/DEAR+970?OpenDocument.

U.S. Office of Management and Budget. (1998). *Implementation of the Federal Activities Inventory Reform Act of 1998 (Public Law 105-270).* Washington, DC: Author.

U.S. Office of Management and Budget. (2001). *The president's management agenda.* Washington, DC: Author.

U.S. Office of Management and Budget. (2003a). *Circular No. A-76* (revised; originally issued in 1983). Washington, DC: Author.

U.S. Office of Management and Budget. (2003b). *Competitive sourcing: Conducting public-private competition in a reasoned and responsible manner*. Washington, DC: Author.

West v. Atkins, 487 U.S. 42 (1988).

Wyatt v. Cole, 504 U.S. 158 (1992).

Zelman v. Simmons-Harris, 536 U.S. 639 (2002).

A Partial Revolution: The Diplomatic Ethos and Transparency in Intergovernmental Organizations (Pp. 53–68)

ActionAid. 2000. *Recommendations for Ways Forward on Institutional Reform of the World Trade Organization*. London: ActionAid.

Alterman, Eric. 1998. *Who Speaks for America? Why Democracy Matters in Foreign Policy*. Ithaca, NY: Cornell University Press.

Archer, Clive. 2001. *International Organizations*. London: Routledge.

Arthurs, Harry. 1997. Mechanical Arts and Merchandise: Canadian Public Administration in the New Economy. *McGill Law Journal* 42(1): 29–62.

Bank Information Center. 2001. The Ongoing Struggle for World Bank Transparency: The Outcome of the Information Disclosure Policy Review. Bank Information Center Update, November 4. http://www.bicusa.org/bicusa/issues/misc_resources/456.php.

Barshefsky, Charlene. 1999. The Trading System of the 21st Century. Speech delivered to the Economic Strategy Institute Conference, April 28, Washington, DC.

Baucus, Max. 2002. Letter to the Honorable Robert B. Zoellick, United States Trade Representative, April 15. Washington, DC: Office of Senator Max Baucus.

Berridge, G. R. 2002. *Diplomacy: Theory and Practice*. New York: Palgrave.

Blanton, Thomas. 2002. The World's Right to Know. *Foreign Policy* 131 (July/August): 50–58.

Blustein, Paul. 2001. *The Chastening: Inside the Crisis that Rocked the Global Financial System and Humbled the IMF*. New York: Public Affairs.

Bretton Woods Project. 2003. *Briefing Note: G-7, Civil Society Press for IMF, World Bank Transparency Reforms*. London: ActionAid.

Camdessus, Michel. 1998. Toward an Agenda for International Monetary and Financial Reform. Remarks to the World Affairs Council, November 6, Philadelphia, PA.

Canada. 2003. Communication from Canada on the Improvement of the Dispute Settlement Understanding. Geneva: World Trade Organization. TN/DS/W/41.

Chamberlain, Chris. 1999. *Fulfilling the IDA -12 Mandates: Recommendations for Expanding Public Access to Information at the World Bank*. Washington, DC: Bank Information Center. http://www.bicusa.org/bicusa/issues/misc_resources/462.php.

Clark, Peter, and Peter Morrison. 1998. Key Procedural Issues: Transparency. *International Lawyer* 32: 851.

Coalition for Open Trade. 2000. Public Participation Barred Once Again in WTO Dispute Settlement. *Tradewatch Bulletin*, March 6. http://www.dbtrade.com/licit/.

Dawson, Thomas. 2003. *Transparency and the IMF: Toward Second Generation Reforms*. Washington, DC: International Monetary Fund.

Debevoise, Whitney. 1998. Key Procedural Issues: Transparency. *International Lawyer* 32: 817.

Doyle, Kate. 2002. Mexico Opens the Files. *The Nation*, August 5, 7.

Draper, Theodore. 1991. *A Very Thin Line: The Iran-Contra Affairs*. New York: Hill and Wang.

Elster, Jon. 1995. Strategic Uses of Argument. In *Barriers to the Negotiated Resolution of Conflict*, edited by K. J. Arrow, 236–57. New York: W. W. Norton.

European Community. 2002. *Communication from the European Community to the Working Group on Trade and Investment: Concept Paper on Transparency*. Geneva: World Trade Organization. WT/WGTI/W/110.

European Union (EU). 2001. *Regulation on Public Access to Documents*. Brussels: European Union. (EC) 1049/2001.

Fischer, Stanley. 2001. *Farewell to the IMF Board*. Washington, DC: International Monetary Fund.

Florini, Ann. 1999. *Transparency in the Interests of the Poor*. Washington, DC: World Bank Summer Research Workshop on Poverty.

Fox, Francis. 1980. Cabinet Discussion Paper on Access to Information. In *The Complete Annotated Guide to Federal Access to Information*, edited by M. Drapeau and M. A. Racicot, 92–120. Toronto: Carswell.

Francois, Joseph F. 1999. *Maximizing the Benefits of the Trade Policy Review Mechanism for Developing Countries*. Rotterdam/London: Tinbergen Institute/Centre for Economic Policy and Research.

Gill, Stephen. 2000. The Constitution of Global Capitalism. Paper presented at the International Studies Association Annual Convention, March 14–18, Los Angeles, CA.

Group of Independent Experts. 1999. *External Evaluation of IMF Surveillance*. Washington, DC: International Monetary Fund.

Hewart, Gordon. 1929. *The New Despotism*. London: Benn.

Horwitz, Morton. 1992. *The Transformation of American Law, 1870–1960*. New York: Oxford University Press.

International Centre for Sustainable Trade and Development (ICSTD). 1999. *Accreditation Schemes and Other Arrangements for Public Participation in International Fora*. Geneva: International Centre for Sustainable Trade and Development.

———. 2002a. DSU Review: Developing Countries Reject U.S. Proposal on Transparency. *Bridges Weekly Trade News Digest,* September 18. http://www.ictsd.org/weekly/.

———. 2002b. EC Proposal under Scrutiny in DSU Negotiations. *Bridges Weekly Trade News Digest*, April 23. http:// www.ictsd.org/weekly/.

———. 2002c. Members Divided over Transparency, Definition at WTO Investment Talks. *Bridges Weekly Trade News Digest*, April 23. http://www.ictsd.org/weekly/.

International Monetary Fund (IMF). 2001a. *Assessing the Implementation of Standards—An IMF Review of Experience and Next Steps*. Washington, DC: International Monetary Fund. PIN 01/17.

———. 2001b. *IMF Reviews the Experience with Publication of Staff Reports and Takes Decisions to Enhance Transparency*. Washington, DC: International Monetary Fund. PIN 01/3.

———. 2001c. *IMF Surveillance: A Factsheet*. Washington, DC: International Monetary Fund.

———. 2002. *Quarterly Report on the Assessments of Standards and Codes—June 2002*. Washington, DC: International Monetary Fund, Policy Development and Review Department.

———. 2003. *The Fund's Transparency Policy: Progress Report on Publication of Country Documents*. Washington, DC: International Monetary Fund.

Japan. 2002. *Communication from Japan to the Working Group on Trade and Investment on Transparency*. Geneva: World Trade Organization. WT/WGTI/W/112.

Keesing, Donald B. 1998. *Improving Trade Policy Reviews in the World Trade Organization*. Washington, DC: Institute for International Economics.

Kuttner, Robert. 2001. The Role of Governments in the Global Economy. In *On the Edge: Living with Global Capitalism*, edited by W. Hutton and A. Giddens, 147–63. London: Vintage.

Larsen, Flemming. 2002. The Global Financial Architecture in Transition. *OECD Observer*, March 11, 10–12.

Marchi, Sergio. 1998. Statement at the Second Session of the WTO Ministerial Conference, May 20. Geneva: World Trade Organization.

Mavroidis, Petros. 2001. Amicus Curiae Briefs before the WTO: Much Ado about Nothing. Working paper, Harvard Law School.

McIntosh, Toby 2002. Release of Secret Loan Document in Uruguay Fuels Public Debate. http://www.freedominfo.org.

Morgenthau, Hans. 1954. *Politics among Nations*. New York: Alfred A. Knopf.

Nader, Ralph, and Lori Wallach. 1996. GATT, NAFTA, and the Subversion of the Democratic Process. In *The Case against the Global Economy*, edited by J. Mander and E. Goldsmith, 92–107. San Francisco: Sierra Club Books.

Office of the United States Trade Representative (USTR). 1998. *1998 Annual Report of the President of the United States on the Trade Agreements Program*. Washington, DC: Office of the United States Trade Representative.

———. 2000. U.S. Pushes for Increased Transparency in the WTO. News release, October 10.

Oxfam UK. 2000. *Discussion Paper: Institutional Reform of the WTO*. Oxford, UK: Oxfam UK.

Pauly, Louis. 1997. *Who Elected the Bankers?* Ithaca, NY: Cornell University Press.

Picciotto, Sol. 2000. Democratizing Globalism. Working paper, Lancaster University.

Qureshi, Asif. 1995. Some Lessons from Developing Countries' Trade Policy Reviews in the GATT Framework: An Enforcement Perspective. *World Economy* 18(3): 489–503.

Raghavan, Chakravarthi. 2000a. *Continuing Conceptual Divides at the WTO*. Penang, Malaysia: Third World Network.

———. 2000b. *NGOs Launch "Shrink or Sink" Campaign against WTO*. Penang, Malaysia: Third World Network.

Roberts, Alasdair. 2001. Structural Pluralism and the Right to Information. *University of Toronto Law Journal* 5 1(3): 243–71.

Rosenbloom, David H. 2000. *Building a Legislative-Centered Public Administration*. Tuscaloosa: University of Alabama Press.

Rozell, Mark. 1994. *Executive Privilege*. Baltimore: Johns Hopkins University Press.

Schattschneider, E. E. 1960. *The Semisovereign People: A Realist's View of Democracy in America*. New York: Holt, Rinehart, and Winston.

Stiglitz, Joseph. 2000. What I Learned at the World Economic Crisis. *New Republic*, April 17, 56–60.

United Nations Development Program (UNDP). 1997. *Public Information Disclosure Policy*. New York: UNDP.

———. 2002. *Human Development Report 2002: Deepening Democracy in a Fragmented World*. New York: Oxford University Press.

United States. 2000. *Submission Regarding Informal Consultations on External Transparency*. Geneva: World Trade Organization. WT/GC/W/4 13/Rev. 1.

———. 2002. *Communication from the United States on the Improvement of the Dispute Settlement Understanding of the WTO Related to Transparency*. Geneva: World Trade Organization. TN/DS/W/13.

United States and Canada. 1998. *Revised Proposals on Procedures for the Circulation and Derestriction of WTO Documents*. Geneva: World Trade Organization. WT/GC/W/106.

U.S. Department of Justice (DOJ). 1999. *Brief for the Petitioners in the Case of U.S. v. Weatherhead*. Washington, DC: U.S. Department of Justice.

U.S. General Accounting Office (GAO). 1998. *Multilateral Development Banks: Public Consultation on Environmental Assessments*. Washington, DC: General Accounting Office. GAO/NSIAD-98-192.

U.S. Mission. 1999. *Communication to the Working Group on the Interaction between Trade and Competition Policy*. Geneva: United States Permanent Mission to the WTO.

Van Houtven, Leo. 2002. *Governance of the IMF*. Pamphlet 53. Washington, DC: International Monetary Fund.

Watson, Adam. 1983. *Diplomacy: The Dialogue between States*. New York: McGraw-Hill.

Weiler, J. H. H. 2000. The Rule of Lawyers and the Ethos of Diplomats: Reflections on the Internal and External Legitimacy of WTO Dispute Settlement. Working paper, Harvard Law School.

Weiner, John, and L. Brennan Van Dyke. 1997. *A Handbook for Obtaining Documents from the World Trade Organization*. Geneva: International Centre for Trade and Sustainable Development.

Wildavsky, Aaron B. 1969. *The Presidency*. Boston: Little, Brown.

World Bank. 2001. World Bank Revises Disclosure Policy. Press release, September 7.

———. 2002. *The World Bank Policy on Disclosure of Information*. Washington, DC: World Bank.

World Trade Organization (WTO). 1996a. *Procedures for the Circulation and Derestriction of WTO Documents*. Geneva: World Trade Organization. WT/L/160/Rev. 1.

———. 1996b. *Singapore Ministerial Declaration*. Geneva: World Trade Organization.

———. 1998. *Report of the Appellate Body: United States—Import Prohibition of Certain Shrimp and Shrimp Products*. Geneva: World Trade Organization. WT/DS58/AB/R.

———. 2000. *Minutes of Meeting of the General Council Held on 22 November 2000*. Geneva: World Trade Organization. WT/GC/M/60.

———. 2001a. *Draft Decision: Procedures for the Circulation and Derestriction of WTO Documents*. Geneva: World Trade Organization. WT/GC/W/464.

———. 2001b. *Report of the Appellate Body: European Communities—Measures Affecting Asbestos and Asbestos-Containing Products*. Geneva: World Trade Organization. WT/DS135/AB/R.

———. 2002a. Director-General's Farewell Speech to the WTO General Council. Press release, July 31.

———. 2002b. *Minutes of Meeting of the General Council held on 13–14 May 2002*. Geneva: World Trade Organization. WT/GC/M/74.

———. 2002c. Moore Pledges to Build on Doha Success in 2002. Press release, January 2.

———. 2002d. *Revised Procedures for the Circulation and Derestriction of WTO Documents*. Geneva: World Trade Organization. WT/L/452.

World Trade Organization, Agriculture Committee. 1999. *Summary Report of the Meeting Held on 25–26 March 1999*. Geneva: World Trade Organization. G/AG/R/18.

World Trade Organization, General Council. 1998. *Minutes of Meeting of the General Council*. Geneva: World Trade Organization. WT/GC/M/28.

———. 2001. *Minutes of Meeting Held on 18 and 19 July 2001*. Geneva: World Trade Organization. WT/GC/M/66.

Zoellick, Robert. 2001. The United States, Europe and the World Trading System. Address to the Kangaroo Group, May 15, Strasbourg, France.

CHAPTER 4: PROACTIVELY RELEASED INFORMATION

Introduction (Pp. 69–71)

Feinberg, L. E. "Mr. Justice Brandeis and the Creation of the Federal Register." *Public Administration Review* 61, no. 3 (2001): 359–70.

Holzer, M., and S.-T. Kim. *Digital Governance in Municipalities Worldwide (2007): A Longitudinal Assessment of Municipal Websites Throughout the World*. Newark, N.J.: E-Governance Institute, National Center for Public Performance, Rutgers University, Campus at Newark, 2007.

Lee, M. "The Agency Spokesperson: Connecting Public Administration and the Media." *Public Administration Quarterly* 25, no. 1 (2001): 103–30.

Lohr, S. "Online Tool Will Track U.S. Tech Spending." *New York Times*. 30 June 2009. http://www.nytimes.com/2009/07/01/technology/01dashboard.html?ref=us (9 July 2009).

Moon, M. J. "The Evolution of E-Government among Municipalities: Rhetoric or Reality?" *Public Administration Review* 62, no. 4 (2002): 424–33.

Piotrowski, S. J., and E. L. Borry. "Governmental Transparency and Websites: The Case of New Jersey Municipalities." Pp. 389–406 in *Strategies for Local E-Government Adoption and Implementation: Comparative Studies* edited by C. G. Reddick. Hershey, Pa.: IGI Global, 2009.

USASpending.gov. "About This Site." http://www.usaspending.gov/aboutthissite.php (5 July 2009).

The Evolution of E-Government among Municipalities: Rhetoric or Reality? (Pp. 71–76)

Anderson, Kim. 1999. Reengineering Public Sector Organizations Using Information Technology. In *Reinventing Government in the Information Age*, edited by Richard Heeks, 312–30. New York: Routledge.

Brown, Douglas. 1999. Information Systems for Improved Performance Management: Development Approaches in U.S. Public Agencies. In *Reinventing Government in the Information Age*, edited by Richard Heeks, 113–34. New York: Routledge.

Cats-Baril, William, and Ronald Thompson. 1995. Managing Information Technology Projects in the Public Sector. *Public Administration Review* 55(6): 559–66.

Daukantas, Patricia. 2000. PTO Starts E-government Shift. *Government Computer News* 19(33). Available at http://www.gcn.com/vol19_no33/news/3327-1.html. Accessed September 7, 2001.

Fountain, Jane. 2001. *Building the Virtual State: Information Technology and Institutional Change.* Washington, DC: Brookings Institution.

Galston, William. 1999. (How) Does the Internet Affect Community? In *Democracy.com? Governance in Networked World*, edited by Elaine Ciulla Kamarck and Joseph S. Nye, Jr., 45–62. Hollis, NH: Hollis Publishing Company.

Gore, Al. 1993. *Creating a Government that Works Better and Costs Less: Reengineering Through Information Technology*. Report of the National Performance Review. Washington DC: Government Printing Office.

Government and the Internet Survey. Handle with Care. 2000. *The Economist* 355(8 176): 33–34.

Heeks, Richard. 1999. Reinventing Government in the Information Age. In *Reinventing Government in the Information Age*, edited by Richard Heeks, 9–21. New York: Routledge.

Hiller, Janine, and France Bélanger. 2001. *Privacy Strategies for Electronic Government*. E-Government Series. Arlington, VA: PricewaterhouseCoopers Endowment for the Business of Government.

Kimberly, John R. 1976. Organizational Size and the Structural Perspective. *Administrative Science Quarterly* 21(4): 577–97.

Landsbergen, Jr., David, and George Wolken, Jr. 2001. Realizing the Promise: Government Information Systems and the Fourth Generation of Information Technology. *Public Administration Review* 61(2): 206–20.

Layne, Karen, and Jungwoo Lee. 2001. Developing Fully Functional E-Government: A Four Stage Model. *Government Information Quarterly* 18(2): 12–136.

Moon, M. Jae, and Stuart Bretschneider. 1997. Can State Government Actions Affect Innovation and Its Diffusion? An Extended Communication Model and Empirical Test. *Technological Forecasting and Social Change* 54(1): 57–77.

———. 2002. Does the Perception of Red Tape Constrain IT Innovativeness in Organizations? Unexpected Results from Simultaneous Equation Model and Implications. *Journal of Public Administration Research and Theory* 12(2): 273–91.

Moon, M. Jae, and Peter deLeon. 2001. Municipal Reinvention: Municipal Values and Diffusion among Municipalities. *Journal of Public Administration Research and Theory* 11(3): 327–52.

Musso, Juliet, Christopher Weare, and Matt Hale. 2000. Designing Web Technologies for Local Governance Reform: Good Management or Good Democracy. *Political Communication* 17(1): 1–19.

Nedović-Budić, Zorica, and David Godschalk. 1996. Human Factors in Adoption of Geographic Information System. *Public Administration Review* 56(6): 554–67.

Nolan, Richard. 1979. Managing the Crises in Data Processing. *Harvard Business Review* 57 (March/April): 115–26.

Norris, Donald, and Kenneth Kraemer. 1996. Mainframe and PC Computing in American Cities: Myths and Realities. *Public Administration Review* 56(6): 568–76.

Norris, Pippa. 1999. Who Surfs? New Technology, Old Voters, and Virtual Democracy. In *Democracy.com? Governance in Networked World,* edited by Elaine Ciulla Kamarck and Joseph S. Nye, Jr., 71–94. Hollis, NH: Hollis Publishing Company.

Nunn, Samuel. 2001. Police Information Technology: Assessing the Effects of Computerization on Urban Police Functions. *Public Administration Review* 61(2): 221–34.

Nye, Jr., Joseph. 1999. Information Technology and Democratic Governance. In *Democracy.com? Governance in Networked World*, edited by Elaine Ciulla Kamarck and Joseph S. Nye, Jr., 1–18. Hollis, NH: Hollis Publishing Company.

Peled, Alon. 2001. Centralization or Diffusion? Two Tales of On-line Government. *Administration and Society* 32(6): 686–709.

Preston, Morag. 2000. E-government U.S.-style. *New Statesman* 129(4517): xxx.

Quinn, Robert, and Kim Cameron. 1983. Organizational Life Cycles and Shifting Criteria of Effectiveness: Some Preliminary Evidence. *Management Science* 29(1): 33–51.

Rogers, Everett. 1995. *Diffusion of Innovations.* 4th ed. New York: Free Press.

Sprecher, Milford. 2000. Racing to E-government: Using the Internet for Citizen Service Delivery. *Government Finance Review* 16(5): 21–22.

Svara, James. 1990. *Official Leadership in the City: Patterns of Conflict and Cooperation.* New York: Oxford University Press.

———. 1999. The Shifting Boundary between Elected Officials and City Managers in Large Council-Manager Cities. *Public Administration Review* 59(1): 44–53.

Tornatzky, Louis G., and Mitchell Fleischer. 1990. *The Process of Technological Innovation.* Lexington, KY: Lexington Books.

United Nations and American Society for Public Administration. 2001. *Global Survey of E-government.* Available at http://www.unpan.org/egovernment2.asp. Accessed November 27, 2001.

Ventura, Stephen J. 1995. The Use of Geographic Information Systems in Local Government. *Public Administration Review* 55(5): 461–67.

Weare, Christopher, Juliet Musso, and Matt Hale. 1999. Electronic Democracy and the Diffusion of Municipal Web Pages in California. *Administration and Society* 31(1): 3–27.

White House Press Office. 2000. President Clinton and Vice-President Gore: Major New E-Government Initiatives. *US Newswire,* June 24. Available at http://web.lexis-nexis.com/ universe... d5=0f245defaacf01afe1 7703e5dfd7da67. Accessed September 7, 2001.

Mr. Justice Brandeis and the Creation of the *Federal Register* (Pp. 76–89)

Austern, H. Thomas. 1934a. The Louis Dembitz Brandeis Papers, 1870–1941. Reel 65, G8-1. University of Louisville, University Archives and Research Center. June 14.

———. 1934b. The Louis Dembitz Brandeis Papers, 1870–1941. Reel 65, G8-1. University of Louisville, University Archives and Research Center. July 19.

Brandeis, Louis D. 1914. *Other People's Money,* 92–108. First published as What Publicity Can Do, *Harper's Weekly,* December 20, 1913.

———. 1934. The Louis Dembitz Brandeis Papers, 1870–1941. Reel 65, G8-1. University of Louisville, University Archives and Research Center.

Celler, Emanuel. 1954. *You Never Can Leave Brooklyn. The Autobiography of Emanuel Celler.* New York: John Day Company.

Code of Federal Regulations.1998.63FR31883. June 1.

de Tocqueville, Alexis. 1969. *Democracy in America.* Edited by J. P. Mayer. New York: Doubleday and Company.

Dickinson, John, to Louis D. Brandeis. 1934a. The Louis Dembitz Brandeis Papers, 1870–1941. Reel 65, G8-1. University of Louisville, University Archives and Research Center. October 8.

———. 1934b. The Louis Dembitz Brandeis Papers, 1870–1941. Reel 65, G8-1. University of Louisville, University Archives and Research Center. November 5.

Dickinson, John, to Donald Richberg. 1934. The Louis Dembitz Brandeis Papers, 1870–1941. Reel 65, G8-1. University of Louisville, University Archives and Research Center. November 5.

Fairlie, John A. 1920. Administrative Legislation, *Michigan Law Review* (January), xviii. Reprinted in *National Emergency.* Hearings before the Special Committee on the Termination of the National Emergency of the United States Senate. 93rd Cong., 1st sess., Part 3—Constitutional Questions Concerning Emergency Powers, November 3, 1973. 615–830.

Frankfurter, Felix, to Cecil T. Carr. 1935a. The Louis Dembitz Brandeis Papers, 1871–1941. Correspondence with Frankfurter. Reel 65, G9–2. University of Louisville, University Archives and Research Center. January 28.

———. 1935b. Papers at the Harvard Law Library, Manuscript Division and Library of Congress Manuscript Division. October 3.

Freund, Paul. 1977/1978. Justice Brandeis: A Law Clerk's Remembrance. *American Jewish History* 67(1–4): 7–18.

Goodhart, Arthur. 1949. *Five Jewish Lawyers of the Common Law.* Freeport, NY: Books for the Library Press.

Griswold, Erwin N. 1934a. Memorandum for Assistant Attorney General Stephens. Griswold, Box 23-7. Harvard Law Library, Manuscript Division. March 20.

———. 1934b. Griswold, Box 23-6. Harvard Law Library, Manuscript Division. December 17, 18, 24.

———. 1935. Griswold, Box 23-5. Harvard Law Library, Manuscript Division. January 2.

———. 1992. *Ould Fields, New Corne.* St. Paul, MN: West Publishing Co., 115–19.

Hawley, Ellis W. 1966. *The New Deal and the Problem of Monopoly. A Study in Economic Ambivalence.* Princeton, NJ: Princeton University Press.

Ickes, Harold L. 1933. *The Secret Diaries of Harold Ickes, V. I, The First Thousand Days, 1933–36.* New York: Simon and Schuster.

Jaffe, Louis. 1965. *Judicial Control of Administrative Action.* Boston, MA: Little, Brown and Company.

Lavery, Urban A. 1941. The Supreme Court—Its Home Past and Present. *American Bar Association Journal* 27(5): 283–89.

Lief, Alfred, ed. 1941. *The Brandeis Guide to the Modern World.* Boston, MA: Little, Brown and Company.

Mason, Alpheus T. 1946. *Brandeis. A Free Man's Life.* New York: Viking Press.

Murphy, Bruce Allen. 1982. *The Brandeis/Frankfurter Connection: The Secret Political Activities of Two Supreme Court Justices.* New York: Oxford University Press.

New York Times. 1934. Oil and Auto Codes in Supreme Court. December 11, 4. Also found in the *Washington Post,* December 11, 1934.

Pearson, Drew, and Robert S. Allen. 1935. The Washington Merry-Go-Round. January 1. Syndicated column.

Relyea, Harold. 1996. Dissemination of Government Information. *Bowker Annual* 41: 220–35.

Richberg, Donald. 1934. The Louis Dembitz Brandeis Papers, 18701941. Reel 65, G8-1. University of Louisville, University Archives and Research Center. November 3.

Ritchie, Donald A. 1980. *James M. Landis: Dean of Regulators.* Cambridge, MA: Harvard University Press.

Roos, Charles F. 1937. *NRA Economic Planning.* Bloomington, IN: Principia Press.

Roosevelt, Franklin D. 1967. *Roosevelt and Frankfurter: Their Correspondence, 1928–1945,* annotated by Max Freedman. Boston, MA: Little, Brown, and Company.

Ruddy, J. C., and B. S. Simmons. 1944. The Federal Register—Forum of the Government and the People. *Georgetown Law Review* 32: 248–63.

Stephens, Harold M., to Erwin Griswold. 1935. Griswold papers, Box 70-12. Harvard Law Library, Manuscript Division. January 7.

Strum, Philippa, ed. 1995. *Brandeis on Democracy.* Lawrence, KS: University of Kansas Press.

U.S. House Sub-Committee No. Il of the Committee on the Judiciary. 1936. Testimony by Harold M. Stephens on H.R. 11337 and H.R. 10932. 74th Cong., 2d sess.

Urofsky, Melvin I. 1986. The Brandeis-Frankfurter Conversations. In *The Supreme Court Review, 1985,* edited by Philip Kurland, Gerhard Casper, and Denis Hutchinson, 299–399. Chicago: University of Chicago Press.

Urofsky, Melvin I., and David Levy, eds. 1991. *Half Brother, Half Son. The Letters of Louis D. Brandeis to Felix Frankfurter.* Norman, OK: University of Oklahoma Press.

Walters, John. 1992. The Official Bulletin of the United States: America's First Official Gazette. *Government Publications Review* 19: 243–56.

Waltman, Franklyn. 1934. NRA Set-Up Made Target in High Court. *Washington Post.* December 11, 1–2.

Wyzanski, Charles, to Erwin Griswold. 1934. Letters to Griswold. Box 32-24. Harvard Law Library, Manuscript Division. September 28, October 1, November 23.

At the Intersection of Bureaucracy, Democracy, and the Media:
The Effective Agency Spokesperson (Pp. 90–98)

Arnette, S. U. (1995). Improving Your Agency's Image. *Journal of Housing and Community Development*, *52*(2), 38–41.

Avery, G. D., Bedrosian, J. M., Brucchi, S. J., Dennis, L. B., Keane, J. F. and Koch, G. (1996). Public Affairs in the Public Sector. In L. B. Dennis (ed.), *Practical Public Affairs in an Era of Change: A Communications Guide for Business, Government, and College*. Lanham, MD: University Press of America for Public Relations Society of America (pp. 169–85).

Barrett, E. W. (1953). *Truth is Our Weapon*. New York: Funk & Wagnalls.

Berding, A. (1962). *Foreign Affairs and You! How American Foreign Policy is Made and What it Means to You*. Garden City, NY: Doubleday.

Blau, P. M. and Meyer, M. W. (1993 [1987]). *Bureaucracy in Modern Society*, 3rd ed. New York: McGraw-Hill.

Brown, D. H. (1976). Information Officers and Reporters: Friends or Foes? *Public Relations Review*, *2*(2), 29–38.

Burns, N. (1996). Talking to the World about American Foreign Policy. *Harvard International Journal of Press/Politics*, *1*(4), 10–14.

Carter, Hodding, III (1984). *Whose News is It?* Manhattan: Kansas State University.

Chittick, W. O. (1970). *State Department, Press, and Pressure Groups: A Role Analysis*. New York: Wiley-Interscience.

Courter, E. M. (1974). Putting the Resident Pollyanna to Work. *Public Welfare*, *32*, 53–56.

Crisis Spokesman (1970, October 5). *Newsweek*, *76*(14), 106.

Cutlip, S. M. (1976). Public Relations in the Government. *Public Relations Review*, *2*(2), 5–28.

Daley, R. (1978 [1973]). *Target Blue: An Insider's View of the N.Y.P.D.* New York: Dell.

Denning, S. (1997). Toward an End to Fear and Loathing of the News: Making the Media Work for You. *The Agenda* (newsletter of the Section on Health and Human Services Administration of the American Society for Public Administration), *4*(2), 4.

Dunn, D. D. (1969). *Public Officials and the Press*. Reading, MA: Addison-Wesley.

Dunwoody, S. and Ryan, M. (1983). Public Information Persons as Mediators between Scientists and Journalists. *Journalism Quarterly*, *60*, 647–56.

Édes, B. W. (2000). The Role of Government Information Officers. *Journal of Government Information*, *23*, 455–69.

Fletcher, J. E. and Soucy, P. E. (1983). Army Public Affairs Officer as Perceived By Press and by Military Colleagues. *Journalism Quarterly*, *60*, 93–97, 204.

Friedman, T. L. (2006). *The World is Flat: A Brief History of the Twenty-First Century*, updated and expanded ed. New York: Farrar, Straus and Giroux.

Garnett, J. L. (1992). *Communicating for Results in Government: A Strategic Approach for Public Managers*. San Francisco: Jossey-Bass.

Goldstein, S. (1981). 'Hi, I'm from Government and I Want to Help You.' *Public Relations Journal*, *37*(10), 22–24.

Gosnell, A. R. (2000). Maximizing Media Coverage. *Fire Engineering*, *153*(5), 93–94.

Goulding, P. G. (1970). *Confirm or Deny: Informing the People on National Security*. New York: Harper & Row.

Graber, D. A. (2003). *The Power of Communication: Managing Information in Public Organizations*. Washington, DC: CQ Press.

Grunig, J. E. (1997). Public Relations Management in Government and Business. In J. L. Garnett and A. Kouzmin (eds.), *Handbook of Administrative Communication*. New York: Marcel Dekker (pp. 241–83).

Helm, L. M., Hiebert, R. E., Naver, M. R. and Rabin, K. (eds.) (1981). *Informing the Public: A Public Affairs Handbook*. New York: Longman.

Hess, S. (1984). *The Government/Press Connection: Press Officers and Their Offices.* Washington, DC: Brookings Institution.

Hiebert, R. E. and Spitzer, C. E. (eds.) (1968). *The Voice of Government.* New York: John Wiley.

Krey, D. (ed.) (2000). *Delivering the Message: A Resource Guide for Public Information Officials*, 2nd ed. Sacramento: California Association of Public Information Officials.

Krohn, C. A. (2004). Confessions of a P.A.O. *Columbia Journalism Review, 42*(6), 35–39.

Lee, M. (1998). Public Relations in Public Administration: A Disappearing Act in Public Administration Education. *Public Relations Review, 24*, 509–20.

———. (1999). Reporters and Bureaucrats: Public Relations Counter-Strategies by Public Administrators in an Era of Media Disinterest in Government. *Public Relations Review, 25*, 451–63.

———. (2000). Public Information in Government Organizations: A Review and Curriculum Outline of External Relations in Public Administration. *Public Administration and Management, 5*, 183–214. Retrieved September 2009, from http://www.spaef.com/file.php?id=314.

———. (2001a). The Agency Spokesperson: Connecting Public Administration and the Media. *Public Administration Quarterly, 25*, 101–30.

———. (2001b). The Image of the Government Flack: Movie Depictions of Public Relations in Public Administration. *Public Relations Review, 27*, 297–315.

———. (2002a). Bureaucracy in the Hebrew Bible: A Neglected Source of Public Administration History. *Public Voices, 5*, 79–88.

———. (2002b). Intersectoral Differences in Public Affairs: The Duty of Public Reporting in Public Administration. *Journal of Public Affairs, 2*(2), 33–43.

———. (2007). Globalization and Media Coverage of Public Administration. In A. Farazmand and J. Pinkowski (eds.), *Handbook of Globalization, Governance, and Public Administration.* Boca Raton, FL: CRC Press/Taylor & Francis (pp. 153–64).

———. (2008a). Media Relations and External Communications during a Disaster. In J. Pinkowski (ed.), *Disaster Management Handbook.* Boca Raton, FL: CRC Press/Taylor & Francis (pp. 387–99).

———. (ed.) (2008b). *Government Public Relations: A Reader.* Boca Raton, FL: CRC Press/Taylor & Francis.

———. (2008c). Public Affairs Enters the US President's Subcabinet: Creating the First Assistant Secretary for Public Affairs (1944–1953) and Subsequent Developments. *Journal of Public Affairs, 8*, 185–94.

Lindsey, R. (1956). *This HIGH Name: Public Relations and the U.S. Marine Corps.* Madison: University of Wisconsin Press.

Manning, R. J. (1966). Journalism and Foreign Affairs. In G. Gross (ed.), *The Responsibility of the Press.* New York: Fleet Publishing (pp. 184–98).

McCamy, J. L. (1939). *Government Publicity: Its Practice in Federal Administration.* Chicago: University of Chicago Press.

McCloskey, R. J. (1990). The Care and Handling of Leaks. In S. Serfaty (ed.), *The Media and Foreign Policy.* New York: St. Martin's (pp. 109–20).

Mecklin, J. (1965). *Mission in Torment: An Intimate Account of the U.S. Role in Vietnam.* Garden City, NY: Doubleday.

Morgan, D. (1978). *The Capitol Press Corps: Newsman and the Governing of New York State.* Westport, CT: Greenwood.

Morgan, D. (1986). *The Flacks of Washington: Government Information and the Public Agenda.* New York: Greenwood.

Mosher, W. E. (chairman) (1941). *Public Relations of Public Personnel Agencies: A Report Submitted to the Civil Service Assembly by the Committee on Public Relations of Public Personnel Agencies.* Chicago: Civil Service Assembly of the United States and Canada.

Moss, J. E. (1968). Future Problems and Prospects. In R. E. Hiebert and C. E. Spitzer (eds.), *The Voice of Government.* New York: John Wiley (pp. 27–36).

Motschall, M. and Cao, L. (2002). An Analysis of the Public Relations Role of the Police Public Information Officer. *Police Quarterly, 5*, 152–80.

Nimmo, D. D. (1964). *Newsgathering in Washington: A Study in Political Communication*. New York: Atherton.

Oldfield, B. (1956). *Never a Shot in Anger*. New York: Duell, Sloan and Pearce.

Peters, B. G. (1988). *Comparing Public Bureaucracies: Problems of Theory and Method*. Tuscaloosa: University of Alabama Press.

Pimlott, J. A. R. (1972 [1951]). *Public Relations and American Democracy*. Port Washington, NY: Kennikat.

Proctor, C. B. (1920). First Marine Corps Publicity Bureau. *Recruiters' Bulletin, 6*(8), 5–6.

Roberts, A. (2006). *Blacked Out: Government Secrecy in the Information Age*. New York: Cambridge University Press.

Rourke, F. E. (1961). *Secrecy and Publicity: Dilemmas of Democracy*. Baltimore: Johns Hopkins Press.

Rubin, B. (1958). *Public Relations and the Empire State: A Case Study of New York State Administration, 1943–1954*. New Brunswick, NJ: Rutgers University Press.

Ruda, S. J. (1998). The PIO: A Position with Infinite Boundaries. *Fire Engineering, 151*(12), 61–63.

Schachter, H. L. (1983). *Public Agency Communication: Theory and Practice*. Chicago: Nelson-Hall.

Sigal, L. V. (1973). *Reporters and Officials: The Organization and Politics of Newsmaking*. Lexington, MA: D.C. Heath.

Starr, P. (2004). *The Creation of the Media: Political Origins of Modern Communications*. New York: Basic Books.

Staszak, D. (2001). Media Trends and the Public Information Officer. *FBI Law Enforcement Bulletin, 70*(3), 10–13.

Stephens, L. F. (1981). Professionalism of Army Public Affairs Personnel. *Public Relations Review, 7*(2), 43–56.

Swartz, J. E. (1983). On the Margin: Between Journalist and Publicist. *Public Relations Review, 9*(3), 11–23.

Weinberger, C. W. (2001). *In the Arena: A Memoir of the 20th Century*. Washington, DC: Regnery.

Williams-Thompson, R. (1951). *Was I Really Necessary?* London: World's Press News.

Willis-Kistler, P. (2003). The Public Information Professional Increases Public Awareness and Understanding. *Western City, 79*(9), 15–18, 54.

Wise, K. (2002–2003). Linking Public Relations Processes and Organizational Effectiveness at a State Health Department. *Journal of Health and Human Services Administration, 25*, 497–525.

Zorthian, B. (1971). A Press Relations Doctrine for the Foreign Service. *Foreign Service Journal, 48*(2), 20–23, 55–56.

CHAPTER 5: OPEN PUBLIC MEETINGS

Introduction (Pp. 99–101)

Adams, B. "Public Meetings and the Democratic Process." *Public Administration Review* 64, no. 1 (2004): 43–54.

Baker, W. H., H. L. Addams, and B. Davis. "Critical Factors for Enhancing Municipal Public Hearings." *Public Administration Review* 65, no. 4 (2005): 490–99.

McComas, K. A. "Theory and Practice of Public Meetings." *Communication Theory* 11, no. 1 (2001): 36–55.

"Open Meeting Statutes: The Press Fights for the 'Right To Know.'" *Harvard Law Review* 75, no. 6 (1962): 1119–1221.

Rhinard, M. "The Democratic Legitimacy of the European Union Committee System." *Governance* 15, no. 2 (2002): 185–210.

The Democratic Legitimacy of the European Union Committee System (Pp. 103–19)

Beetham, David. 1991. *The Legitimation of Power*. Basingstoke: Macmillan.

Beyers, Jan, and Guido Dierickx. 1998. The Working Groups of the Council of the European Union: Supranational or Intergovernmental Negotiations. *Journal of Common Market Studies* 36: 289–317.

Black, Ian. 2001. People Losing Faith in "Anonymous" EU. *The Guardian* 18 July. Available online at http://www.guardian.co.uk/international/story/0,3604,523270,00.html.

Cardozo, Rita. 1987. The Project for a Political Community. In R. Pryce, ed., *The Dynamics of European Union*. London: Croom Helm.

Christiansen, Thomas. 1996. A Maturing Bureaucracy? The Role of the Commission in the Policy Process. In J. Richardson, ed., *European Union: Power and Policy-Making*. London: Routledge.

Christiansen, Thomas, and Emil Kirchner. 2000. Introduction. In T. Christiansen and E. Kirchner, eds., *Committee Governance in the European Union*. Manchester: Manchester University Press.

Council of the European Union. 1999. Council Decision Laying Down the Procedures for the Exercise of Implementing Powers Conferred on the Commission (1999/468/EC of 28 June 1999). *Official Journal* 17 July.

———. 2000. Council Decision Adopting the Council's Rules of Procedure (2000/396/EC of 5 June 2000). *Official Journal* L 149, 23 June.

———. 2001. Council Decision on Standard Committee Rules of Procedure (1999/468/EC). *Official Journal* 2 February.

Dahl, Robert A. 1994. A Democratic Dilemma: System Effectiveness versus Citizen Participation. *Political Science Quarterly* 109: 23–34.

———. 1998. *On Democracy*. New Haven, CT: Yale University Press.

Dehousse, Renaud. 1995. Institutional Reform in the European Community: Are There Alternatives to the Majoritarian Avenue? In J. Hayward, ed., *The Crises of Representation in Europe*. London: Frank Cass.

Docksey, Christopher, and Karen Williams. 1994. The Commission and the Execution of Community Policy. In G. Edwards and D. Spence, eds., *The European Commission*. London: Longman.

Dogan, Rhys. 2000. A Cross-Sectoral View of Comitology: Incidence, Issues, and Implications. In T. Christiansen and E. Kirchner, eds., *Committee Governance in the European Union*. Manchester: Manchester University Press.

Dryzek, John S. 1996. *Democracy in Capitalist Times: Ideals, Limits, and Struggles*. Oxford: Oxford University Press.

The Economist. 2001. The European Union: Can It Work and Be Popular? 16–22 June:15.

European Commission. 1991. Commission Proposal for a Council Directive Concerning Common Rules for the Internal Market in Electricity (COM[91]548). *Official Journal* C 65, 14 March.

———. 1997. Commission Decision Setting up Scientific Committees in the Field of Consumer Health and Food Safety (97/579/EC of 23 July 1997). *Official Journal* L 237, 28 August.

———. 1999. Internal Memorandum from the Commission: Commission Expert Groups, Annual List of Authorization (SEC[1999]1149). 14 July.

Franchino, Fabio. 2000. Control of the Commission's Executive Functions: Uncertainty, Conflict, and Decision Rules. *European Union Politics* 1: 63–92.

Haibach, Georg. 1999. Council Decision 1999/468—A New Comitology Decision for the 21st Century? *EIPAscope, Journal of the European Institute for Public Administration* 1999: 10–18.

Hayes-Renshaw, Fiona, and Helen Wallace. 1997. *The Council of Ministers*. The European Union Series. London: Macmillan.

Hayward, Jack. 1996. Conclusion: Has European Unification by Stealth a Future? In J. Hayward, ed., *Elitism, Populism, and European Politics*. Oxford: Clarendon Press.

Héritier, Adrienne. 1999. Elements of Democratic Legitimation in Europe: An Alternative Perspective. *Journal of European Public Policy* 6:269–282.

Hermann, F. 1994. *Second Report of the Institutional Committee on the Constitution of the European Union: European Parliament*. Brussels: European Parliament Publication.

Höreth, Marcus. 1999. No Way Out for the Beast? The Unsolved Legitimacy Problem of European Governance. Journal of European Public Policy 6: 249–68.

Jachtenfuchs, Markus. 1997. *Democracy and Governance in the European Union.* European Integration Online Papers 1. Available online at http://eiop.or.at/eiop/texte/1997–002a.htm.

Joerges, Christian. 1997. Scientific Expertise in Social Regulation and the European Court of Justice: Legal Frameworks for Denationalised Governance Structures. In C. Joerges, K. H. Ladeur, and E. Vos, eds., *Integrating Scientific Expertise into Regulatory Decision-Making.* Baden-Baden: Nomos.

Joerges, Christian, and Jurgen Neyer. 1997a. From Intergovernmental Bargaining to Deliberative Political Processes: The Constitutionalisation of Comitology. *European Law Journal* 3: 272–99.

———. 1997b. Transforming Strategic Interaction into Deliberative Problem-Solving: European Comitology in the Foodstuffs Sector. *Journal of European Public Policy* 4: 609–25.

———, and Ellen Vos, eds. 1999. *EU Committees: Social Regulation, Law and Politics.* Oxford: Hart.

Kassim, Hussein, B. Guy Peters, and Vincent Wright, eds. 2000. *The National Co-ordination of EU Policy: The Domestic Level.* Oxford: Oxford University Press.

King, Anthony. 1981. What Do Elections Decide? In D. Butler, H. R. Penniman, and A. Ranney, eds., *Democracy at the Polls: A Comparative Study of Competitive National Elections.* Washington, DC: American Enterprise Institute.

Lenaerts, Koen, and Amaryllis Verhoeven. 2000. Towards a Legal Framework for Executive Rule-Making in the EU? The Contribution of the New Comitology Decision. *Common Market Law Review* 37: 645–86.

Lewis, Jeffrey. 1998. Is the "Hard-Bargaining" Image of the Council Misleading? The Committee of Permanent Representatives and the Local Elections Directive. *Journal of Common Market Studies* 36(4): 479–504.

Lipset, Seymour M., Martin A. Trow, and James S. Coleman. 1956. *Union Democracy: the Internal Politics of the International Typographical Union.* Glencoe, IL: The Free Press.

Lord, Christopher. 1998. *Democracy in the European Union.* Contemporary European Studies Series. Sheffield: Sheffield Academic Press.

Majone, Giandomenico. 1994. Independence vs. Accountability? Nonmajoritarian Institutions and Democratic Government in Europe. EUI Working Papers in SPS Series. Florence: European University Institute.

———. 1996. *Regulating Europe.* London: Routledge.

Mancini, G. Federico. 1998. Europe: The Case for Statehood. *European Law Journal* 4: 29–42.

Mazey, Sonia, and Jeremy Richardson. 2001. Institutionalizing Promiscuity: Commission-Interest Groups Relations in the EU. In A. S. Sweet, W. Sandholtz, and N. Fligstein, eds., *The Institutionalization of Europe.* Oxford: Oxford University Press.

———, eds. 1993. *Lobbying in the European Community.* Oxford: Oxford University Press.

Mill, John Stuart. 1972. *Utilitarianism: On Liberty and Representative Government.* London: Dent.

Monnet, Jean. 1978. *Mémoires.* London: Collins.

Nugent, Neill. 1999. *The Government and Politics of the European Union.* The European Union Series. Basingstoke: Macmillan.

Pedler, Robin H., and Guenther F. Schaefer, eds. 1996. *Shaping European Law and Policy: The Role of Committees and Comitology in the Political Process.* Maastricht, The Netherlands: European Institute of Public Administration.

Peters, Guy. 1996. Agenda-Setting in the European Union. In J. Richardson, ed., *European Union: Power and Policy-Making.* London: Routledge.

Plamenatz, John. 1973. *Democracy and Illusion: An Examination of Certain Aspects of Modern Democratic Theory.* London: Longman.

Radaelli, Claudio M. 1999. The Public Policy of the European Union: Whither the Politics of Expertise? *Journal of European Public Policy* 6: 757–74.

Richardson, Jeremy. 1996. Policy-Making in the EU: Interests, Ideas, and Garbage Cans of Primeval Soup. In J. Richardson, ed., *European Union: Power and Policy-Making.* London: Routledge.

Rometsch, Dietrich, and Wolfgang Wessels. 1994. The Commission and the Council of the Union. In G. Edwards and D. Spence, eds., *The European Commission.* London: Carterhill.

Rose-Ackerman, Susan. 1992. *Rethinking the Progressive Agenda: The Reform of the American Regulatory State*. New York: Free Press.

Schaefer, Guenther F. 1996. Committees in the EC Policy Process: A First Step Towards Developing a Conceptual Framework. In R. H. Pedler and G. F. Schaefer, eds., *Shaping European Law and Policy: The Role of Committees and Comitology in the Political Process*. Maastricht, The Netherlands: European Institute of Public Administration.

Scharpf, Fritz W. 1999. *Governing in Europe: Effective and Democratic?* Oxford: Oxford University Press.

Schattschneider, E. E. 1960. *The Semisovereign People: A Realist's View of Democracy in America*. Hinsdale: Dryden Press.

Schmitter, Philippe C. 1989. Corporatism Is Dead—Long Live Corporatism. *Government and Opposition* 24: 54–73.

Schumpeter, Joseph Alois. 1943. *Capitalism, Socialism, and Democracy*. London: Allen & Unwin.

Shapiro, Martin. 1988. *Who Guards the Guardians? Judicial Control of Administration*. Athens: University of Georgia Press.

Siedentop, Larry. 2000. *Democracy in Europe*. London: Allen Lane/Penguin Press.

Swedish Presidency Web Site. 2001. Meetings in Brussels and Luxembourg. Available online at http://eu2001.se/static/eng/sweden/motenibryssel.asp.

van der Knaap, Peter. 1996. Government by Committee: Legal Typology, Quantitative Assessment, and Institutional Repercussions of Committees in the European Union. In R. H. Pedler and G. F. Schaefer, eds., *Shaping European Law and Policy: The Role of Committees and Comitology in the Political Process*. Maastricht, The Netherlands: European Institute of Public Administration.

van Schendelen, M. P. C. M. 1996. EC Committees: Influence Counts More Than Legal Powers. In R. H. Pedler and G. F. Schaefer, eds., *Shaping European Law and Policy: The Role of Committees and Comitology in the Political Process*. Maastricht, The Netherlands: European Institute of Public Administration.

Vos, Ellen. 1997. The Rise of Committees. *European Law Journal* 3: 210–29.

Wallace, William. 1996. Has Government by Committee Lost the People's Confidence? In J. Hayward, ed., *Elitism, Populism, and European Politics*. Oxford: Clarendon Press.

Wallace, William, and Julie Smith. 1995. Democracy or Technocracy? European Integration and the Problem of Popular Consent. In J. Hayward, ed., *The Crisis of Representation in Europe*. London: Cass.

Weale, Albert. 1996. Environmental Rules and Rule-Making in the European Union. Journal of *European Public Policy* 3: 594–611.

———. 2000. Government by Committee: Three Principles of Evaluation. In T. Christiansen and E. Kirchner, eds., *Committee Governance in the European Union*. Manchester: Manchester University Press.

Weber, Max. [1918] 1942. Politics as a Vocation. In H. H. Gerth and C. W. Mills, eds., *From Max Weber: Essays in Sociology*. Oxford: Oxford University Press.

Weiler, Joseph H. H. 1997. Legitimacy and Democracy of Union Governance. In G. Edwards and A. Pijpers, eds., *The Politics of European Union Treaty Reform*. London: Pinter.

Weiler, Joseph H. H., Ulrich R. Haltern, and Franz C. Mayer. 1995. European Democracy and Its Critique. *West European Politics* 18: 4–39.

Wessels, Wolfgang. 1998. Comitology: Fusion in Action. Politico-administrative Trends in the EU System. *Journal of European Public Policy* 5: 209–34.

Critical Factors for Enhancing Municipal Public Hearings (Pp. 119–32)

Balla, Steven J. 2000. Legislative Success and Failure and Participation in Rule Making. *Journal of Public Administration Research and Theory* 10(3): 633–53.

Bryson, John M., and Sharon R. Anderson. 2000. Applying Large-Group Interaction Methods in the Planning and Implementation of Major Change Efforts. *Public Administration Review* 60(2): 143–62.

Burby, Raymond J. 2003. Making Plans that Matter: Citizen Involvement and Government Action. *Journal of the American Planning Association* 69(1): 33–49.

Carson, Lyn. 1999. The Telephone as a Participatory Mechanism at a Local Government Level. In *Technology and Public Participation*, edited by Brian Martin, 37–60. Wollongong, Australia: University of Wollongong.

Chipman, Helen, Patricia Kendall, Michael Slater, and Garry Auld. 1996. Audience Responses to a Risk Communication Message in Four Media Formats. *Journal of Nutrition Education* 28(3): 133–39.

Covey, Stephen R. 1991. *Principle-Centered Leadership*. New York: Simon and Schuster.

Crewson, Philip E., and Bonnie S. Fisher. 1997. Growing Older and Wiser: The Changing Skill Requirements of City Administrators. *Public Administration Review* 57(5): 380–86.

Crosby, Ned, Janet M. Kelly, and Paul Schaefer. 1986. Citizens Panels: A New Approach to Citizen Participation. *Public Administration Review* 46(2): 170–78.

Davis, Richard. 2000. The Net Effect. *Brigham Young Magazine*, Fall, 40–46.

Ebdon, Carol. 2002. Citizen Participation in the Local Government Process. *Journal of Public Budgeting, Accounting, and Financial Management* 14(2): 273–94.

Fiorino, Daniel J. 1990. Citizen Participation and Environmental Risk: A Survey of Institutional Mechanisms. *Science, Technology, and Human Values* 15(2): 226–43.

Frewer, Lynn J., Chaya Howard, Duncan Hedderley, and Richard Shepherd. 1996. What Determines Trust in Information about Food-Related Risks? Underlying Psychological Constructs. *Risk Analysis* 16(4): 473–86.

Golding, Dominic, Sheldon Krimsky, and Alonzo Plough. 1992. Evaluating Risk Communication: Narrative vs. Technical Presentations of Information about Radon. *Risk Analysis* 12(1): 27–35.

King, Cheryl S., Kathryn M. Feltey, and Bridget O'Neill Susel. 1998. The Question of Participation: Toward Authentic Public Participation in Public Administration. *Public Administration Review* 58(4): 317–26.

Lando, Tom. 2003. The Public Hearing Process: A Tool for Citizen Participation, or a Path toward Citizen Alienation? *National Civic Review* 92(1): 73–83.

Lowndes, Vivien, Gerry Stoker, Lawrence Pratchett, David Wilson, Steve Leach, and Melvin Wingfield. 1998. *Enhancing Public Participation in Local Government*. London: U.K. Department of the Environment, Transport and the Regions.

McCombs, Maxwell. 1997. Building Consensus: The News Media's Agenda-Setting Roles. *Political Communication* 14(4): 433–43.

McLeod, Jack M., Dietram A. Scheufele, and Patricia Moy. 1999. Community, Communication, and Participation: The Role of Mass Media and Interpersonal Discussion in Local Political Participation. *Political Communication* 16(3): 315–36.

Midden, Cees J. H. 1995. Direct Participation in Macro-Issues: A Multiple Group Approach; An Analysis and Critique of the Dutch National Debate on Energy Policy, Fairness, Competence, and Beyond. In *Fairness and Competence in Citizen Participation*, edited by Ortwin Renn, Thomas Webler, and Peter Wiedemann, 305–20. Dordrecht, Netherlands: Kluwer Academic.

Middendorf, Gerad, and Lawrence Busch. 1997. Inquiry for the Public Good: Democratic Participation in Agricultural Research. *Agriculture and Human Values* 14(1): 45–57.

Nalbandian, John. 1999. Facilitating Community, Enabling Democracy: New Roles for Local Government Managers. *Public Administration Review* 59(3): 187–97.

Pew Research Center. 1998. Internet News Takes Off. http://people-press.org/reports/display.php3?PageID=566.

———. 2000. Performance and Purpose: Constituents Rate Government Agencies. http://people-press.org/reports/display. php3?ReportID=41.

Rowe, Gene, and Lynn J. Frewer. 2000. Public Participation Methods: A Framework for Evaluation. Science, *Technology and Human Value* 25(1): 3–27.

Sei-Hill Kim, Dietram A. Scheufele, and James Shanahan. 2002. Think About It This Way: Attribute Agenda-Setting Function of the Press and the Public's Evaluation of a Local Issue. *Journalism and Mass Communication Quarterly* 79(1): 7–25.

Smith, L. Graham, Carla Y. Nell, and Mark V. Prystupa. 1997. The Converging Dynamics of Interest Representation in Resources Management. *Environmental Management* 21(2): 139–46.

Thomas, John C. 1995. *Public Participation in Public Decisions*. San Francisco: Jossey-Bass.

Walters, Lawrence C., James Aydelotte, and Jessica Miller. 2000. Putting More Public in Policy Analysis. *Public Administration Review* 60(4): 349–59.

Young, Iris Marion. 2001. Activist Challenges to Deliberative Democracy. *Political Theory* 29(5): 670–90.

CHAPTER 6: WHISTLEBLOWING AND LEAKED INFORMATION

Introduction (Pp. 133–34)

Bok, S. "Whistleblowing and Leaks. Pp. 210–29 in *Secrets: On the Ethics of Concealment and Revelation*. New York: Vintage Books, 1989.

Ellsberg, D. *Secrets: A Memoir of Vietnam and the Pentagon Papers*. New York: Penguin, 2003.

Heuvel, G. V. D. "The Parliamentary Enquiry on Fraud in the Dutch Construction Industry Collusion as Concept Between Corruption and State-Corporate Crime." *Crime, Law & Social Change* 44 (2005): 133–51.

Jos, P., M. Tompkins, and S. Hays. "In Praise of Difficult People: A Portrait of the Committed Whistleblower." *Public Administration Review* 49, no. 6 (1989): 552–61.

Lovell, A. "The Enduring Phenomenon of Moral Muteness." *Public Integrity* 5, no. 3 (2003): 187–204.

"Nuclear Whistleblower Wins Compensation." *DutchNews.nl*, 1 May 2009. http://www.dutchnews.nl/news/archives/2009/05/nuclear_whistleblower_wins_com.php (8 July 2009).

Prados, J., and M. P. Porter. *Inside the Pentagon Papers*. Lawrence, Kan.: University Press of Kansas, 2004.

Wald, M. L. "Inspector Predicted Danger Before Buffalo Crash." *New York Times*, 3 June 2009. http://www.nytimes.com/2009/06/04/nyregion/04colgan.html?_r=1&emc=eta1 (7 July 2009).

Weiner, T. "W. Mark Felt, Watergate Deep Throat, Dies at 95." *New York Times*, 19 December 2008.

Woodward, B., and C. Bernstein. *All the President's Men*. Pocket, 2005.

The Enduring Phenomenon of Moral Muteness (Pp. 147–62)

Anderson, A. 1999. *Ethical Concerns and Reputation Risk Management: A Study of Leading UK Companies*. London: London Business School.

Bartels, L. K., E. Harrick, K. Martell, and D. Strickland. 1998. "The Relationship Between Ethical Climate and Ethical Problems Within Human Resource Management." *Journal of Business Ethics* 17: 799–804.

Bauman, Z. 1994. Alone Again: Ethics After Certainty. London: Demos.

Beardshaw, V. 1981. *Conscientious Objectors at Work: Mental Hospital Nurses—A Case Study*. London: Social Audit.

Bird, F. B., and Waters, J. A. 1989. "The Moral Muteness of Managers." *California Management Review* (Fall): 73–88.

Fisher, C., and A. Lovell. 2000. "Accountants' Responses to Ethical Issues at Work." London: CIMA.

Franke, G. R., D. F. Crown, and D. F. Spake. 1997. "Gender Differences in Ethical Perceptions of Business Practices: A Social Role Theory Perspective." *Journal of Applied Psychology* 82, no. 6: 920–34.

Fritzsche, D. J. 2000. "Ethical Climates and the Ethical Dimension of Decision Making." *Journal of Business Ethics* 24: 125–40.

Harrison, R. 1988. "Quality of Service: A New Frontier in Organizations." In *Executive Integrity: The Search for High Human Values in Organizational Life*, ed. S. Srivastva, 45–67. San Francisco: Jossey-Bass.

Hunt, G. (ed.). 1995. *Whistleblowing in the Social Services: Public Accountability and Professional Practice.* London: Edward Arnold. 1998. *Whistleblowing in the Health Service: Accountability, Law & Professional Practice.* London: Edward Arnold.

Jos, P. H., M. E. Tomkins, and S. W. Hays. 1989. "In Praise of Difficult People: A Portrait of the Committed Whistleblower." *Public Administration Review* (November/December): 552–61.

Legge, K. 1998. "Is HRM Ethical? Can HRM Be Ethical?" In *Ethics & Organizations*, ed. M. Parker, 150–72. London: Sage.

Miceli, M., and J. P. Near. 1992. *Blowing the Whistle: The Organizational & Legal Implications for Companies and Employees.* Lanham, Md.: Lexington Books.

Prasad, J. N., N. Marlow, and R. E. Hattwick. 1998. "Gender-based Differences in Perception of a Just Society." *Journal of Business Ethics* 17, no. 3: 219–28.

Schroeder, K. 2001. "A Whistleblower's Perspective." In *Whistleblowing at Work*, ed. D. B. Lewis, 128–40. London: Athlone Press.

Sims, R. I., and J. P. Keenan. 1998. "Predictors of External Whistleblowing: Organizational and Intrapersonal Variables." *Journal of Business Ethics* 17: 411–21.

Soeken, K., and D. Soeken,1987. *A Survey of Whistleblowers: Their Stresses and Coping Strategies.* Laurel, Md.: Association of Mental Health Specialties.

Srivastva, S., and D. L. Cooperrider. 1988. "The Urgency for Executive Integrity." In *Executive Integrity: The Search for High Human Values in Organizational Life*, ed. S. Srivastva, 1–28. San Francisco: Jossey-Bass.

Stevenson, T. H., and C. D. Bodkin. 1998. "A Cross-National Comparison of University Students' Perceptions Regarding the Ethics and Acceptability of Sales Practices." *Journal of Business Ethics* 17, no. 1: 45–55.

Straughan, R. 1984. "Why Act on Kohlberg's Moral Judgements? (or, How to Reach Stage 6 and Remain a Bastard)." In Lawrence Kohlberg: *Consensus and Controversy*, ed. S. Modgil and C. Modgil, 149–57. Brighton, UK: Falmer Press.

Titmuss, R. 1970. *The Gift Relationship: From Human Blood to Social Policy.* London: Allen & Unwin.

Tsaliki, J., and M. Ortiz-Buonafina. 1990. "Ethical Belief Differences of Males and Females." *Journal of Business Ethics* 9, no. 6: 509–18.

Vinten, G. (ed.). 1994. *Whistleblowing: Subversion or Corporate Citizenship?* London: Chapman Hall.

Waters, J. A., F. Bird, and P. D. Chant. 1986. "Everyday Moral Issues Experienced by Managers." *Journal of Business Ethics* 5: 373–84.

Winfield, M., 1990. *Minding Your Own Business: Self-Regulation and Whistleblowing in British Companies.* London: Social Audit.

Index

About the Editor

Suzanne J. Piotrowski is an associate professor of public affairs and administration at Rutgers University–Newark. For the 2009/2010 academic year she holds the position of Faculty Fellow in the Office of the Chancellor. Professor Piotrowski founded and moderates the International Transparency and Secrecy Research Network listserv. She earned a PhD in political science from School of Public Affairs at American University, Washington, D.C., and a master of public administration degree from the University of Delaware.

Dr. Piotrowski's research focuses on nonmission-based values in public administration, including administrative transparency and ethics. Her current research focuses on defining and measuring municipal transparency. She authored the book *Governmental Transparency in the Path of Administrative Reform* from the State University of New York Press (2007).

Professor Piotrowski has written widely on public management, accountability, and transparency issues, including book chapters, journal articles, case studies, and encyclopedia articles. Dr. Piotrowski's work is published in *Public Administration Review*, the *American Review of Public Administration, Journal of Public Administration Research and Theory, Government Information Quarterly, Public Administration Quarterly,* the *Chinese Public Administration Review,* the *Syracuse Journal of International Law and Commerce, Open Government: A Journal on Freedom of Information,* the *Journal of Cooperative Education,* and the *Journal of Public Works Management and Policy.*